European Portrait Photography since 1990

European Portrait Photography since 1990

Edited by Frits Gierstberg

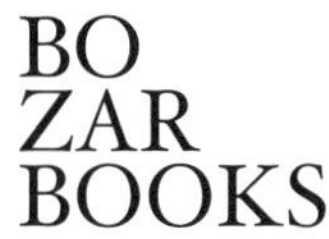

PRESTEL

MUNICH · LONDON · NEW YORK

Europe not only represents a continent. It also gives its name to the most successful regional peace project, the European Union. So Europe is more than a continent, a project, an organization. It is also a dream or a *state of mind*. Being European refers to whoever *feels* European.

Identity is not eternally fixed. People can toy with the different layers of an identity. That is why the European Union has adopted the motto 'unity in diversity'. Precisely this unity in diversity – and the diversity of individual unity – surfaces in the work of these photographers.

This exhibition is inspired by the fall of the Berlin Wall and the disappearance of the Iron Curtain. These pivotal events reunited our continent. They led to a new Europe and a new global order. In a world that is no longer divided into two opposing blocks, the European project has gone full speed ahead. Today many of the Central and Eastern European industries that were on the frontline of this divide are blossoming. The end of the Cold War gave Europe a new, common future. The works of the artists originating from these countries reflect this new departure.

Aside from geographic togetherness, there are many other elements that contribute to a feeling of community, like family and lifestyle. Take a look, for example, at the women at the side of the road, as portrayed by my compatriot Paola De Pietri: pregnant, seemingly desolate or abandoned in suburban areas – or are they perhaps willingly choosing new roads, new options ahead of them, carrying the future of Europe?

This exhibition looks for a compromise between feelings of understanding and distance, between the community and the individuals. It is this careful balance that drives our everyday work in the European Union. Our European culture is cherished in many corners of this world and works of art, such as the ones we see in this exhibition, help us relate to our partners around the globe.

This collection of photographs is a wonderful celebration of our shared past. It also gives a glimpse into our common future. I wish to congratulate the three co-producers – the Centre for Fine Arts in Brussels, the Nederlands Fotomuseum in Rotterdam and the Museum of Photography in Thessaloniki – with this multi-coloured cross-section of 25 years of European portrait photography.

Federica Mogherini
High Representative of the European Union
for Foreign Affairs and Security Policy

'People, people, people', said the writer James Joyce.

Every day, we encounter faces. Every day, our eyes meet the gaze of other people. Every day, we smile. Every day, we experience what it is to be human.

Thanks to the career I chose in my early youth, I have been able to meet many people during my lifetime; thousands of faces, each of them unique, yet some of them similar. Many faces remind me of others I know, or they look like a collage of parts of different faces. They evoke memories and bring the distant or recent past to life. They never leave me untouched.

The philosopher Emmanuel Levinas claimed that all our humanity is present in our face. It is the most revealing part of our body. The mouth, gaze, eyebrows, wrinkles, frowns and respiration all express humanity. The face 'speaks', as it were. It exceeds the sum of its various parts, and words always fall short in expressing what we feel when we are confronted with a face. This is because each face is expressive and expressiveness cannot be described. It is experienced. After all, behind every face there lies an awareness, and that awareness looks inwards, at oneself, as well as at other faces.

This catalogue is a sort of herbarium. It is a collection of faces of people of all ages, ranks, walks of life and origins. Those portrayed are clothed or bare. They are photographed or painted in the most varied frames and poses: traditional, theatrical, static, bizarre, comical, and so forth.

These faces have been photographed in Europe over the past 25 years. The chief merit of this exhibition lies in showing us that the differences between faces are unrelated to time and space. Indeed, the people who came up with the idea of this exhibition have put a number of recently photographed faces alongside painted portraits from 16th-century Renaissance Europe. The similarities are striking.

We can draw one conclusion from this: people are both different and identical. They are different because there is an incredible variety of heads, mouths, noses, eyebrows, et cetera. The possible combinations are virtually countless. They are identical in that the similarities between certain faces are unrelated to the cultural or geographical situation of those portrayed. In ths exhibition, we certainly see people in all sorts of 'situations': families at home, children on the beach, aristocrats in their monumental drawing rooms, schoolboys and girls in the playground, Orthodox priests against the backdrop of the azure Greek sea, farmers in their golden-brown fields, and so on. Even if these scenes show a certain closeness between people, they take nothing away from their individuality. If we just note similarities between faces, these transcend borders and centuries, which becomes clear when we see a young swimmer in her bathing suit alongside Botticelli's Venus, or the portrait of the Duke of Urbino by Piero della Francesca next to a woman with a resolute, eagle-like gaze.

It is in this respect that people are the same the world over. What I mean is that while there are certain differences in face, character, stature, and so forth, there are also 'types', and it is these types that are common to all mankind. Incidentally, Jean de La Bruyère tried to draw these 'characters' in a book of the same name: *Les Caractères*. The intrigues in the comedies of Plautus remind us of the films of Woody Allen. The tragedies of Aeschylus have much in common with some modern television series that present powerful men and women. Everywhere we find psychological motives that human behaviour has in common across different periods and genres.

All these faces tell us something, yet we cannot fully fathom them. They still conceal a certain confidentiality within them, an inner life that we imagine, but cannot reach simply by looking carefully. To do that, we have to interact with the person and enter into a relationship. We assume that behind all these faces there is finiteness, fragility and vulnerability.

Another common feature of these faces is that they are all portraits. These people all adopt a pose. Time stands still. Movements become rigid. This is characteristic of a portrait *in itself*. A genre that has existed for centuries. After all, a portrait has to record an image – the image we have of ourselves whenever we think of ourselves.

This last point raises the question of our identity. Who are we really? When we pose for a portrait, we are not our natural selves. But then are we actually anything by nature? A portrait is always a construction. We try to live up to the image of ourselves that we wish to project. But what this exhibition also demonstrates is that we come across differently to others because of the gaze they cast in our direction: the different photographers, each in their own way, reconstruct the reality they deal with. There is no such thing as unprocessed reality. There are only gazes on faces. Only faces. Different yet similar.

Charles Michel
Prime Minister of Belgium

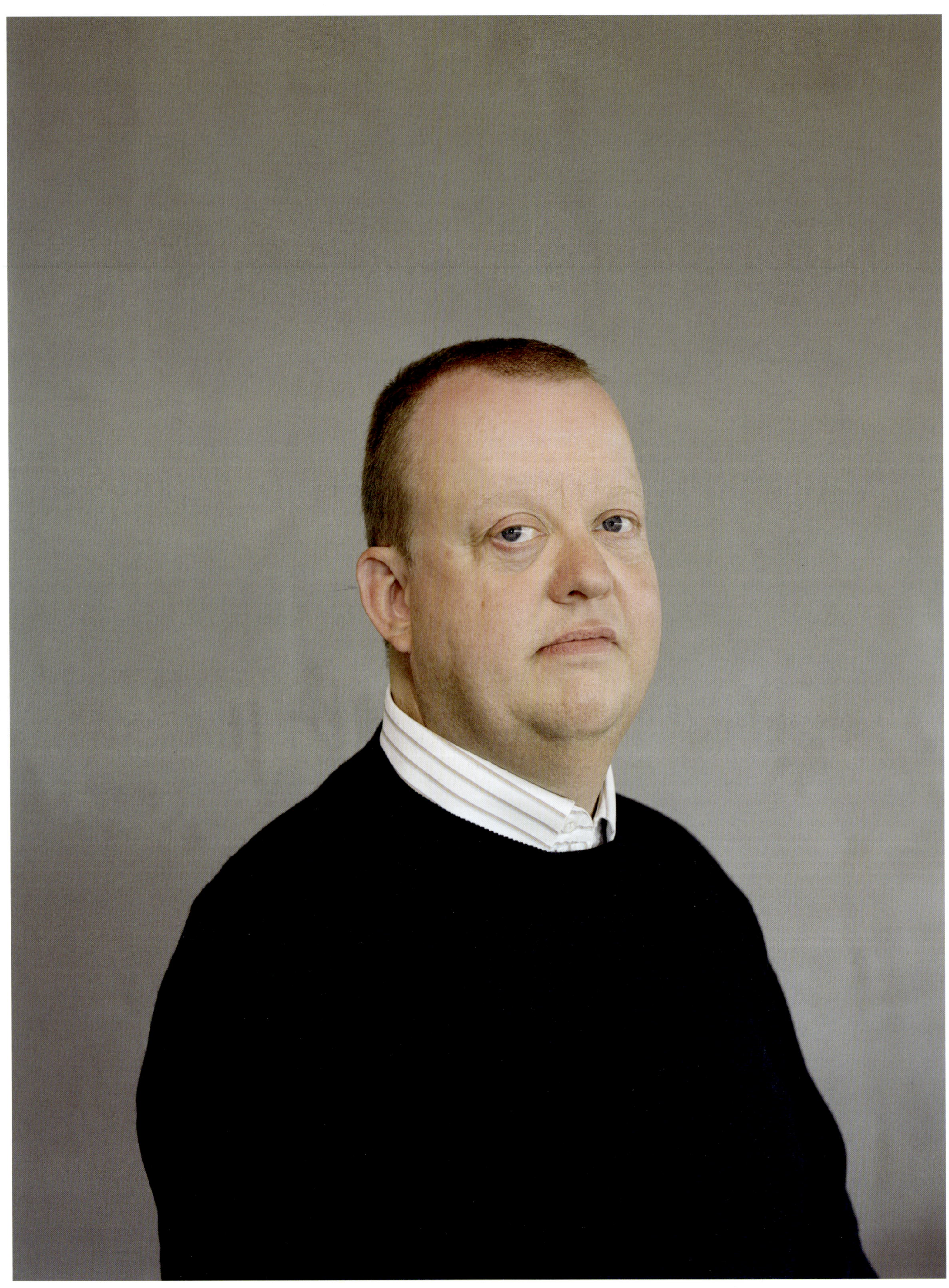

Jitka Hanzlová, *Untitled (Holger)*, in 'There is something I don't know', 2011. Archival pigment print on cotton, 35.4 × 27 cm. Courtesy the artist

Portrait photography has a long history of both documenting and creating identities of individual people, thereby harking back to important European painterly traditions of the Renaissance. In this tradition, the individual and his or her personal development, expression and vision lie at the heart of community life, with no loss to social coherence and community spirit. Looking at a portrait, one is confronted with 'the other' as a fellow human being.

Although artistic changes and renewal of the photographic medium have taken place throughout the 20th century at different stages, the period starting in the early 1990s seems to have been extremely inspiring for artists and photographers. This period coincided with major social and political changes in Europe after the collapse of the communist and socialist states and the opening up of borders between East and West. This exhibition links these two developments – artistic and social – by placing the work of portrait artists in the light of Europe's new search for identity and its shared historical and cultural values.

The exhibition is travelling from Brussels to Rotterdam to Thessaloniki. In each venue it resonates in another environment, with a different history, identity and outreach. The Centre for Fine Arts in Brussels (BOZAR) stimulates the dialogue between cultural heritage and the living arts. It encourages reflection on and research into Europe's cultural commons. As a pendant to *European Portrait Photography since 1990*, BOZAR is simultaneously staging the exhibition *Renaissance Portraits from the Low Countries*. Visitors are invited to make mental connections between the photographs and the 16th-century paintings, and to compare the changing views on individuality, intimacy and community-building.

The Nederlands Fotomuseum in Rotterdam is keeper of a major part of the photographic heritage in the Netherlands. As such, it aims to reach out to a large audience with the story of photography, connecting the past with the present and placing the medium and its social, political and artistic implications in the broader context of our society. *European Portrait Photography since 1990* is a perfect illustration of this ambition, as well as an ideal example of a successful international collaboration between European cultural institutions.

The Museum of Photography in Thessaloniki is the only state institution in Greece dedicated to photography and falls under the supervision of the Ministry of Culture and Sports. The museum's goals are to present photography in all its uses, preserve the national photographic heritage, collect Greek and international works, and to support contemporary activity. Part of its mission is to endorse collaboration between other institutions, especially when it yields projects, like this one, that stimulate dialogue and bring unanswered questions to the fore.

This book and its accompanying exhibition showcase work by more than 30 artists who have been living and working in Europe since 1990. Both the publication and the exhibition were realized through a unique collaboration between three cultural institutions that share the ambition to play a role in the ongoing artistic and cultural debates of our time. We would like to thank all these institutions and their teams, for their efforts, energy and vision, and especially the following: Sophie Lauwers from BOZAR EXPO and her team – Exhibition Coordinator Christophe De Jaeger and Publication Coordinator Gunther De Wit; also Barbara Basdeki from the Museum of Photography in Thessaloniki. Furthermore, we wish to thank all the lenders, without whom this exhibition would not have been possible; the head curator, Frits Gierstberg, and the board of advisors, consisting of Christophe De Jaeger (BOZAR), Gautier Platteau (Hannibal), Alexandra Athanasiadou and Vangelis Ioakimidis (Museum of Photography, Thessaloniki) and Olga Sviblova (House of Photography, Moscow); the publishers Hannibal and Prestel for the wonderful catalogue; and of course, a very big thank you to all the galleries with which we collaborated for this exhibition.

Last but not least, we thank the artists for accepting our invitation to show their work and to share it with people all over Europe. We hope their work will be inspirational, serve as a mirror, tell us something about Europe and its people – even if this raises new questions in our minds. Whatever the outcome or effect, we are sure these portraits will touch you.

Paul Dujardin
Director-General and Artistic Director, BOZAR, Centre for Fine Arts, Brussels

Ruud Visschedijk
Director, Nederlands Fotomuseum, Rotterdam

Vangelis Ioakimidis
Director, Museum of Photography, Thessaloniki

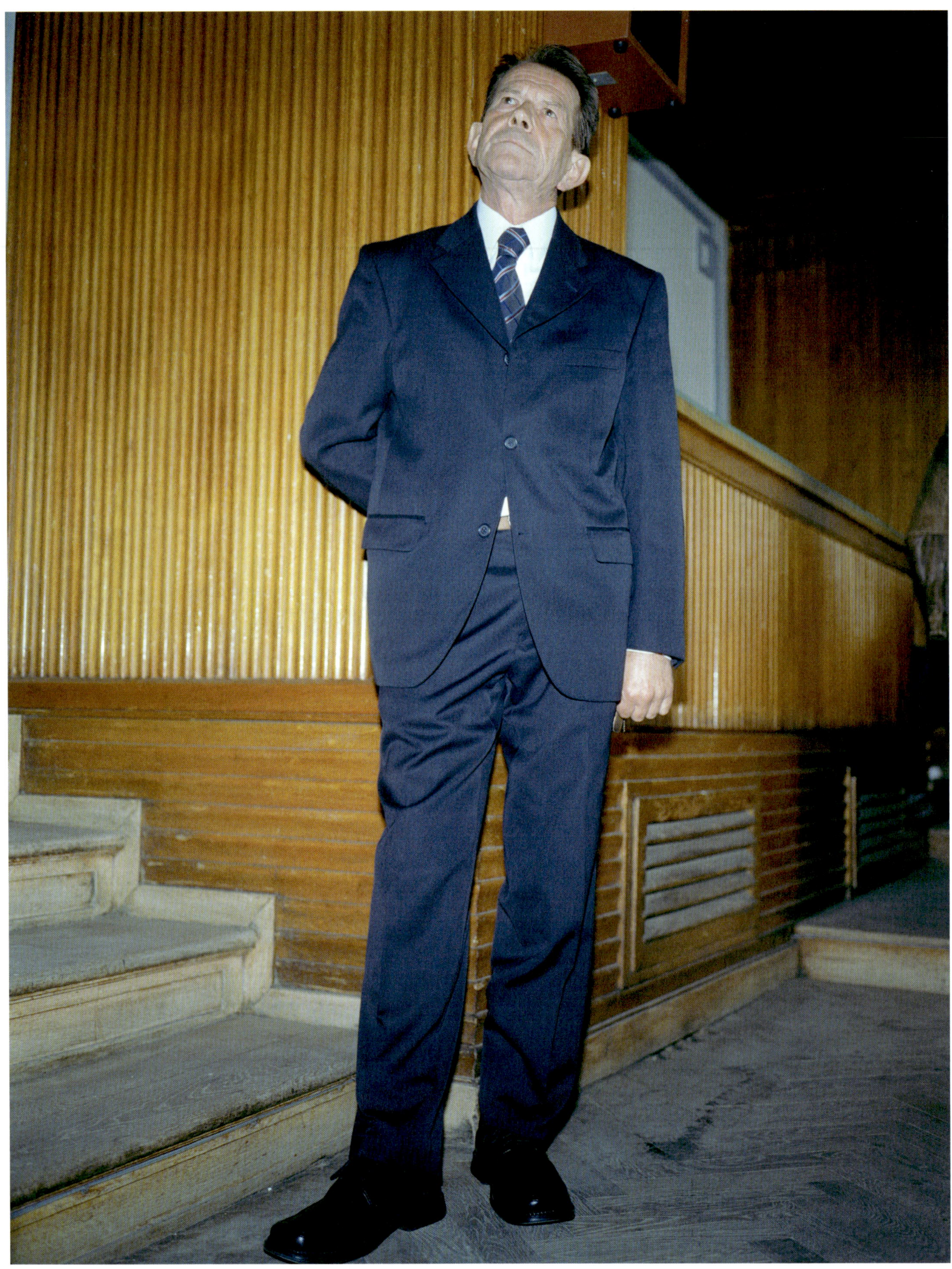

Lucia Nimcova, *Principal*, in 'Unofficial', 2007. Archival ink-jet print, 80 × 60 cm. Courtesy the artist and Krokus Galéria, Bratislava

European Portraits:
an Introduction

Frits Gierstberg

Renaissance

We live in the age of the portrait. Never before in history have portraits been so popular, albeit mainly in the form of a selfie. Similarly, never has it been so incredibly simple to make a portrait to show to the whole world. The rise of the Internet, social media and the smartphone have all given the photographic portrait an unprecedented strong impetus. Yet not all portraits are the same. There are many different sorts of photo portraits (passport photographs, family portraits, self-portraits, profile photographs, writer portraits, glamour portraits, official portraits, etc.) and just as many applications and uses (the pop idol in a teenager's bedroom, the king in the courtroom, the mayor in the town hall, the dictator in the town square, the loved one in the purse, the deceased on the mantelpiece, the writer on the back cover, the artist in the museum, and so on). Portraits often have great personal or social significance. They are part of social customs, rituals and protocols.

This book brings together the work of a number of photographers and visual artists who have made photo portraits somewhere in Europe over the last 25 years. The selected works stand in a long European tradition of the portrayal or imagination of an individual person or a group of individuals. That tradition includes certain stylistic aspects and social customs that arose with the portraiture of the Renaissance in the 15th and 16th centuries. We think here, for example, of the lifelike depiction of an existing person, the symbolic image of his or her social or public status, and the specific place where, or the way in which, the portrait is created, depending on the purpose for which it was intended. The Renaissance tradition is based on the view that the individual human being takes on value and significance within the wider community of people.

Renaissance portraits were clearly physically framed and meant to be hung on the wall, and with good reason. They possess an intensity, stratification and measure of elaboration, but also a significance that demands more than a fleeting glance from the viewer. The same applies to the portraits in this book. In the 21st century, however, people no longer go to church buildings, palaces or town halls to look at public portraits, but rather to the consecrated hall of the art museum. It is possible that every (photo) portrait might in some way or other find a place in the Renaissance tradition. Basically, every portrait is based on the lifelike reproduction of an individual, usually with a focus on the face. On the other hand, today's photographic portraits, as compared with portraits at the time of the Renaissance, are so omnipresent and 'common' that further comparisons soon fall down. In the context of journalism, commerce, publicity, fashion, glamour and the private sphere (such as the aforementioned selfie), millions of portraits are produced every day all over the world. However, the majority of them are doomed to a brief and fleeting existence or, typically for our modern age, no one will ever see them. Yet this in no way detracts from the fact that the social significance of the photographic portrait can be properly understood only within all the functions and customs in the field between art and the mass media.

I myself, the other person, and the maker

Looking at a portrait is like looking at another person. Whether full-length, frontal (face, head and shoulders), three-quarter or in profile, a portrait 'communicates' a look, a glimpse, a facial expression, and even more. It expresses something, aims to tell us something about the person or persons portrayed: a presence, a status, a type or 'character', or a frame of mind – but then why are there so few portraits of people laughing or crying?

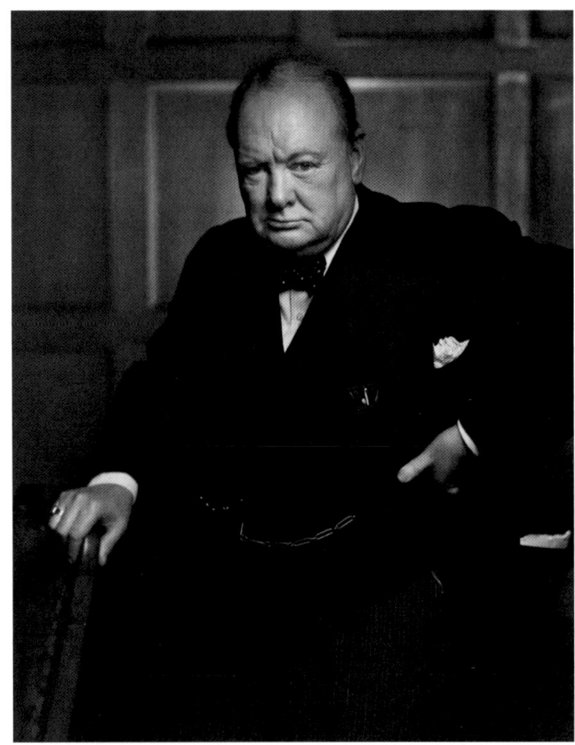

Yousuf Karsh, *Winston Churchill*, 1941. Gelatin silver print, on fibre paper, 50.8 × 40.6 cm. © Yousuf Karsh / Camera Press

With photographs, we are perfectly aware that what we are looking at is an image, a fabrication, a construction, and not a person as such. Yet a portrait does allow us to experience a confrontation with 'the other person'. As we look at a portrait, we see the look first of all. We search out the eyes first, almost instinctively. Within a fraction of a second, we have assessed that look, his or her facial expression and the posture. The image then becomes the fleeting abstract substitute for a meeting *in the flesh*. This gives a portrait a special aura, which is foreign to photographic landscapes, still lifes and street scenes. This makes a photo portrait an exceptional genre, even within photography itself. The portrait has an effect on our experience of being human. It appeals to our sense of humanity. It postulates an identity for the other person or it raises questions, which leads to a degree of empathy as we put ourselves, rationally or emotionally, in the depicted person's place. Secondly, in questioning our identity as a beholder, the portrait acts as a mirror. We have to relate to the other person, and by doing so, we see ourselves. This happens only if the image of that other person is a credible one.

Sometimes, the person being portrayed does not look the viewer in the eye, gazing instead at a point outside the frame. Such portraits belong to a different category, one that is less confrontational: since there is no eye contact, we are free to observe unobserved, like a voyeur. Yet we still feel that the person in the portrait really is present in some way or other. The powerful presence of the depicted person, that aura, compels us to treat the portrait with respect, to cherish and preserve it by embedding it into our personal or social rituals. We do not tear up portraits of loved ones. Portraits of hated dictators, however, get stamped on.

When a portrait is being made, both the sitter and the photographer try to anticipate the (desired) effects that the portrait will have on the viewer – engaging in a mutual endeavour to channel the way it will be interpreted. They do this without revealing their 'bag of tricks': pose, incidence of light, facial expression, camera angle, background, clothing and, if necessary, any relevant props. The pose relates the portrait genre to that of the theatre, where people act and pretend, projecting something with their bodies and facial expressions. Context, culture and tradition form the broader connection in which portraits are made, understood, used and appreciated. Like a painted or sketched portrait, a photo, too, is the product of a relationship – however transient it may be – between the maker of the portrait and the person depicted. A legendary example is when photographer Yousuf Karsh plucked the cigar out of Winston Churchill's mouth, provoking a scowl that Karsh was able to capture just a split second later. Portrait photographers look for a certain intensity or radiance in their subjects, the aim being to create an expressive image that conveys a particular feeling, although a special feeling or look can also be achieved by distant and seemingly neutral facial expressions. To get the right result, a photographer may decide to interview his subject, use a cue word, simply wait until the sitter's nerves have settled down – or resort to a provocation, which is how Karsh got the photo he wanted of Britain's wartime leader in 1941. The big difference between now and then is that in our image culture, we are all too aware of the ubiquitous presence of cameras and what they are capable of. Today, in 2015, there is no such thing as an innocent glance.

Image of mankind

Contemporary artistic photography embraces many styles, views and methods. This diversity has come about not only through artistic developments, but also through changing views on the concept of identity over the last three or four decades: the fact that identity is not tied down, the importance of context for the establishment of identity, the manipulability of identity, and the 'post-human' concept of the cyborg. Also playing a part is the undermining of photography as a reality-bound medium. Countless expressive artists and photographers have reflected on these developments in their work and treated the portrait as a phenomenon and/or in a conceptual manner. Moreover, since the early 1990s, there has been a striking (and in some respects rather 'traditional') movement within portrait photography, in which real, existing persons and their individuality take centre stage. Here, old values and myths surrounding the portrait (the exposure of character, the capture and portrayal of the soul) are not naively restored to a place of honour, but there is still a belief in the power of the portrait in the relationship between subject and beholder, between the one who looks and the one being 'looked at'. Portraits are regarded as encounters in which the individuals are seen and shown implicitly or explicitly as human beings who are part of a community, culture and history. Attention is paid to their humanity, human dignity, vulnerability, and the uncertain and fluid nature of their identities. In other words, this appeals expressly to a humanistic view of mankind and thereby searches implicitly or explicitly for a link with the Renaissance tradition.

The common man

What is most striking about contemporary and autonomous portrait photography is the attention paid to ordinary people, or people doing ordinary, everyday things. Obviously, portraits of prominent figures and celebrities (from politicians to artists and pop stars) are still being made, and we have selected some of them for this book. Nevertheless, a substantial proportion of portrait photographers and expressive artists are interested in ordinary men, women and children, albeit perhaps those with an unusual 'story'. Rineke Dijkstra photographed adolescents she saw on the beach in summer. Jitka Hanzlová photographed inhabitants of a small Czech village going about their daily lives. Beat Streuli photographed passers-by in the street, while Luc Delahaye concentrated on metro passengers (exceptional portraits because the people in the pictures were unaware of the camera). At one point, Thomas Ruff was taking photographs of his fellow students. Juergen Teller pointed his camera at young ladies who came to his door in the hope of becoming photographic model. Boris Mikhailov has immortalized his compatriots in Charkov, Ukraine, who were at the bottom end of society and ended up in abject poverty. Clare Strand invited the homeless to come and pose in her studio. Nikos Markou gave a face to the multitudes of Greeks who suffered badly during the economic crisis of 2008. Stratos Kalafatis ventured to Mount Athos to photograph monks there who had opted for isolation within a small and sharply defined religious community. Koos Breukel and Stephan Vanfleteren have put into pictures those who have visibly lived life to the full.

Setting, culture, history – context

As with other photography practices since the 1990s, styles, methods and genres are increasingly overlapping and hybrid forms are emerging. Contemporary photography has long ceased to define 'portrait' according to traditional aesthetic or stylistic criteria. More photographers are applying greater stratification to their portraits by putting them in certain cultural and historical contexts. In her *Rokytník* series, Jitka Hanzlová combined spontaneous portraits with the immediate rural setting in and around a small Czech village in order to illustrate the close connection between the inhabitants and the location. Manfred Willmann also photographed countryside dwellers, in the Austrian province of Weststeiermark, during their daily life and work on 'the land', where the strong interaction between tradition, culture and nature shapes their identity. Like Hanzlová's photographs, Willmann's portraits, too, are part of a bigger series, which includes different topics (such as landscapes and interiors). In both cases, the work was created during years of personal involvement, or even 'participation', in the scenes depicted, resulting in a special combination of intimacy, naturalism and poetry. These important works are thus connected specifically to those people and locations; at the same time, however, they serve to illustrate the changes under way in rural communities and local cultures that have existed for centuries throughout large parts of Europe. In a village in eastern Poland (on the same spot where the photographer's grandfather once worked the land), Adam Pańczuk created a series of theatrical portraits in which the inhabitants express their ties to the land they culti-vate. Lucia Nimcova had her characters play out 're-enactments' of everyday situations in the days of communism, as remembered by them. In this way, both Pańczuk and Nimcova incor-porate history in their work, a decisive factor in the experience of one's own identity, and make it an explicit part of the portrait. Something similar occurs in the works of Paola De Pietri, but *in reverse*: she portrays pregnant women in anonymous settings in suburbia, linking the future and (the loss of) history.

Involvement

Photographers are often committed to their subject for a lengthy period of time. This measure of personal involvement is crucial to many photographers for what they want to achieve with their portraits. Anton Corbijn made friends with the members of the pop group U2 while lay-ing the foundation for their public image with his portrait photos, which were unconventional for pop photography. For years, Rineke Dijkstra followed the progress of the young immigrant Almerisa as she grew up in the Netherlands and made the local culture her own. Such a series of portraits is possible only if there is mutual trust between the two parties. For his *Act* series, Denis Darzacq began photographing people with mental disabilities. They were allowed to decide how and where they wanted to have their portrait made, an unusual freedom that found strong expression in the portraits. To that end, the photographer first had to win their trust, to a greater degree than is necessary when making a regular portrait. This requires a certain men-tality and personality, and also a particular view about the so frequently praised 'democratic aspect' of photography. One could say that in many portraits the identity of the maker creeps into the final result as a recognizable signature. In this respect, every portrait is a self-portrait. The real self-portrait is a special genre that has long been practised in painting. For painters, expressive artists and photographers, the self-portrait means much more than just a look in the mirror. Apart from a reflection of one's own person, a self-portrait is also a reflection of one's identity *as an artist*. At the same time, it is also an investigation of the medium, since the maker is now also looking from the perspective of the subject and is in a better position to understand the workings of his or her mode of artistic expression. Inevitably, the self-portrait is thereby also a test of one's own technical ability. The artistic and existential challenge thus formed explains the importance of the self-portrait for many image makers. They expose and subject themselves to critical scrutiny of their extraordinary position as mediators of identities. Often, that self-portrait is part of a greater whole. Anders Petersen's self-portraits recur with some regularity in his often intense depiction of life around him. Konstantinos Ignatiadis includes his own picture, taken at an archaeological location that speaks of culture and history, in a long series of international artist portraits. Alberto García-Alix places himself within his own imagin-ary community of equally powerful and exceptional personalities. The Portuguese artist Jorge Molder does not make self-portraits, although he himself is often in the picture. Molder uses his own face as a mask, or persona (in Latin, *persona* means 'actor's mask'), beneath which 'identity' takes shape, but also changes constantly, depending on social and artistic influences, the life lived, and the emotions and memories that are activated.

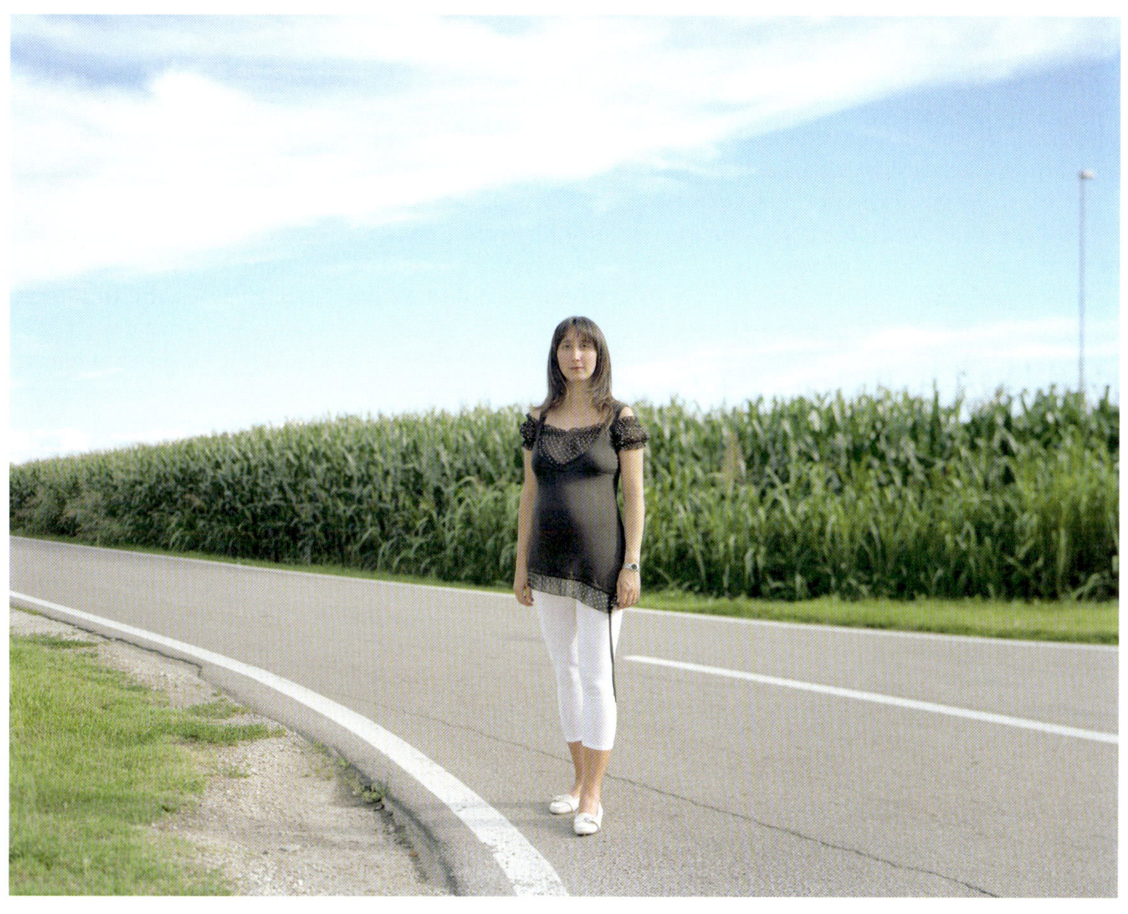

Paola De Pietri, *Untitled*, in 'Io parto', 2007. Archival digital pigment print on cotton rag, 108 × 135.5 cm.
Courtesy the artist, Alberto Peola - Galleria d'Arte Contemporanea, Turin, and Galerie Les Filles du Calvaire, Paris

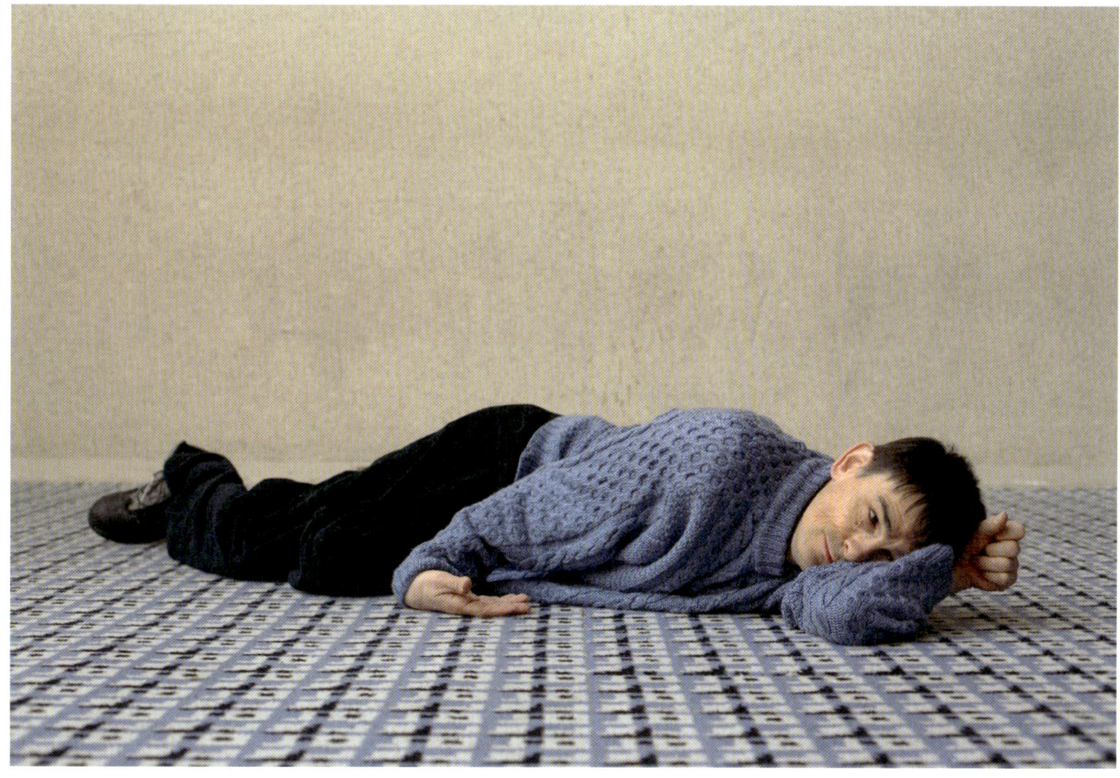

Denis Darzacq, *Paul Ronam, Act 44*, in 'Act', 2010. Digital C-print, 100 × 130 cm. Courtesy the artist and Galerie RX, Paris

Tabula rasa

Portraiture after World War II certainly enjoyed several moments of renewal, such as with Irving Penn, Richard Avedon, Robert Mapplethorpe and other photographers mainly from the USA, but their artistic inventions did not substantially affect the foundations of the portrait genre. Not until the 1980s was there a fundamental reassessment of photography as a so-called truthful and democratic medium. The criticism that photography was a component of more or less established public, social and political structures that had previously lain at the foundation of portrayal became the starting point from which artists and photographers set off in new directions. While it is not possible to give a simple summary of developments within the visual arts and photography at that time – for they did not arise from just one movement or trend – it is possible to point to a number of leading players whose work had a big influence in Europe on the way people thought about photographic portraiture. In the USA, such figures include Cindy Sherman and Nan Goldin, who come from completely different and perhaps radically opposed positions, namely the conceptual as opposed to the personal. With her series *Untitled Film Stills*, Sherman posed questions about authenticity and identity in a modern media society. To what extent does identity differ from a construction, piece of fiction or picture, instead of being something that stays inside a core? By repeatedly photographing herself as a figure in a fictitious film story, she points out the flexibility and instability of the notion. Goldin portrayed her 'family of friends' from the inside out, that is to say, from her intimacy with and emotional involvement in the occasionally dramatic events in the lives of her immediate friends, initially even without explicit artistic ambitions.

Forming an important bridge between these artists and those from the 1990s who would occupy themselves with the portrait and identity was the work of the German artist Thomas Ruff, who in the early 1980s began a series of portraits of fellow students, initially in black and white and switching to colour later on. He portrayed them the way the police would have photographed them, based on the identification system developed by the French photographer and criminologist Alphonse Bertillon (1853-1914): frontal view, no facial expression, even and undramatic exposure. In the first series, Ruff allowed his sitters to choose a background colour from a sample card for colour photography, but later opted for a less expressive, more neutral background. From 1986, he started to present his large-scale portraits measuring 165 × 210 centimetres, exhibiting them as a uniform series hanging rigidly in line – a form and strategy he took over from his tutors, Bernd and Hilla Becher, who had used this approach for their extensive photography project on industrial monuments. The remote, uniform shape of Ruff's portraits make a detached, almost scholarly impression. They are 'empty'. By removing as much significance and connotation as possible from the images, as a sort of zero-degree portrait, his *Porträts* series created a blank slate for the genre and smoothed the way for new possibilities. Rineke Dijkstra, Hellen van Meene, Paola De Pietri, Sergey Bratkov, Ari Versluis & Ellie Uyttenbroek, Juergen Teller, Dita Pepe and many others have been able to build on Ruff's 'blank slate' approach.

Renaissance

It is possible to argue that the question about one's own identity (with regard to the other person, the group and the community) is more important and pressing than ever before in history. At the same time, we know better than ever how complex the subject of 'identity' really is. It appears that we do not have a hard core in ourselves; what we consider to be our own 'I' is also constantly subject to change. The postmodernism that controlled the discourse in expressive art in the 1980s has announced the 'end of great stories' (Lyotard), which mankind had kept together until then as an almost mystical unity – albeit from a Western perspective. The bankruptcy of communism and socialism became visible, and in 1989, the Berlin Wall fell. The period in which this revolution took place also marked the start of the wild growth of the Internet and the World Wide Web in the 1990s. Digitalization and globalization went hand in hand. Marshall McLuhan's concept of a 'global village' became a reality. People were able to communicate with each other beyond the borders of cities, countries and continents, and form new communities separated from time and space. All this would radically change our awareness of identity, with various forms of our 'I' wandering around in the virtual world like avatars.

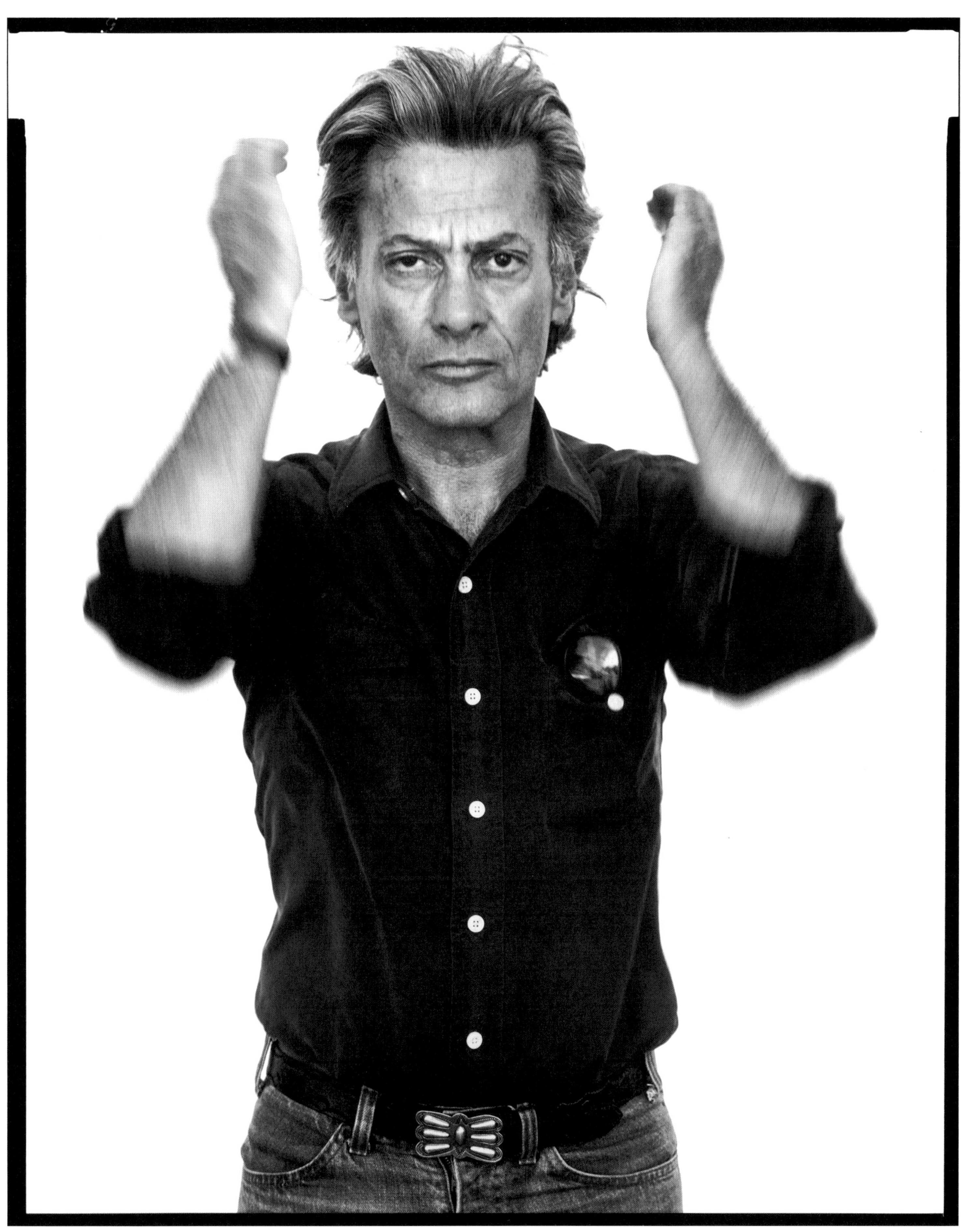

Richard Avedon, *Richard Avedon, Self-portrait, Photographer, Provo, Utah, August 20, 1980*, 1984–85. Gelatin silver print, mounted on aluminium, 127.3 × 99.7 cm
© The Richard Avedon Foundation

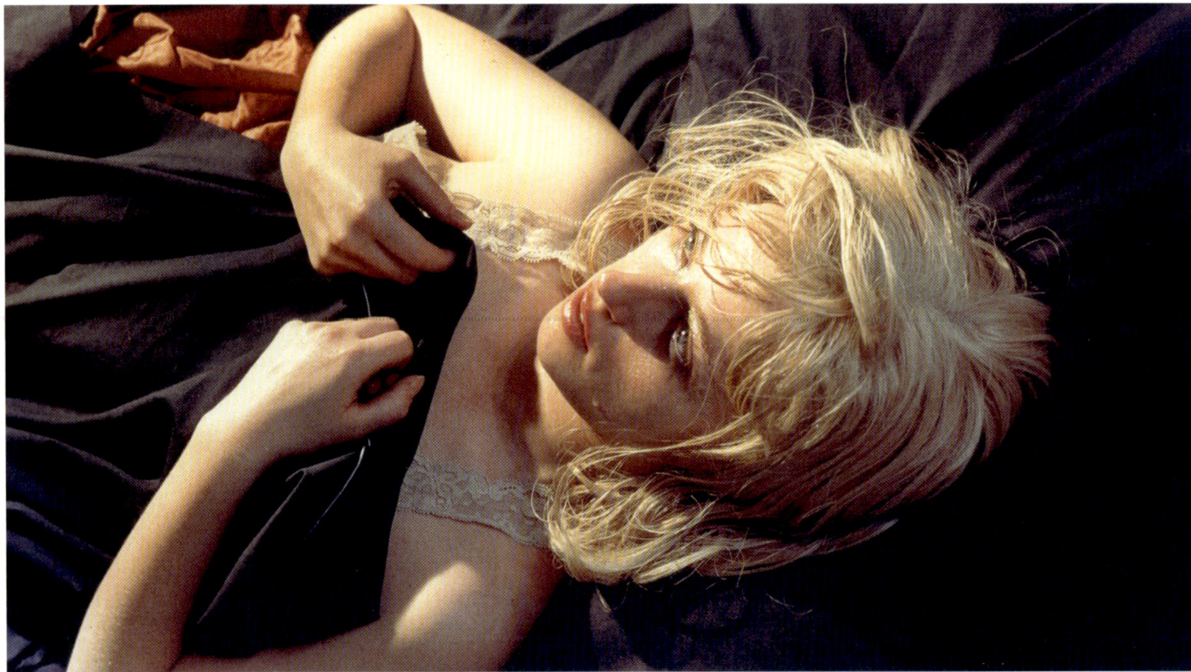

Cindy Sherman, *Untitled Film Still 93*, in 'Untitled Film Stills', 1981. Cibachrome colour print, 61.7 × 123.7 cm. Museum Boijmans Van Beuningen, Rotterdam, courtesy the artist

Yet the dilution and disappearance of borders between countries and continents, between regions and communities, and between locations and time zones also has a snag, namely the fear of losing something: identity, individuality, local culture, the small stories. Traditional communities are falling apart, and historical links are breaking down. In Europe, the cradle of the Renaissance and the humanistic view of mankind, the issue of identity is also taking centre stage with regard to history, landscape, culture, even the soil. Who am I and who is that other person? To what extent are we formed by where we are? By what we do? By where we come from? Am I a Frenchman or a European? An Italian or a Sicilian? Or am I merely a digital world citizen? Developments in which notions of identity change so rapidly (the above is merely a rough sketch) form the context of the current artistic and social significance of portraiture, in so far as it poses the question of identity. An interesting parallel then emerges with the Renaissance, when portraitists looked for a way to depict newly-born mankind.

Catalogue

Tina Barney (born 1945, United States)

The Europeans

Photographer Tina Barney acquired international fame for her large-scale colour photographs of her wealthy family at home on the American east coast. With a large-size camera, she portrayed the members of her family in the midst of their daily lives and family gatherings. The informal moments she chose, such as breakfast, getting dressed or a day at the beach, contrast handsomely with the voluminous nature of the pictures. Barney is interested in human relations, how harmony within a family takes shape, but also how family traditions continue, such as in certain rituals or the way in which a house is designed. For *The Europeans*, Barney travelled through Germany, France, Italy, Austria and Spain between 1996 and 2004 to depict 'upper-class' families in her incomparable manner. These were people who, in times past, would probably have sat for an artist's portrait, or would at least have had, and still have, the means to do so. The series presents an ostensibly documentary image of the upper class in Europe, with scores of references to the artistic and cultural traditions of 'the old Europe'. Barney's photographs strike a perfect balance between an unprompted discovery of an intimate moment and a rehearsed and orchestrated scene. With her precise exposure and composition, she has captured not only the details of the person or persons, but also those of the interiors and objects in view. That's why the latter inevitably affect how people 'read' and interpret the pictures. Barney always strikes a visual balance between the people and the interiors in which they find themselves. Both make their presence felt equally strongly, and in this way the photographer urges us to make connections between aspects like character and possession, upbringing and taste, tradition and renewal, and identity and material culture.

FG

p. 21
The Brocade Walls, in 'The Europeans', 2003.
Chromogenic colour print, 122 × 152 cm

p. 22
The Two Students, in 'The Europeans', 2001.
Chromogenic colour print, 122 × 152 cm

p. 23
The Ancestors, in 'The Europeans', 2001.
Chromogenic colour print, 122 × 152 cm

Courtesy the artist and Paul Kasmin Gallery, New York

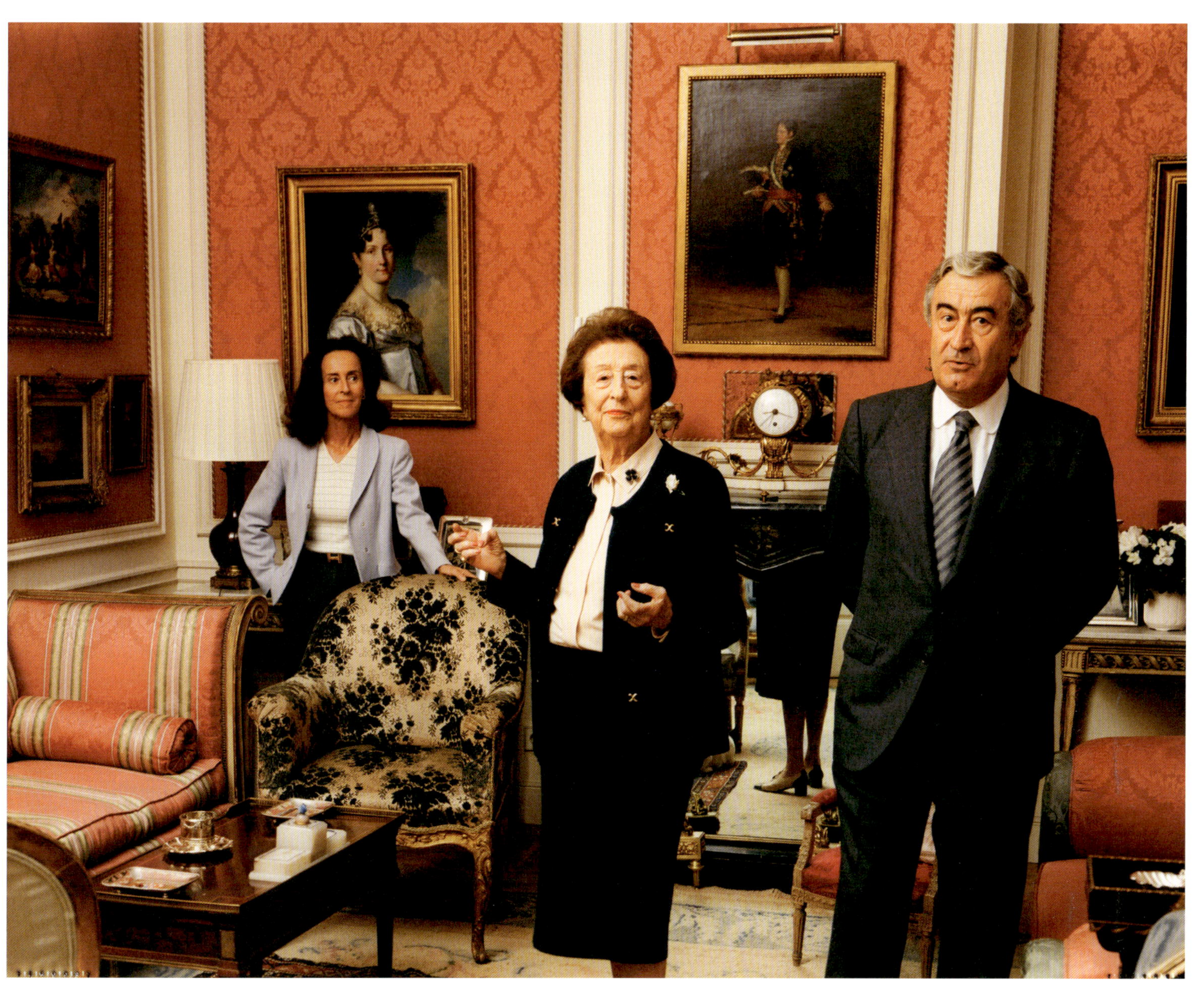

Tina Barney

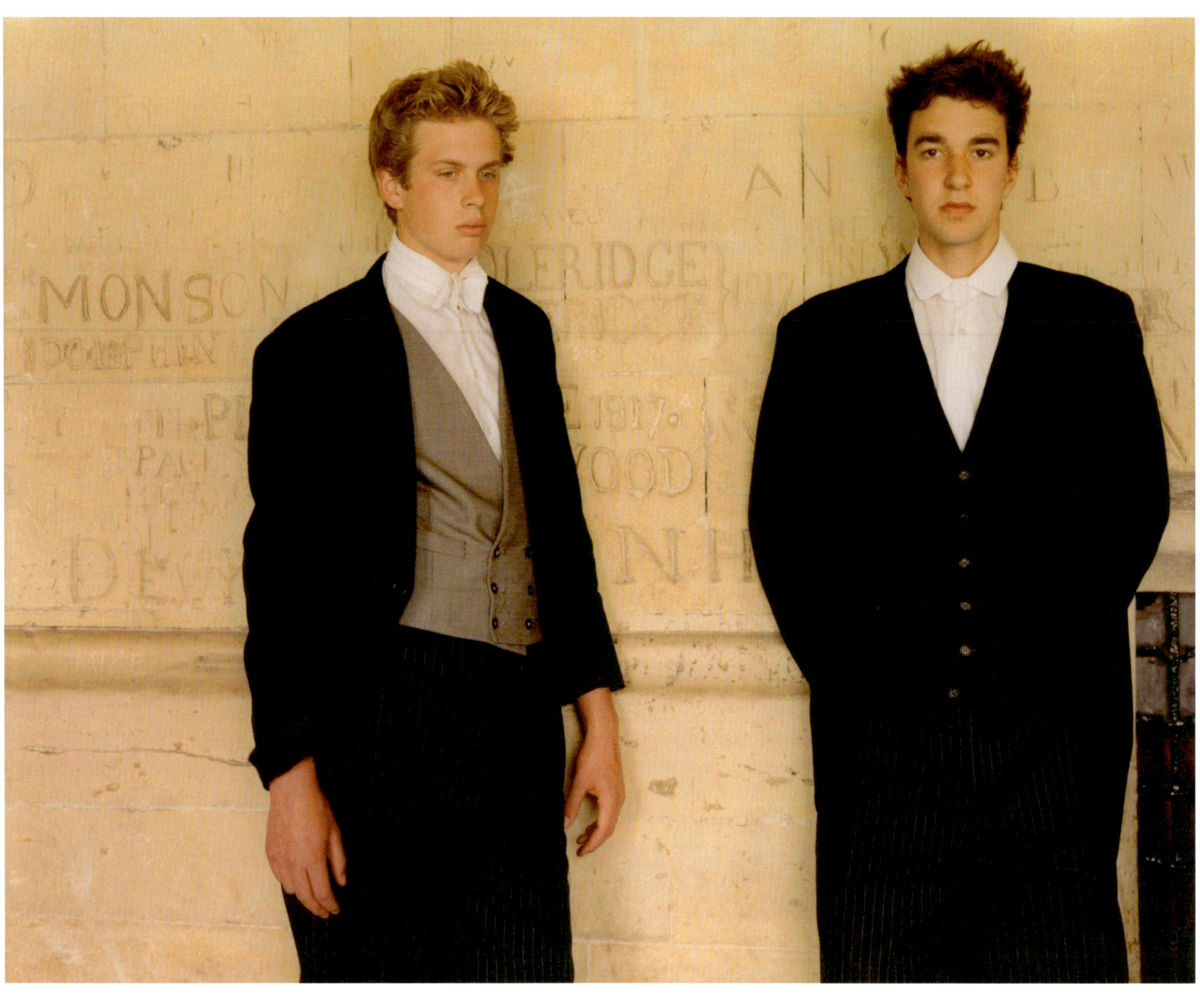

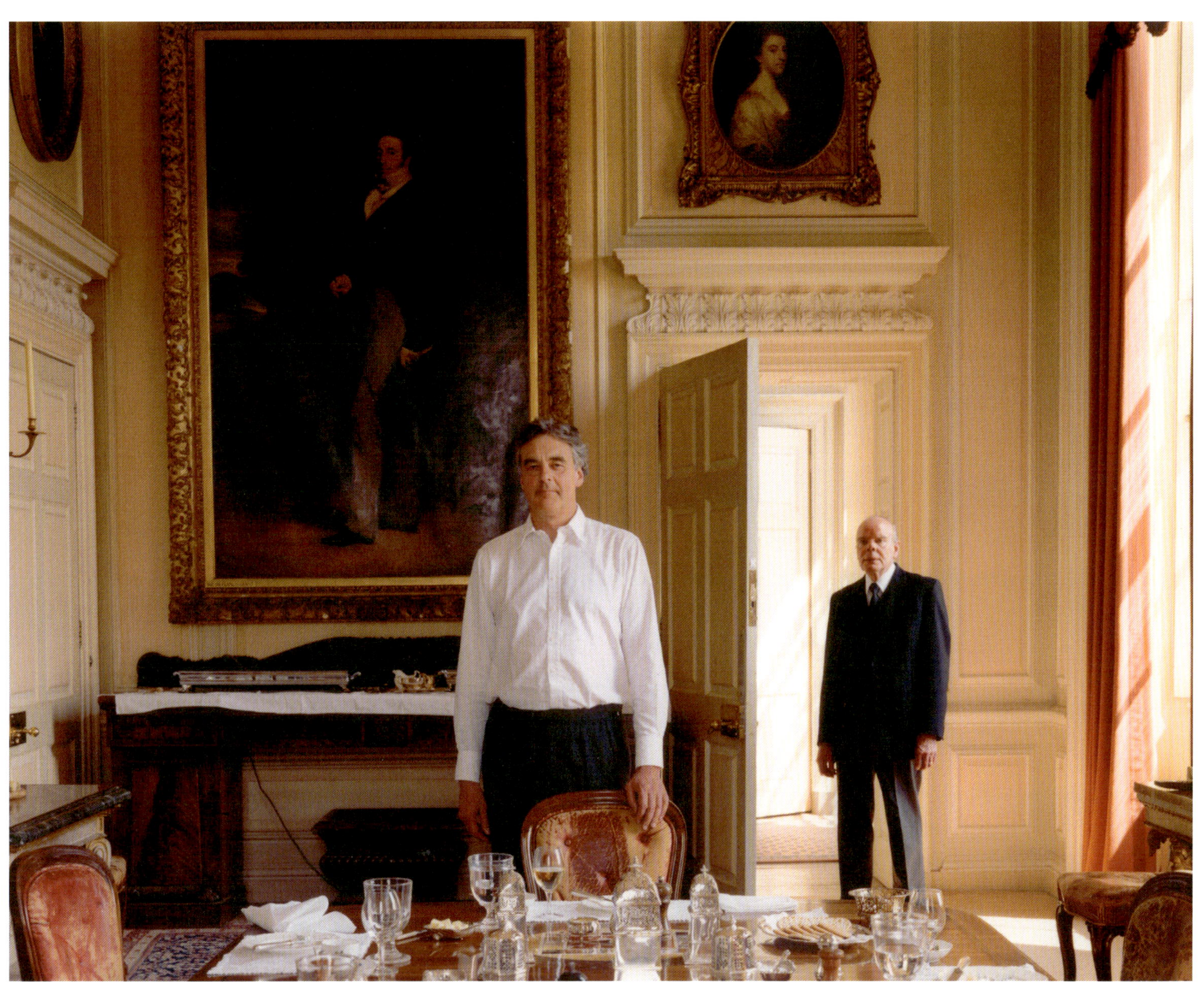

Tina Barney

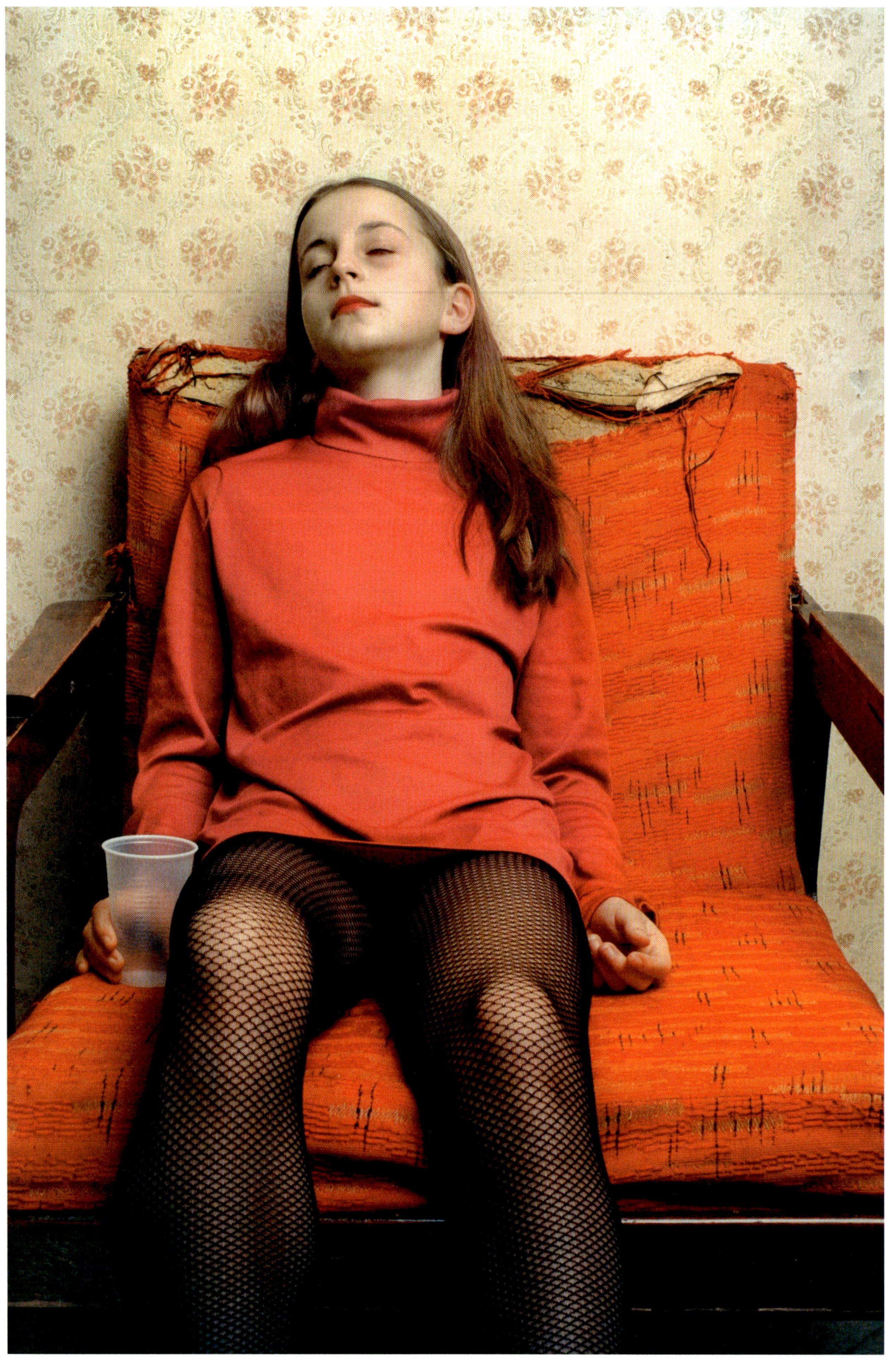

Sergey Bratkov (born 1960, Ukraine)

KIDS

Sergey Bratkov belongs to a group of Ukrainian artists who have developed a radical and realistic style and raised controversial social issues. At first, Bratkov reacted to the propaganda clichés of the Soviet regime, but soon also became critical of the West's visual culture, which took root quickly in the East after the collapse of the Soviet Union. Bratkov used to do graphics, collages and paintings, but later concentrated on photography, with the emphasis on portraits. He produced images of soldiers, children and heroes, or anti-heroes who were the victims of successive ideologies. The *KIDS* series shows Russian child models, whose parents took them to modelling agencies in the hope of building a future and earning some income for themselves or their children. Male and female Lolita-like figures adopt adult and often sensual poses for the camera. Here, Bratkov breaks through moral and aesthetical taboos in both East and West and alludes to a hard, adult world that has lost all its innocence. In these pictures, we see the dreams of a generation that, after the fall of the Berlin Wall, was unexpectedly but inevitably exposed to Western mass media and popular visual culture, including publicity – and which then began to believe in the fairy tales of capitalism.

CDJ

p. 24
Alyona, in 'KIDS', 2000.
Colour photo, 40 × 27 cm. M HKA, Antwerp

p. 26
Zhenya, in 'KIDS', 2000.
Colour photo, 40 × 27 cm. M HKA, Antwerp

p. 27
Sasha, in 'KIDS', 2000.
Colour photo, 40 × 27 cm. M HKA, Antwerp

p. 28
Sonya, in 'KIDS', 2000.
Colour photo, 40 × 27 cm. M HKA, Antwerp

p. 29
Vera, in 'KIDS', 2000.
Colour photo, 40 × 27 cm. M HKA, Antwerp

p. 30
Zakhar, in 'KIDS', 2000.
Colour photo, 40 × 27 cm. M HKA, Antwerp

Courtesy Regina Gallery, London and Moscow

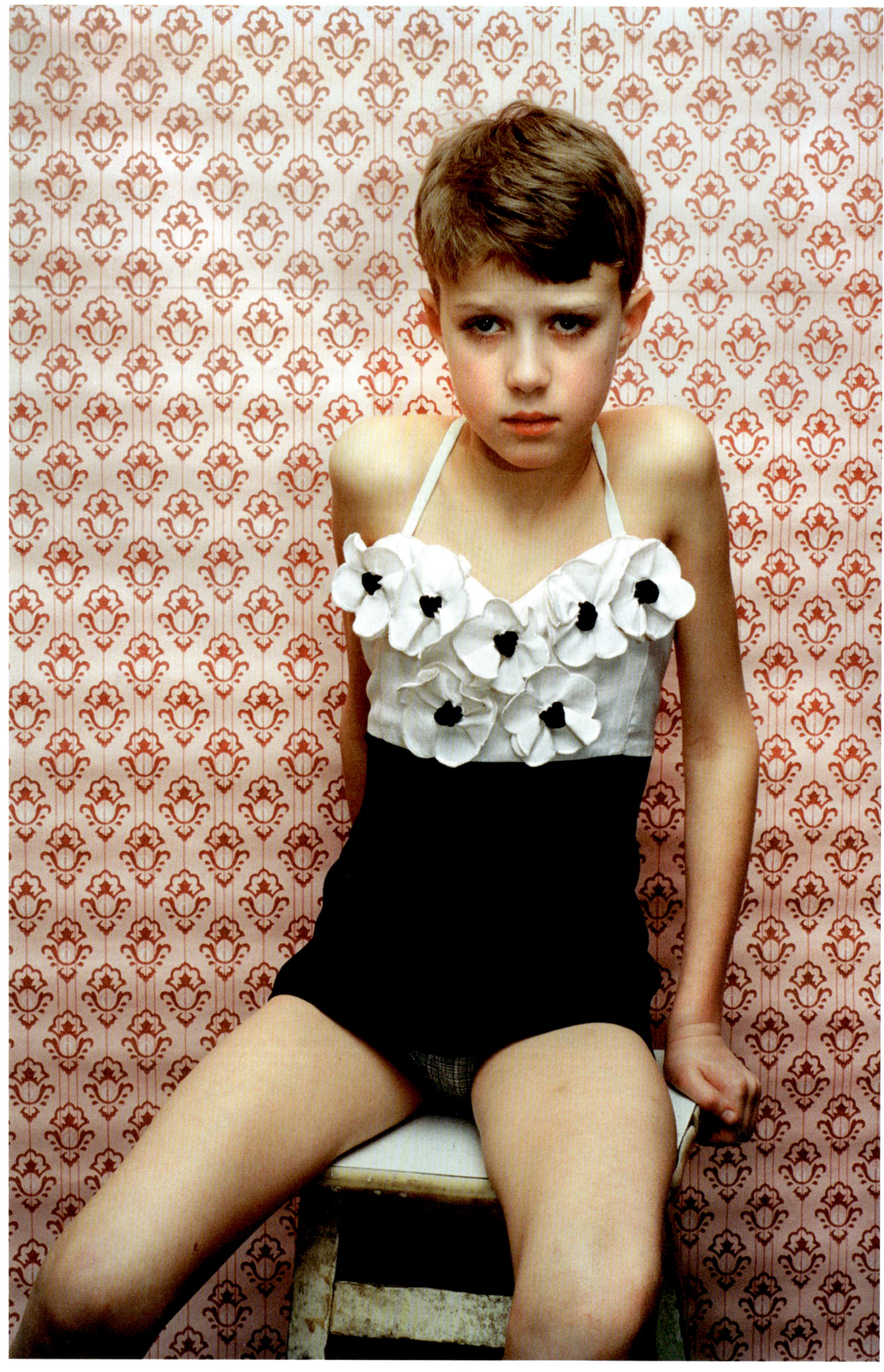

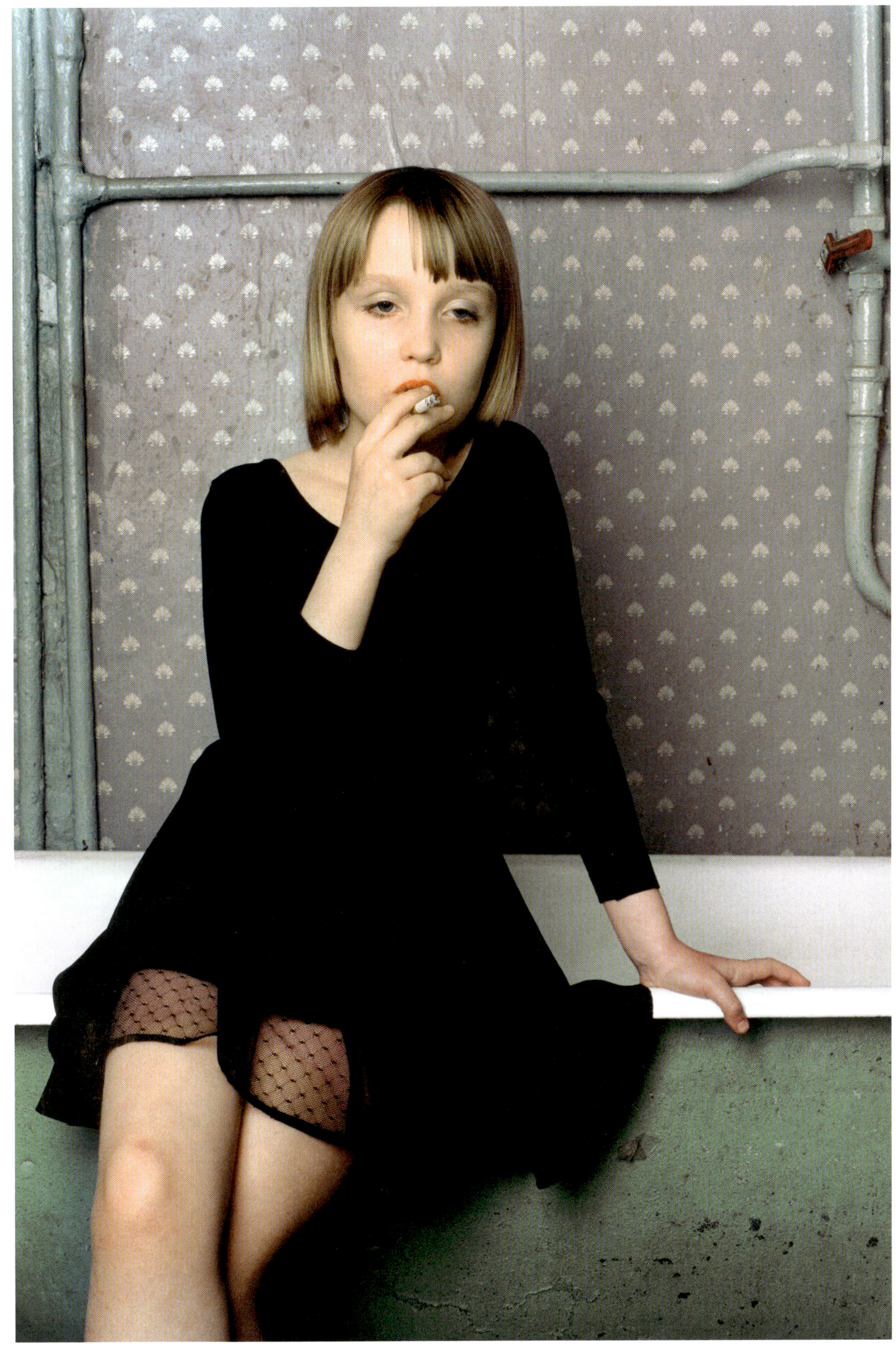

Sergey Bratkov

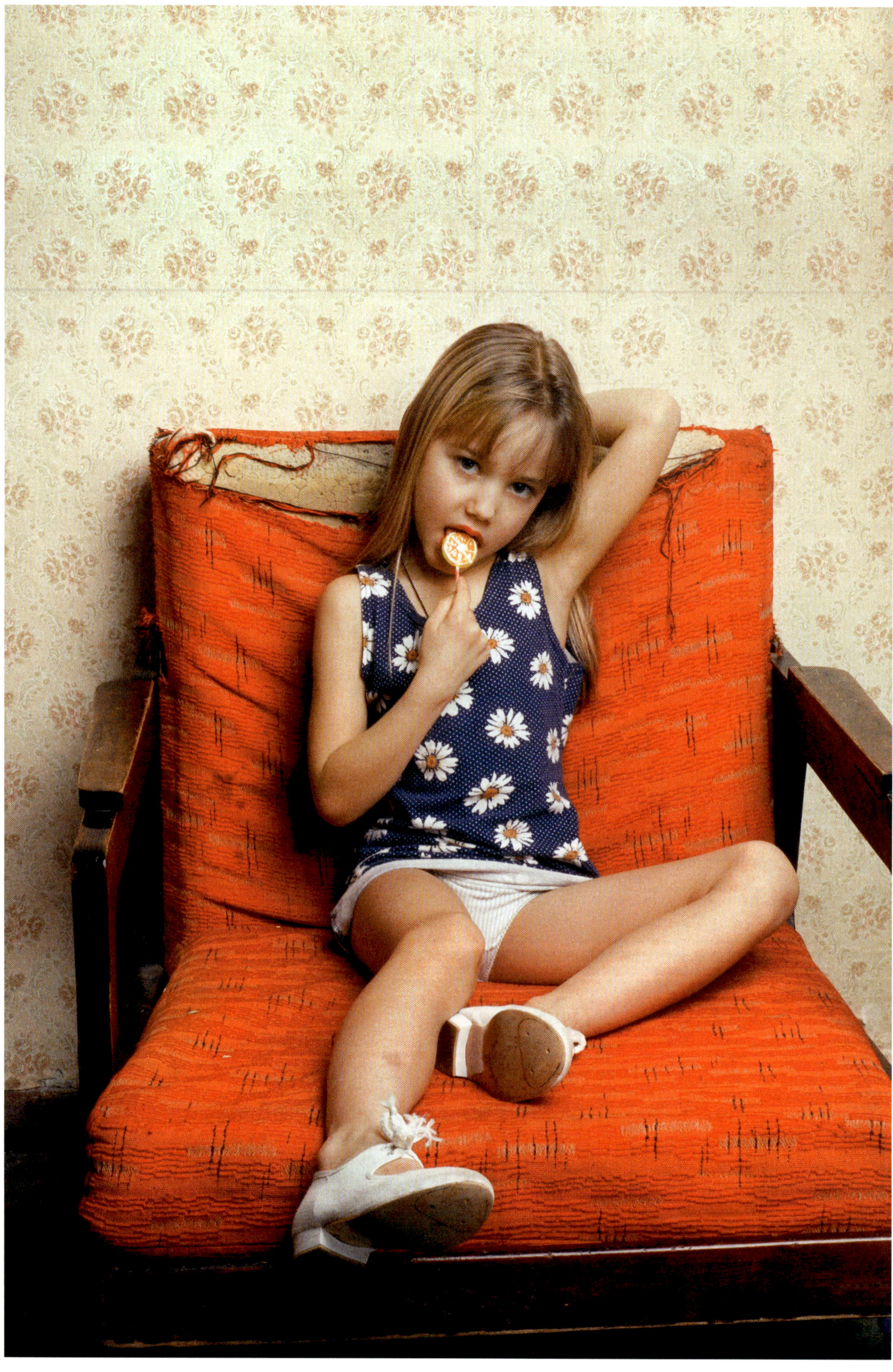

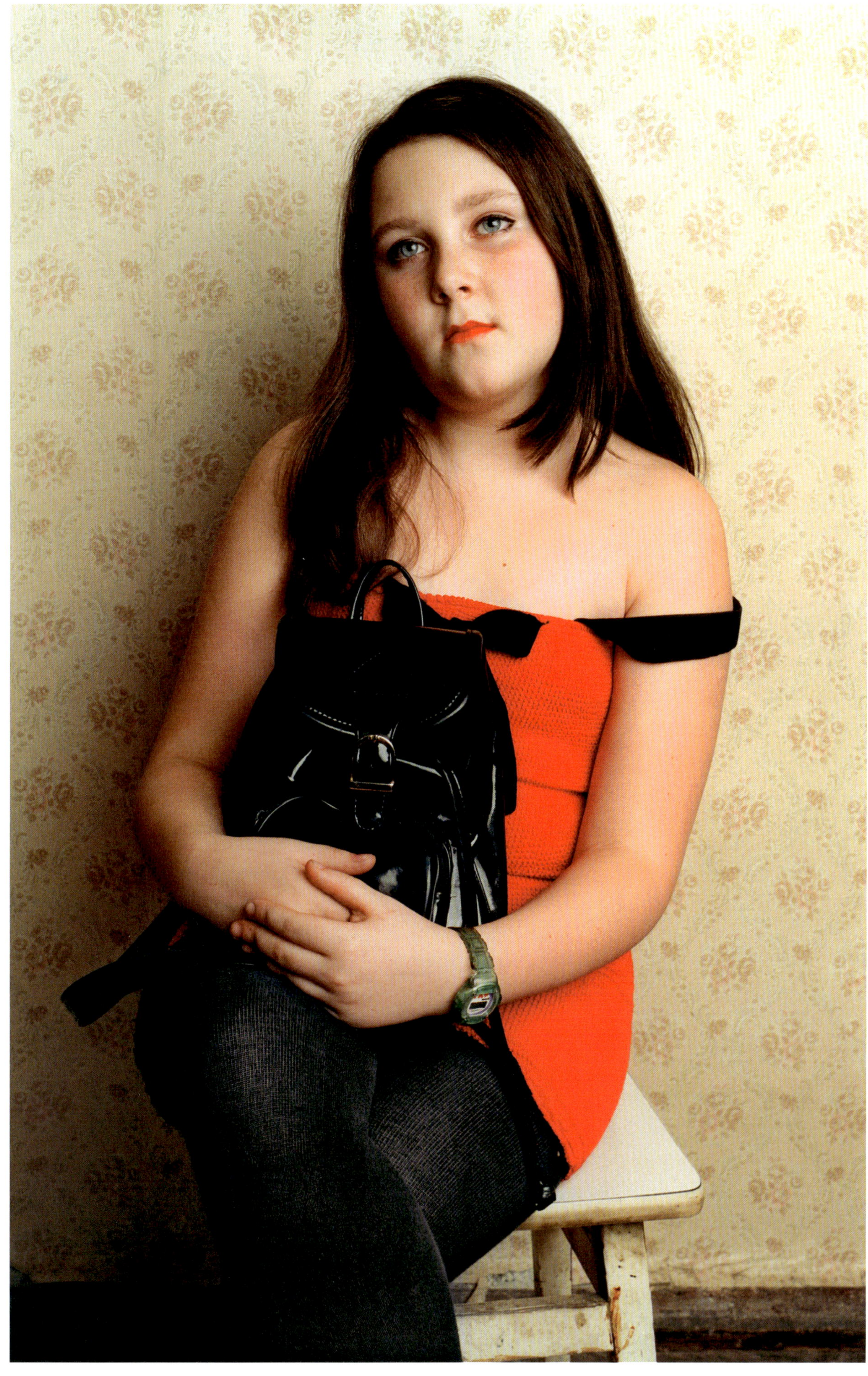

Sergey Bratkov

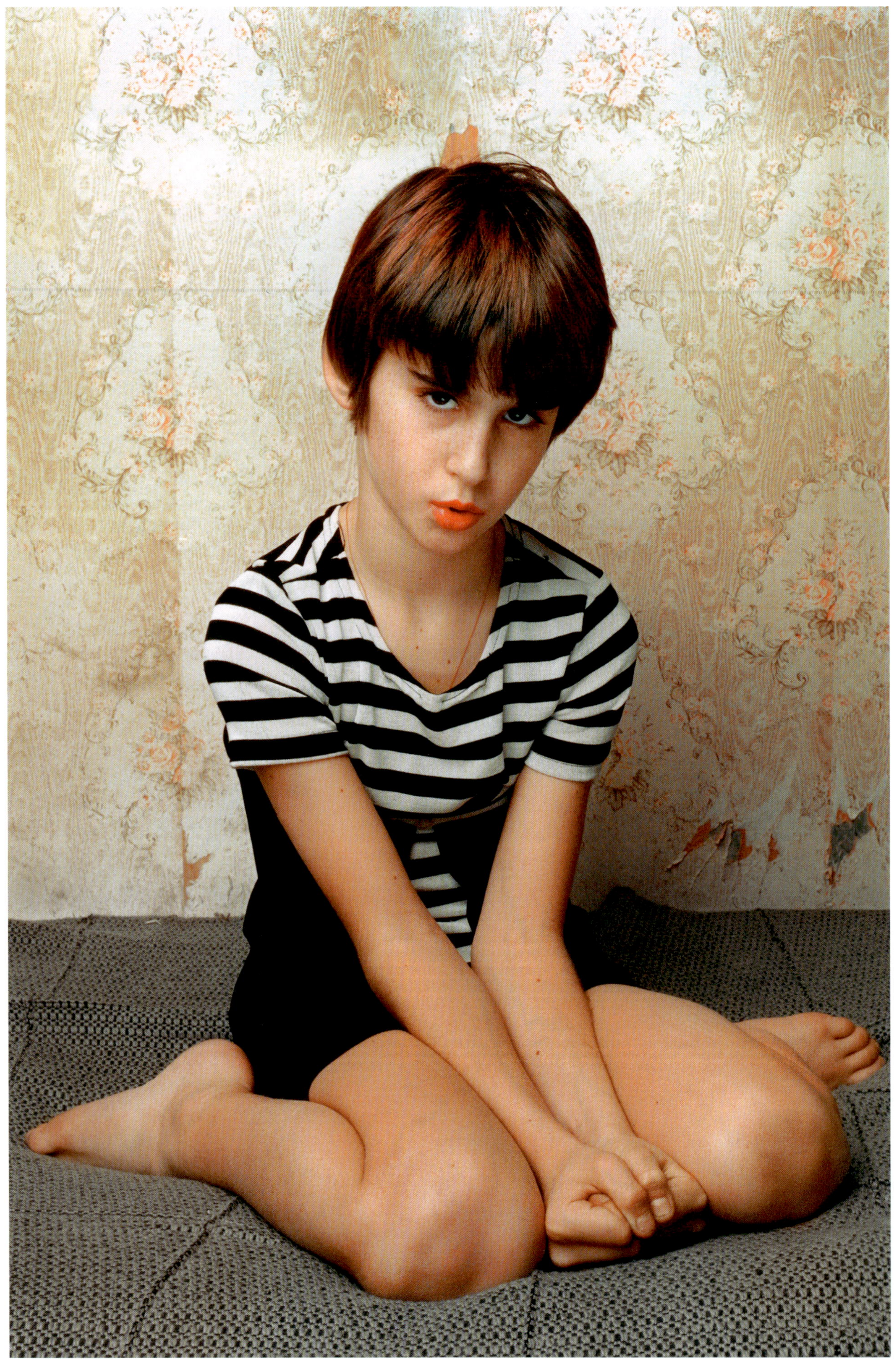

Koos Breukel (born 1962, the Netherlands)

From the very start of his career as a photographer, Koos Breukel never occupied himself with trends in photography or the public who might look at his pictures. He simply photographed life with all its blemishes, from the cradle to the grave. As a result of events in his own personal life, he developed a sensitivity to signs in others of emotions that he had experienced himself. His work reflects his life, as it were, and he refers to himself as a 'photographic anthropologist'. Breukel records the outside, but his pictures go deeper, straight through the façade. With a faultless radar and deep compassion, he shows the beauty and the scars, the hope, fear, love, heaviness of heart and, with great dignity, death and mourning. His early photographs were invariably taken against a dark background, which creates a certain drama, with the contours of his models sometimes barely visible. Later, he also took colour photographs, first with large-format Deardorff and Sinar cameras; he now uses a Canon digital camera. Breukel's work includes series for museums and galleries, and the first state portraits, taken in April 2013, of King Willem-Alexander and Queen Máxima of the Netherlands.

GP

p. 33
Mother, 1992.
Gelatin silver print, 143 × 104 cm

p. 34
Sandra Derks en Ellev, Bergen (NH), 2000.
Gelatin silver print, 108 × 83 cm

p. 35
Gerard Petrus Fieret, Den Haag, 2005.
Gelatin silver print, 120 × 100 cm

pp. 36–37
Hendrien Adams, Amsterdam, 1997.
Gelatin silver print, 100 × 120 cm

Courtesy the artist

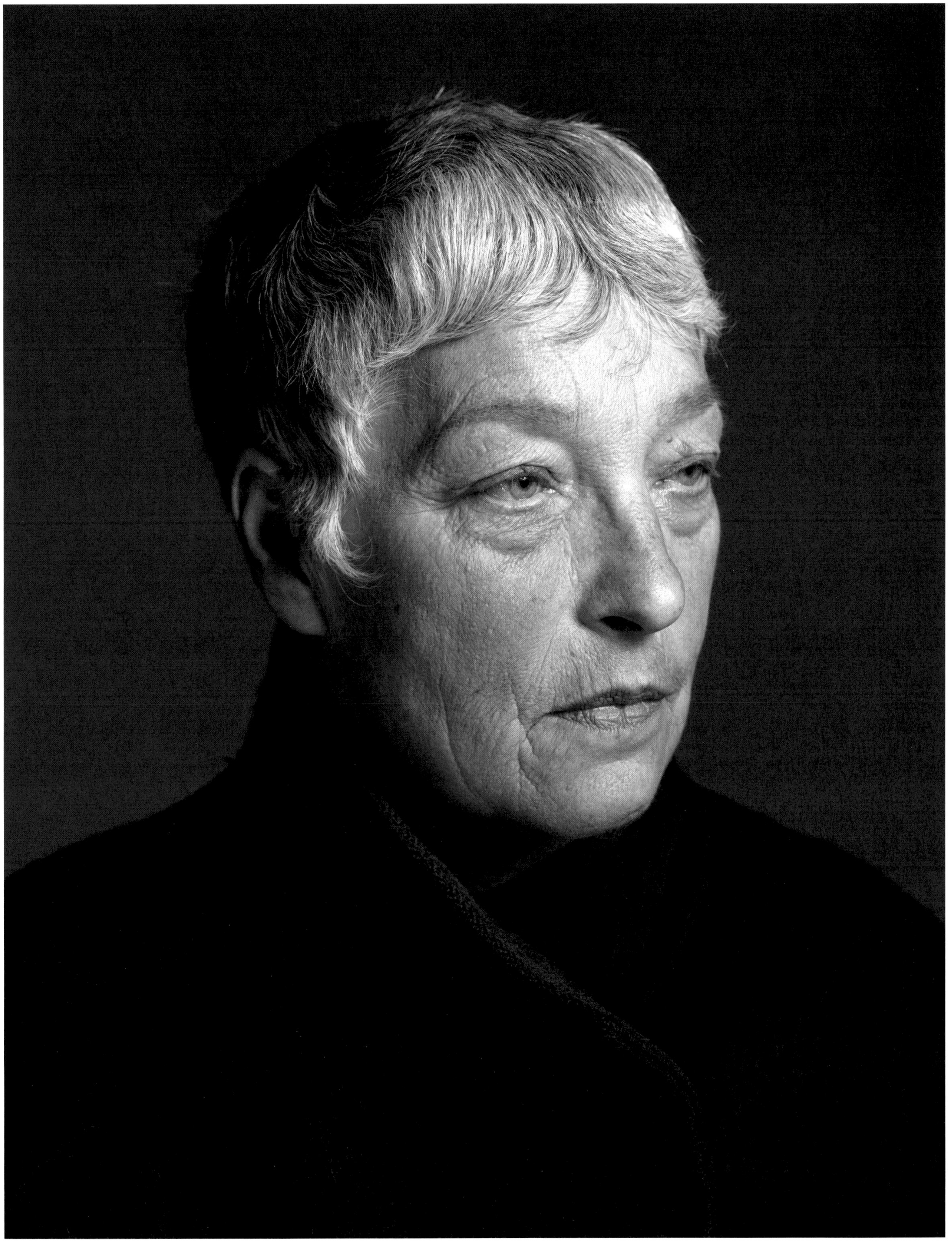

Koos Breukel

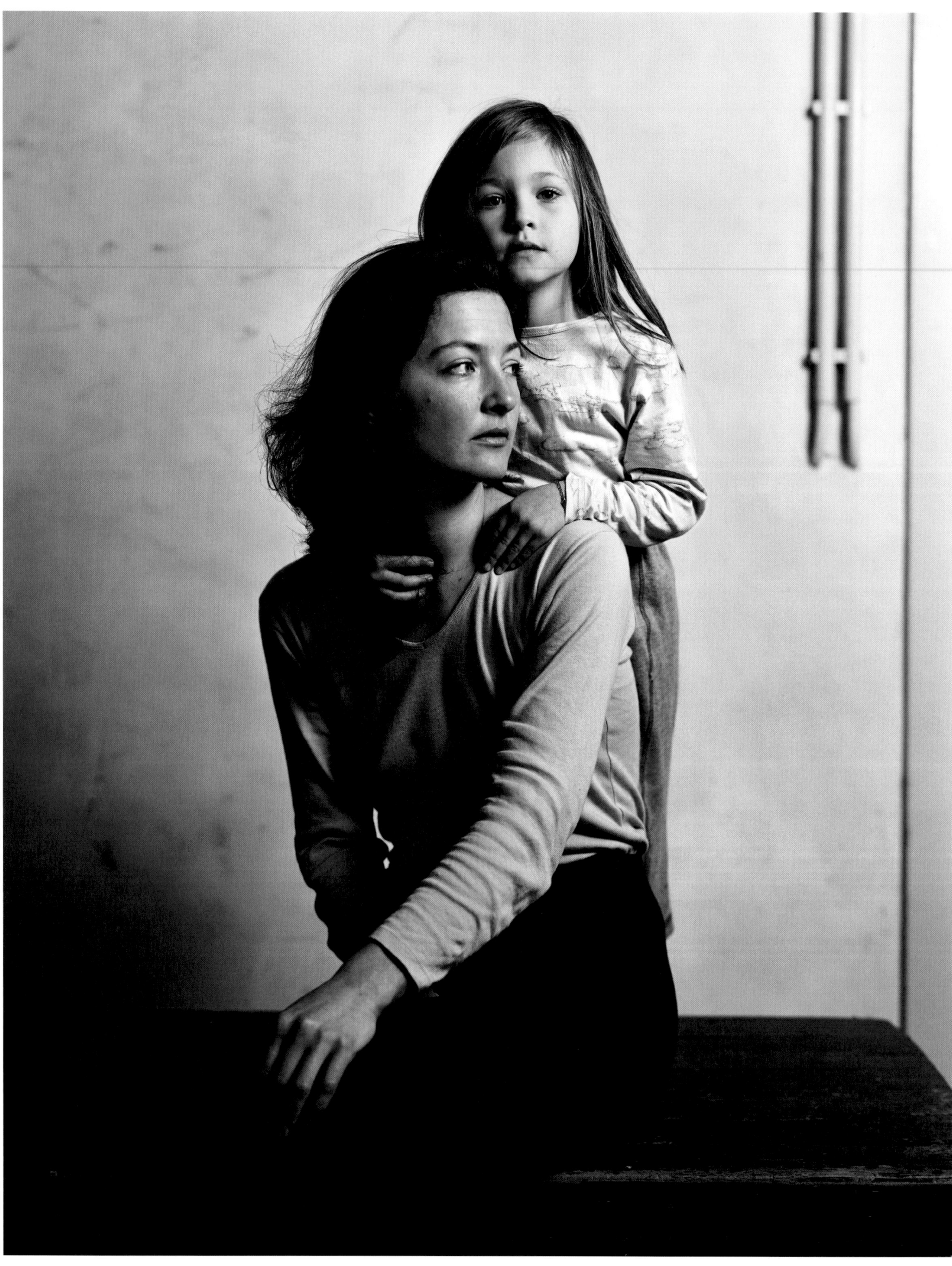

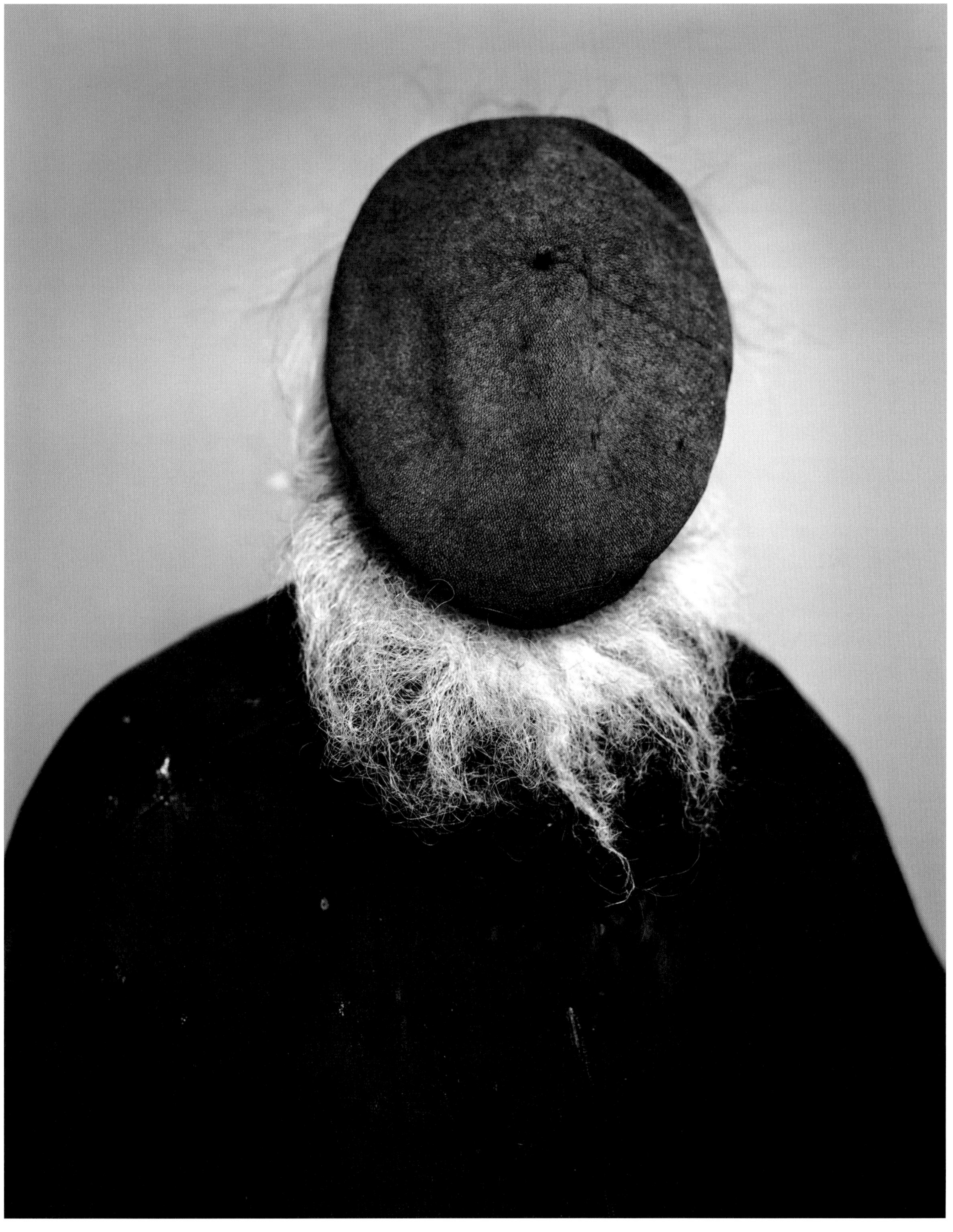

Koos Breukel

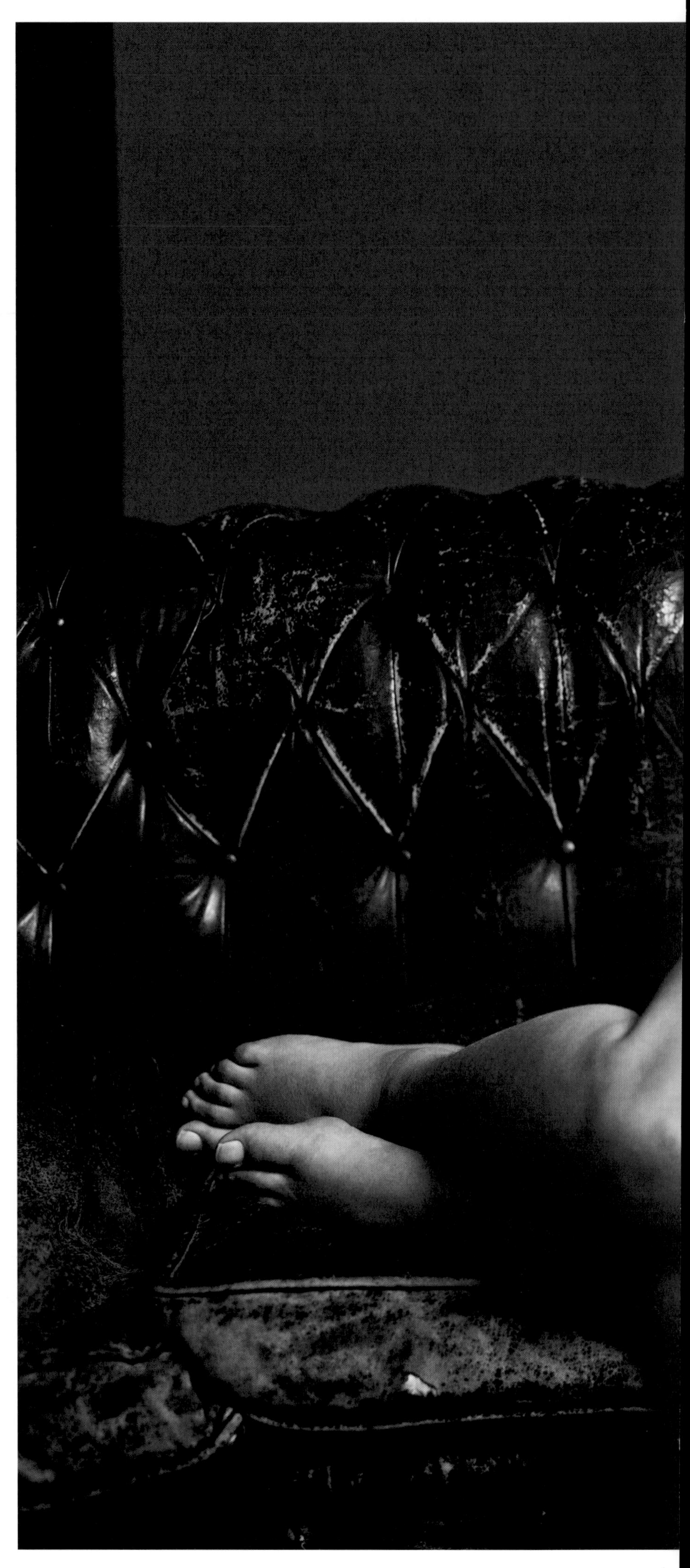

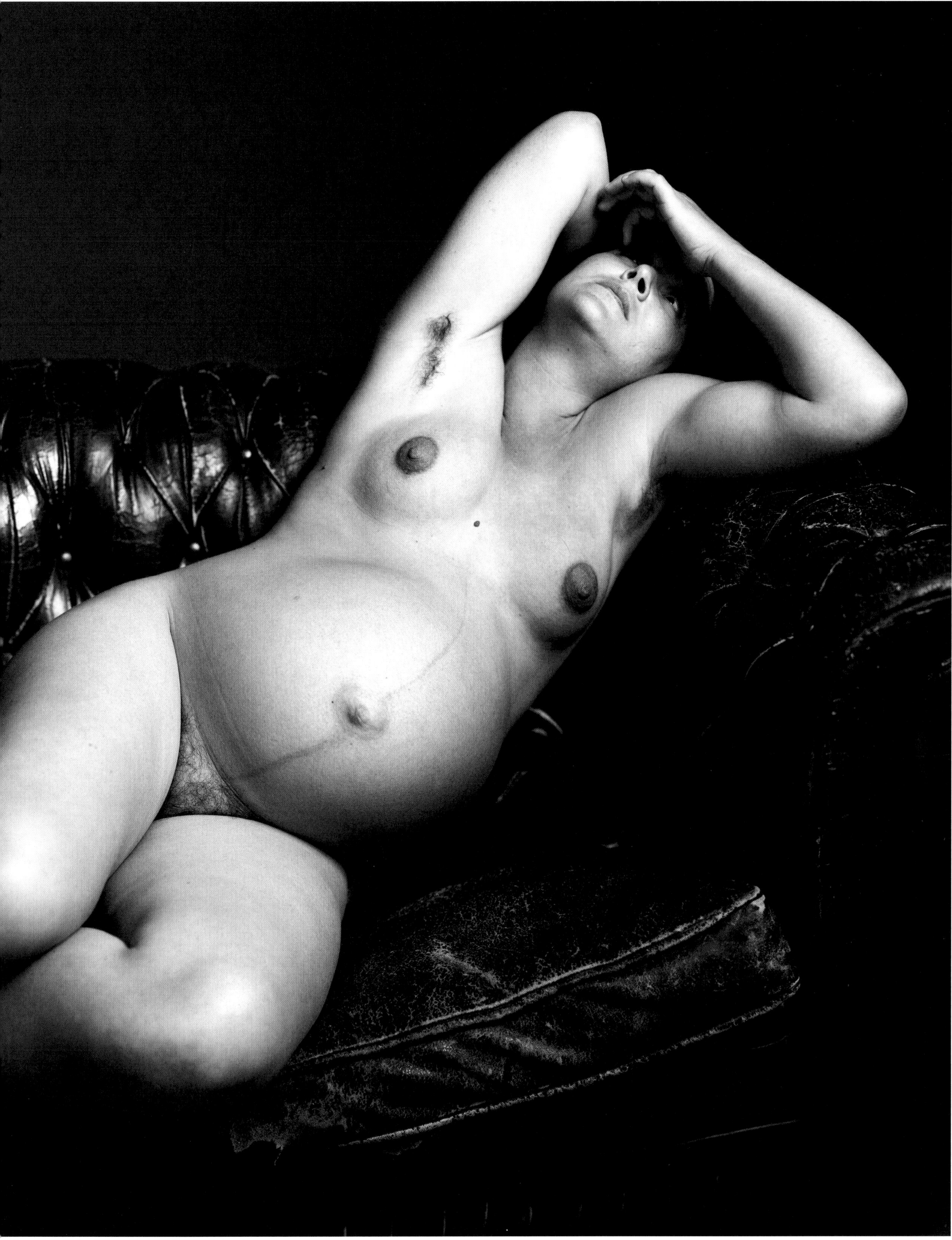

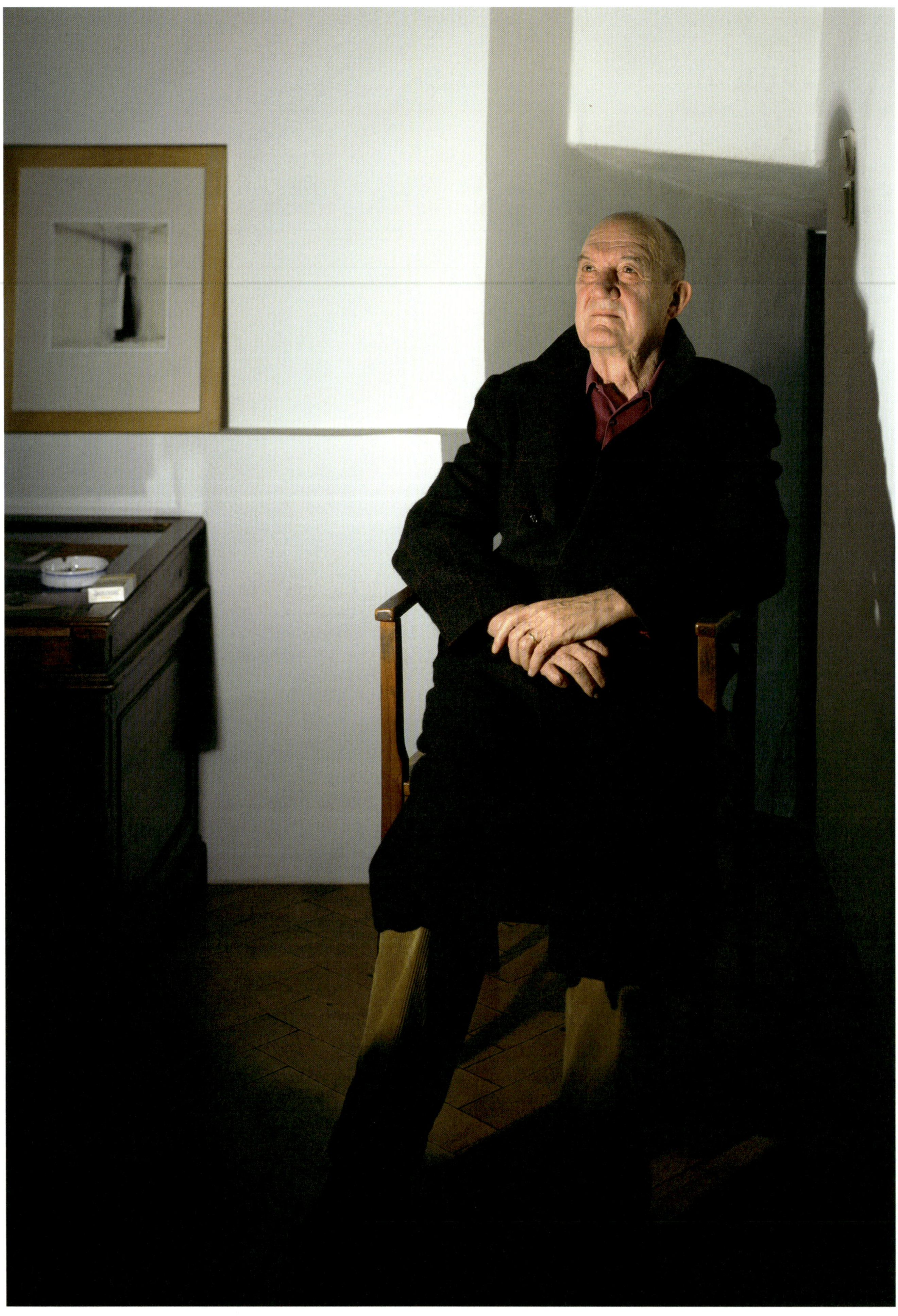

Clegg & Guttmann (born 1957, Ireland; born 1957, Israel)

Clegg & Guttmann are an artist duo consisting of Michael Clegg (born in Dublin) and Martin Guttmann (born in Jerusalem), who have been working on portraiture for more than 20 years. Their portraits shed light not only on the representational mechanisms of power, but also on the cornerstone on which the tradition of portraiture is based: the commission. The relationship between artist and client is a fragile one, in which artists have always had to walk a tightrope, as those commissioning the work usually have a firm idea of what their image is and what they would like to convey. In the case of Clegg & Guttmann, this becomes even more challenging, for their portraits are all about the process itself, revealing the unbearable lightness, as it were, of the long tradition of portrait painting and the tradition of photographic portraiture that superseded it. Power is conditioned by relationships; it is not solid, coming out in one piece. Once it is out in the open, nothing remains the same. Within this context, Clegg & Guttmann have managed to place themselves at the intersection between conceptual art and the rules of the market by blending the two together. The titles of their works are generic, as they do not seek to affirm status, but to create social types, and their clients are usually members of the art world. Clegg & Guttmann use as their frame the poses, gestures, symbols of power and slightly sinister looks typical of 16th- and 17th-century group portraits. They often process the images and create assemblages of different pictures that end up looking like a single work. The initial impression is what one would expect, but the more attentive viewer will see that the power that is supposedly being depicted is actually quite elusive. In fact, we wonder if it was ever there at all.

AA

p. 38
The Artist and His Studio, 2009.
Lambda print, 188 × 139 cm

Courtesy Galerie Elisabeth & Klaus Thoman, Innsbruck/Vienna and Galerie Nagel Draxler, Berlin and Cologne

pp. 40–41
Board of Directors (version 2), 2007.
Lambda print, 172 × 298 cm

Courtesy Galerie Nagel Draxler, Berlin and Cologne

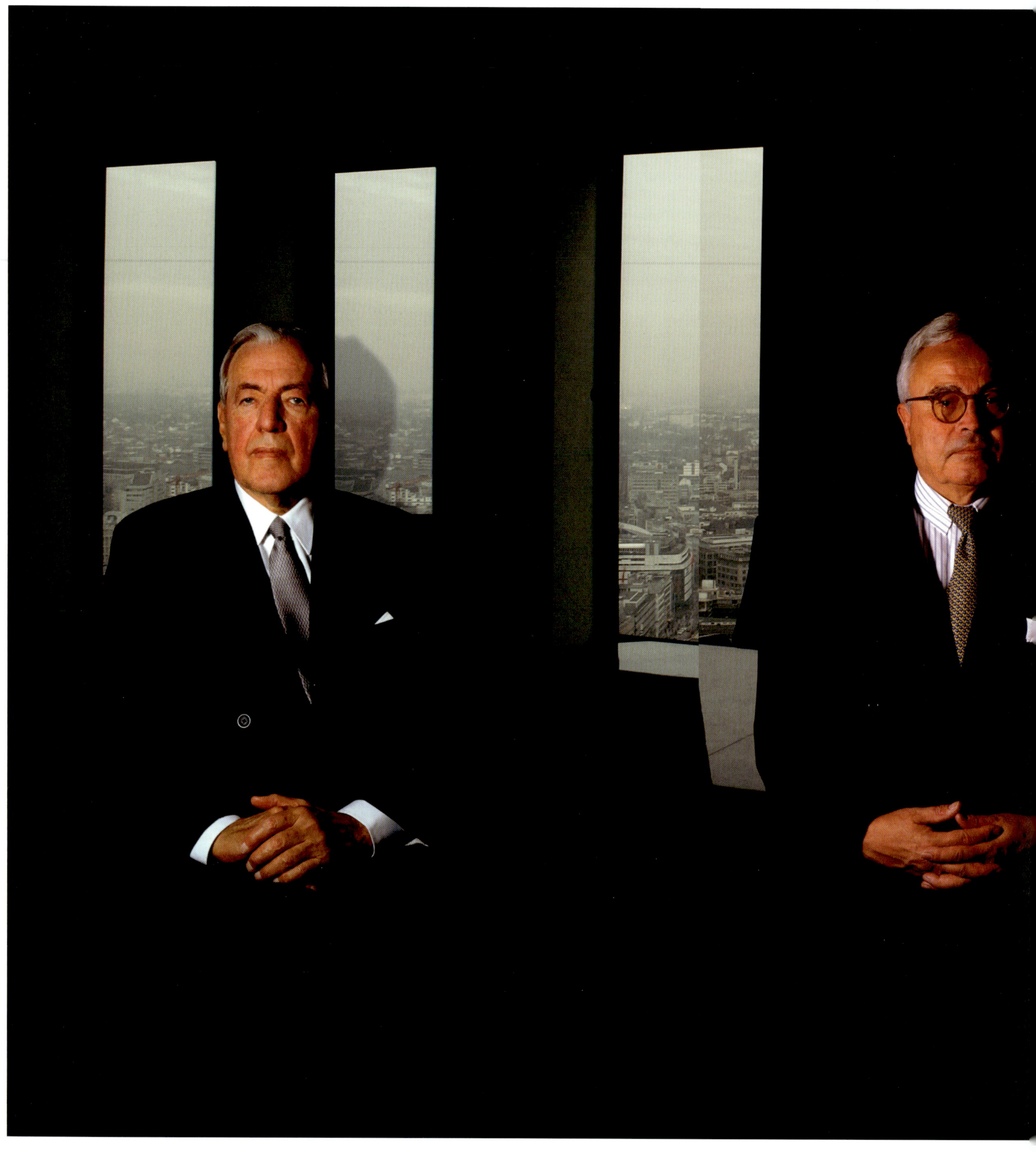

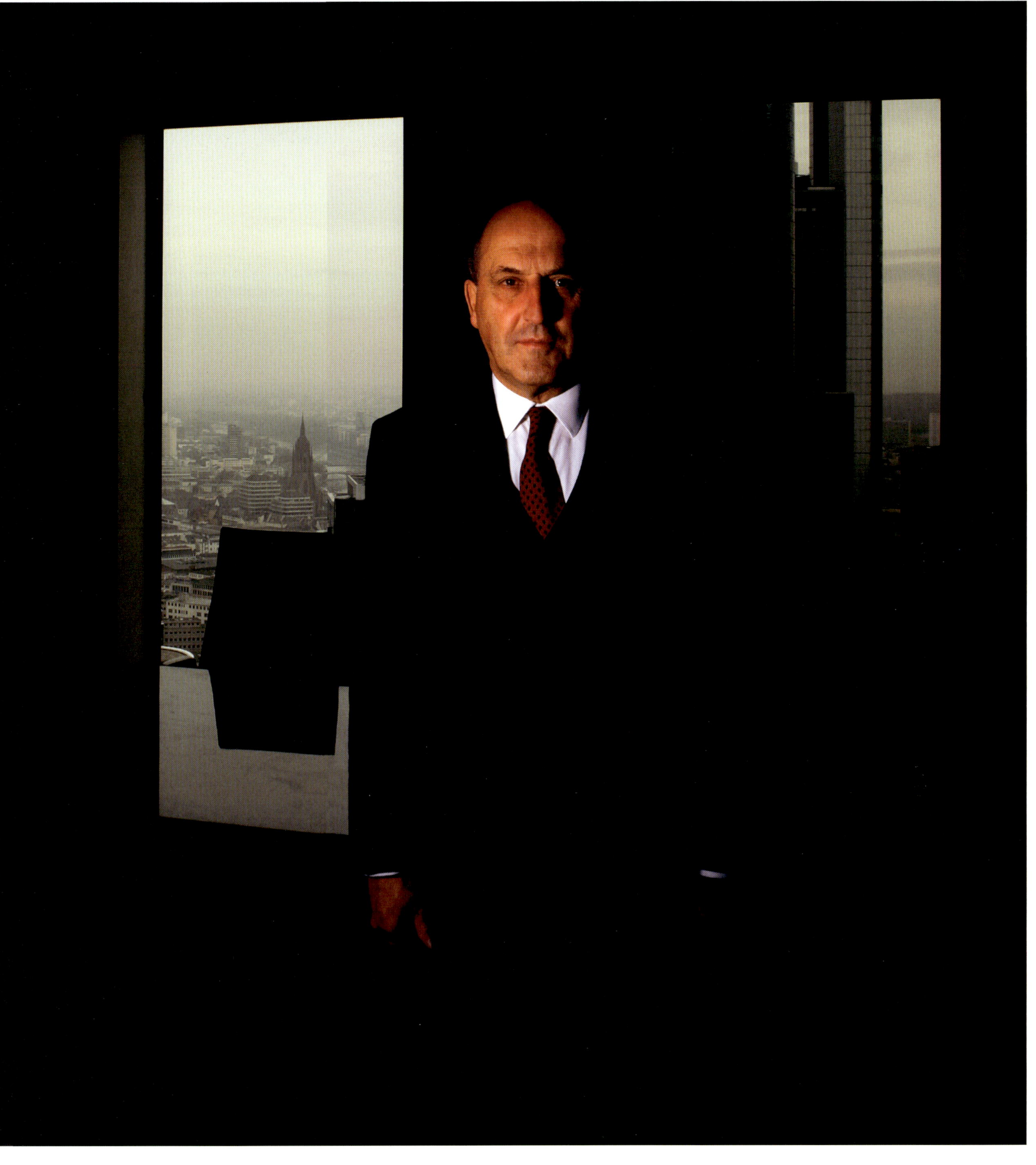

Clegg & Guttmann

Anton Corbijn (born 1955, the Netherlands)

Anton Corbijn is a Dutch photographer who has made numerous portraits of rock and pop musicians. He is also a graphic designer and renowned as a director of feature films such as *Control*, about the life of Joy Division singer Ian Curtis. From 1972 to 1989 he photographed only musicians and bands. In 1990, he broadened his range to include artists, models, writers, and actors. Bono, Bruce Springsteen, Tom Waits, Iggy Pop, Kate Moss, Ai Weiwei, Lucian Freud and Luc Tuymans are just some of the many celebrities who have posed for him. Corbijn tries to fathom the people behind the star personas, establishing a personal link with them and creating portraits that look both poised and natural. A portrait of Marianne Faithfull shows her wearing a black bra and smoking her first cigarette at breakfast, presumably after a turbulent night. Corbijn strips the stars of glamour and glitter and shows them in a sober style that evokes both melancholy and earnestness. Corbijn's black-and-white pictures are analogue, usually made with a Hasselblad camera and coarse-grained film. His later images were sharper and Corbijn also started working in colour. Today, Corbijn is one of the leading photographers and image makers of popular culture of his generation.

CDJ

p. 43
Marlene Dumas, Amsterdam, 2000.
Ink-jet print on fine art pearl photo paper
(Hahnemühle 285 g), mounted on dibond,
146 × 146 cm

p. 44
Luc Tuymans, Antwerp, 2004.
Ink-jet print on fine art pearl photo paper
(Hahnemühle 285 g), mounted on dibond,
146 × 146 cm

p. 45
Lucian Freud, London, 2008.
Ink-jet print on fine art pearl photo paper
(Hahnemühle 285 g), mounted on dibond,
146 × 146 cm. Private collection

p. 46
Marianne Faithfull, Los Angeles, 1990.
Lith print, 69 × 68 cm. Private collection

p. 47
Isabella Rossellini, New York, 1993.
Lith print, 69 × 68 cm. Private collection

Courtesy Zeno X Gallery, Antwerp

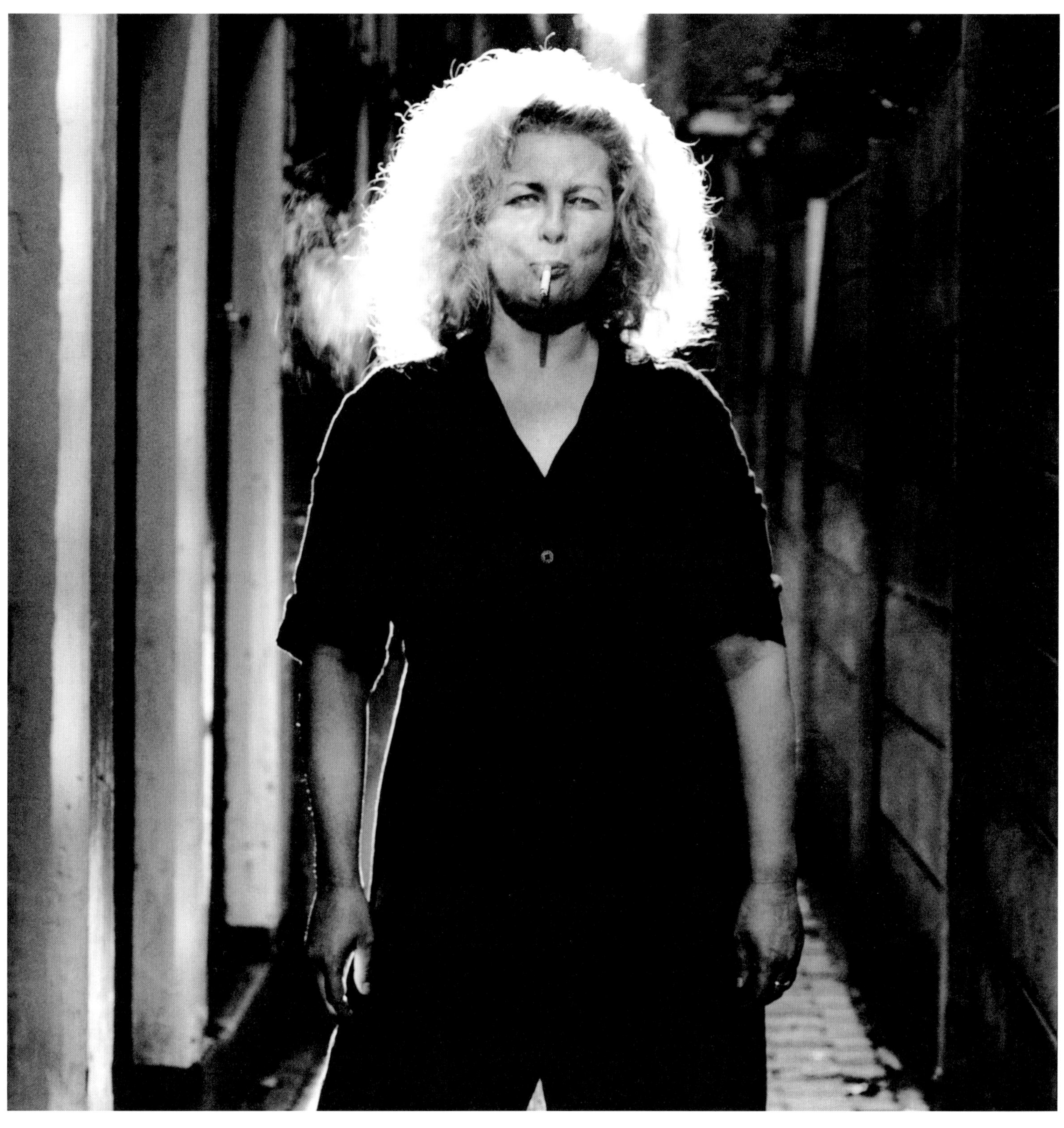

Anton Corbijn

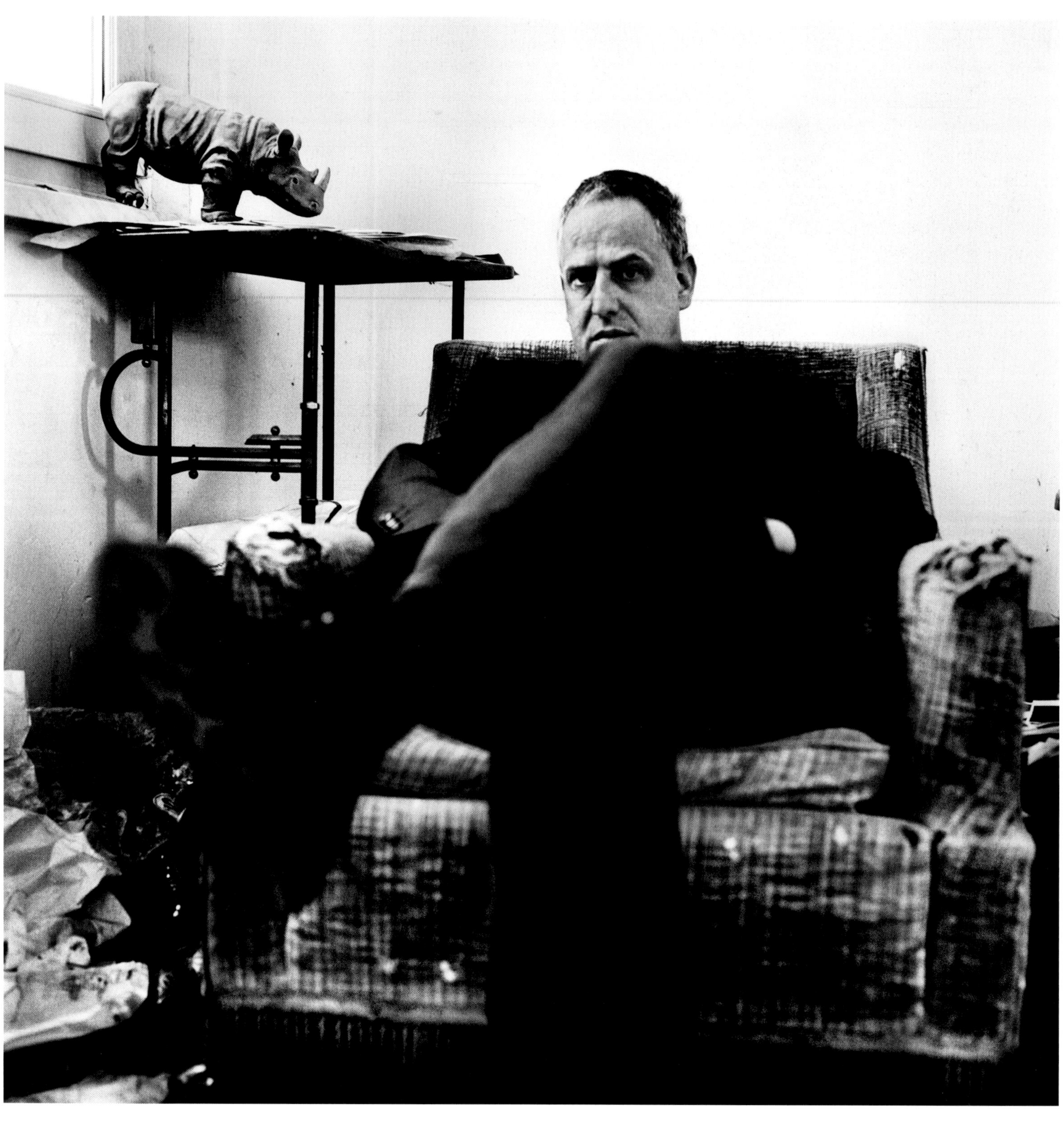

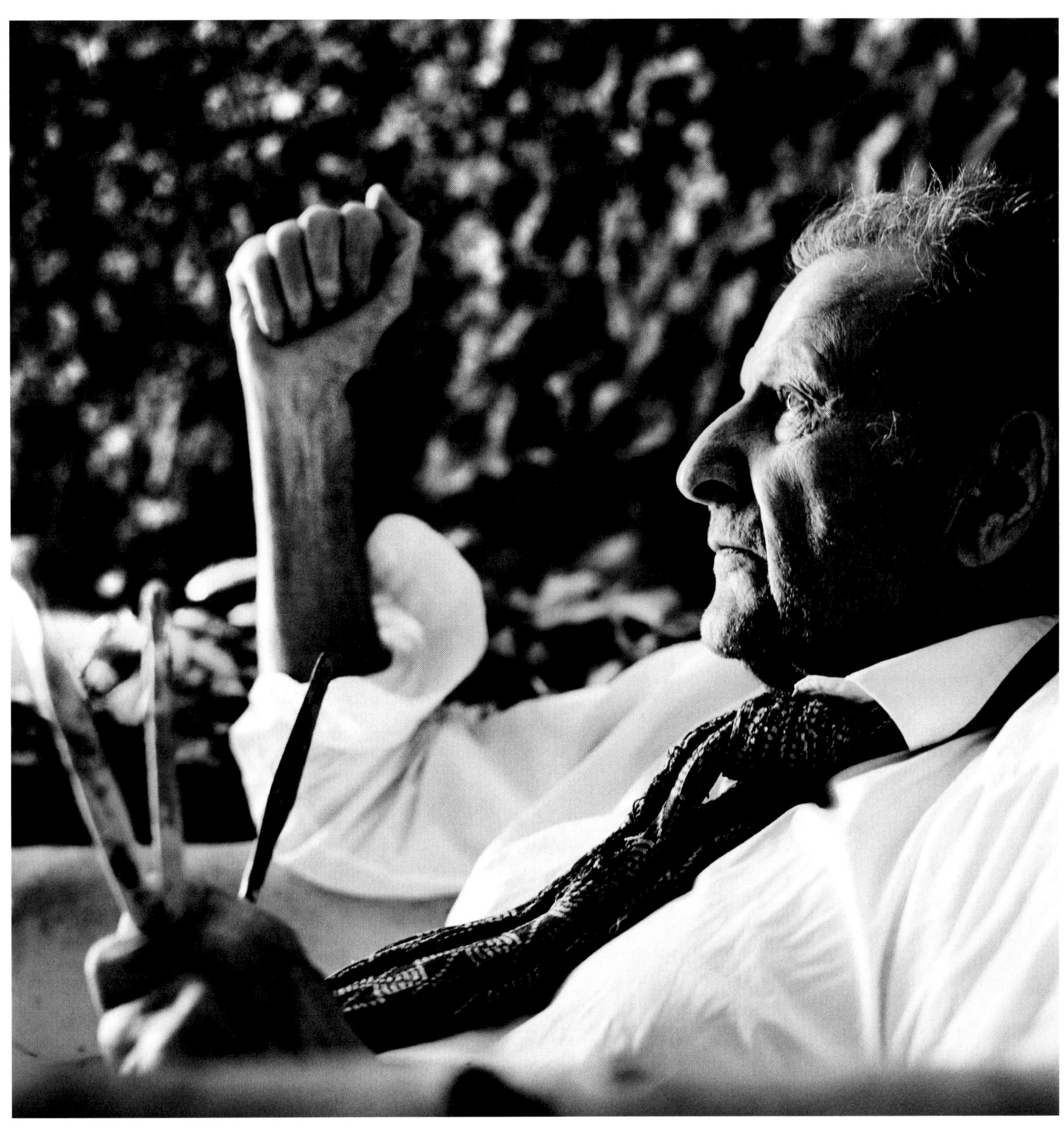

Anton Corbijn

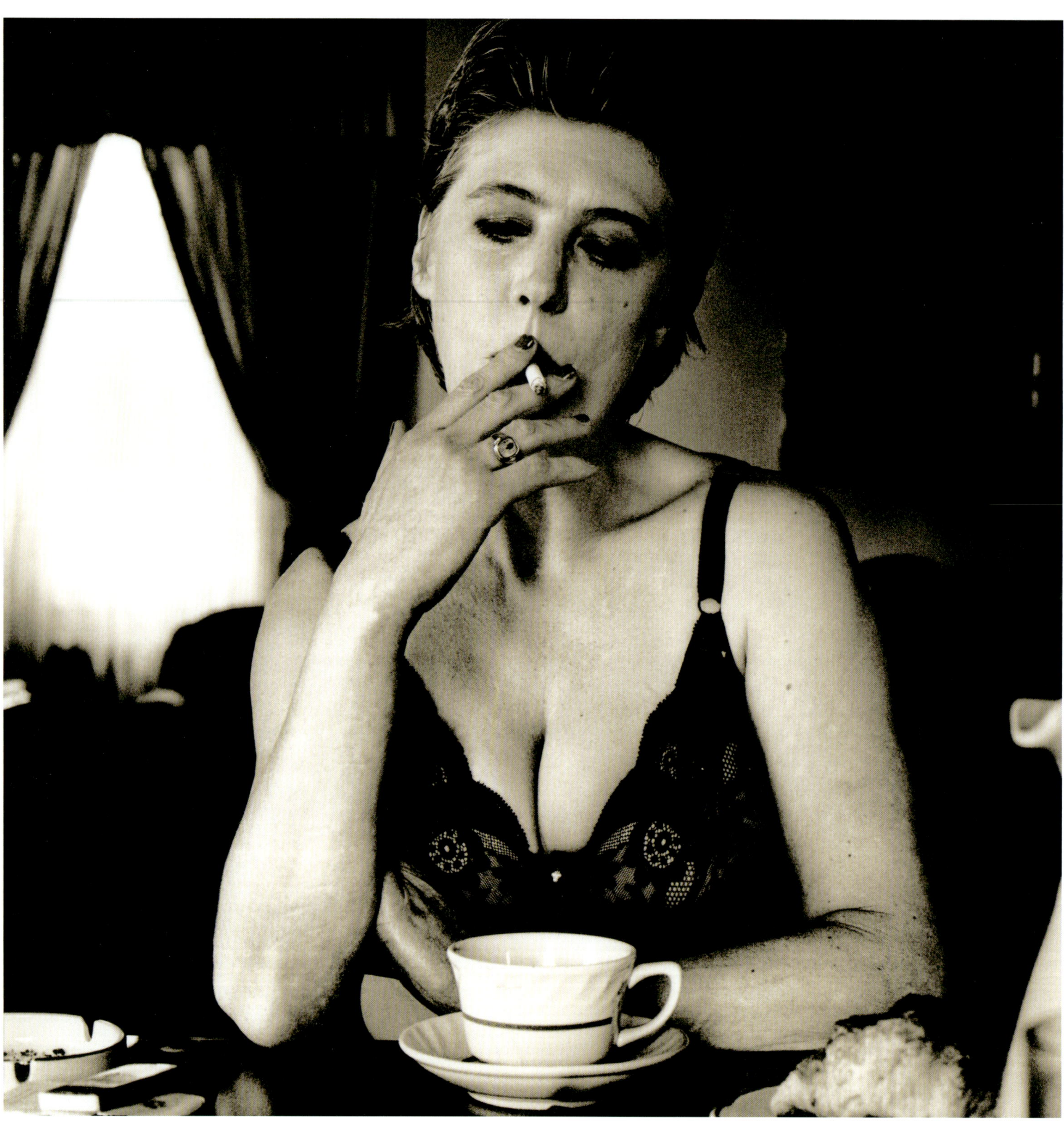

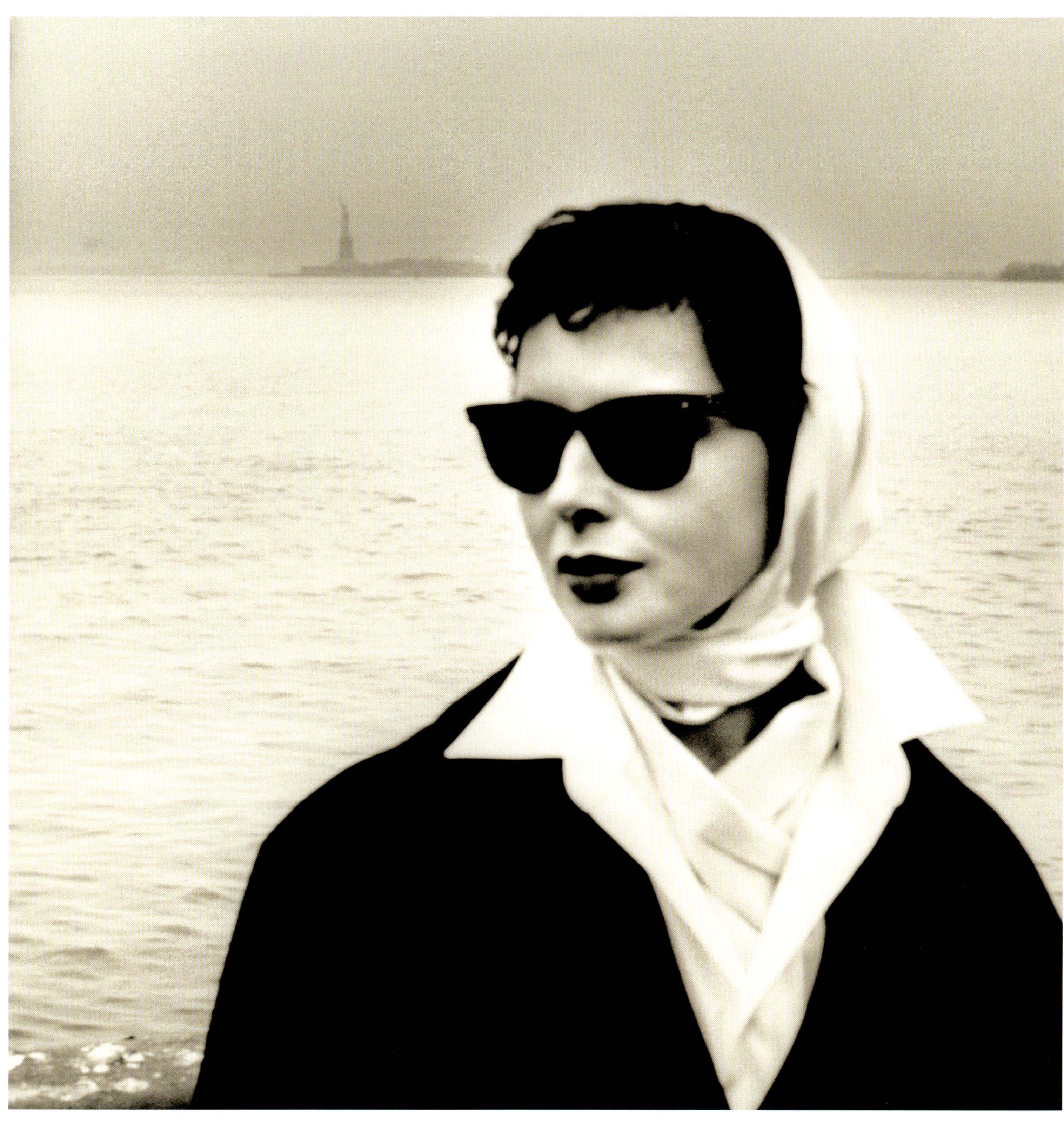

Anton Corbijn

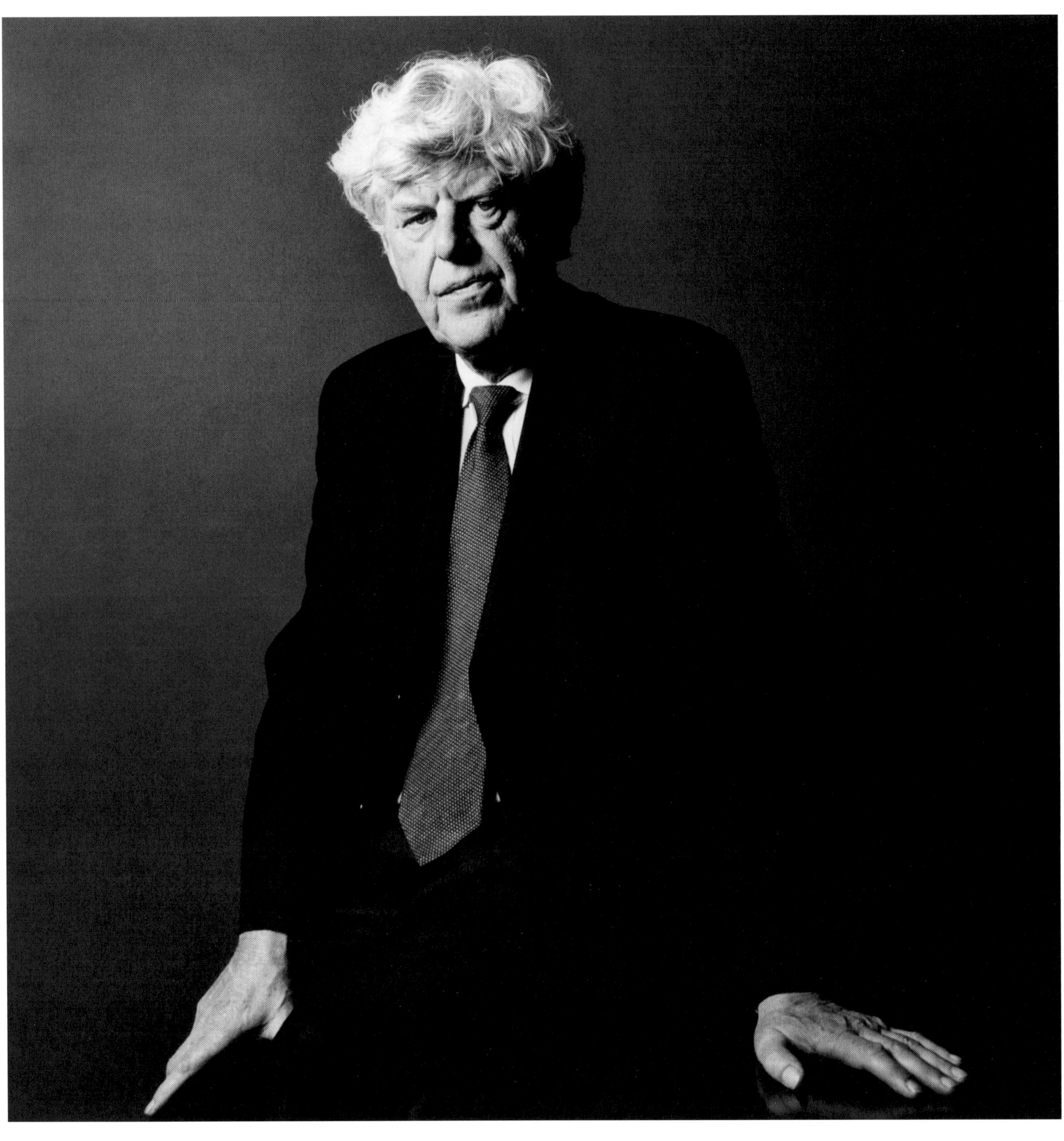

Christian Courrèges (born 1950, France)

Capitale Europe

Power and visionary leadership are qualities one can immediately sense but not easily depict. Architects and sculptors were the first to try to lend them form. Photographers are the last in the lineage of artists to take up the challenge. Finding the nuances in which such attributes are expressed in a face is a multilevel endeavour. What we see is merely the surface; what the artist tries to depict lies deep, the result of many factors, struggles, power games. This is what Christian Courrèges has succeeded in doing with his portraits of famous personalities, men and women who have played an important role in the process of European unification. The portraits selected here were commissioned by the Centre Régional de la Photographie Nord – Pas-de-Calais (1998). No backdrop, no props, just the persona/person looking directly and self-assertively at the viewer. Most of them are sitting down, but there is nothing relaxed in this posture. There is, however, something regal and dominating about them. We sense this even if we do not know who they are. And then there is the aim of the photographer, who wants to capture not the person, but the power that he or she communicates. Here, the face is a mediator, a vehicle, so to speak, conveying the force and vision of each of the prominent figures being portrayed.

VI

p. 48
Wim Duisenberg, in 'Capitale Europe', since 1990.
Gelatin silver print on barite paper, 46.7 × 46.7 cm

p. 50
Simone Veil, in 'Capitale Europe', since 1990.
Gelatin silver print on barite paper, 46.7 × 46.7 cm

p. 51
Jacques Delors, in 'Capitale Europe', since 1990.
Gelatin silver print on barite paper, 46.7 × 46.7 cm

p. 52
Valéry Giscard d'Estaing, in 'Capitale Europe',
since 1990.
Gelatin silver print on barite paper, 46.7 × 46.7 cm

p. 53
Emma Bonino, in 'Capitale Europe', since 1990.
Gelatin silver print on barite paper, 46.7 × 46.7 cm

p. 54
Catherine Lalumière, in 'Capitale Europe', since 1990.
Gelatin silver print on barite paper, 46.7 × 46.7 cm

p. 55
Helmut Schmidt, in 'Capitale Europe', since 1990.
Gelatin silver print on barite paper, 46.7 × 46.7 cm

Courtesy the artist and the Centre Régional
de la Photographie Nord – Pas-de-Calais

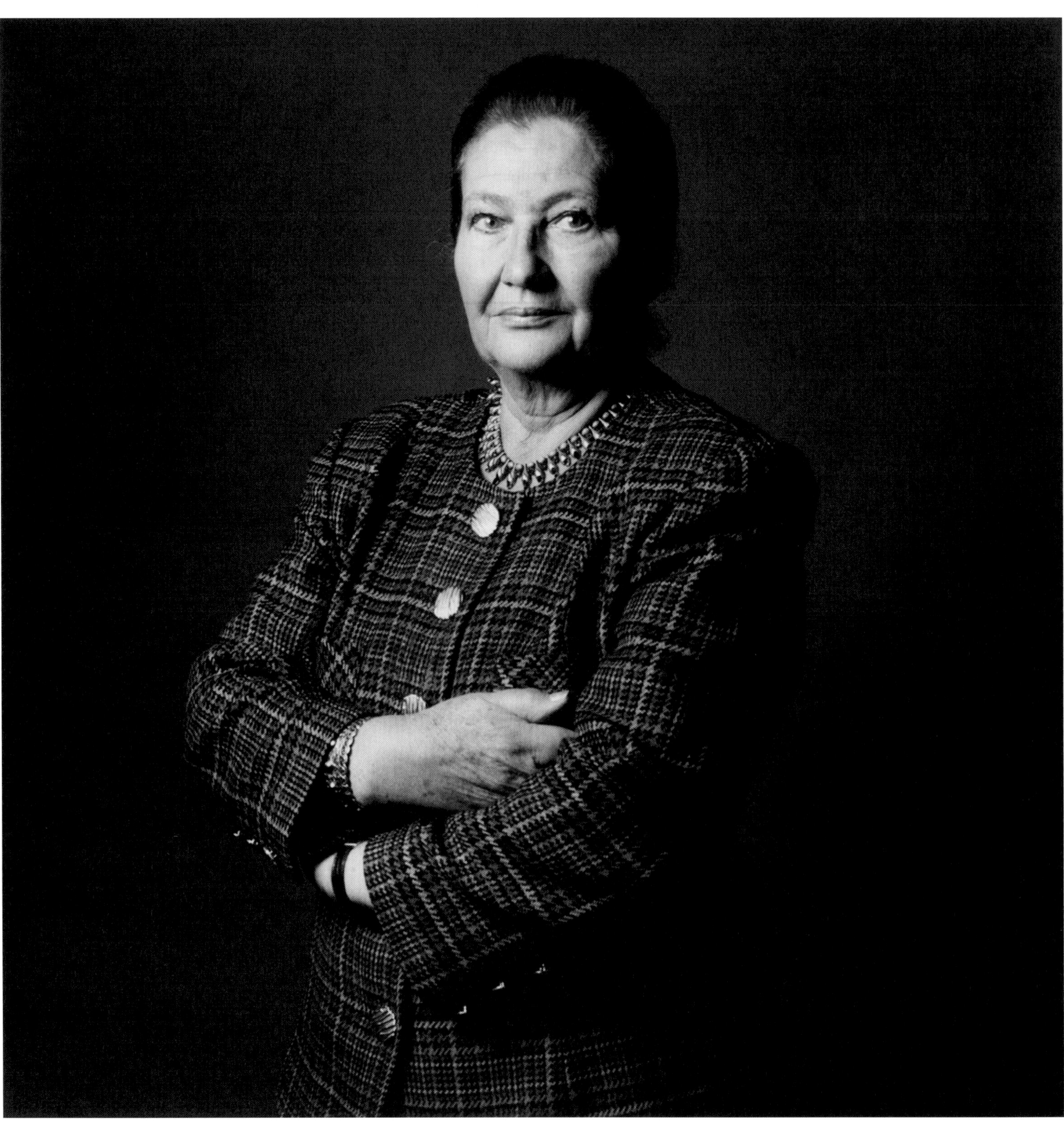

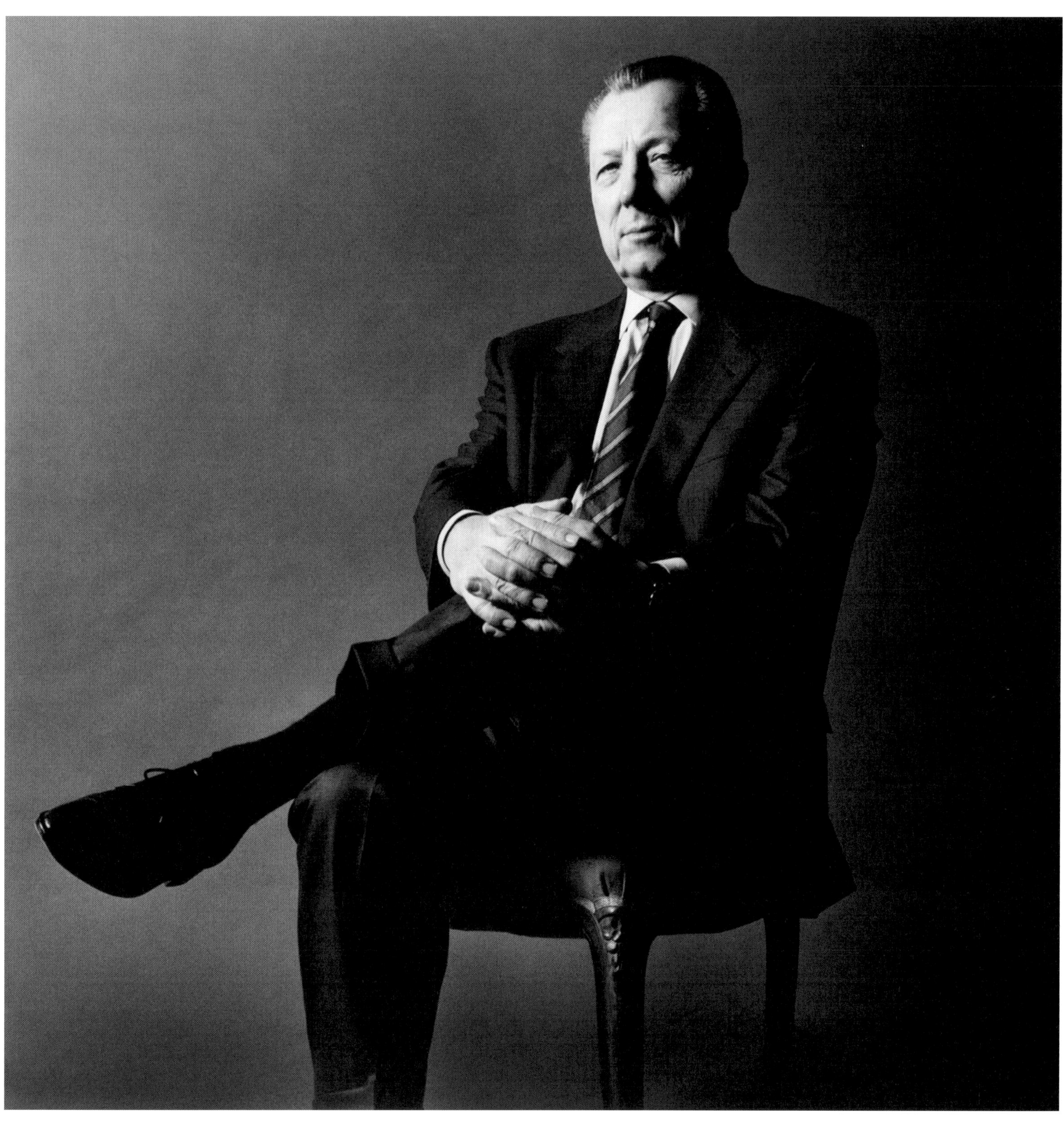

 Christian Courrèges

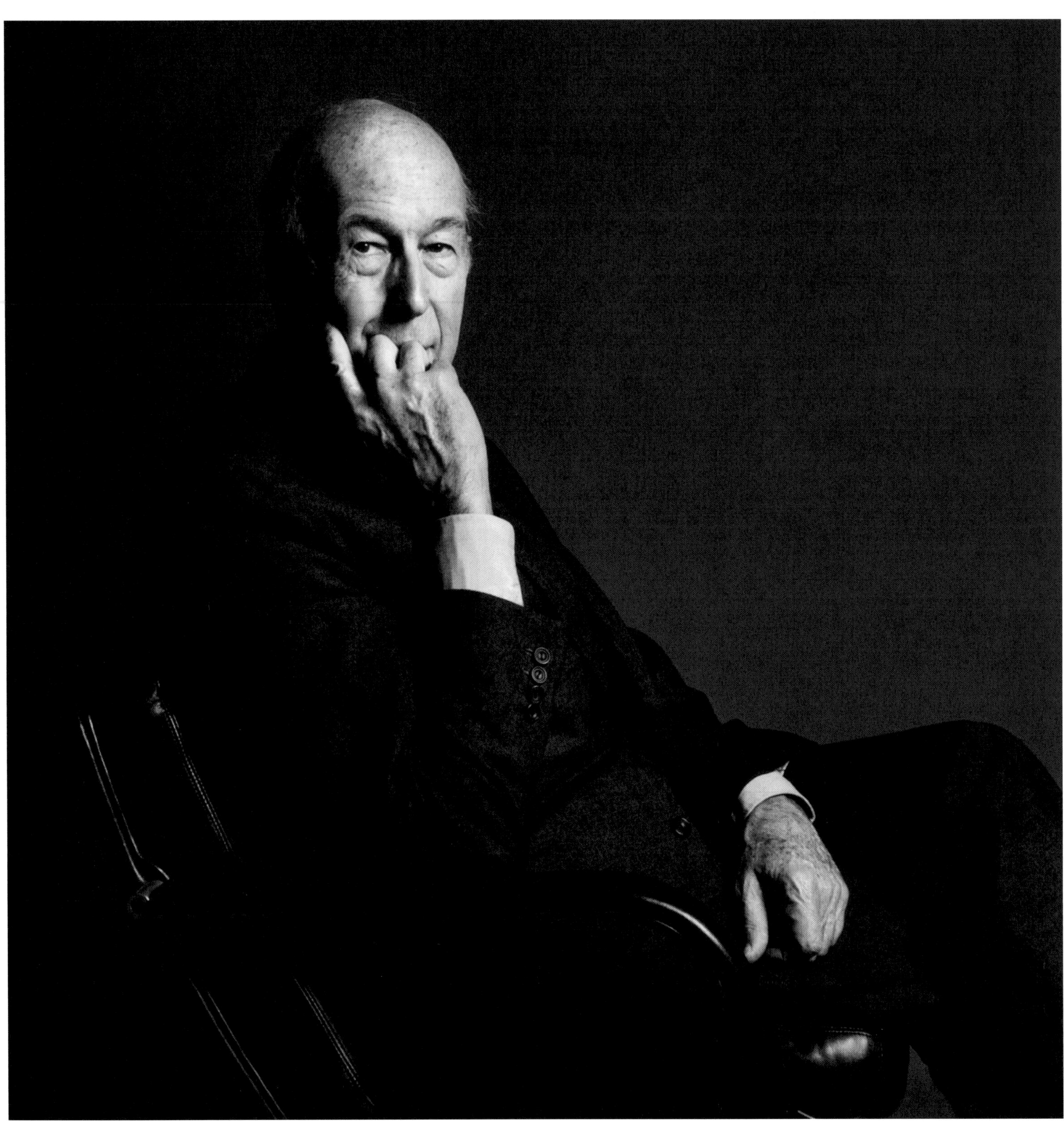

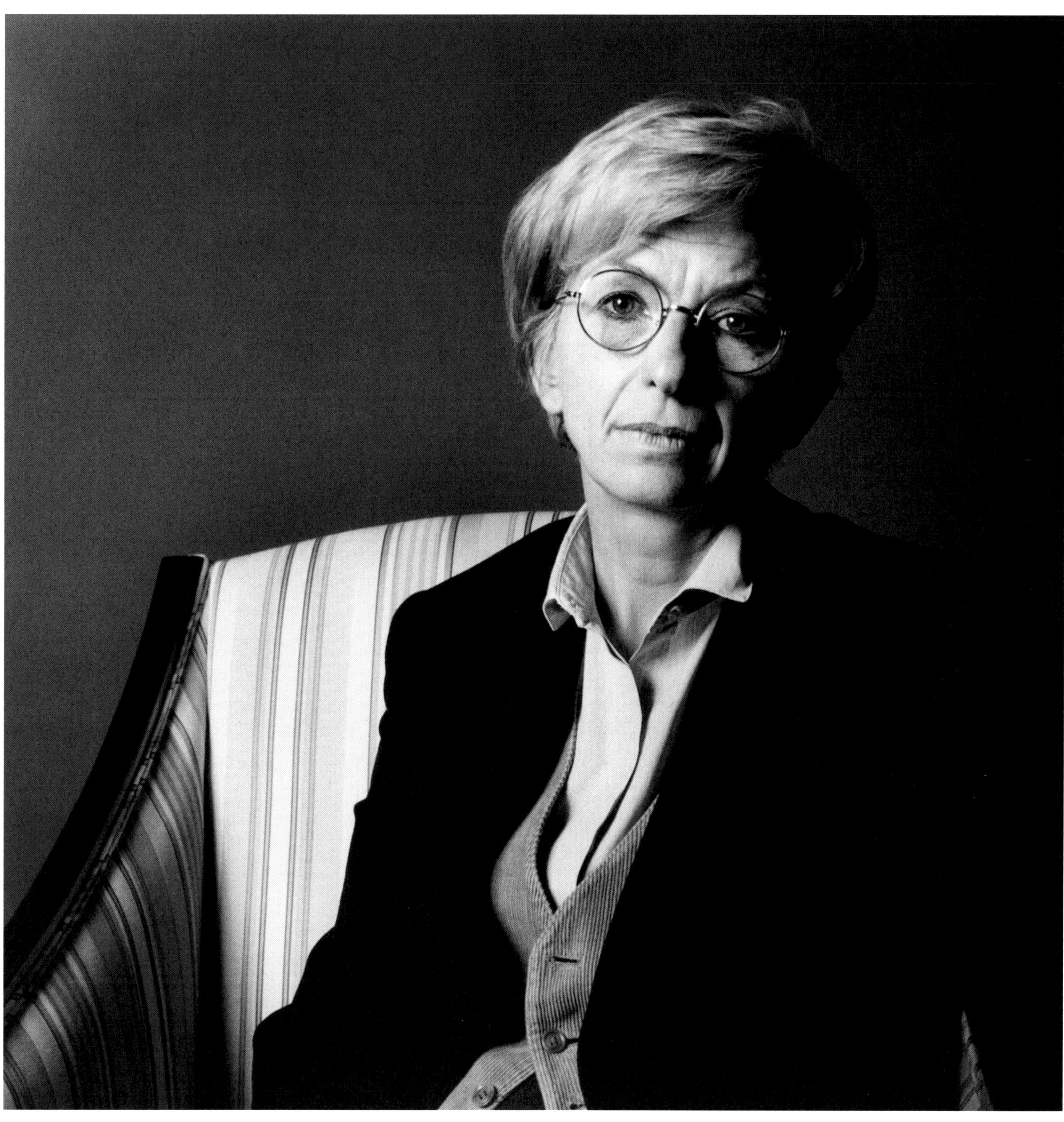

 Christian Courrèges

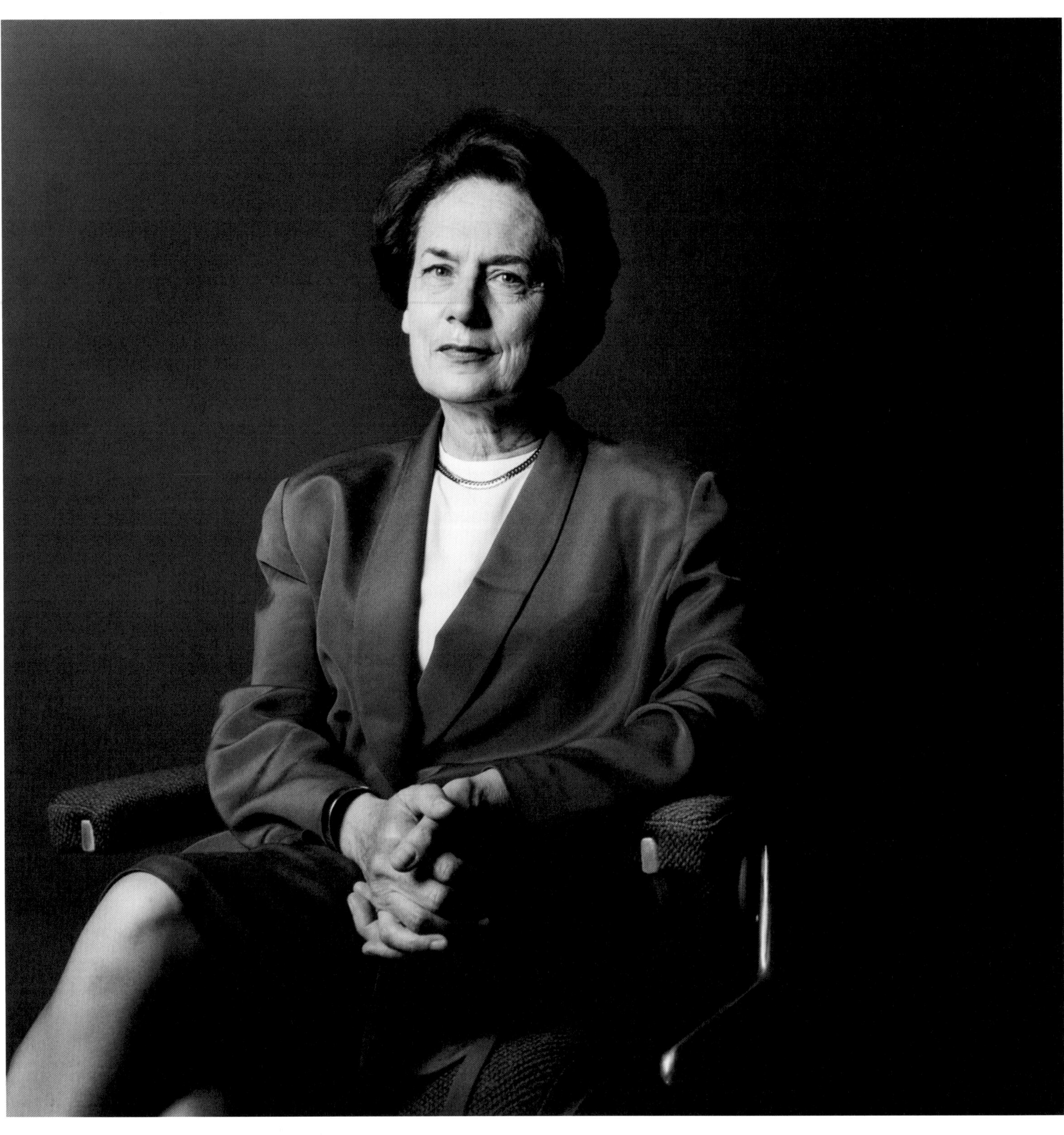

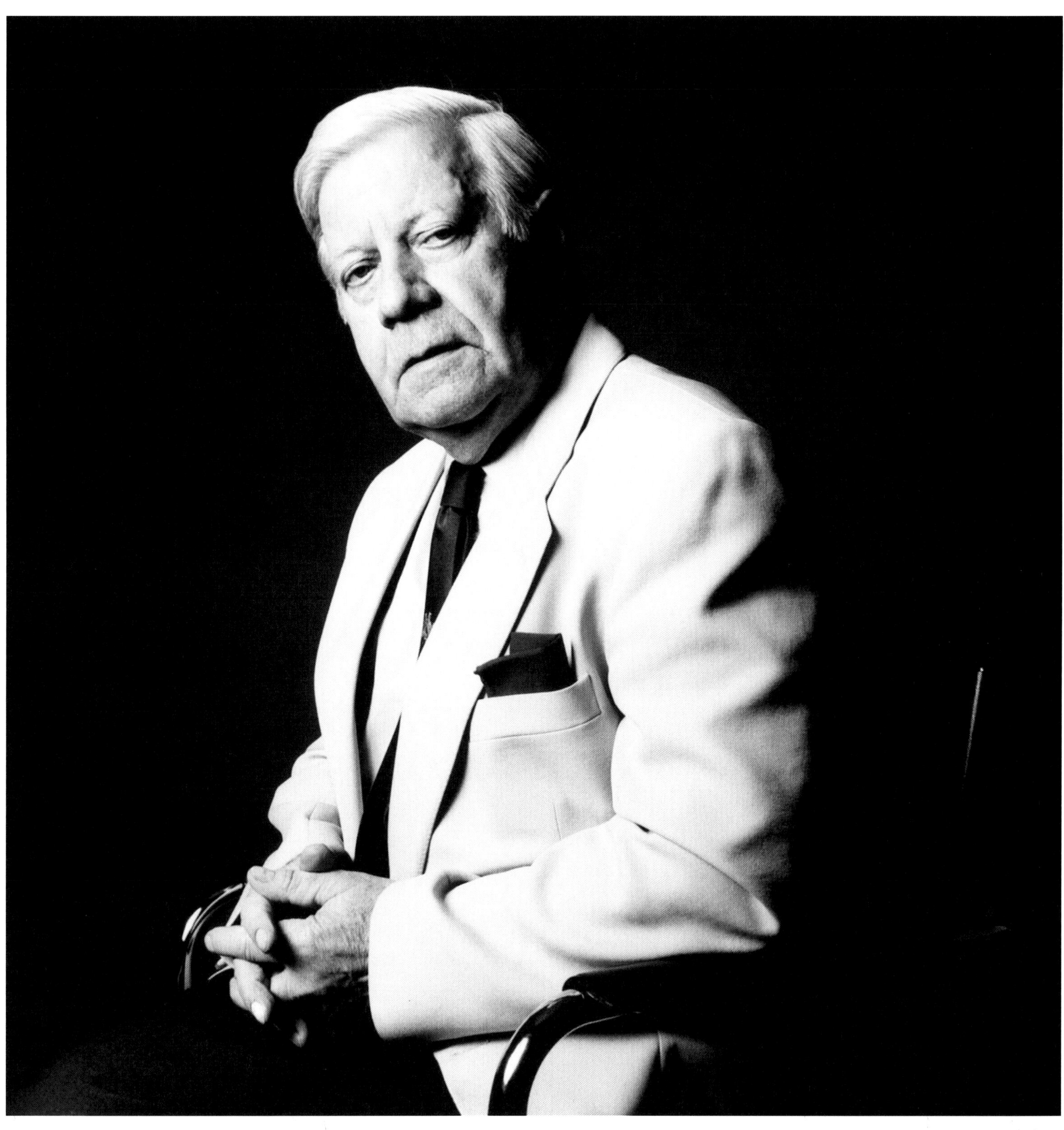

Christian Courrèges

Denis Darzacq (born 1961, France)

Act

In portrait photography, the relationship between the photographer and the model is crucial to the result. Is there an understanding, a personal click, does the subject of the portrait feel at ease or not, and how does the photographer react to that? Does he give precise instructions in the studio or does he 'steal' a fleeting snapshot in the street? *Act* is a series of portraits that emerged from the photographer's work with the mentally disabled. Actors, dancers and athletes also appear in *Act*, but photographer Denis Darzacq made no distinction between them as he produced these warm and human portraits, which also radiate a certain pleasure. The people he portrayed were all given the opportunity to express themselves for the camera spontaneously or after brief instructions by means of individual promptings and body language at a spot of their choice in a public or semi-public area. Sometimes the result is highly expressive, in other cases extremely modest. By giving his subjects the freedom to relate to themselves and the space around them, Darzacq was able to present the classic relationship between photographer and model in a new light. Here, the traditional boundaries between spontaneous and orchestrated, between formal and nonchalant, and between street and studio photography are no longer important. Even more important than their historical artistic or photographic classification, however, is the effect these pictures have on those viewing them, who are not only confronted with their own prejudices, but are also challenged to consider the existential freedom they themselves have.

FG

Courtesy the artist and Galerie RX, Paris

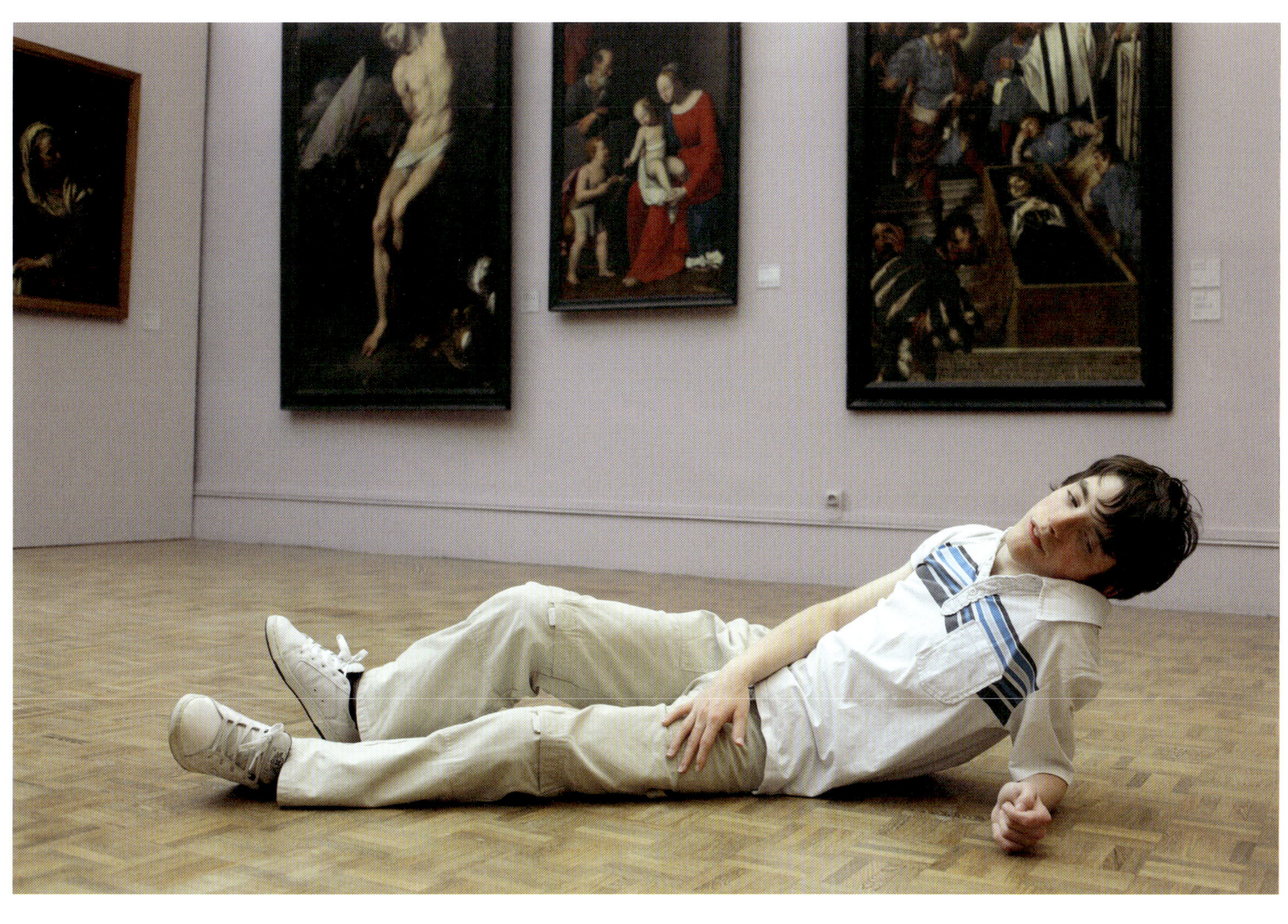

Denis Darzacq

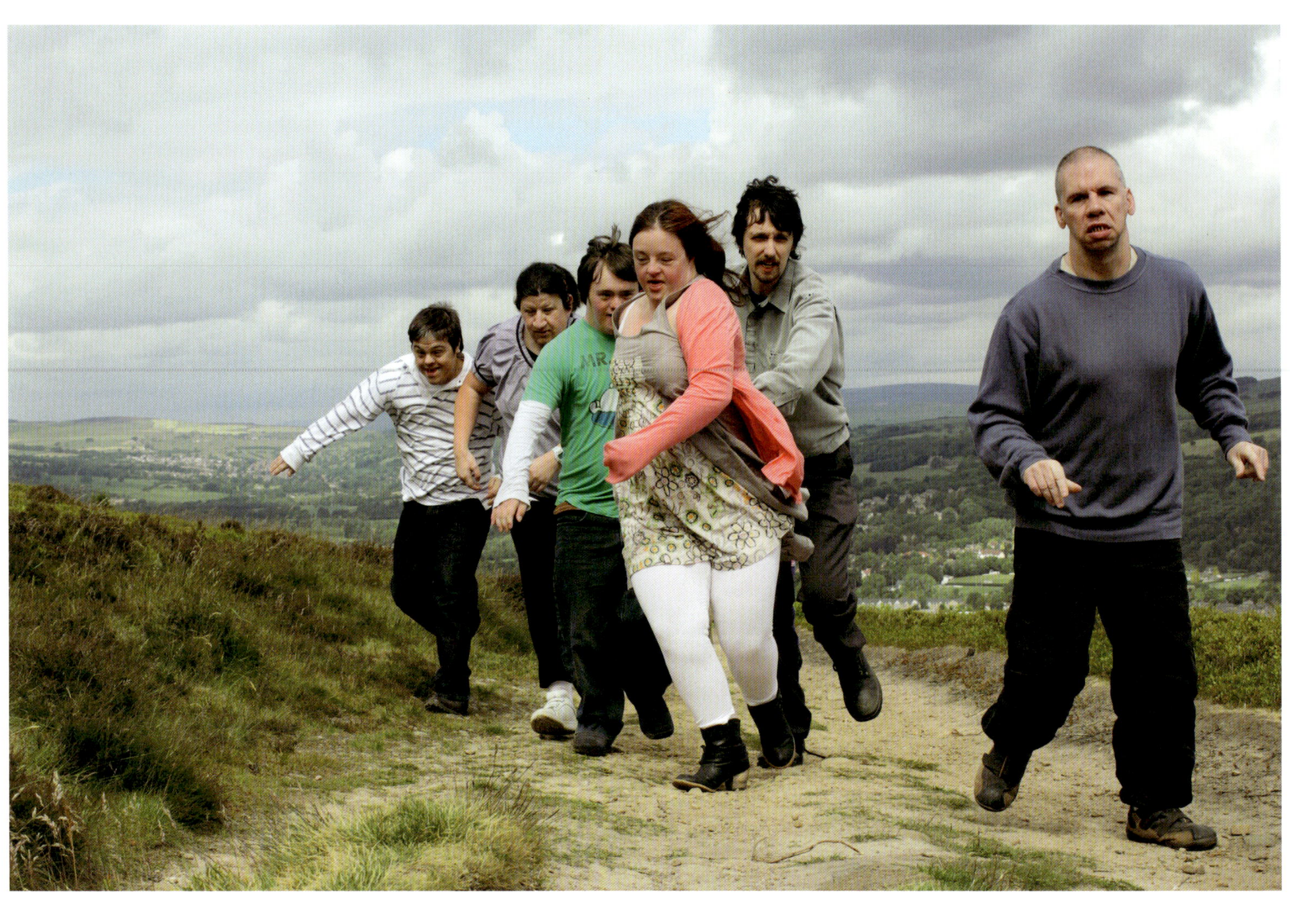

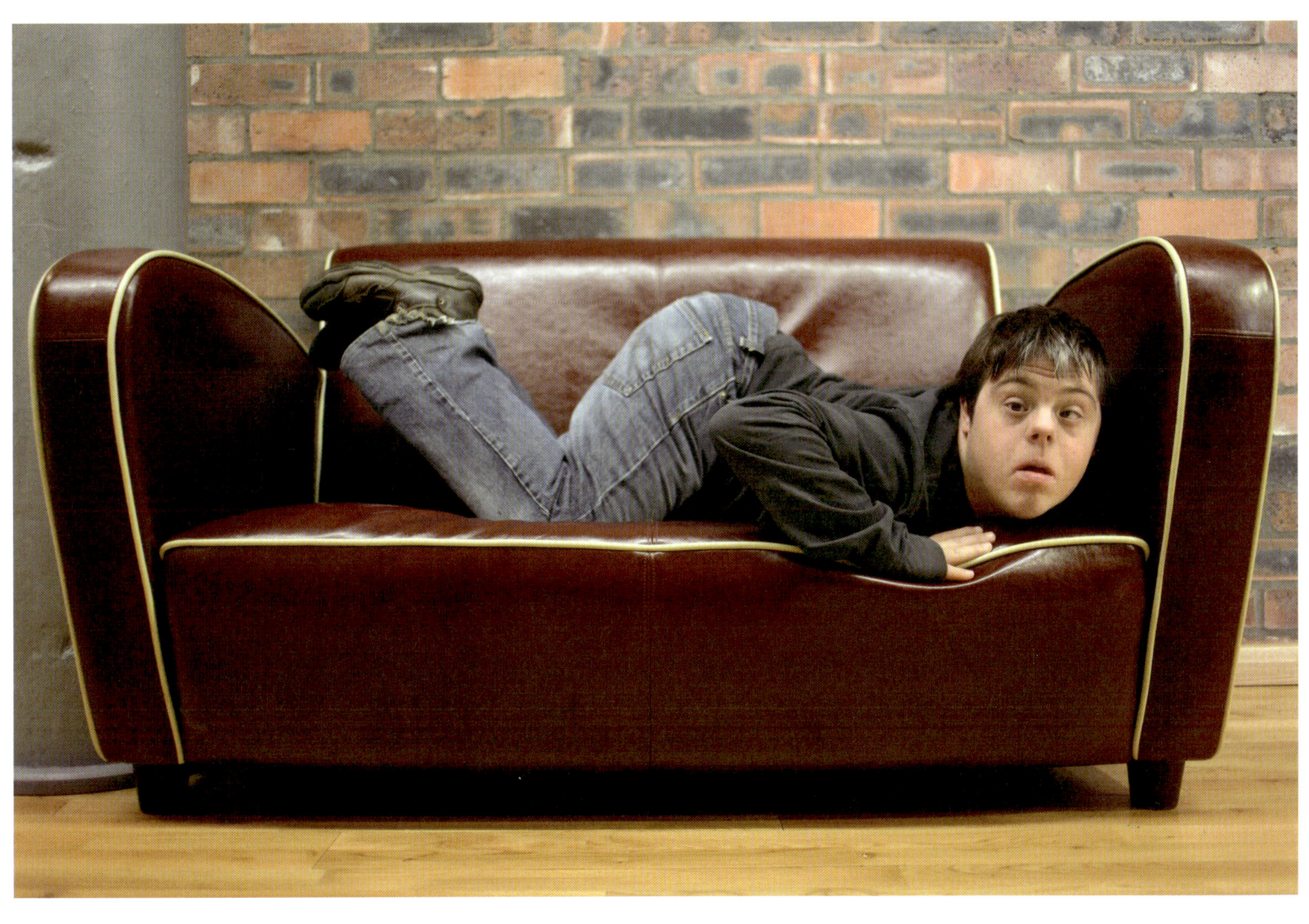

Denis Darzacq

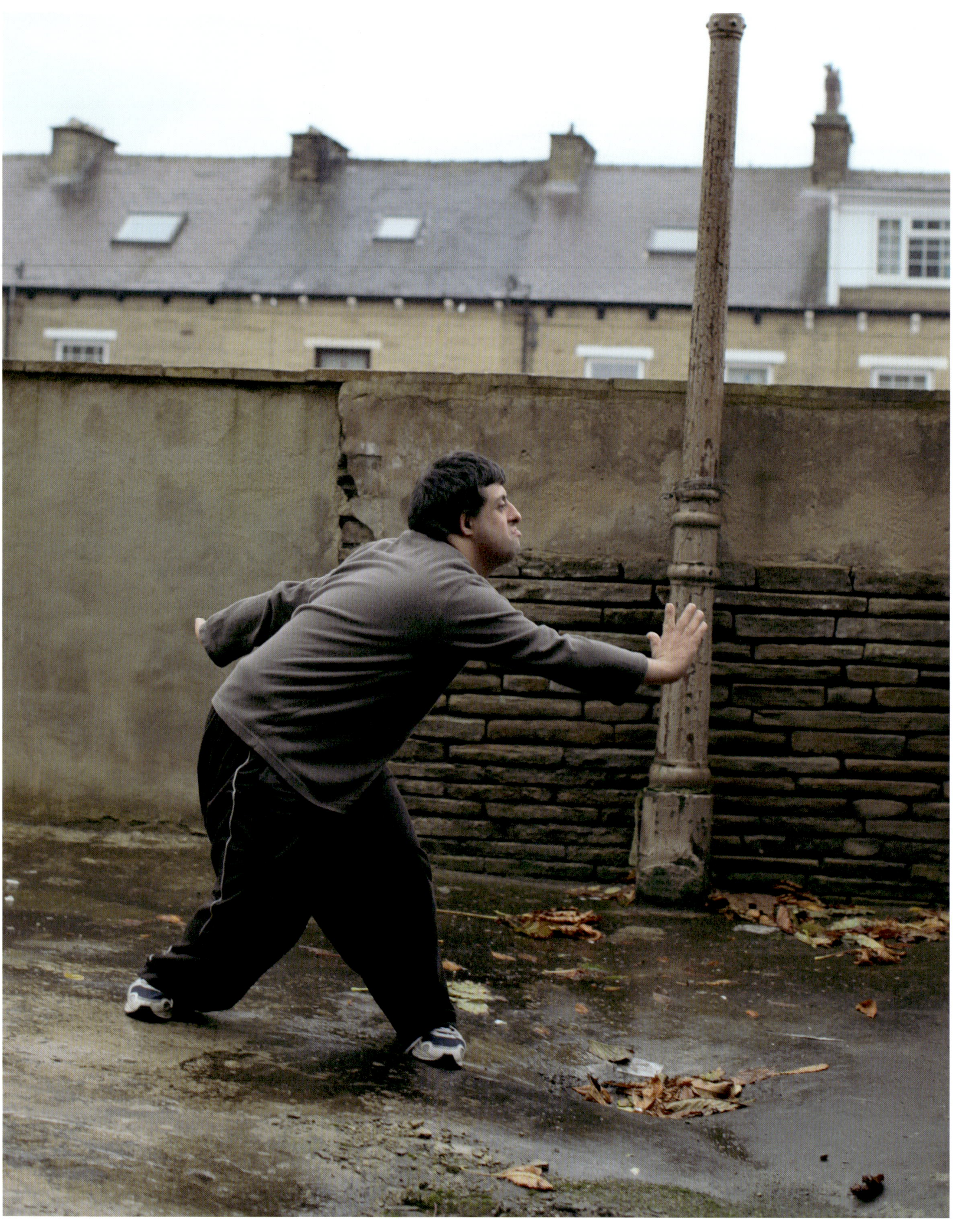

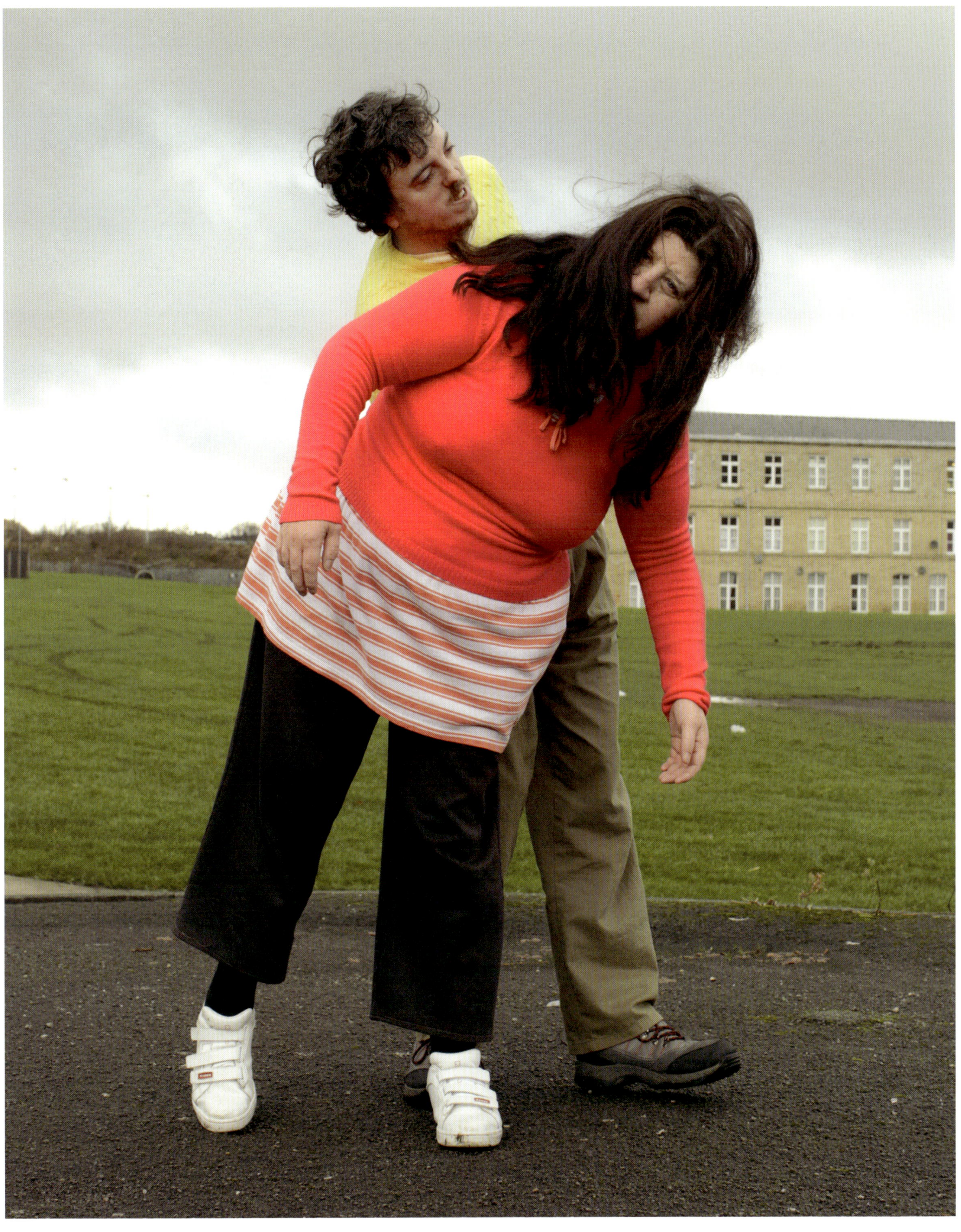

Denis Darzacq

Casques de Thouars

Like many of the projects Denis Darzacq has undertaken, this
one, too, springs from the heart of the suburban setting. The
photographer's interests span urban culture and the unvarying
ways, habits and, ultimately, even the scenery of modern cities.
With *Casques de Thouars* (2007), he provides yet another way of
viewing faces: hidden and protected and at the same time anonymous behind a symbol of speed, somehow reflecting much
of contemporary culture. Just like the superheroes in animated
films, or like cyborgs, these helmeted teenagers are transformed
into powerful figures. *Casques de Thouars* is a commentary on
how young people in suburban environments – where there
is nothing for them to do, and where they feel is trapped by
inertia – pass their time. It underlines the need for a sense of
belonging, a temporary illusion of self-assertiveness, which, of
course, continues beyond the complicated transitional phase of
adolescence. The images can also be viewed as an allegory of the
many faceless masks that people put on today, as adults, in order
to belong – functional masks, like the helmets – following strict
rules in order to stay the course. In the end, though, the image
created is a distant one, provoking the viewer to unmask the
subject, to see what is hidden beneath the rigid helmet, where
insecurity lurks.

VI

Courtesy the artist and Galerie RX, Paris

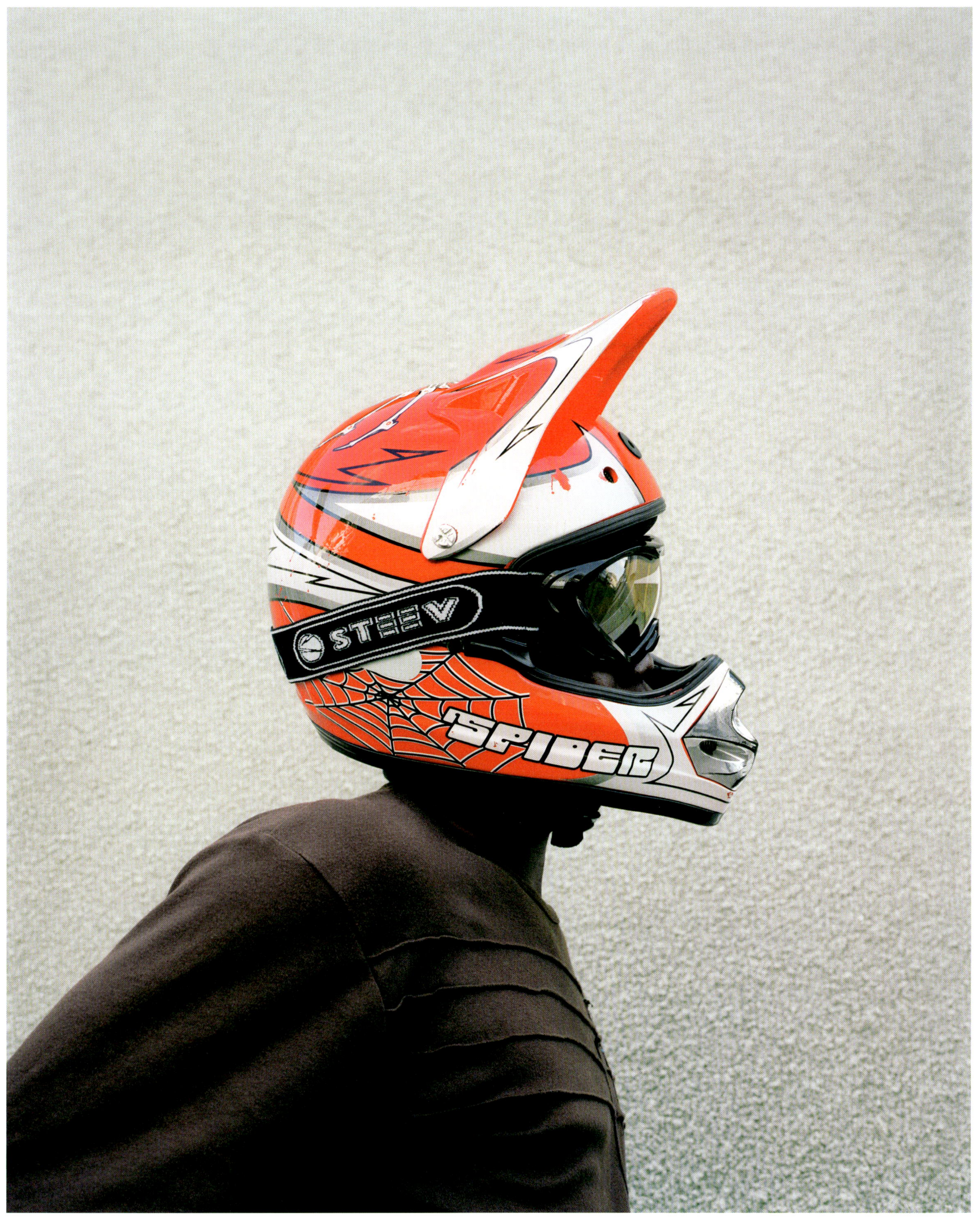

Denis Darzacq

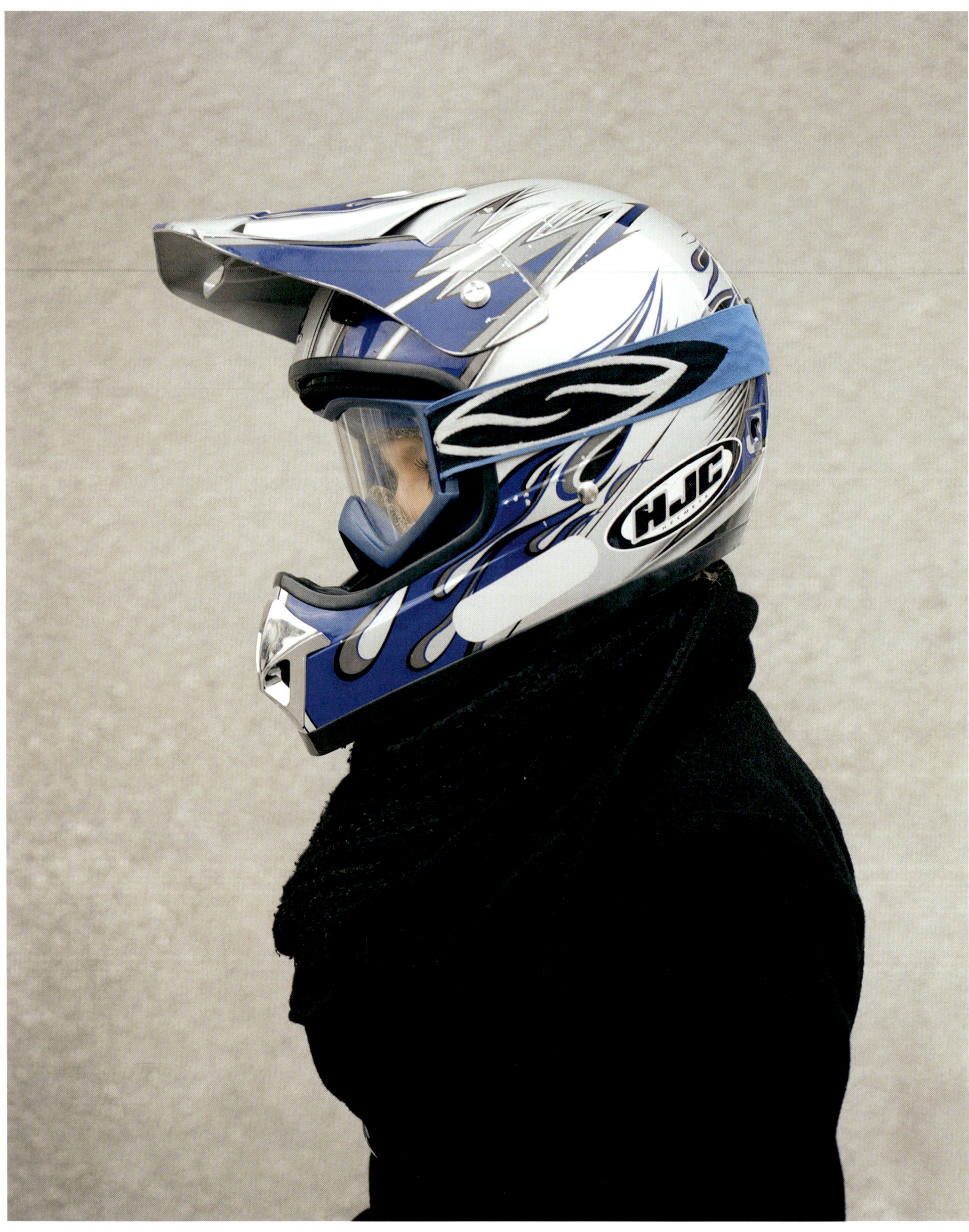
HJC

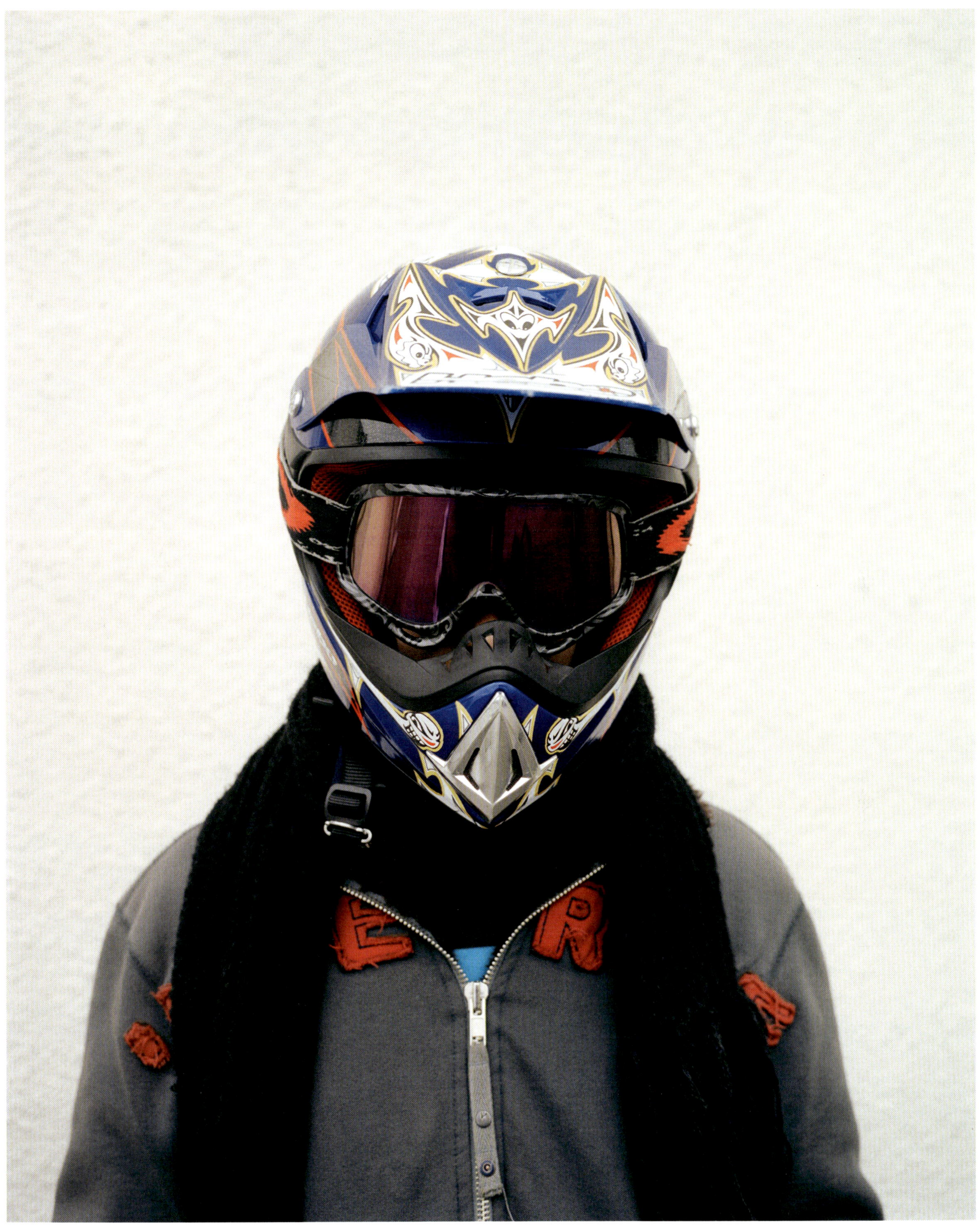

65

Denis Darzacq

Luc Delahaye (born 1962, France)

pp. 67–70
Untitled, in 'L'Autre', 1995–97.
Gelatin silver print, 22 × 16.8 cm

Courtesy the artist and Galerie Nathalie Obadia,
Paris and Brussels

L'Autre

Susan Sontag once wrote that 'There is something on people's
faces when they don't know they are being observed that never
appears when they do.' That is one way of looking at this famous
series by Luc Delahaye. It shows certain similarities to Walker
Evans's photographic study *Many Are Called* (1938–41), in which
Evans photographed New York subway passengers without their
knowledge, using a camera hidden in his coat. From 1995 to
1997, Delahaye also used a hidden camera to secretly take pictures of passengers on the Paris metro.

In Delahaye's case, however, the photographer was not interested in shedding light on the thoughts and moods of everyday
people. His metro portraits are cropped in such a way that we
can see only the unsmiling faces. Delahaye's interest lies in
penetrating the spaces these faces hide behind, even when fully
exposed. As he points out, we follow an unwritten social rule
that prevents us from staring at others. This - along with the fact
that under French law, everyone owns his or her own image -
became the springboard for the project, prompting Delahaye to
'steal' these pictures, as he describes it. What he photographs are
these unspoken and basically unseen 'spaces'. This raises questions about the 'Other' and our constant quest 'to read meaning into these faces, to force signification onto them', as Jean
Baudrillard states in his text accompanying the photographs
in *L'Autre* (The Other). We no longer try to force ourselves on
the other, but hope that, from their 'otherness', we can assert
ourselves.

VI

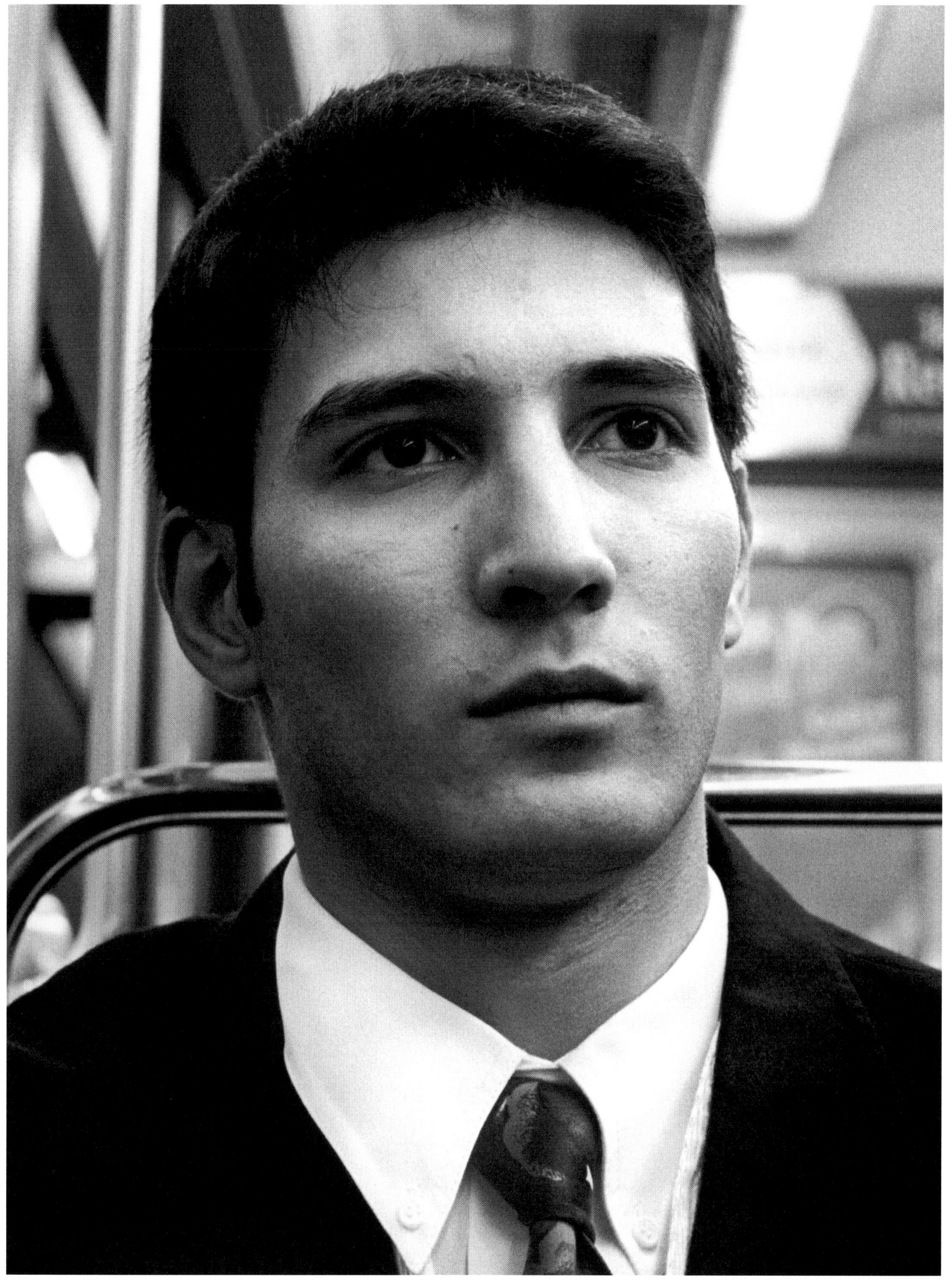

67   Luc Delahaye

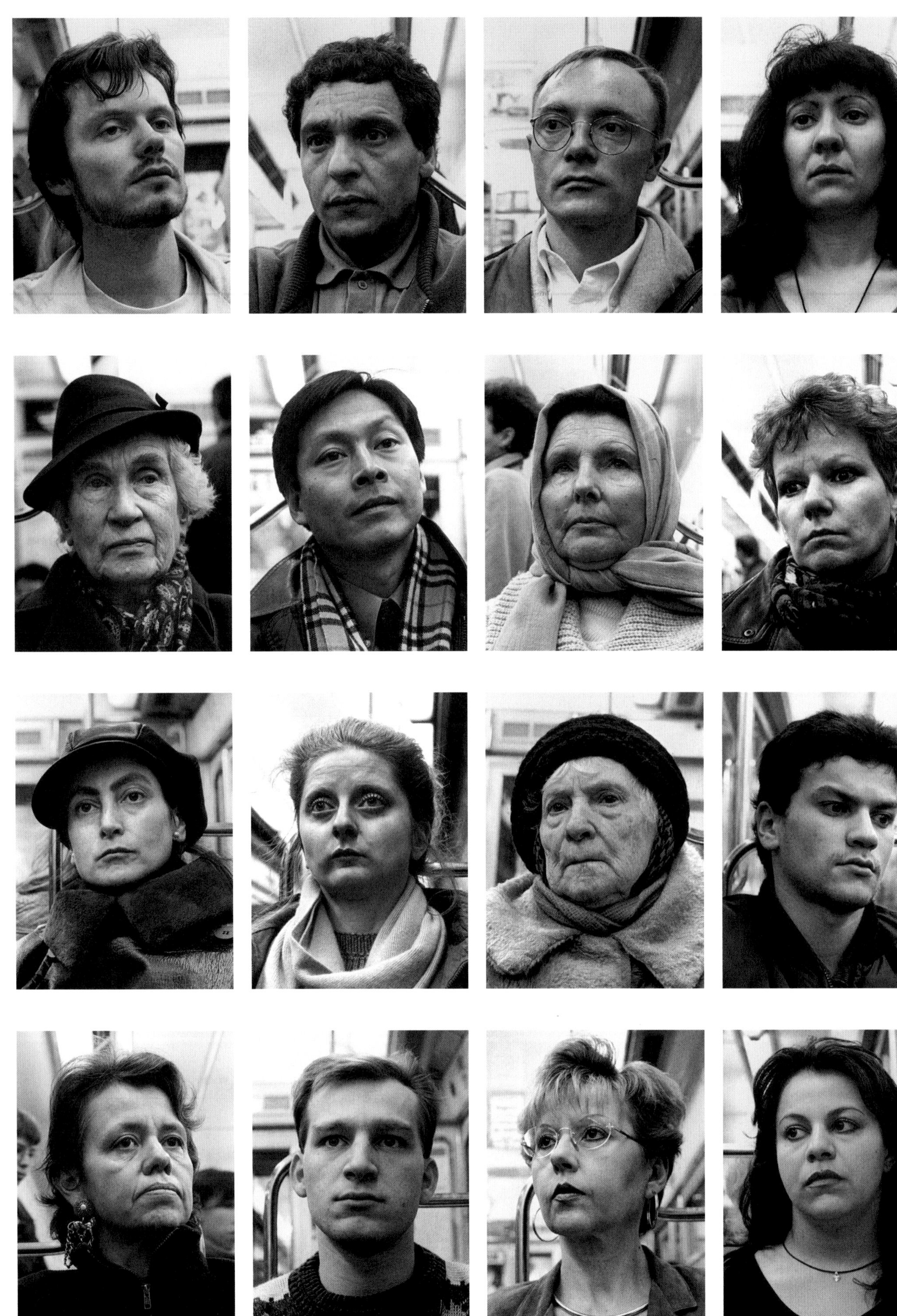

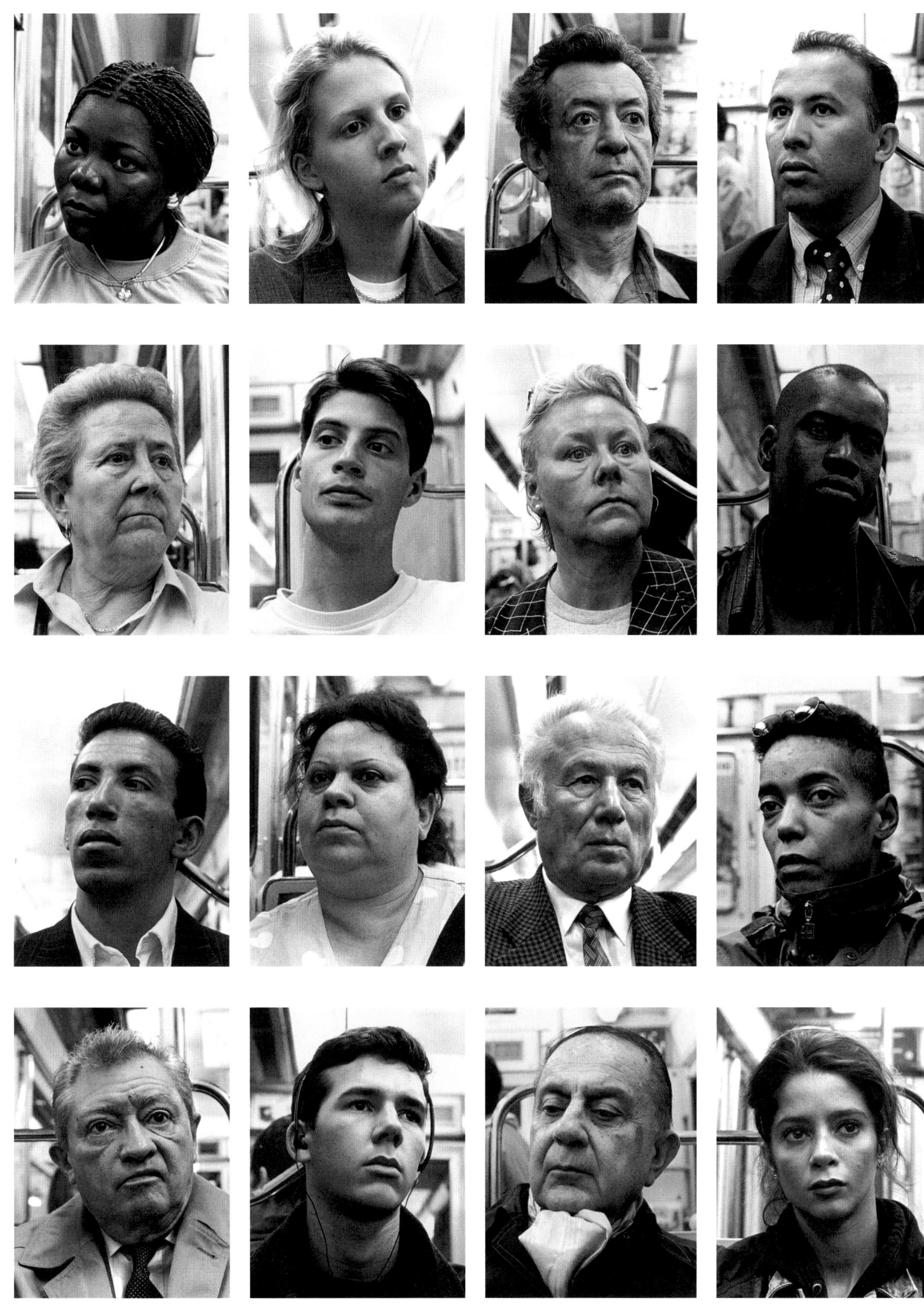

Luc Delahaye

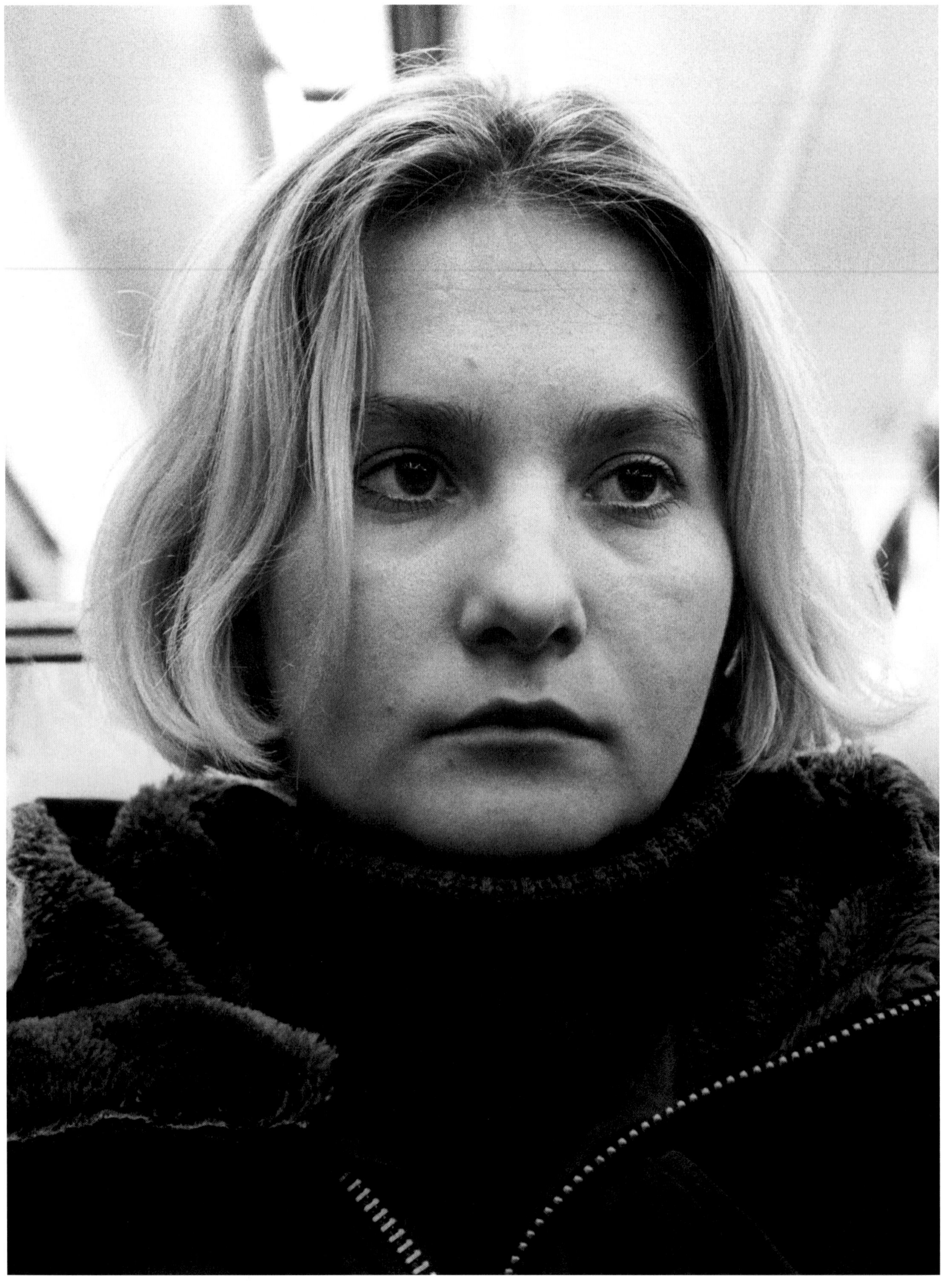

Paola De Pietri (born 1960, Italy)

Io parto

Young mothers-to-be in a suburban setting: the Italian photographer Paola De Pietri is particularly interested in the position of women in modern society. Here, she sees the urban setting of a new estate (in this case in and around Milan) as an important and formative environment for (young) mothers and their children. In her photography, De Pietri aims to investigate in more detail and focus on the relationship between mankind (especially women) and its surrounds. She questions the influence and significance of such impersonal settings, where any trace of history is obliterated and which are being built all over Italy and elsewhere in Europe. The mothers are on their own, full of expectations. Despite their visible personal strength, they exude an air of vulnerability.

Paola De Pietri regards documentary photography as a tool for analysing intricate social issues. The photographs from the series *Io parto* (I'm leaving) are documentary by nature and portraits at the same time, or actually a combination of the two genres. With this work she has one foot in a tradition of (Italian) landscape photography and the other in that of the portrait photograph. She stresses the reality of those two sides in the photographs. It's precisely the notional space in between that creates opportunities for the beholder to reflect on the image and grasp the complexity of what appear at first sight to be simple pictures. De Pietri points her analytical method at modern architecture and urban development, which she regards as part of current culture and politics. Here, she implicitly involves certain Italian traditions in literature and film, from Pavese to Pasolini, where the relationship between man and his place in the landscape plays a central role.

FG

pp. 73–75
Untitled, in 'Io parto', 2007.
Archival digital pigment prints on cotton rag, mounted on dibond, 108 × 135.5 cm

Courtesy the artist, Alberto Peola – Galleria d'Arte Contemporanea, Turin, and Galerie Les Filles du Calvaire, Paris

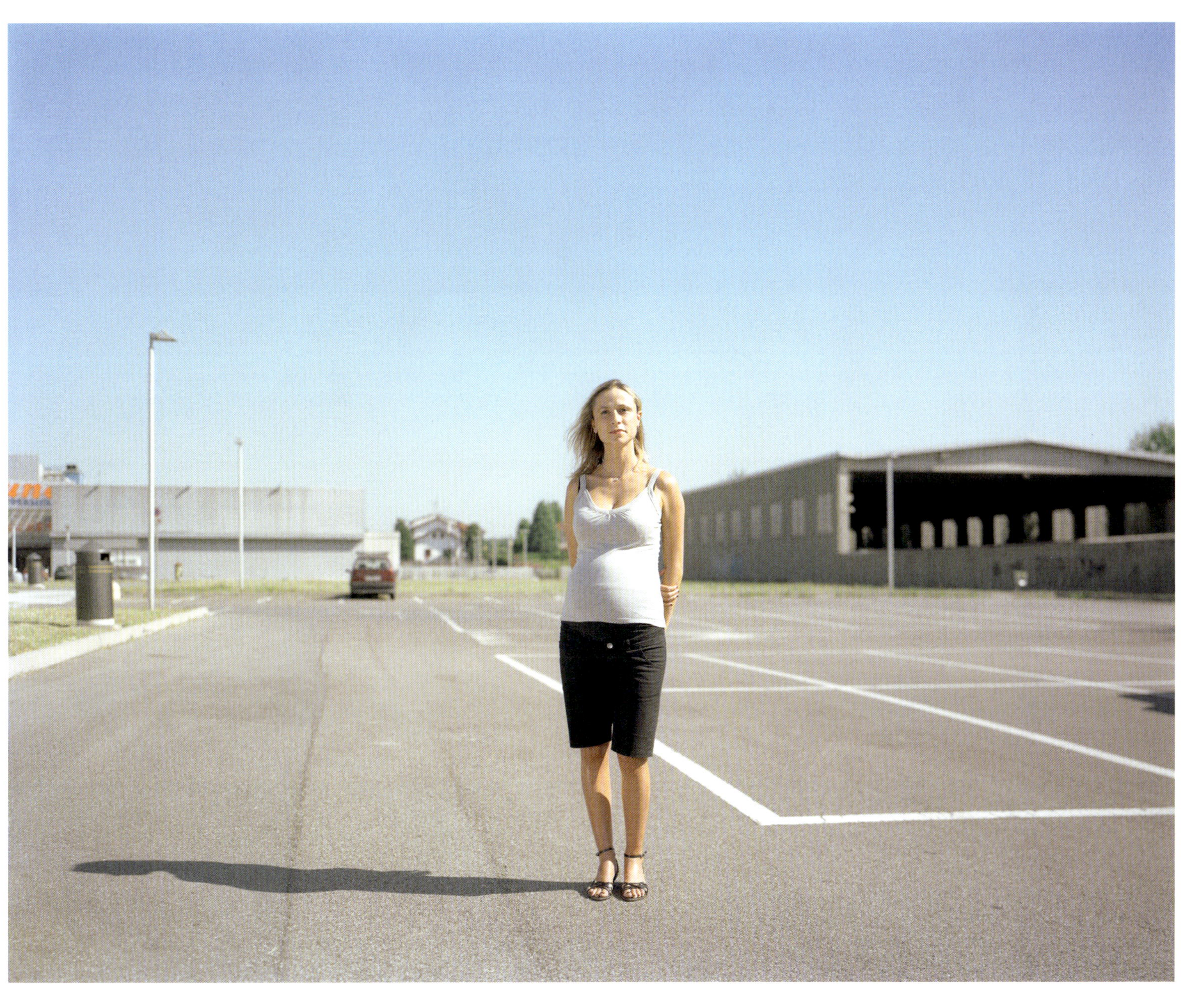

Paola De Pietri

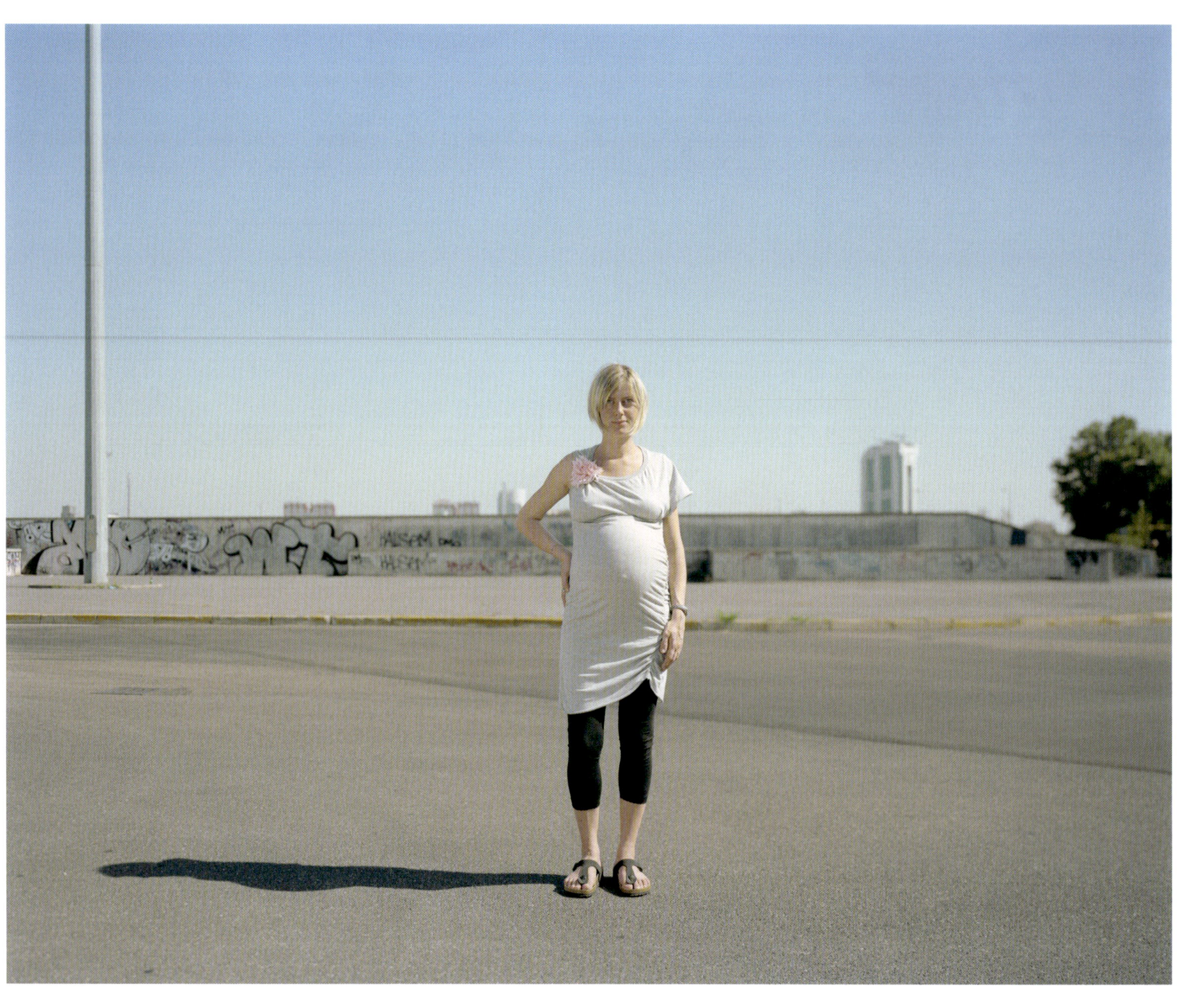

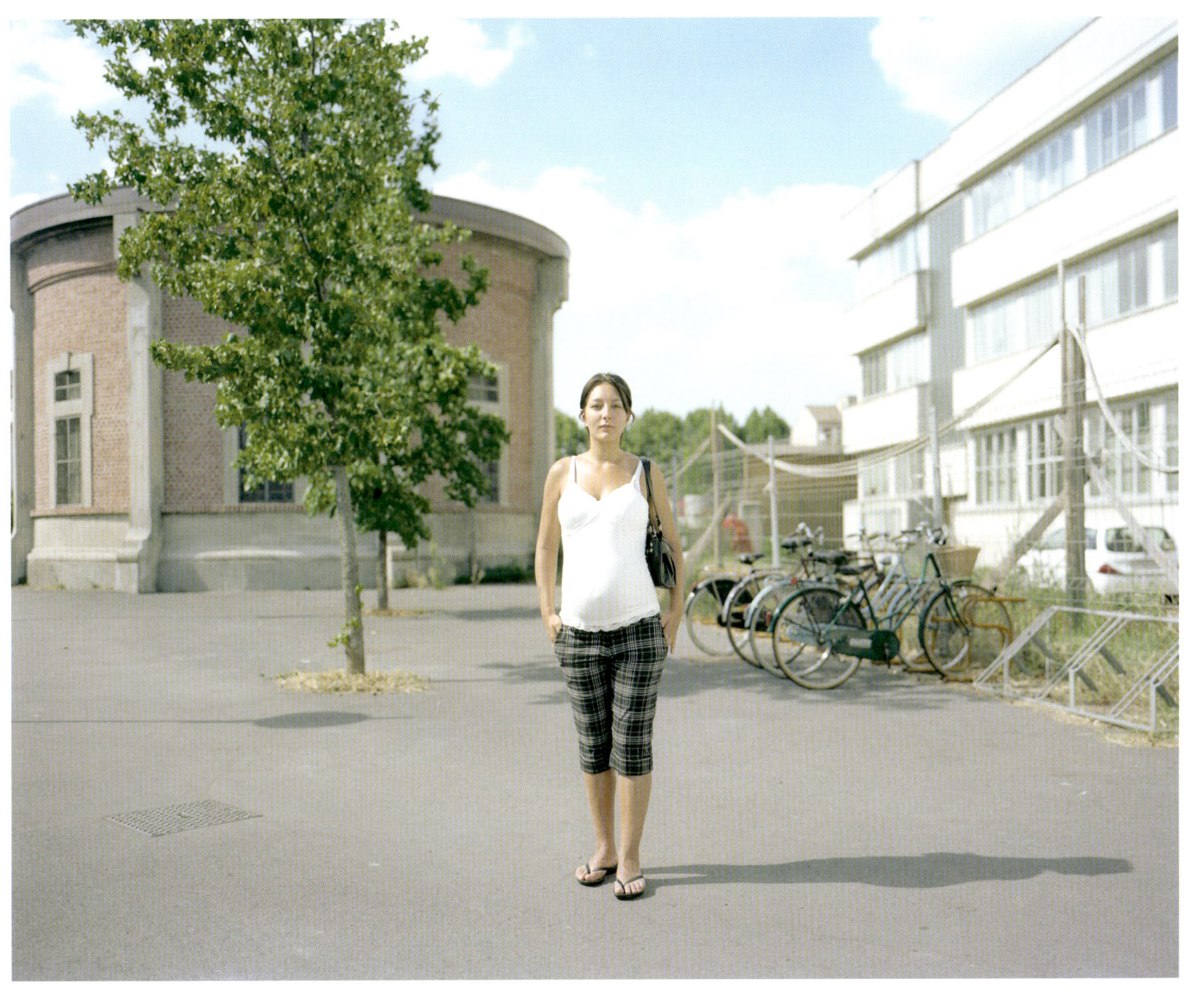

Paola De Pietri

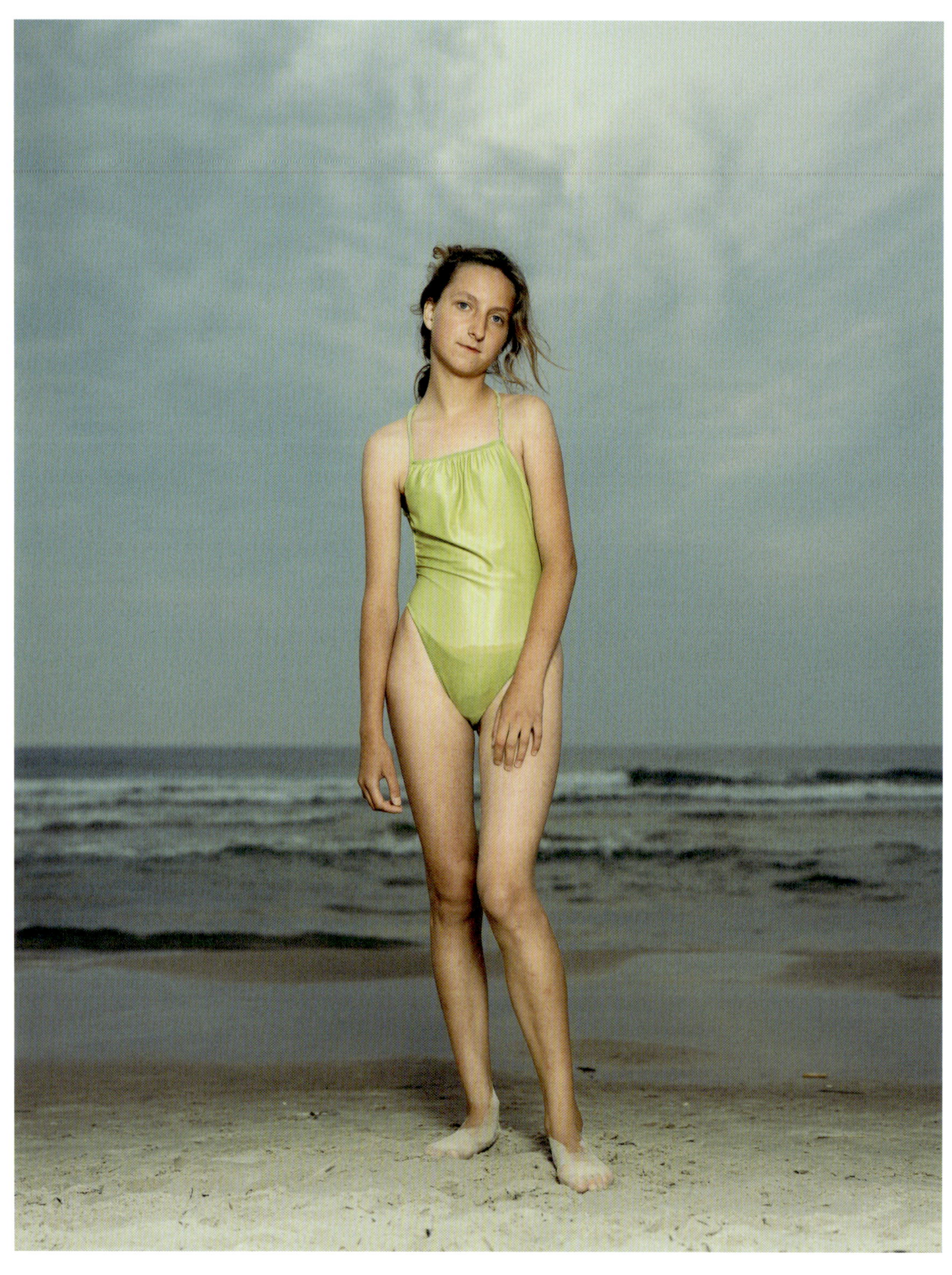

Rineke Dijkstra (born 1959, the Netherlands)

Beach Portraits

The beach may not be the most obvious place in which to take a portrait photograph, yet the series of pictures the Dutch photographer Rineke Dijkstra managed to create on that border of land and sea were to have a big influence on portrait photography in the late 1990s and the first decade of the 21st century. It was not so much the effect of the location as the way she captured in the utmost detail the awkward poses and facial expressions of adolescents in swimwear and a sense of their vulnerability. Between 1992 and 2002, she visited beaches all around the world, taking a large-format Deardorff camera with her to photograph some of the young people she met there. Dijkstra always included the sea in the background. She showed us how a photograph can be the expression of both the physique of an individual and of a universal sense of humanity and human vulnerability. She reinforced this powerful portrait photography by making a typological series of equally large, similar pictures in which the subjects are always put in the middle of the picture, in the same position in relation to the sea and the horizon behind them.

It is remarkable how Dijkstra's beach portraits were soon associated with works of art from earlier periods in the history of art. They have been linked with those of Johannes Vermeer (17th century), her (group) portraits in parks with Édouard Manet's *Le Déjeuner sur l'herbe* (19th century), and one of the beach portraits with Sandro Botticelli's *The Birth of Venus* (15th century). Although it is debatable whether we can call *The Birth of Venus* a real portrait, these comparisons are a good indication of the rich and vivid tradition in which Dijkstra's now iconic portraits stand.

FG

p. 76
Kolobrzeg, Poland, July 26, 1992, 1992.
C-print, 128 × 100 cm

p. 78
De Panne, Belgium, August 7, 1992, 1992.
C-print, 128 × 100 cm

p. 79
Kolobrzeg, Poland, July 23, 1992, 1992.
C-print, 128 × 100 cm

p. 80
Kolobrzeg, Poland, July 23, 1992, 1992.
C-print, 128 × 100 cm

Courtesy the artist and Marian Goodman Gallery, New York, London and Paris

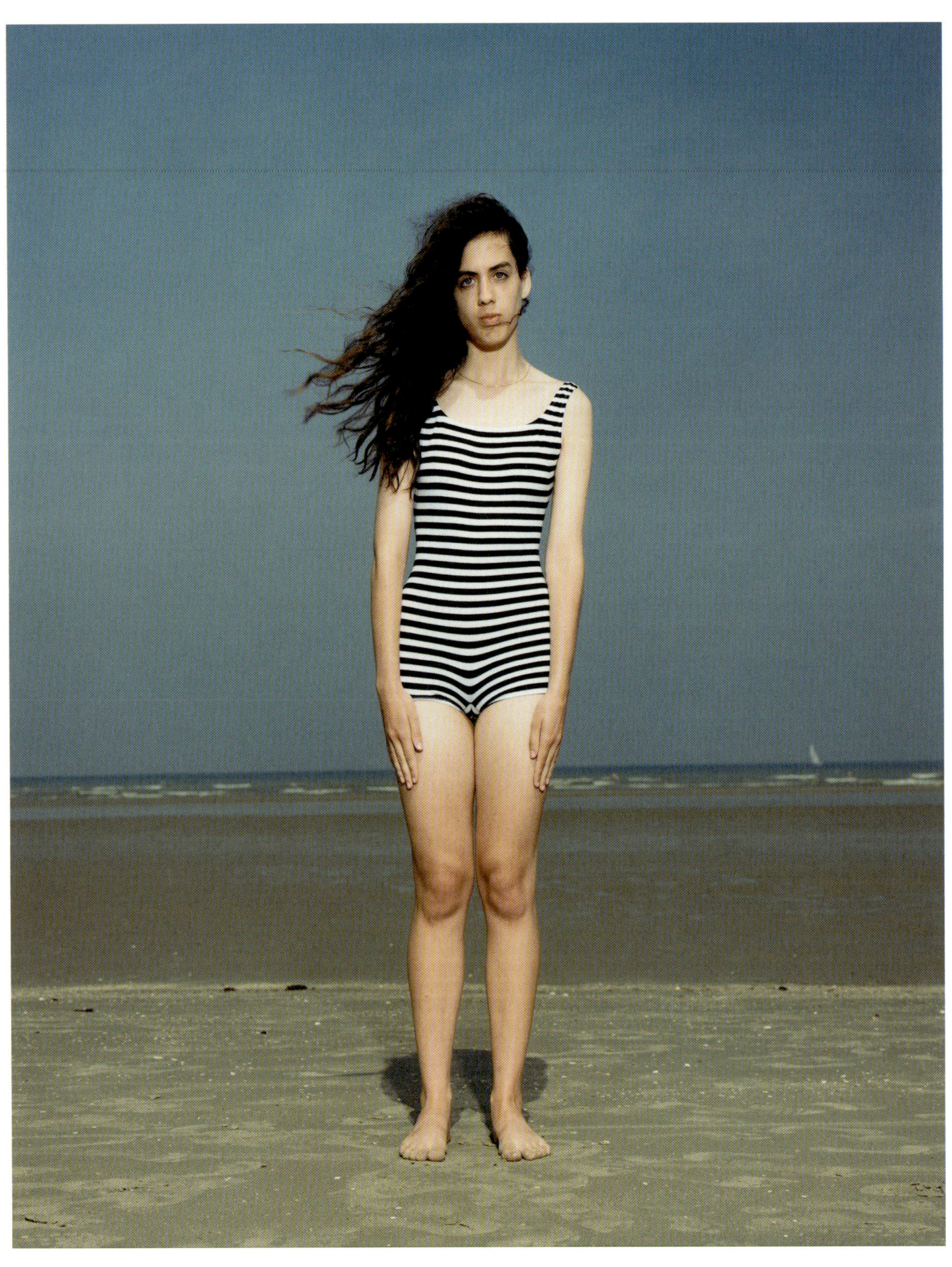

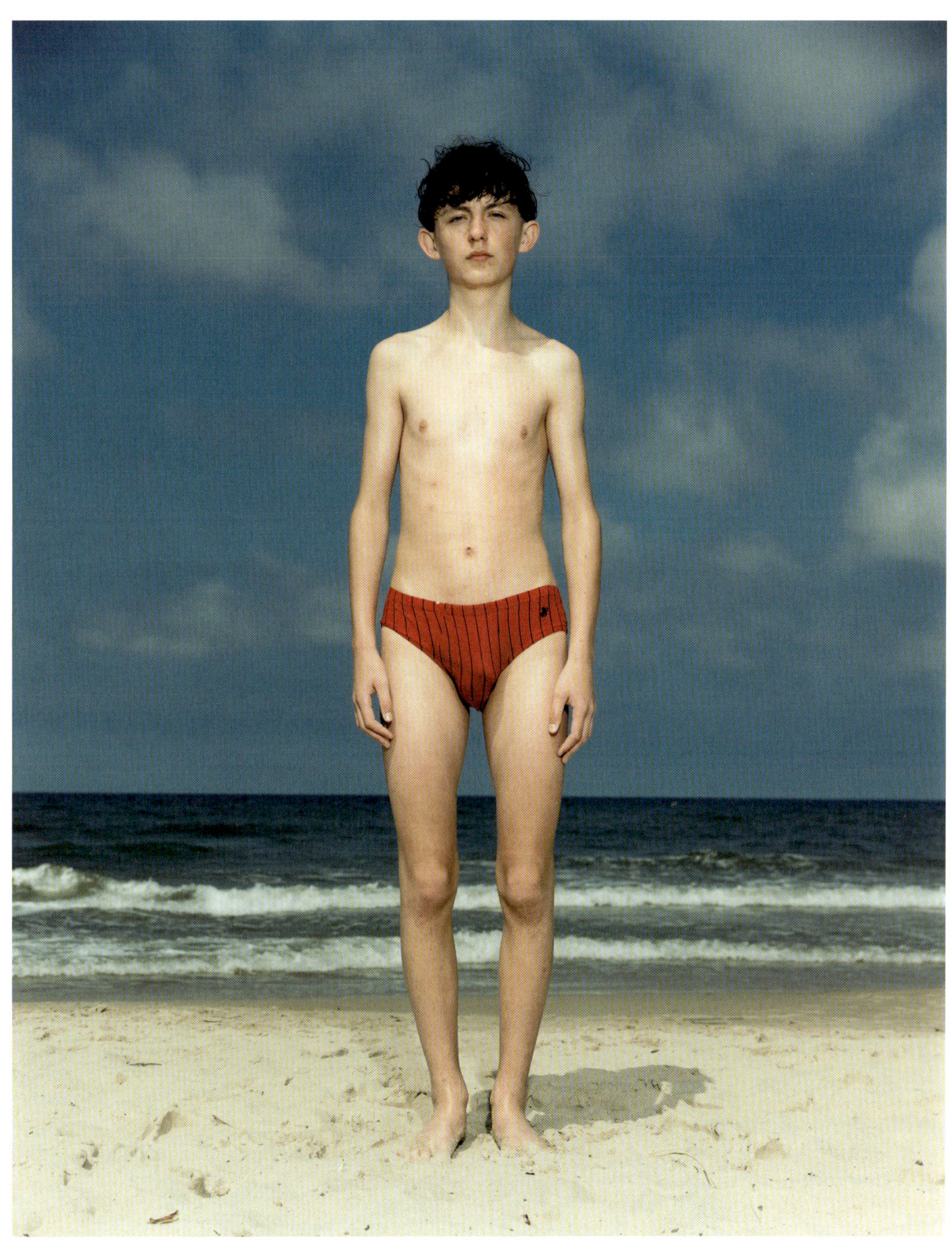

Rineke Dijkstra

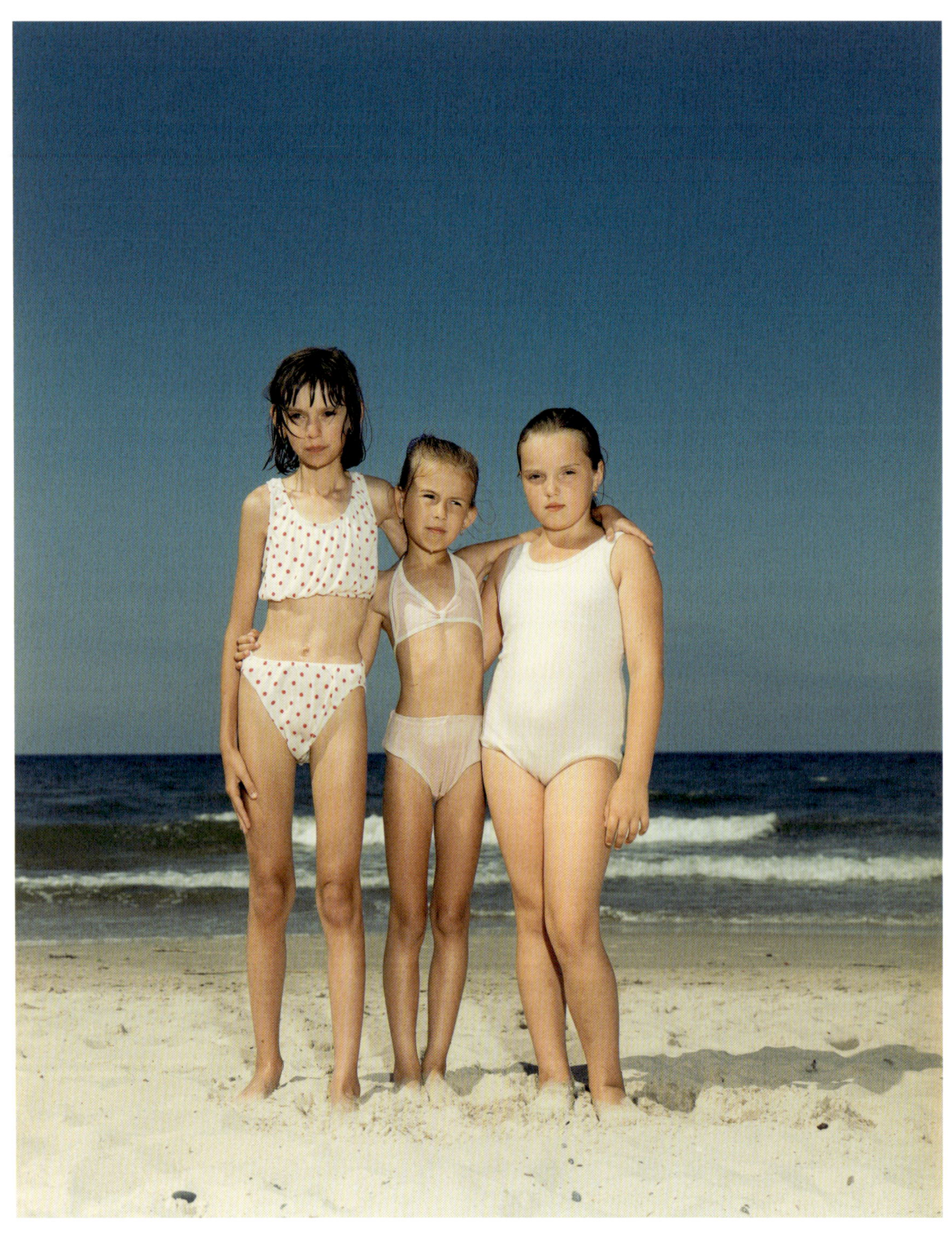

Alberto García-Alix (born 1956, Spain)

When Alberto García-Alix began taking photographs, he used to pose for his own pictures – his initial point of reference being the self-portrait. Through his body and his long journey in the labyrinth of drug addiction, and, most importantly, through his ability to let 'joie de vivre' take precedence over weakness and survival, he mastered a style that is as bright and as dark as the edge of a knife. The portraits shown here, most of them from his series *The Place of No Return*, 'seem to have been extracted from this web of memories', as he states in the audiovisual work of the same name: fragmented yet interlinked – following his life stories and also his view on life. They are like vivid shadows, evoking a world that is real and raw but which, at the same time, always creates an atmosphere that has something surreal, distorted about it. The faces are direct and powerful, with a dynamism that transcends the frame and makes them come alive. Yet they appear to emerge from a fictitious reality, like characters in a movie or a play. This approach seems attuned to the subconscious mind while simultaneously depicting its most lucid consciousness. They are unconventional, simple, black and white, able to create a story of their own, a story that comes from backstage, from the margin, from a place known only to a few – from García-Alix's own life.

AA

p. 83
Autorretrato. Mi lado femenino, 2002.
Gelatin silver print, 110 × 110 cm

p. 84
La Gata, 2001.
Gelatin silver print, 110 × 110 cm

p. 85
Tav Falco, 2003.
Gelatin silver print, 47 × 47 cm

p. 86
Los Irreducibles, 1991.
Gelatin silver print, 47 × 47 cm

p. 87
Marga, 2002.
Gelatin silver print, 47 × 47 cm

p. 88
Isa es así, 2000.
Gelatin silver print, 47 × 47 cm

Courtesy the artist

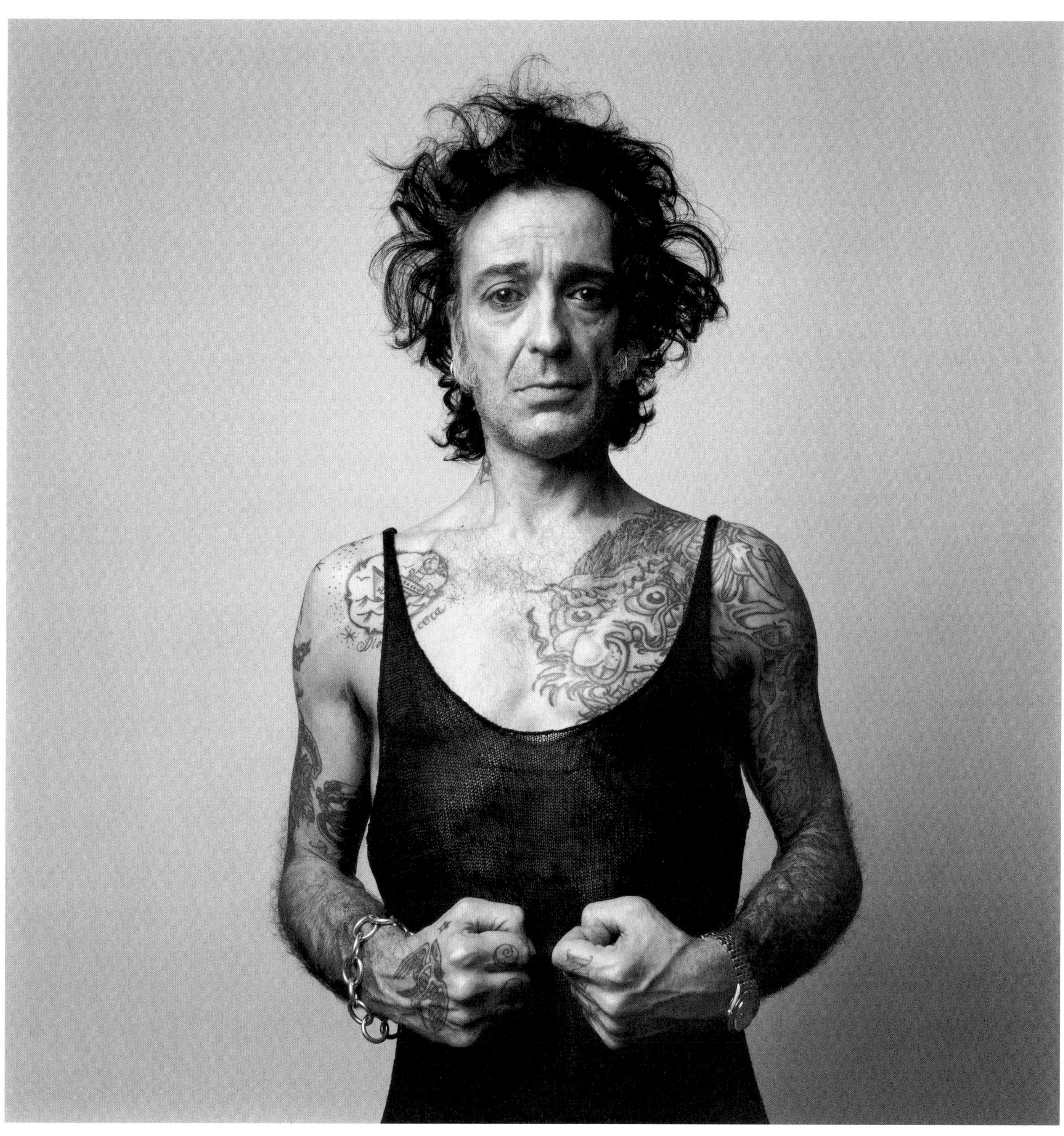

Alberto García-Alix

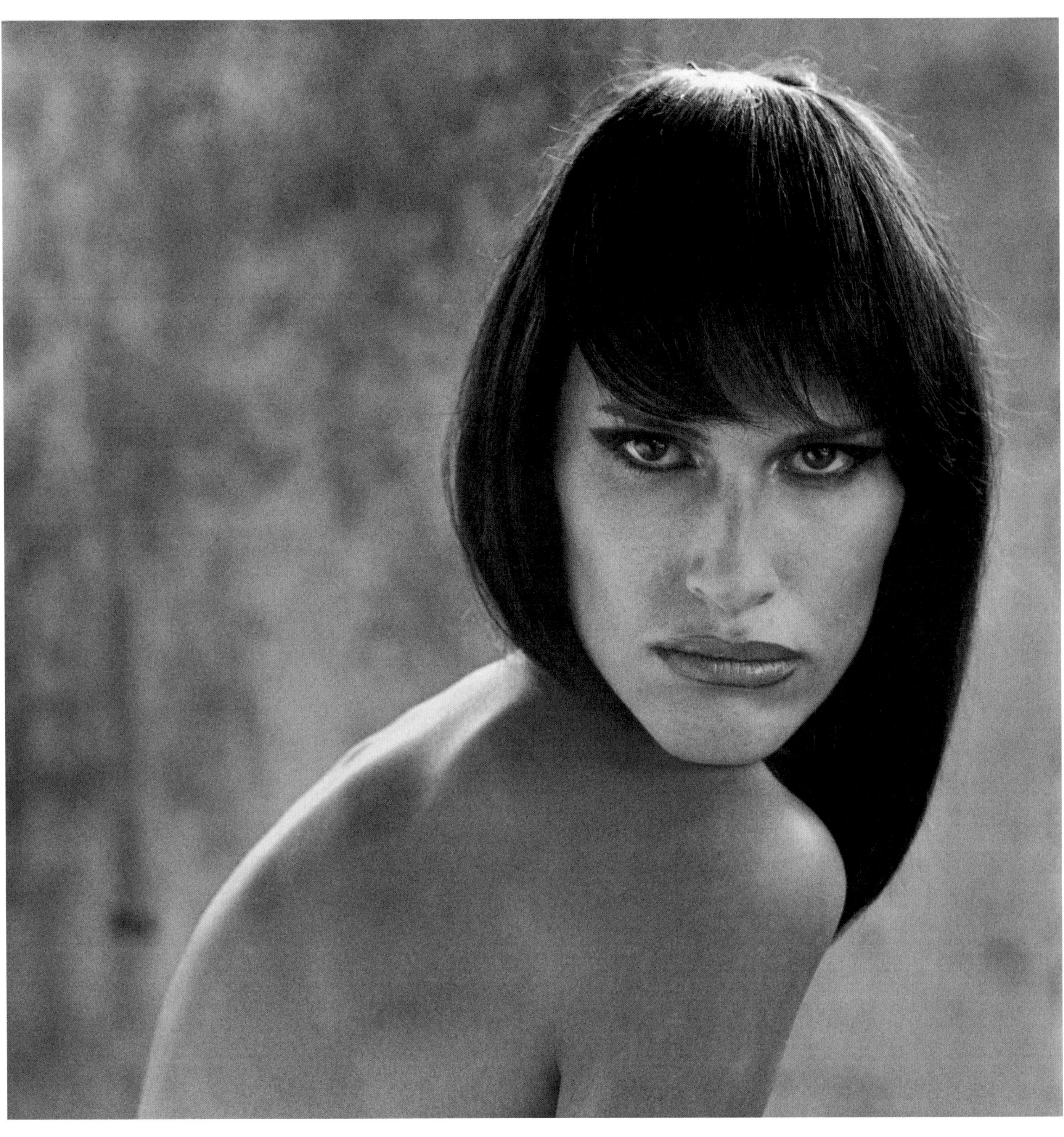

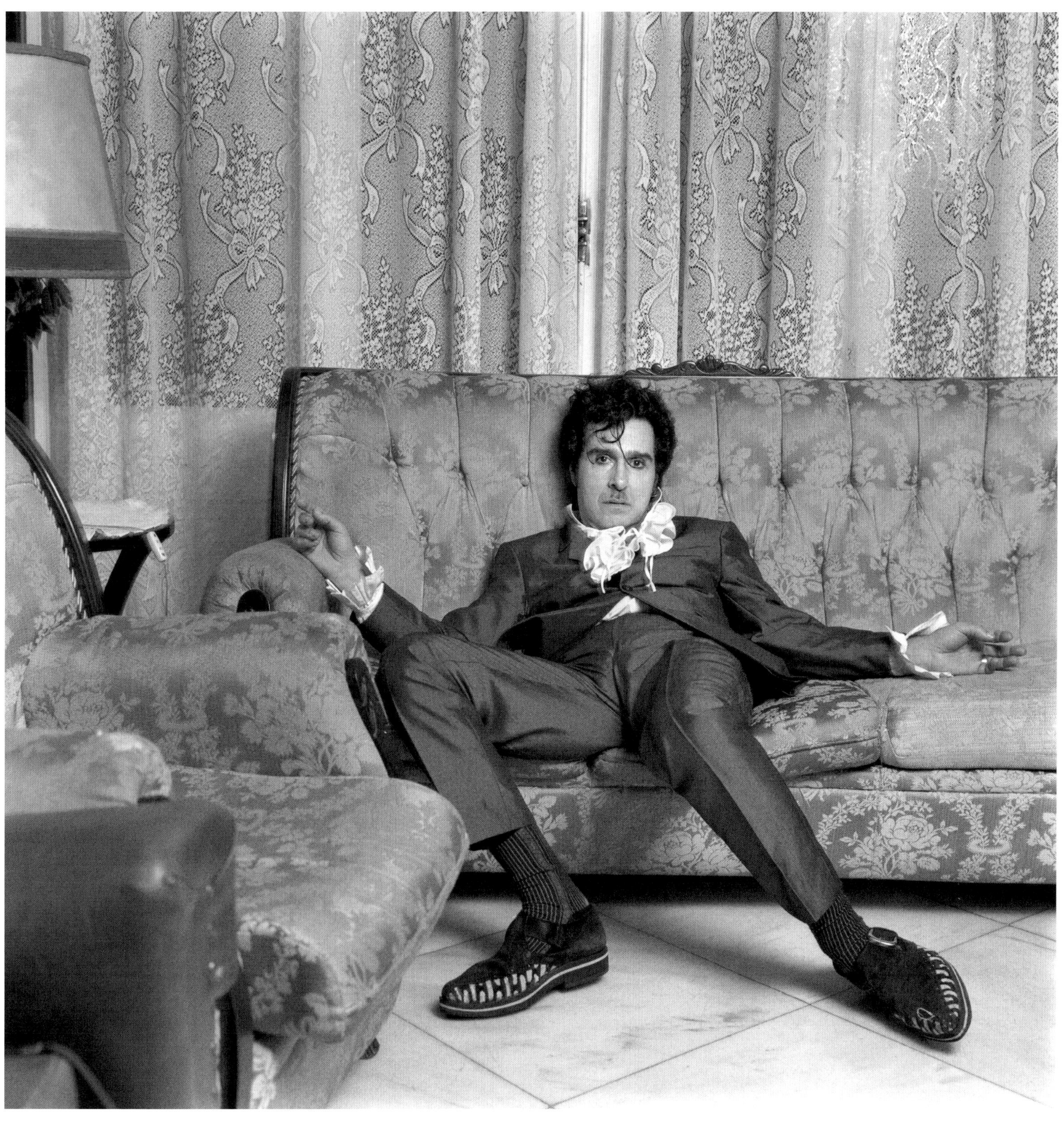

85 Alberto García-Alix

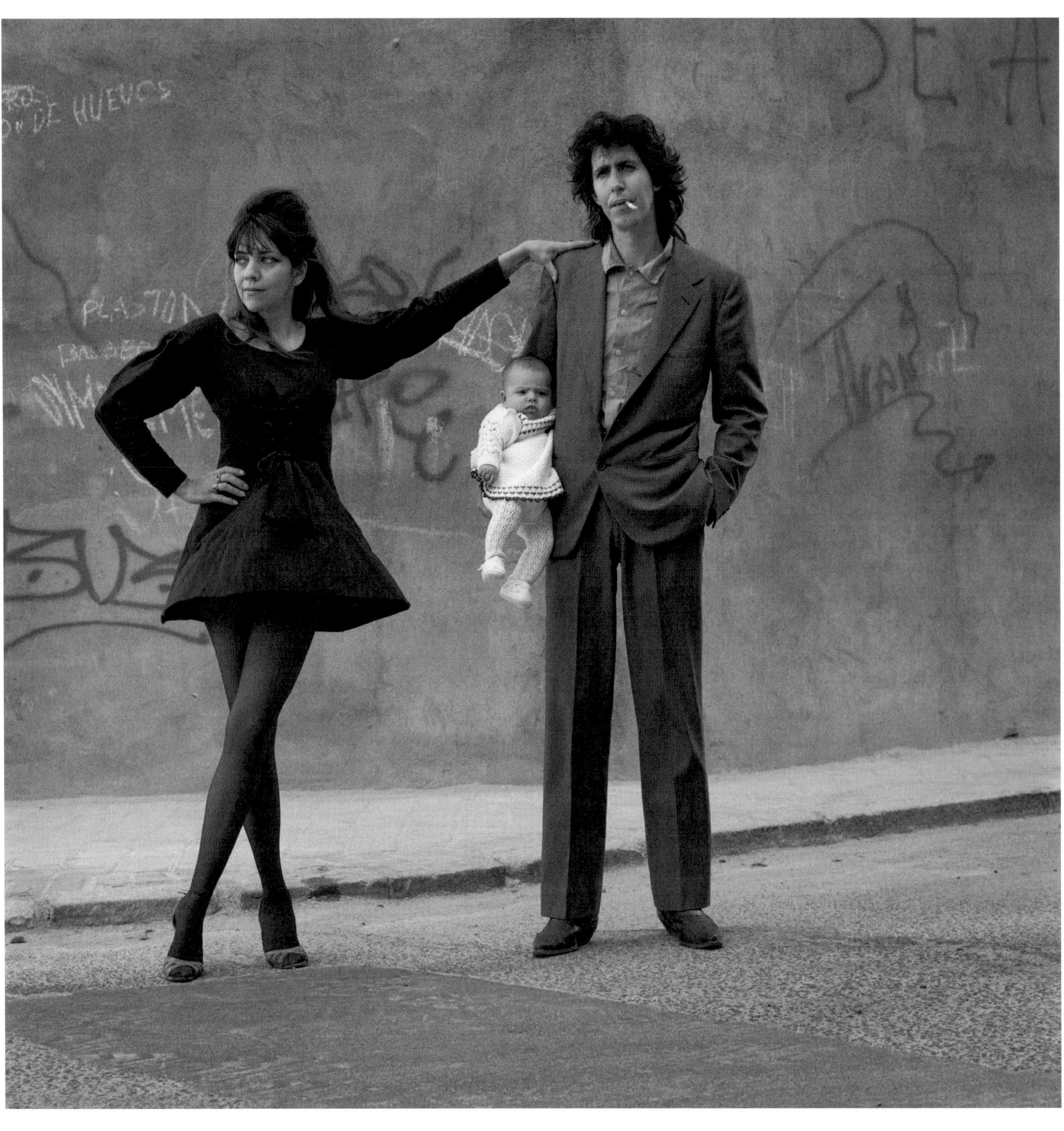

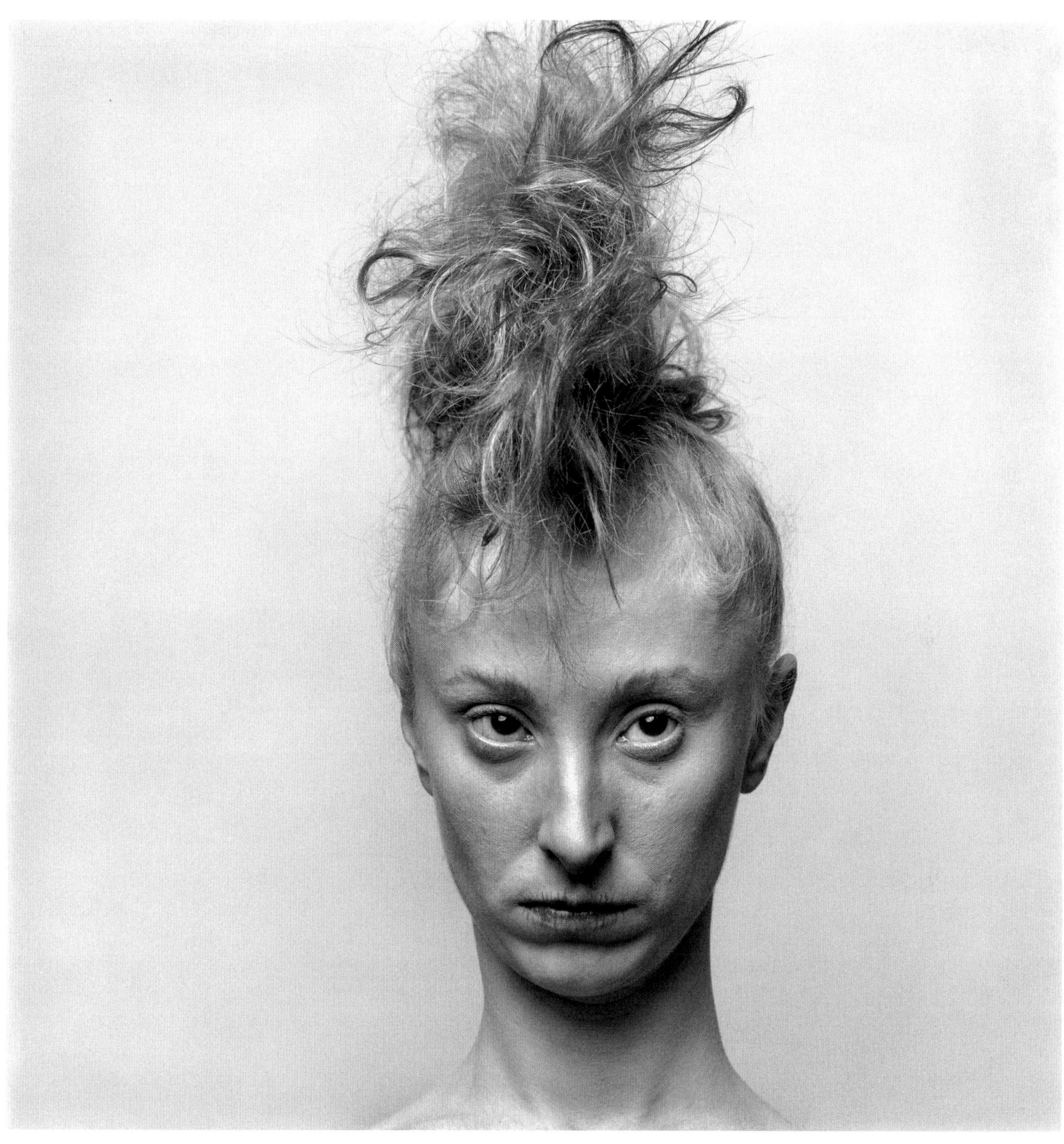

Alberto García-Alix

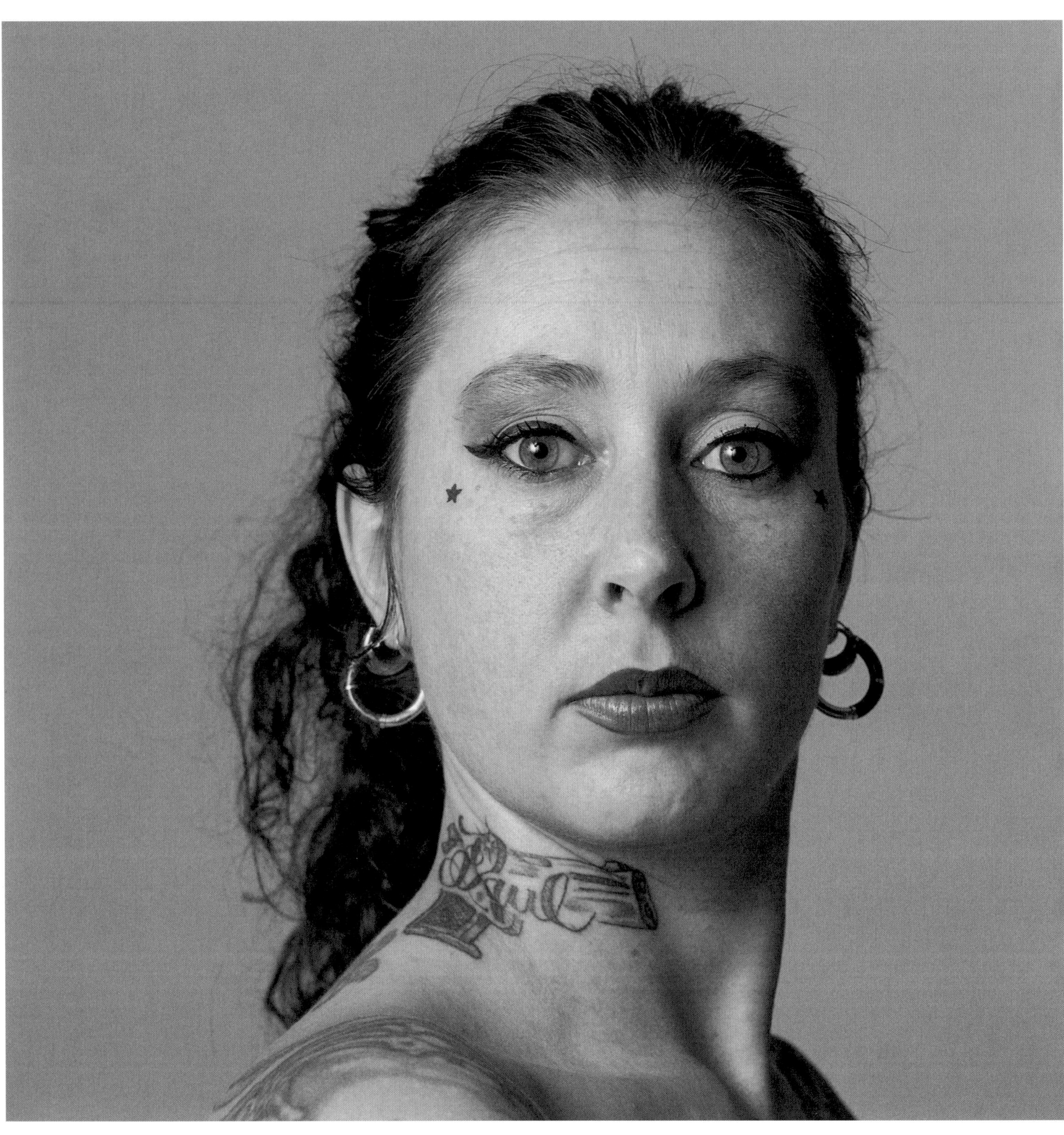

Jitka Hanzlová (born 1958, Czech Republic)

There is something I don't know

In this series, Jitka Hanzlová uses tools from traditional Renaissance portraiture to create contemporary photographic portraits. At first glance, one can detect the conventional style: the pose of the subjects, mostly three-quarter, and torso views, framed in natural light with generally nondescript coloured backgrounds. The details in her compositions also allude to paintings by the great masters, such as Piero della Francesca or even Leonardo da Vinci. In this case, however, the people she has photographed in various cities, including Milan, Essen and Madrid, are not people of status or power but ordinary individuals with a deadpan look, who nonetheless 'had something of that time', as she put it. There are no props or symbols included, no signs of power that then have to be interpreted, such as the wigs, clothing or rings one often sees in paintings. Details – whenever they appear – are there to underline the appropriation. So what matters is not who is being photographed, but what their faces tell us. As the title of the series from 2000–12 says: 'There is something I don't know' and perhaps never will, since these portraits are not intended to capture the faces for eternity. Hanzlová's motto is: 'The way I go is the way back to see the future', but the portraits still manage to withhold something that we don't know. Can we tell anything about the future from these Quattrocento appropriations? Cryptic as ever, these faces preserve their secret.

AA

p. 91
Untitled (Julia), in 'There is something I don't know', 2000. Archival pigment print on cotton, 50 × 34 cm

p. 92
Untitled (Leonardo), in 'There is something I don't know', 2007.
Archival pigment print on cotton, 60 × 43 cm

p. 93
Untitled (Conca), in 'There is something I don't know', 2011.
Archival pigment print on cotton, 52 × 37 cm

p. 94
Untitled (Jule), in 'There is something I don't know', 2011. Archival pigment print on cotton, 41 × 30 cm

p. 95
Untitled (Isabel), in 'There is something I don't know', 2007.
Archival pigment print on cotton, 52 × 37 cm

p. 96
Untitled (Boy), in 'There is something I don't know', 2011. Archival pigment print on cotton, 44 × 33 cm

p. 97
Untitled (Greco), in 'There is something I don't know', 2011.
Archival pigment print on cotton, 41 × 30 cm

Courtesy the artist

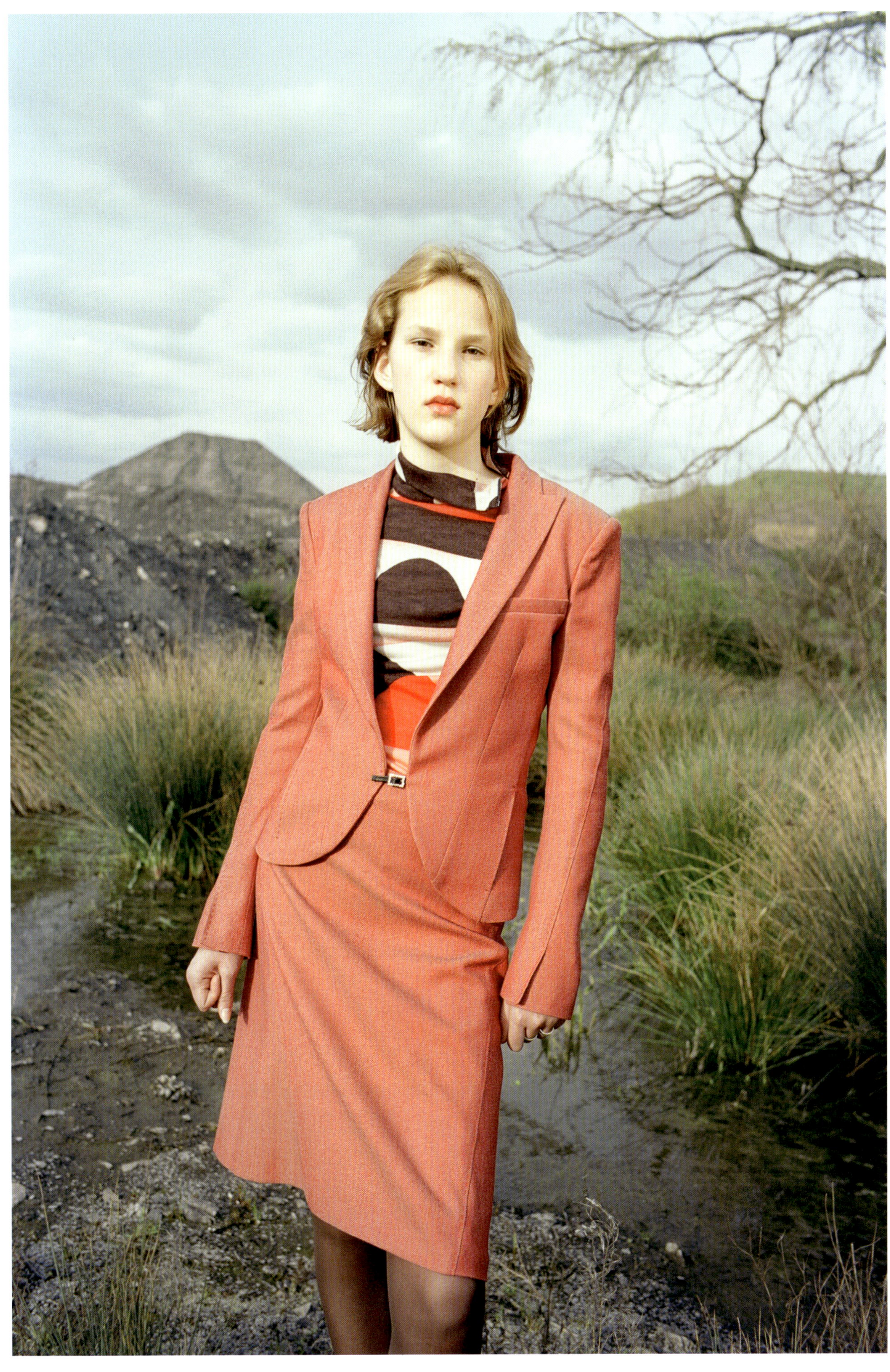

Jitka Hanzlová

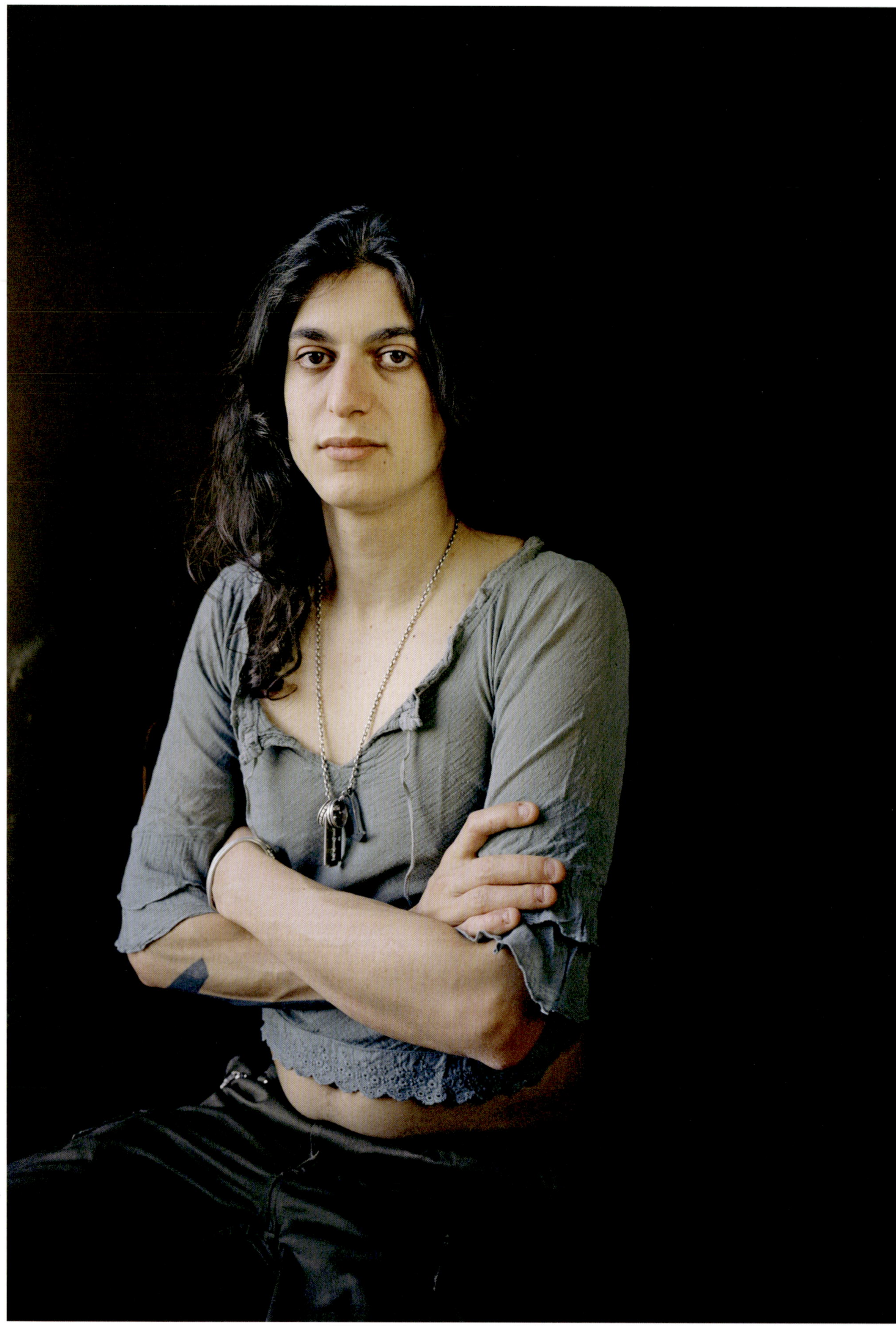

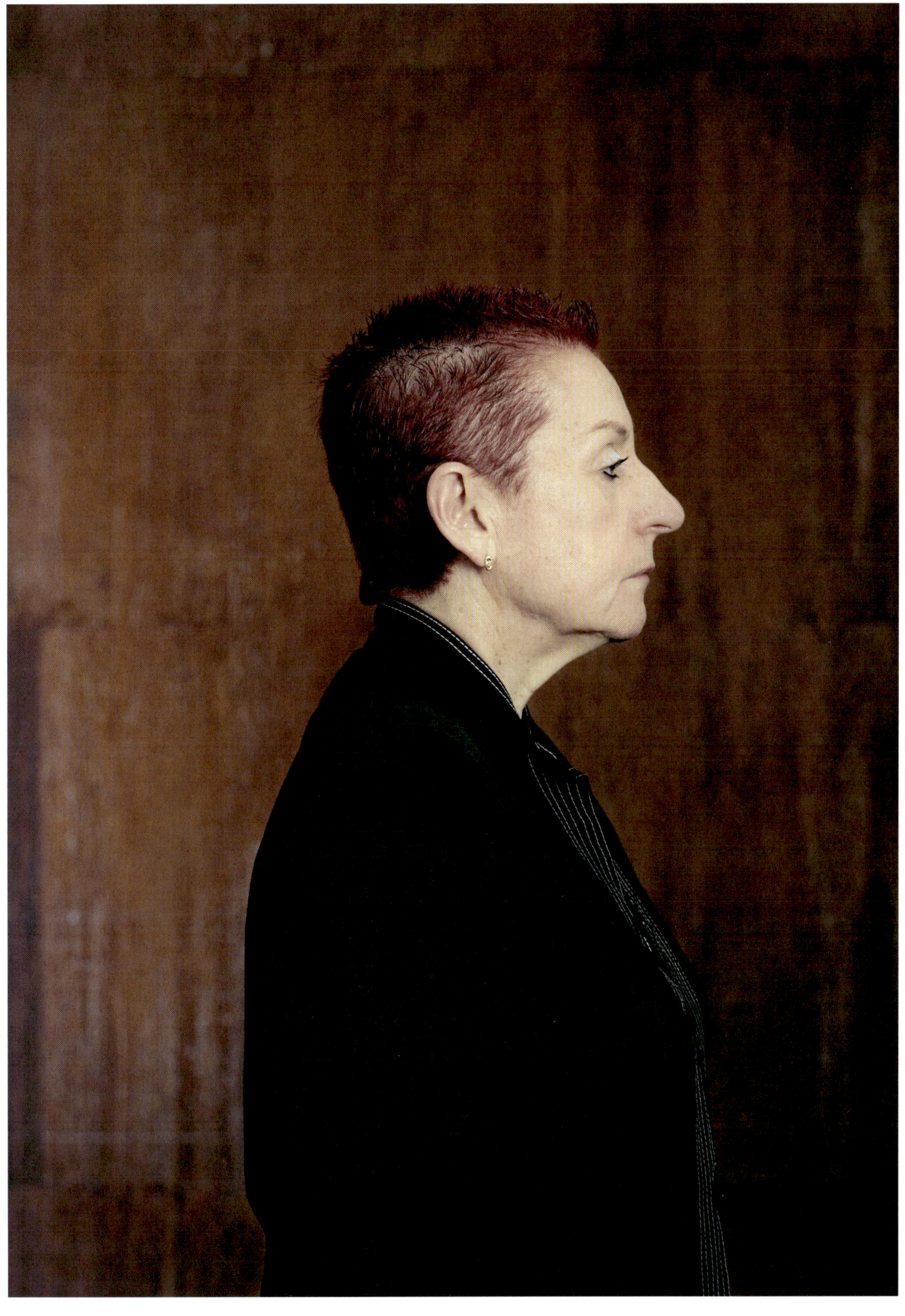

    Jitka Hanzlová

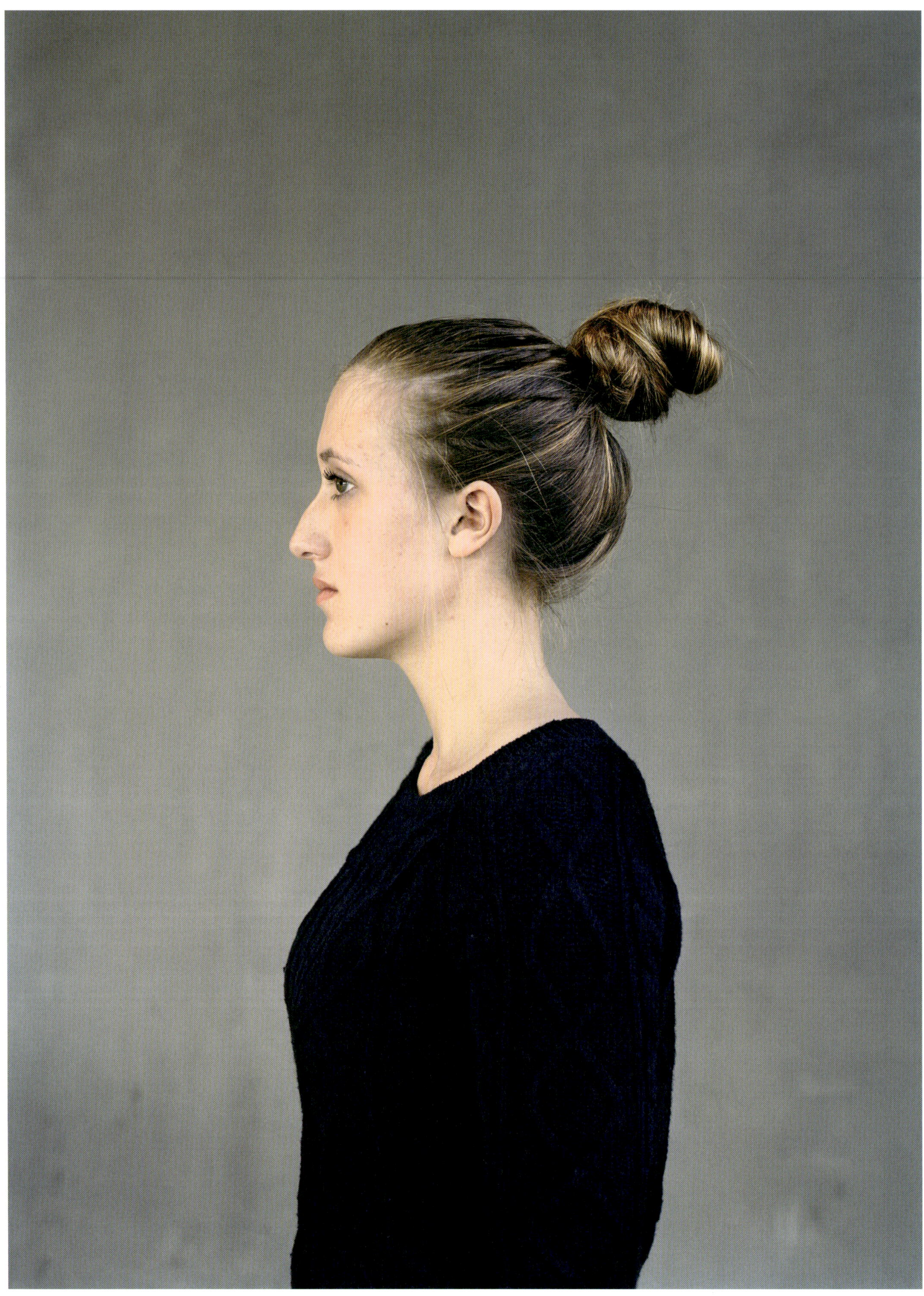

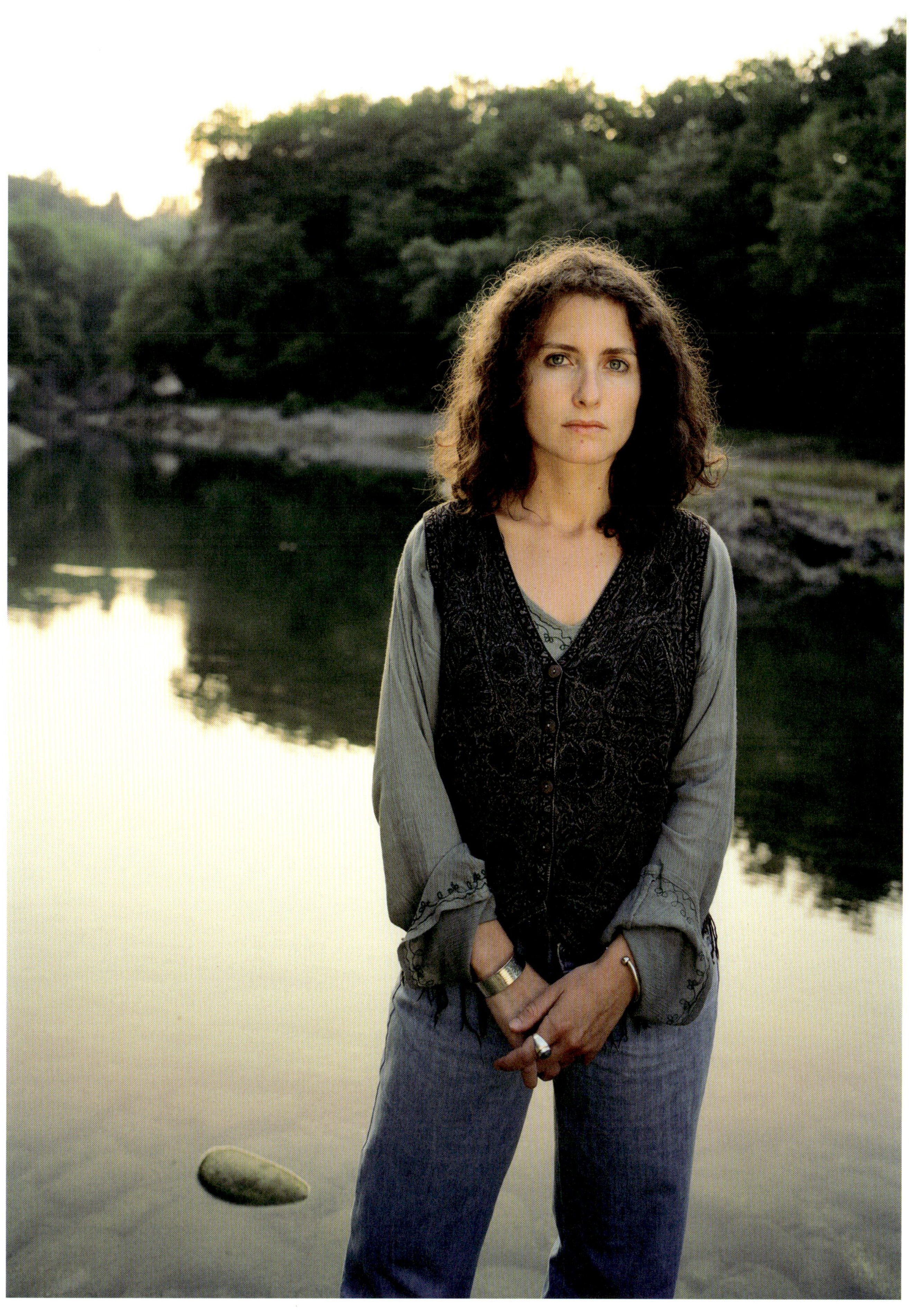

Jitka Hanzlová

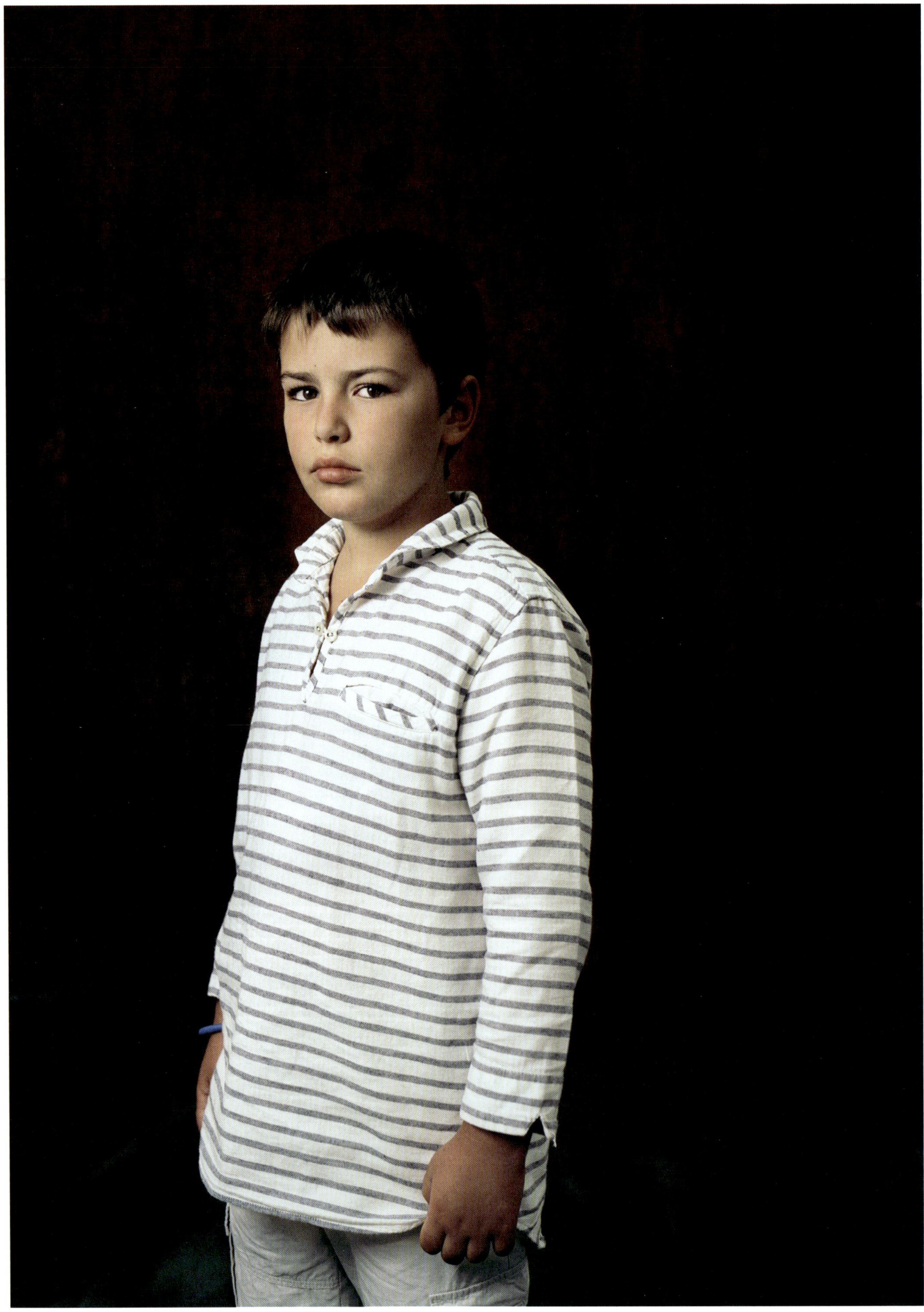

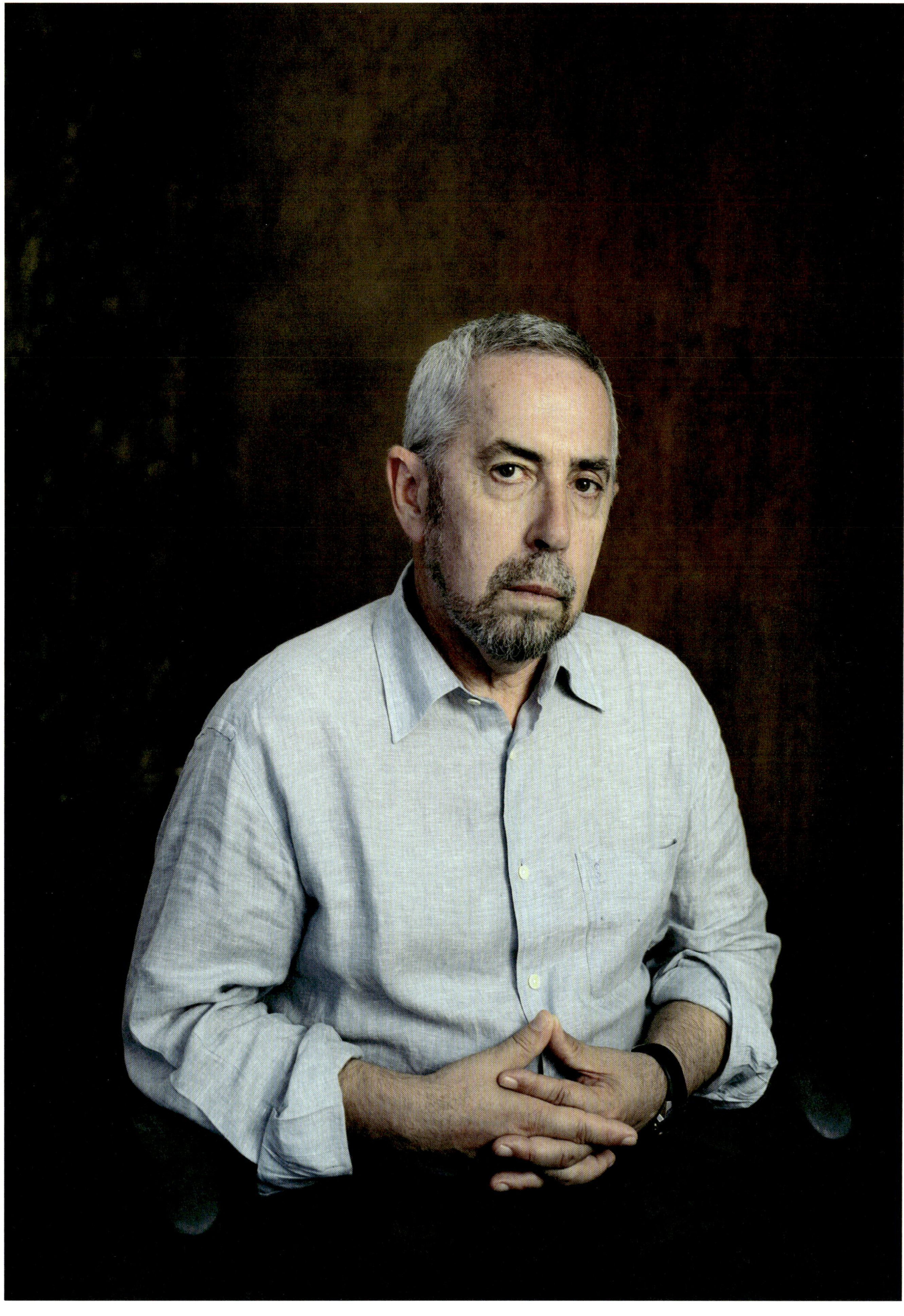

Jitka Hanzlová

Rokytnik

In 1982, at the age of 24, Jitka Hanzlová fled Soviet-dominated
Czechoslovakia to seek refuge in Germany. She studied communication technology, specializing in photography, at Essen
University. After the fall of the communist regime back home
in 1989, she returned to her birthplace, Rokytnik, in eastern
Bohemia – a village replete with memories of her youth, but
also a place where time had stood still. The intricate confrontation between the artist, her past and the local reality resulted
in the *Rokytnik* series of photographs, consisting of landscapes
and pictures of the people who live there. Their lifestyle stands
in stark contrast to the rhythm of big cities in the West, so the
images express both melancholy and criticism. While this series
still gives broad expression to the concept of a 'portrait', the
series *There is something I don't know* considers the genre of the
portrait itself in more depth, with more explicit references to
the Renaissance.

CDJ

pp. 99–105
'Rokytnik', 1990-94.
Original C-prints, 48 × 37.5 cm

Courtesy the artist

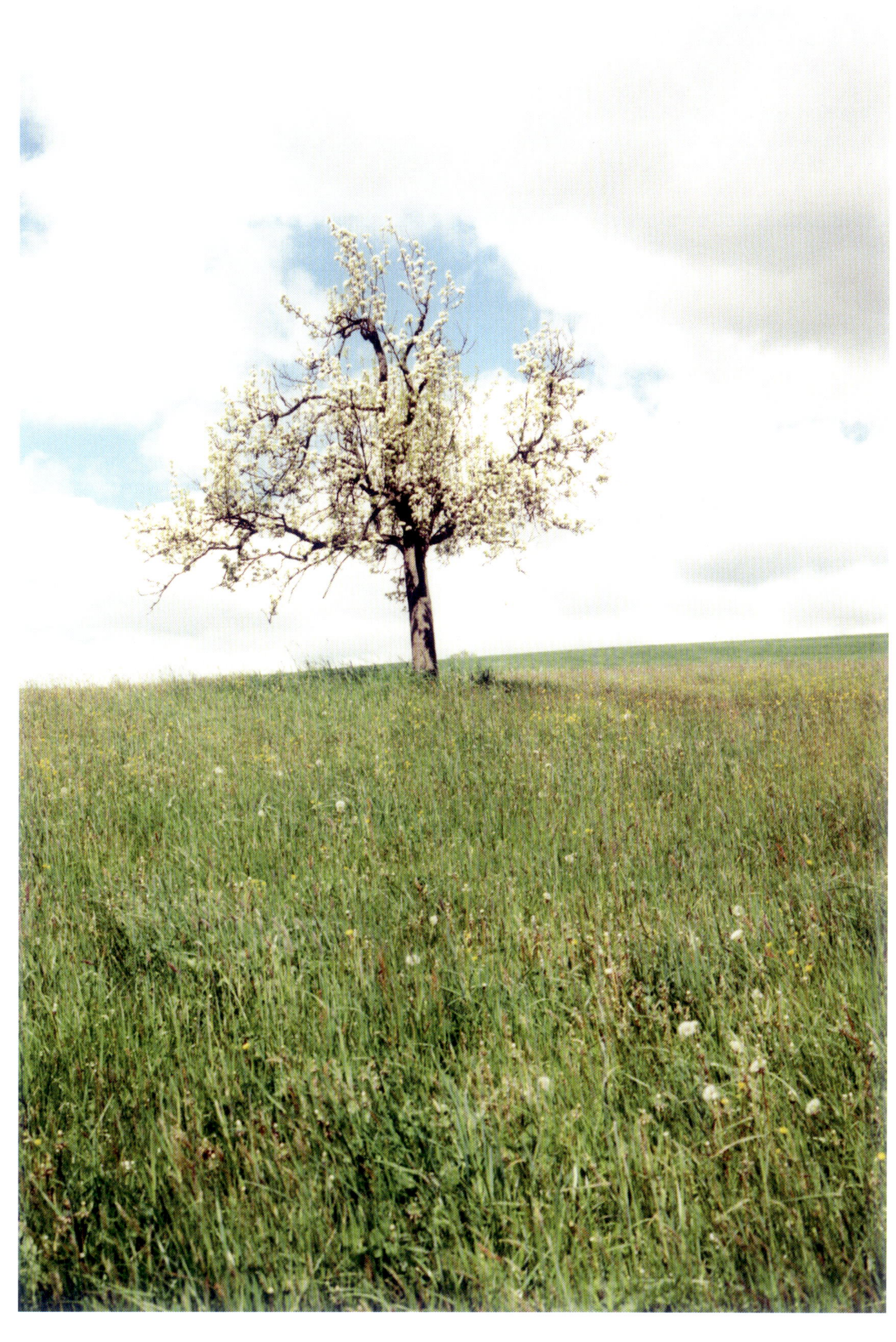

Jitka Hanzlová

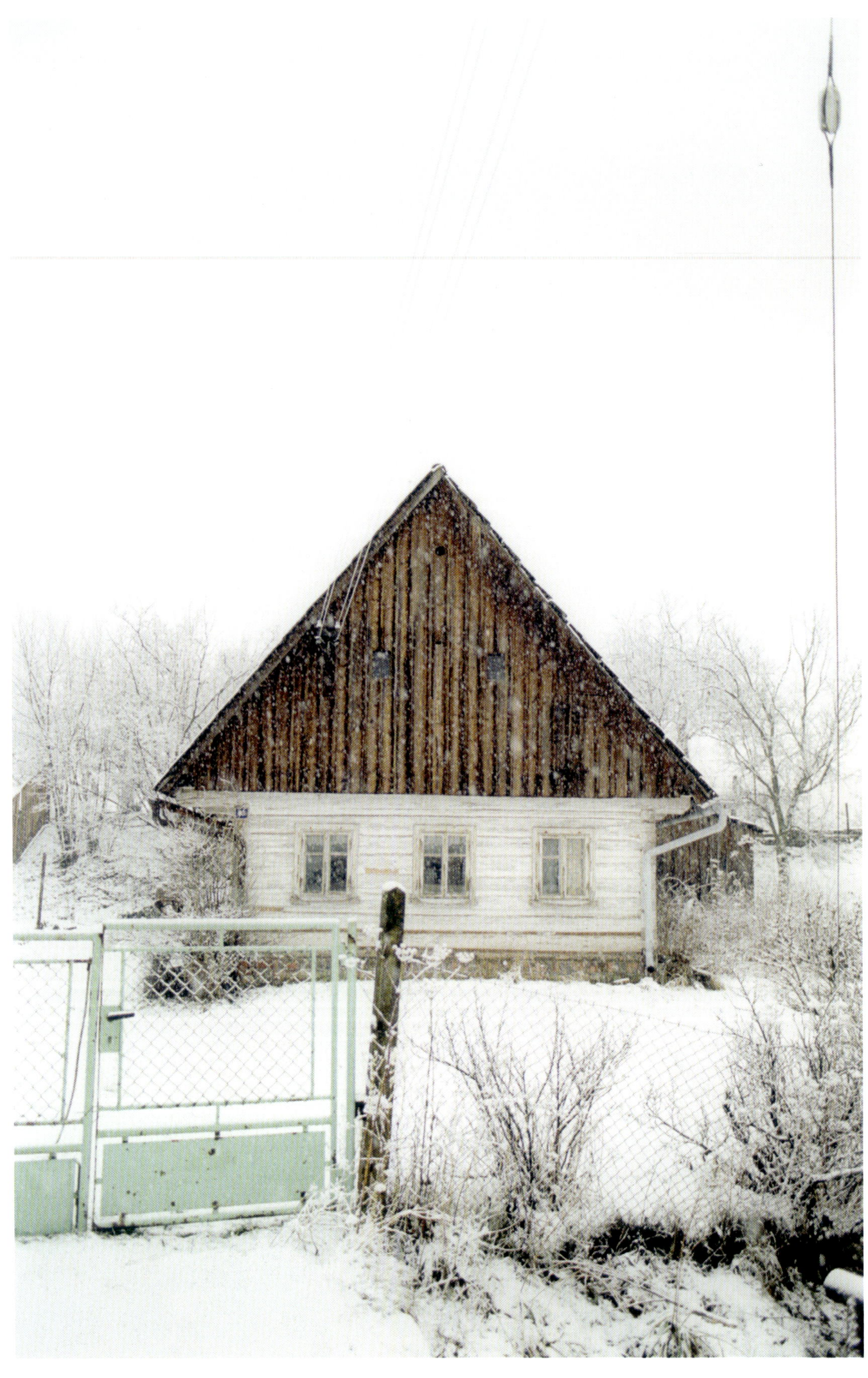

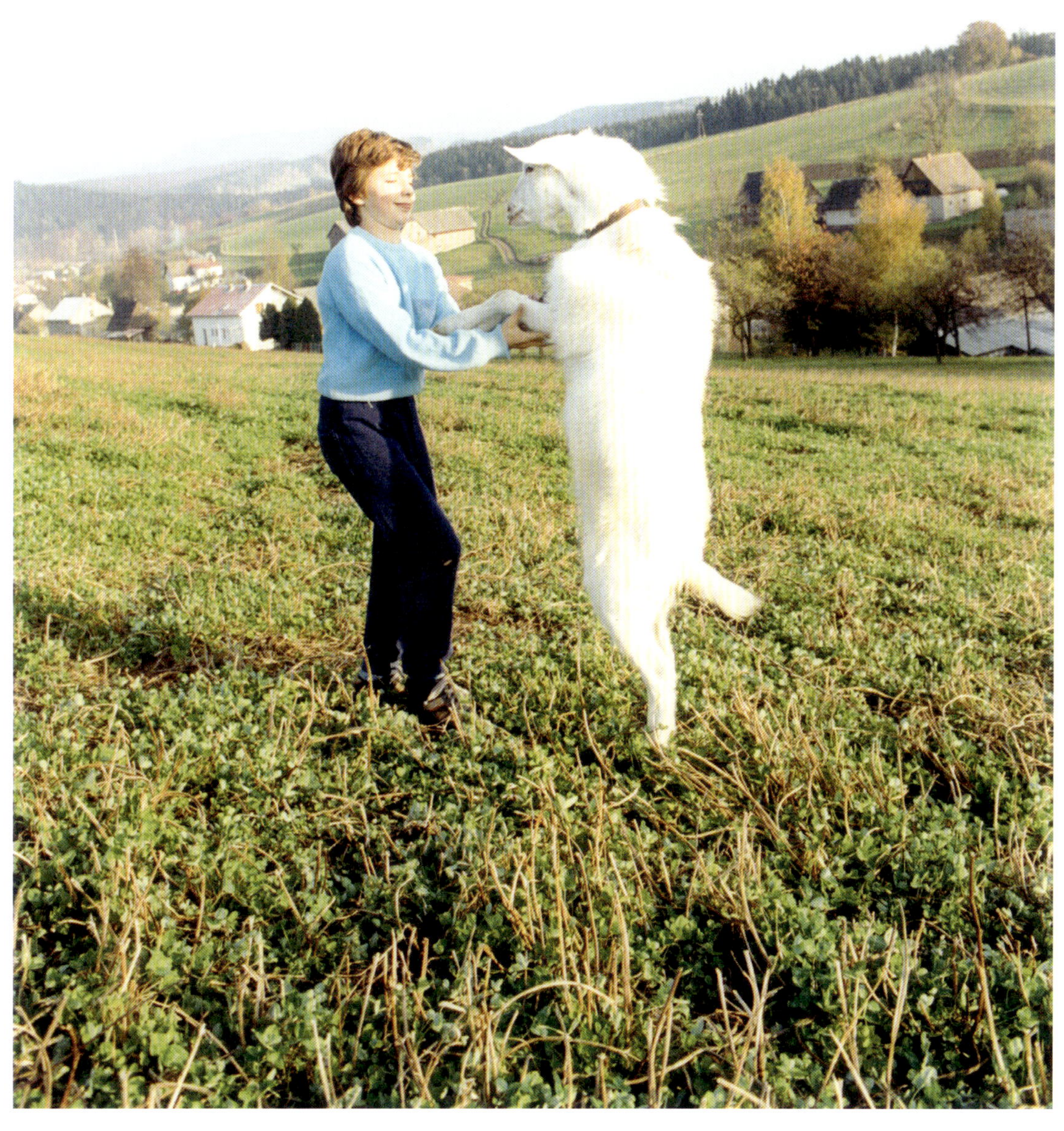

Jitka Hanzlová

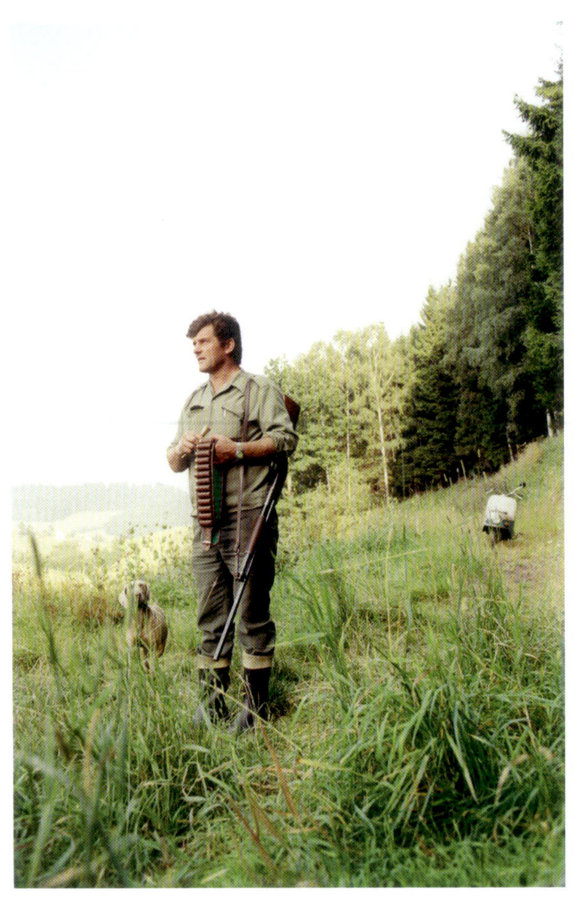
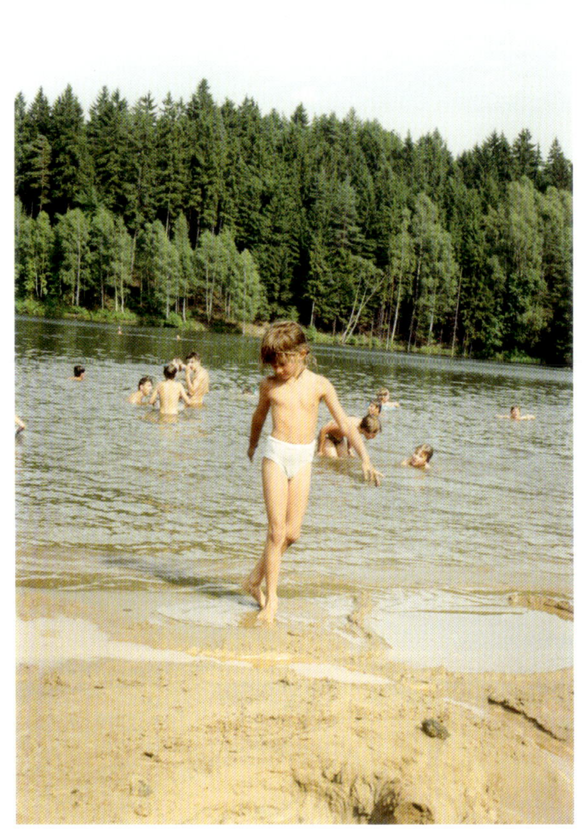
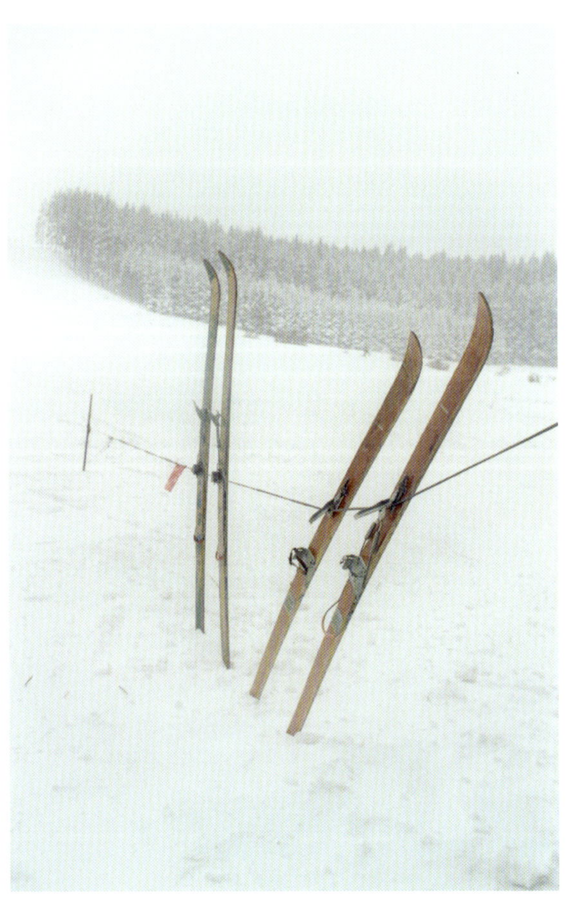
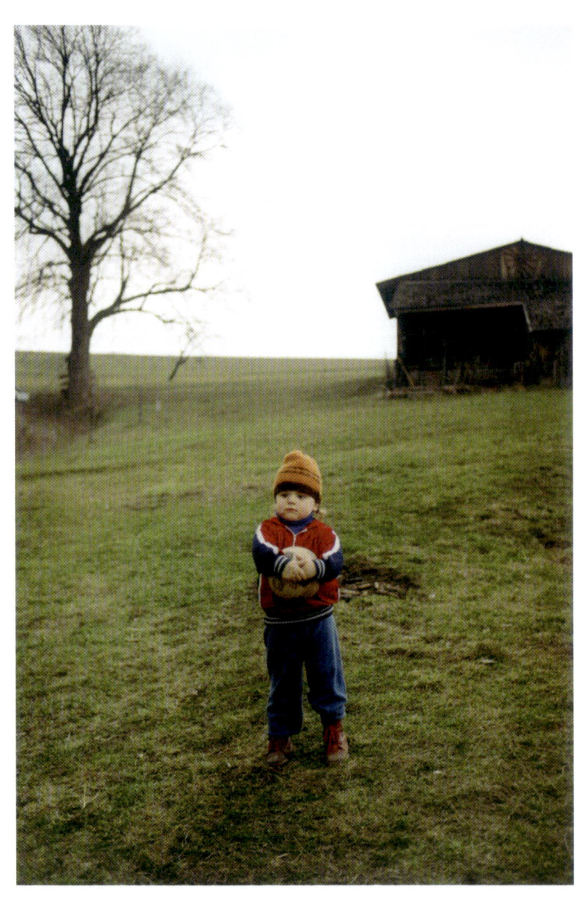

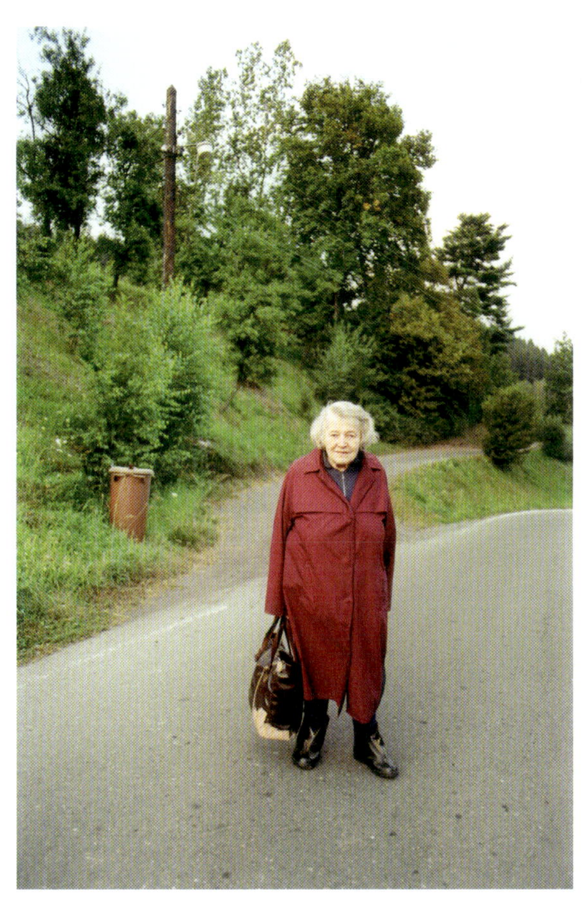
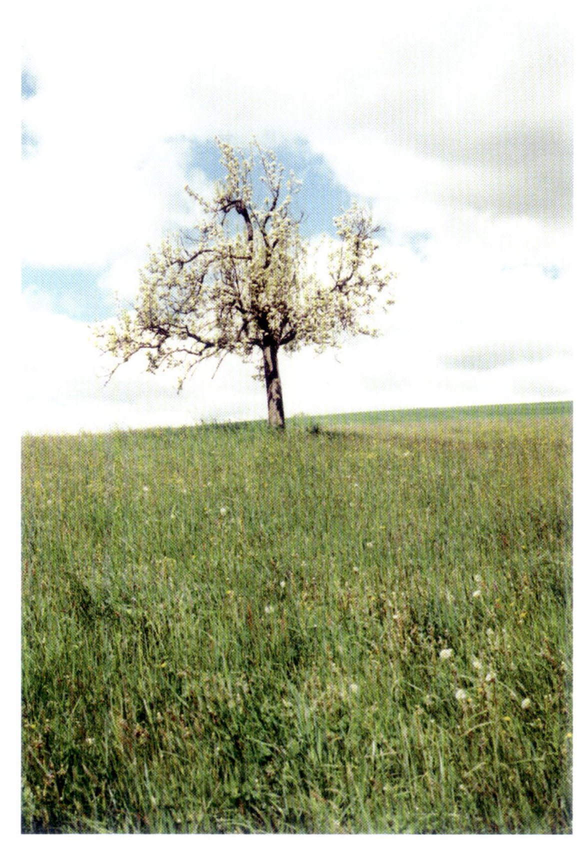
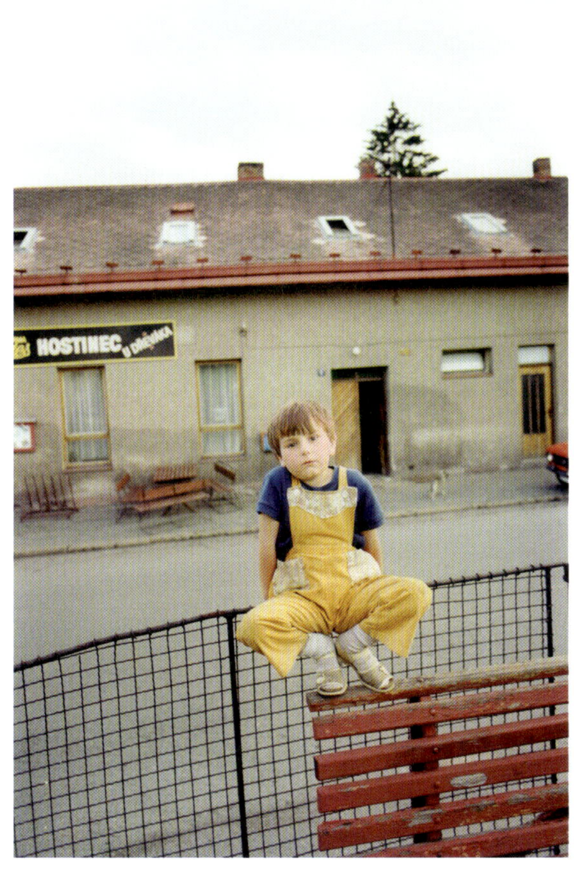
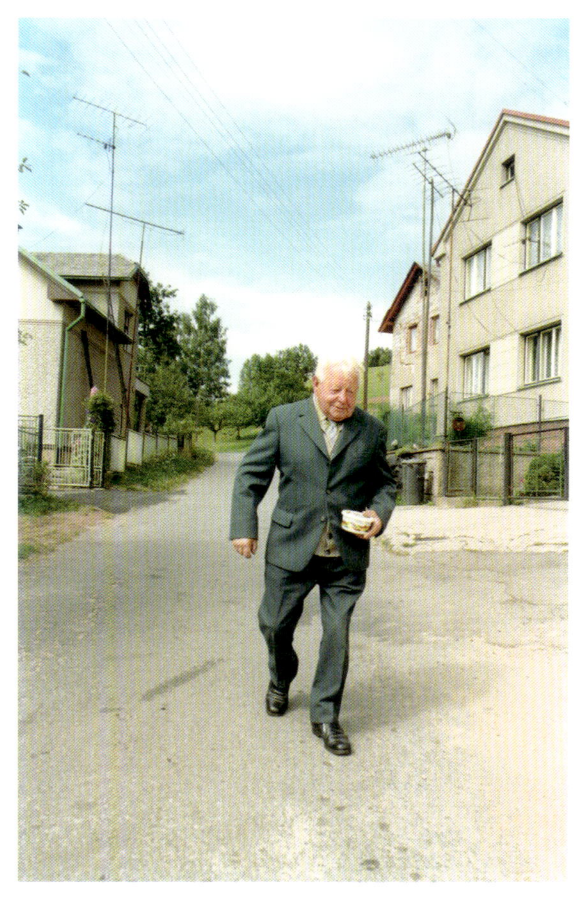

Jitka Hanzlová

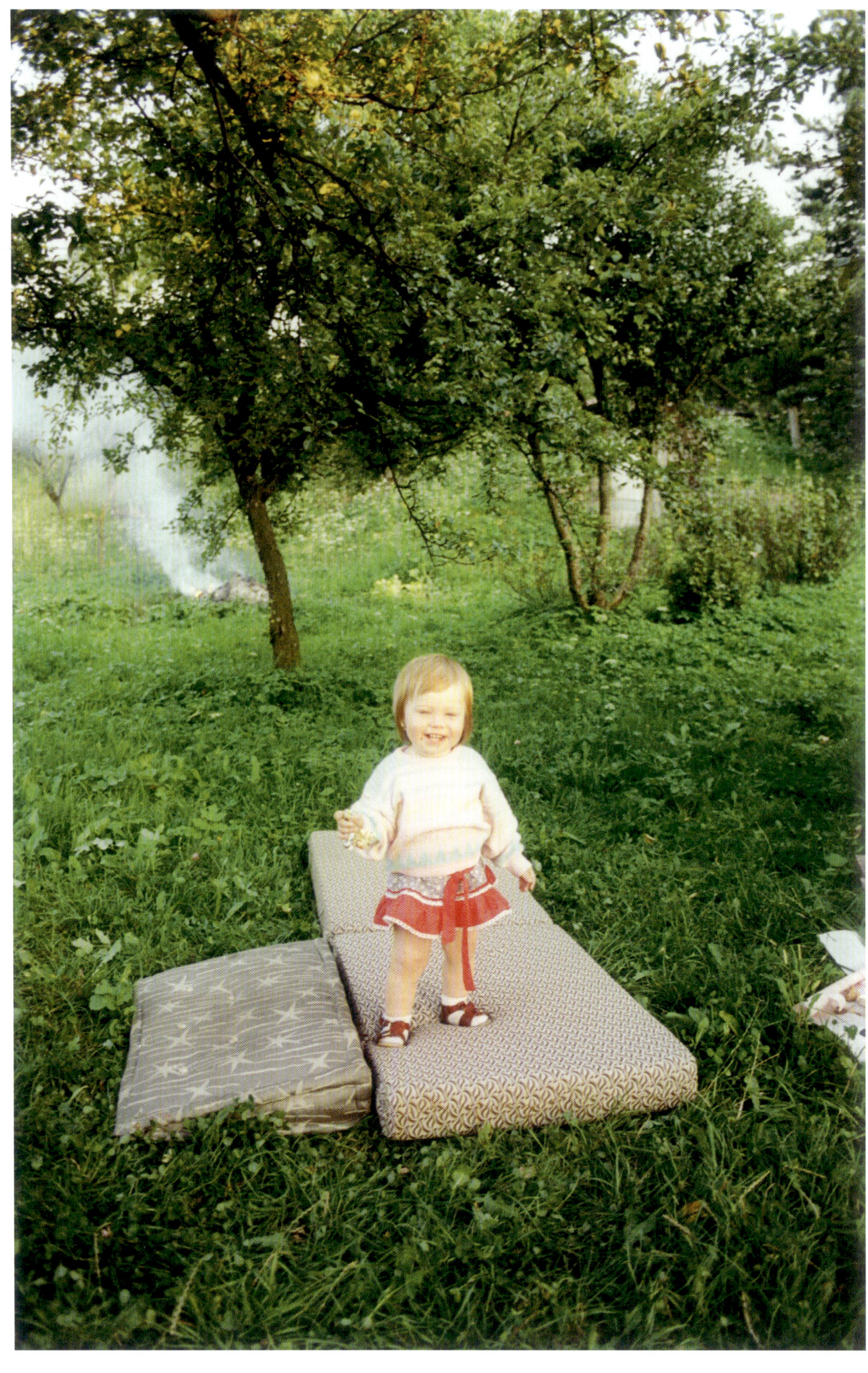

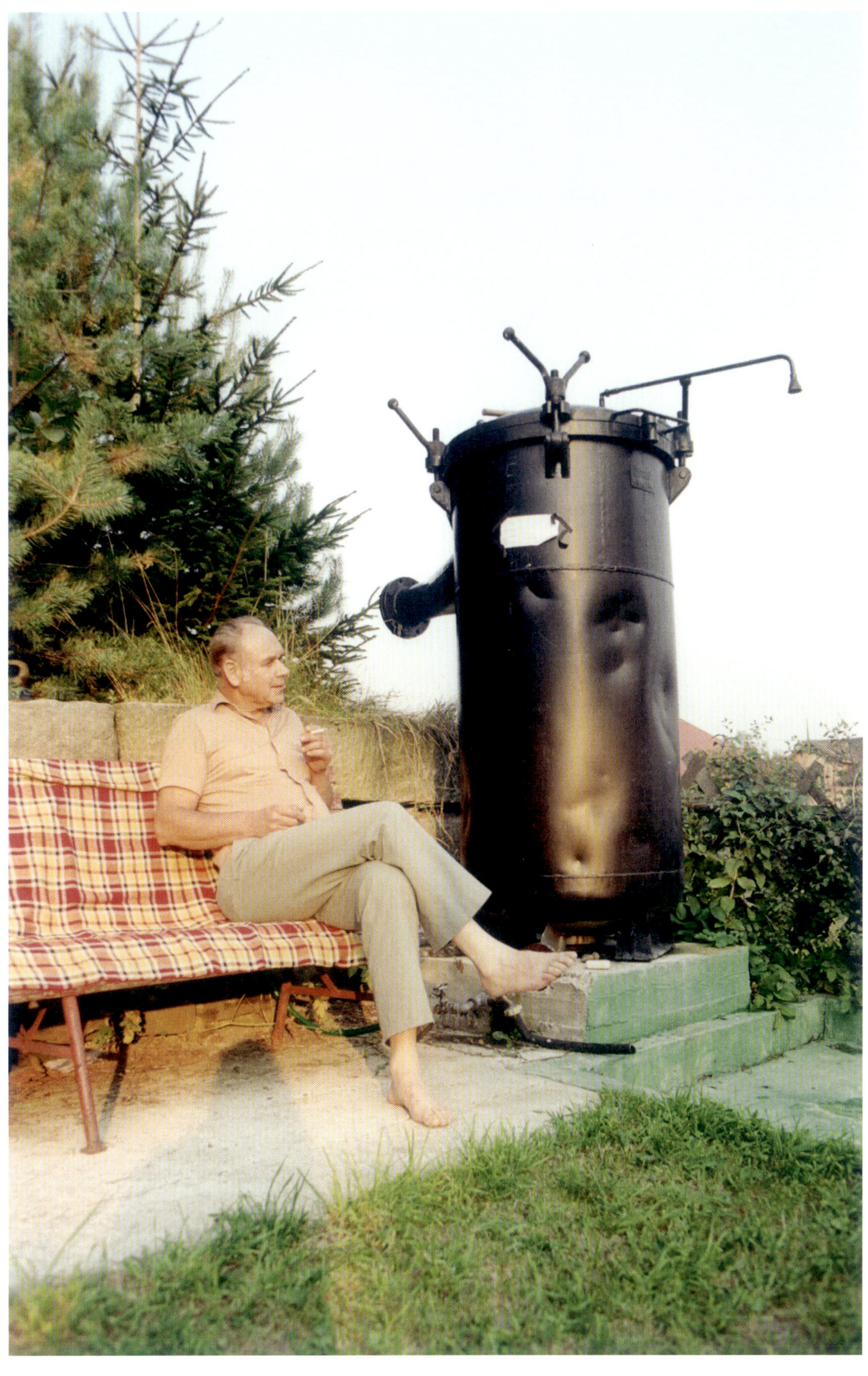

Jitka Hanzlová

Konstantinos Ignatiadis (born 1958, Greece)

Konstantinos Ignatiadis's career began and evolved mostly in
Paris, where he made, among other things, portraits of international intellectuals and artists whose work interested him.
His images seem to highlight the idea that it is one's actions that
define one's character. Most of his portraits include an element
that functions as an extension of his subjects' activity or, con-
versely, as the nucleus of their identity. Made *à l'ancienne*, with a
studio camera, the photographs are taken mostly in the artist's
working place, or personal environment. Ignatiadis's outlook on
photography is traditional: the moment captured stays for ever
and his endeavour is to instil everything in his composition.
The portraits capture fully what the artist saw, felt and, most
of all, thought about the subject matter. They reflect his deci-
sion-making and bring to the forefront the relevant gravitas.
That said, one must also bear in mind that these moments are
extremely significant for Ignatiadis too: his attention to detail,
to the composition, to the tonalities and the juxtapositions that
are created go hand in hand with the lack of reverie he shows
in his approach to his subjects. Most important to Ignatiadis
are the encounters with the people portrayed, his conversations
with them, the memories that remain, which is also something
that Ignatiadis brings out in these portraits. They are not about
the photograph as such, or even about himself, but mainly about
the people being photographed and their craftsmanship, their
talent – his aim is to communicate this by serving his own art
and revealing their greatness through his work.

AA

p. 107
*Marina Abramović, Musée National d'Art Moderne –
Centre Georges Pompidou, Paris 1990*, 1990.
Digital print on archival paper, 92 × 92 cm

p. 108
*Francesco Clemente, Château de Chenonceau,
24 June 1995*, 1995.
Digital print on archival paper, 92 × 92 cm

p. 109
Michel Haas, Paris, n.d.
Digital print on archival paper, 92 × 92 cm

p. 110
Francis Bacon, Paris, n.d.
Digital print on archival paper, 117 × 92 cm

p. 111
Auto-Portrait at Nicopolis, August 1999, 1999.
Digital print on archival paper, 92 × 92 cm

Courtesy the artist

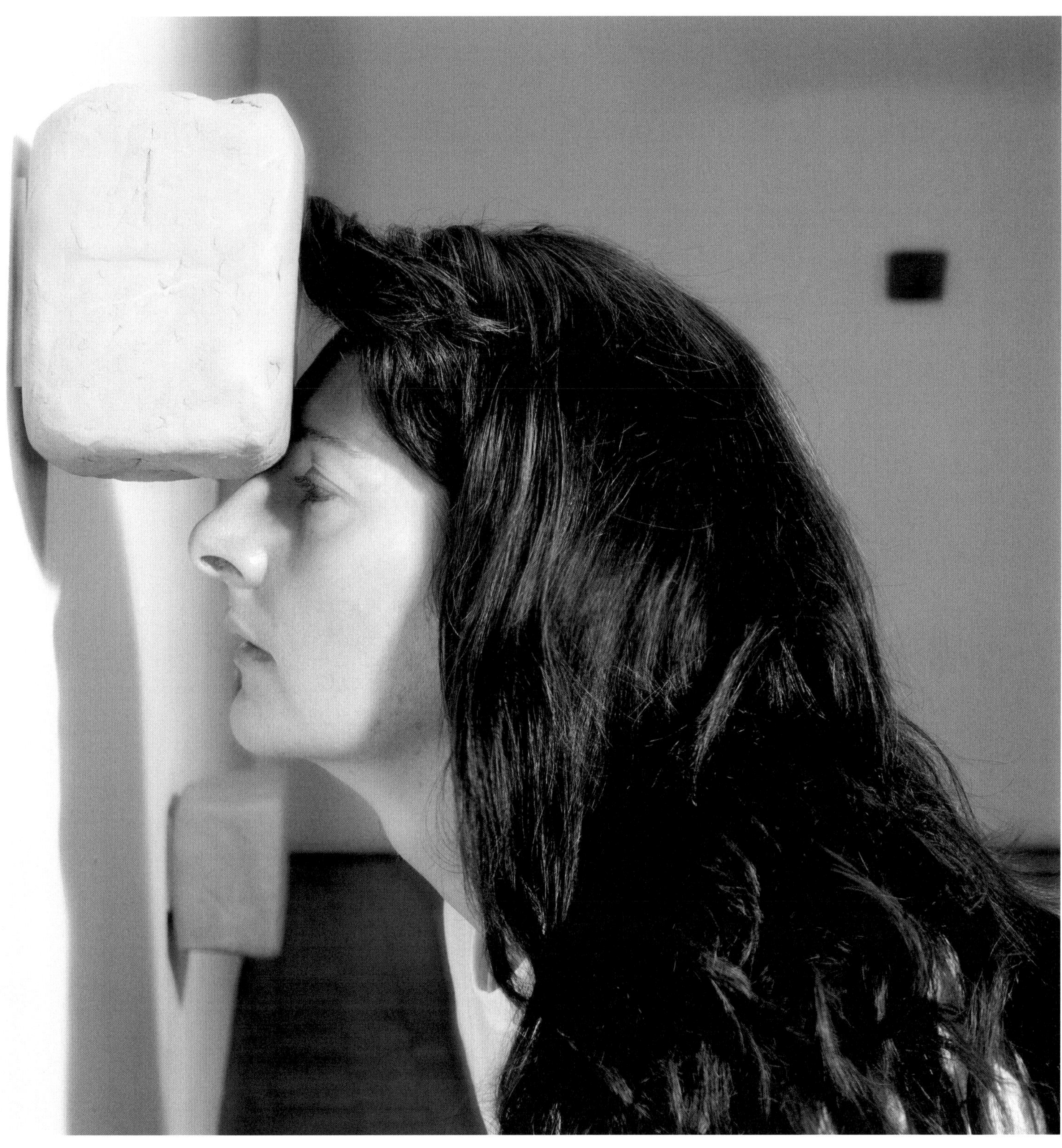

Konstantinos Ignatiadis

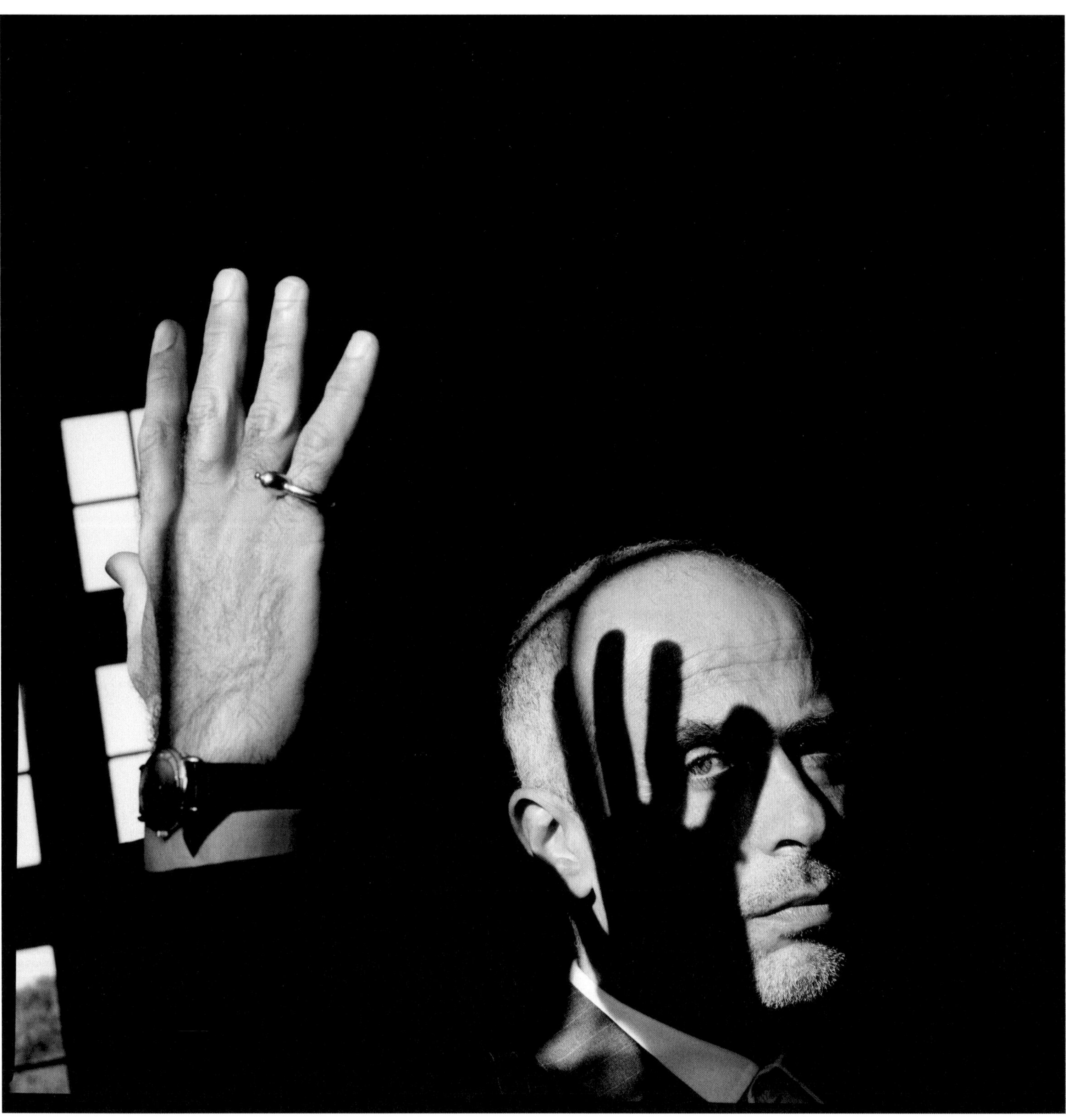

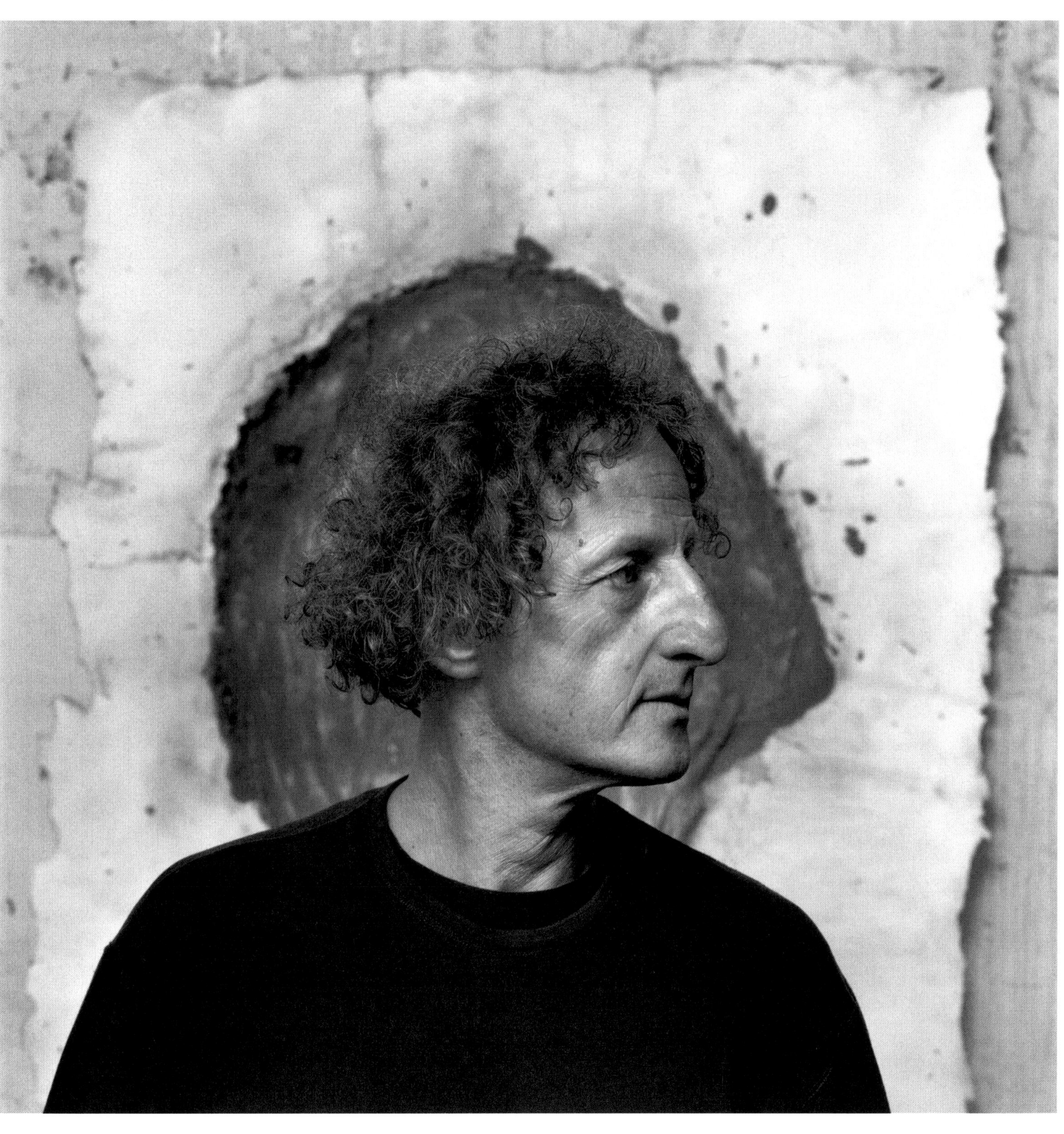

Konstantinos Ignatiadis

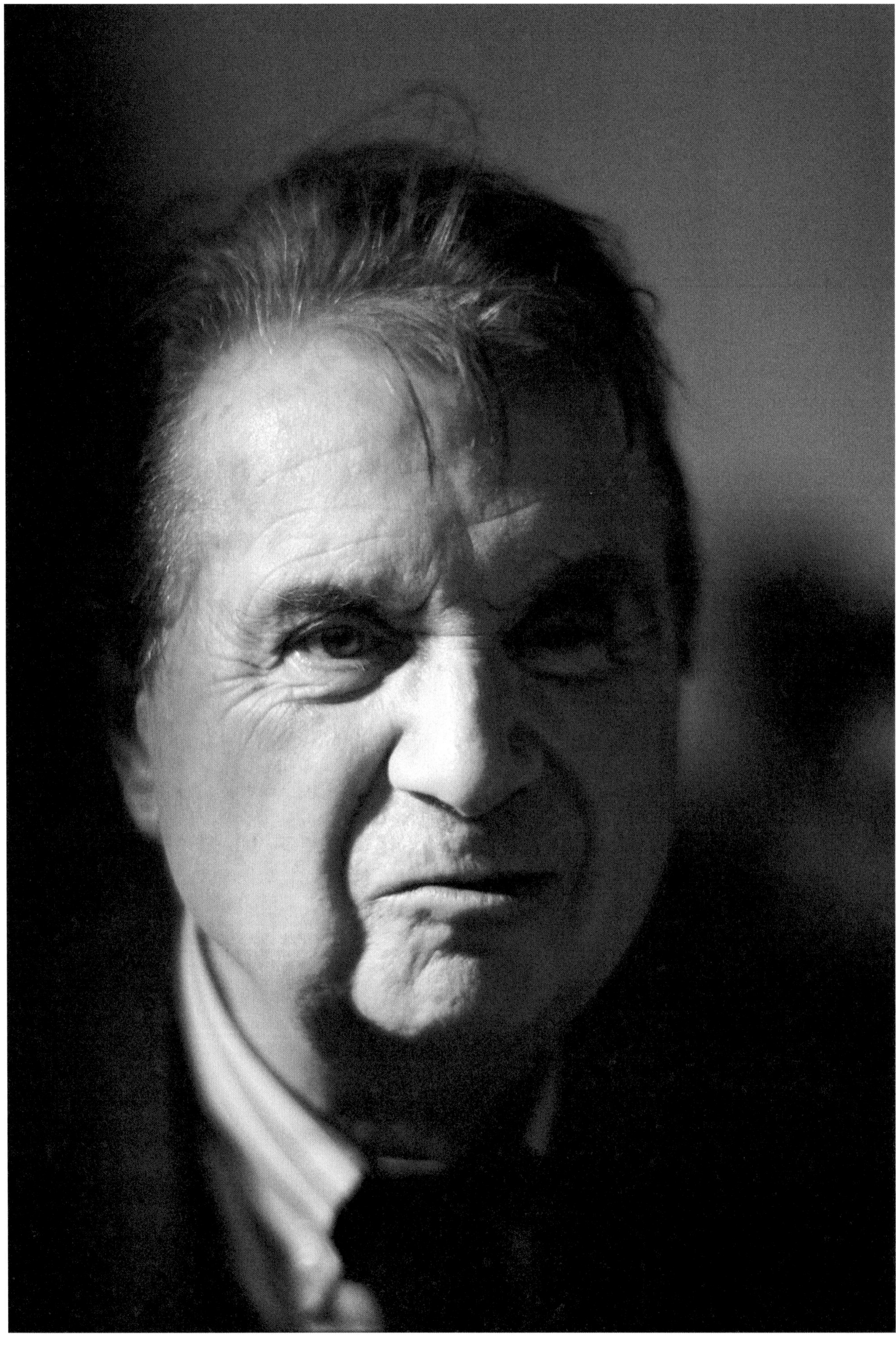

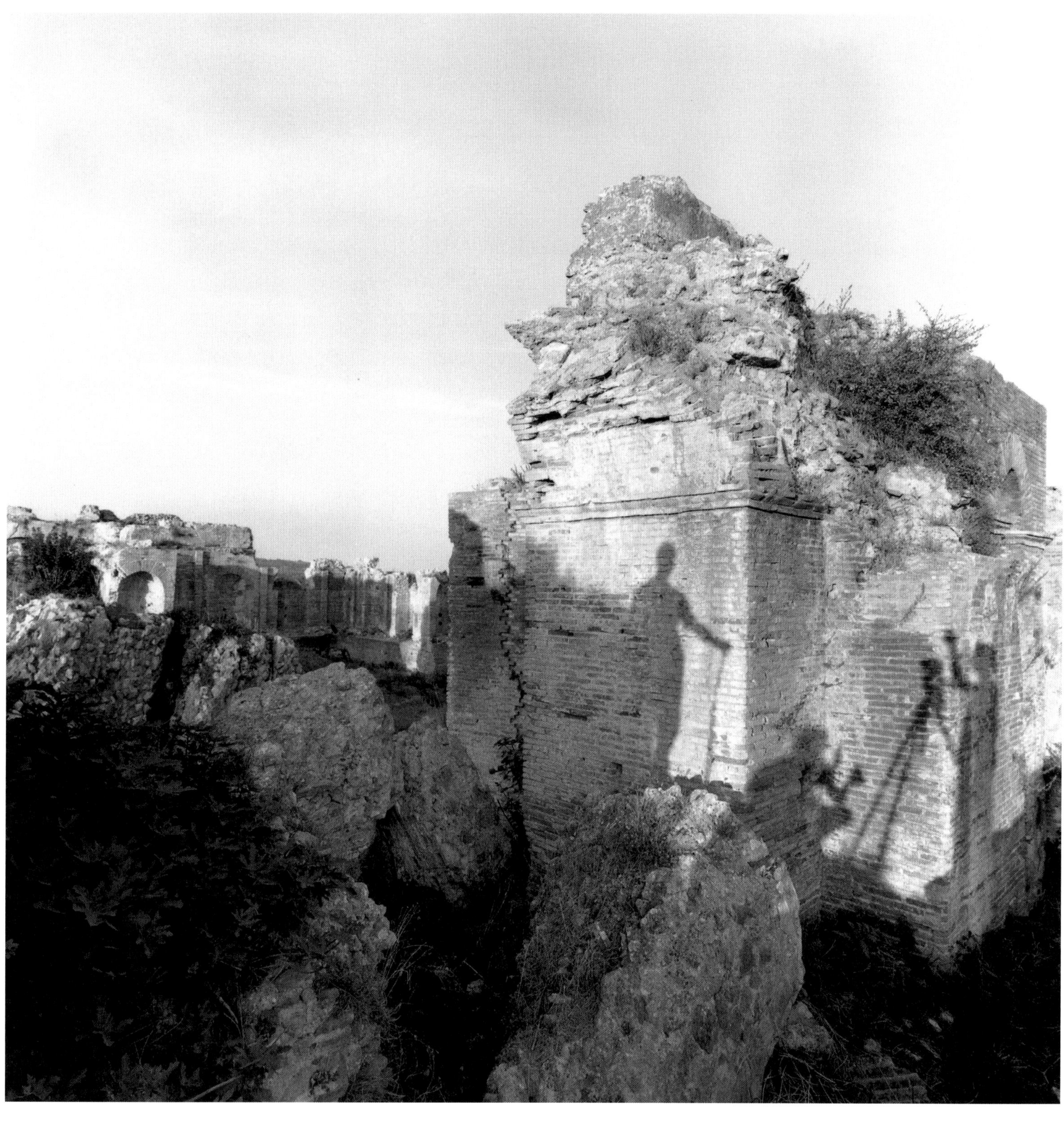

Konstantinos Ignatiadis

Stratos Kalafatis (born 1966, Greece)

Athos/Colors of Faith

Athos/Colors of Faith sets out to explore and disclose. That,
at least, is what viewers expect when confronted with such a
project. Mount Athos – a holy sanctuary founded during the
Byzantine Empire – is an autonomous region covering most of
the Athos peninsula in northern Greece. This mini-state lies
within an unspoiled natural habitat, accessible only to men so as
to maintain the religious and historical tradition of the Eastern
Orthodox Church. For centuries, this 'monastic republic' has
provided a haven for those seeking seclusion in order to reach
the divine, but it has at times also served as a refuge for outcasts.

This series of photographs is the outcome of a long-time
project (2008–14) that brings to the forefront the inhabitants
of Mount Athos. Kalafatis's strong use of colour, distinctive of
his style, enhances his endeavour to present his personal experience of this esoteric world, which has all the elements of any
other microcosm. Those portrayed here may come across more
as icons, but they are in fact real people, and this should disap-
point no one. This has to do with the topic, but also with the
photographer's style. Kalafatis's portraits always linger between
the secular and the divine, creating an aura, and framing characters out of time. These aspects are naturally more intense here
because of the nature of the project. In the end, the distinction
between icon and portrait, the real and the divine, remains an
open question. One can, however, occasionally detect these terms
changing places, depending on the context and the look of both
the artist and his subject. It is this fleeting power game between
the two that ultimately determines where the portrait belongs:
to this side or that side.

VI

p. 113
Pupil at the Athonias Academy, Karyes,
in 'Athos/Colors of Faith', 2008.
Digital print on archival paper, mounted on dibond,
103 × 100 cm

p. 114
Thomas, a priest-monk, in 'Athos/Colors of Faith',
2008. Digital print on archival paper, mounted
on dibond, 103 × 100 cm

p. 115
*Pupils at the Athonias Academy in a 19th-century
photo studio, Serai,* in 'Athos/Colors of Faith', 2008.
Digital print on archival paper, mounted on dibond,
103 × 100 cm

p. 116
Zacharias, a priest-monk from Megisti Lavra,
in 'Athos/Colors of Faith', 2010.
Digital print on archival paper, mounted on dibond,
103 × 100 cm

p. 117
Zacharias, a priest-monk from Megisti Lavra,
in 'Athos/Colors of Faith', 2010.
Digital print on archival paper, mounted on dibond,
103 × 100 cm

Courtesy the artist and Agra Publications

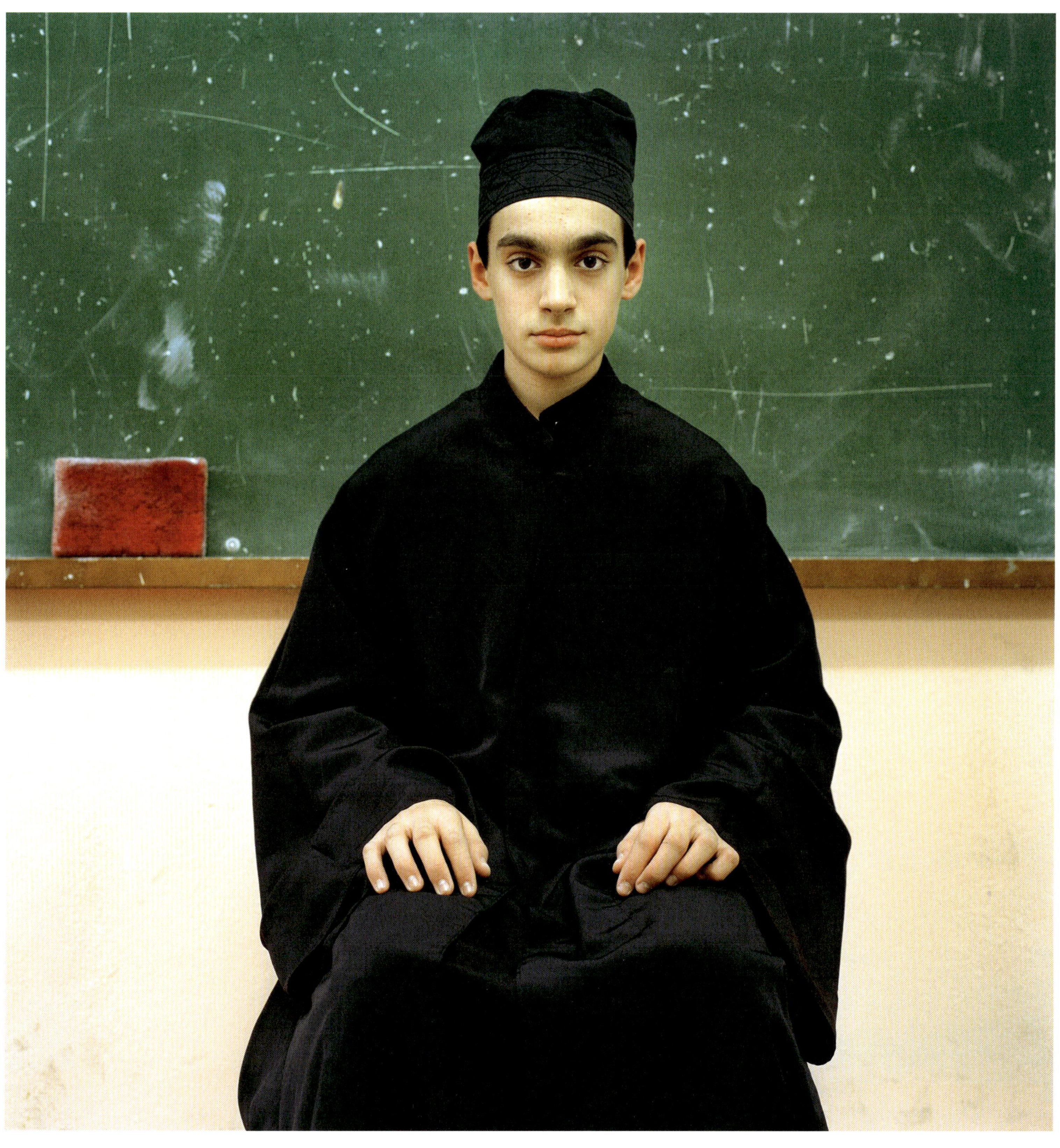

Stratos Kalafatis

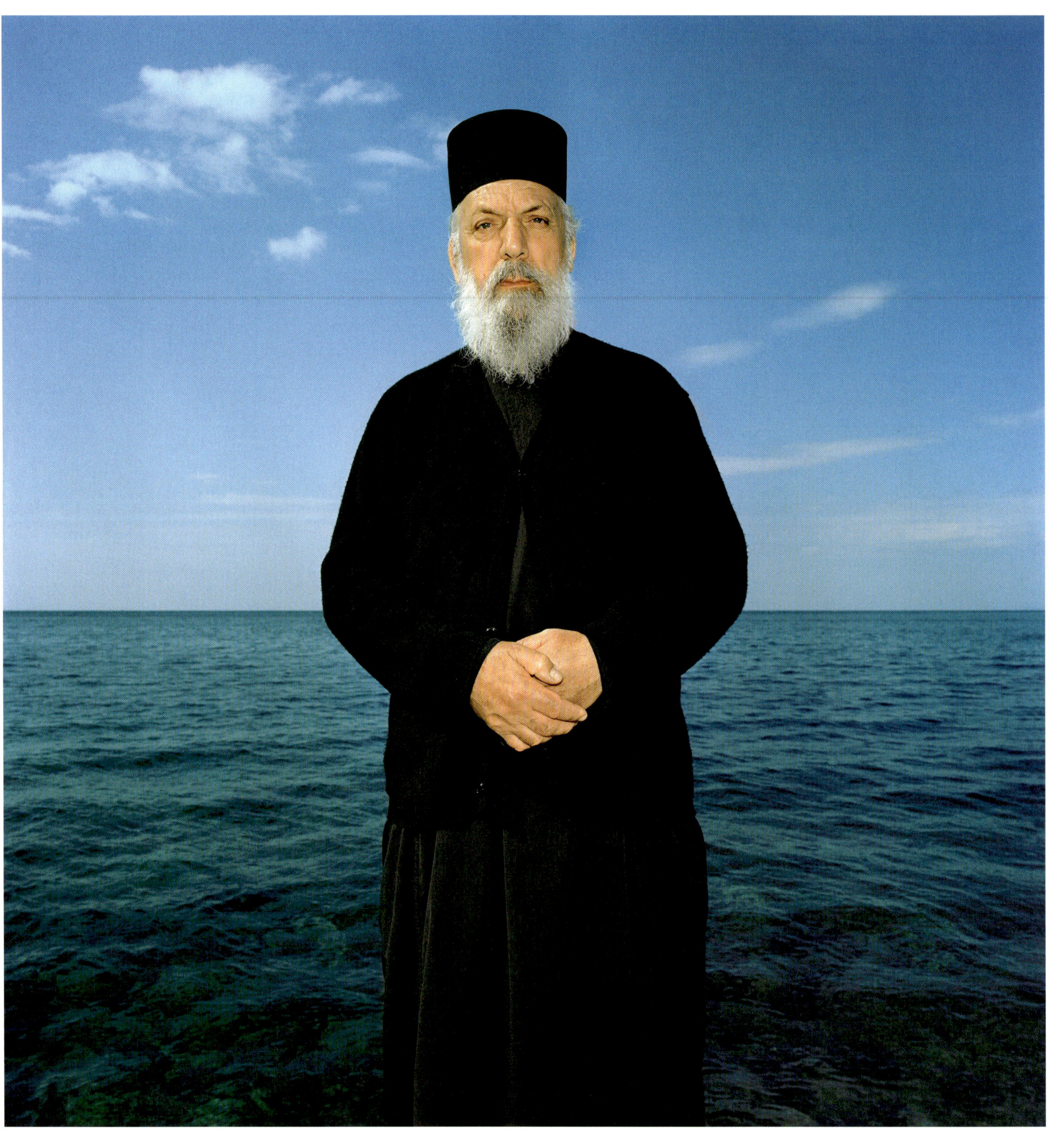

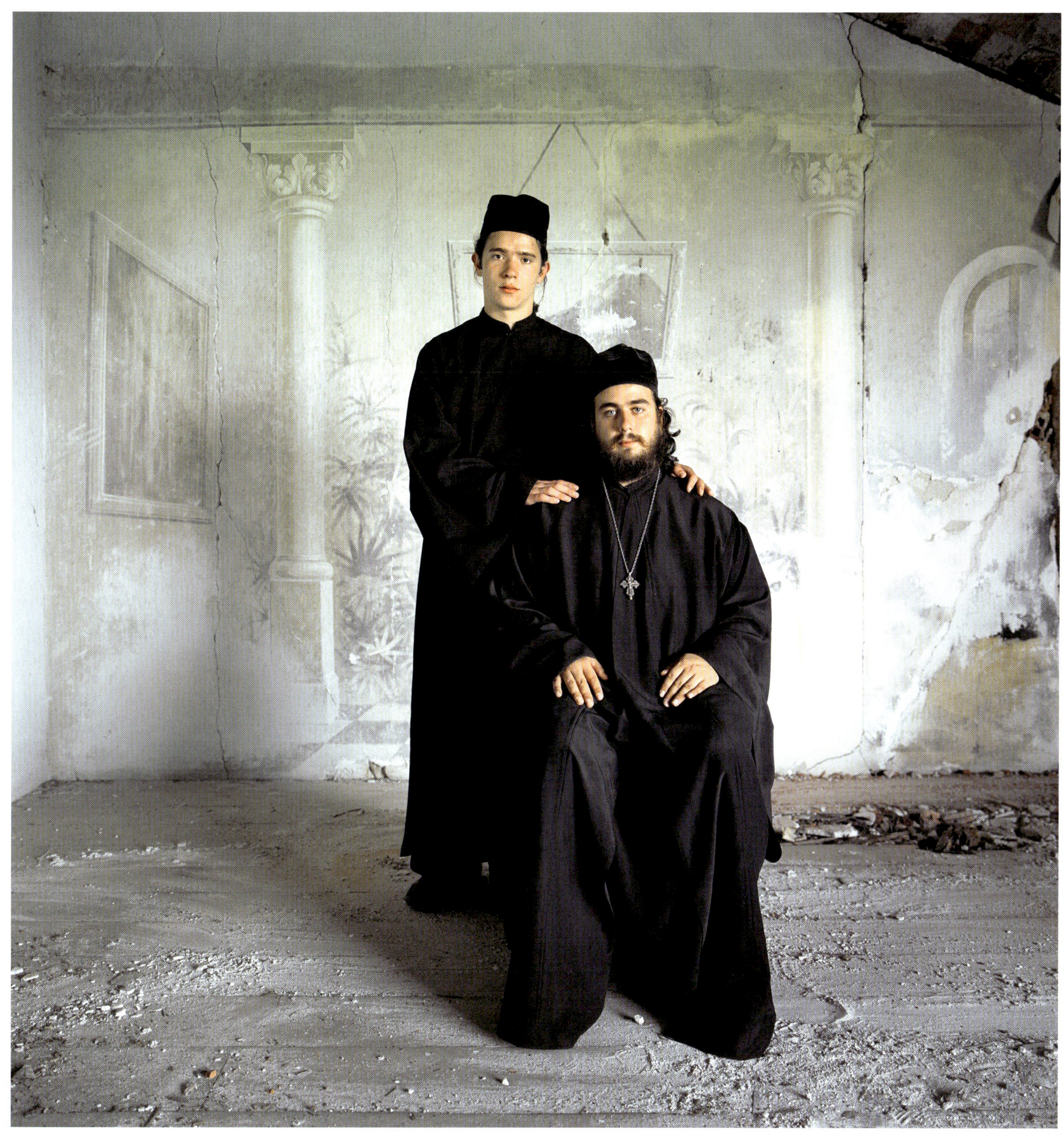

Stratos Kalafatis

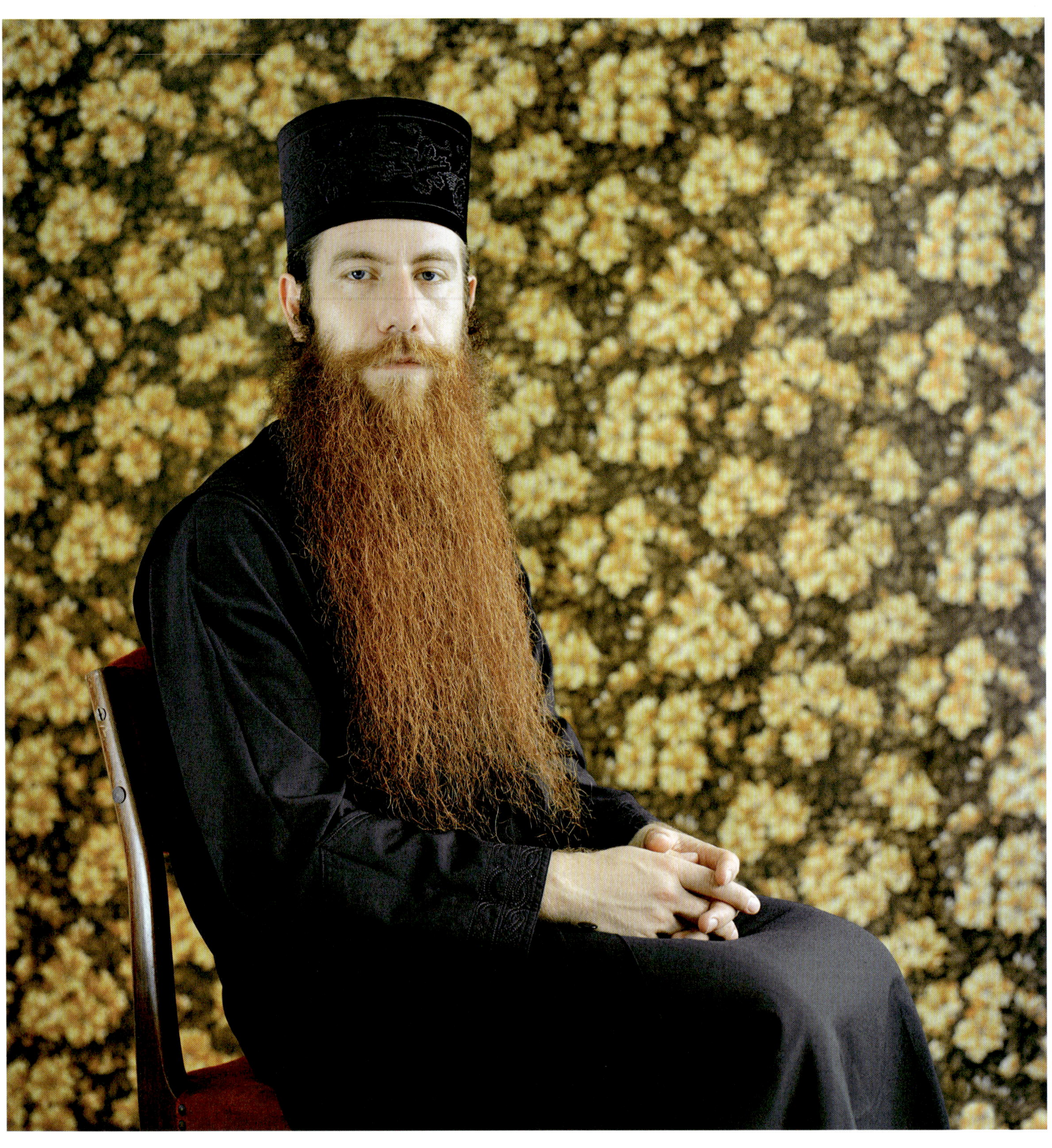

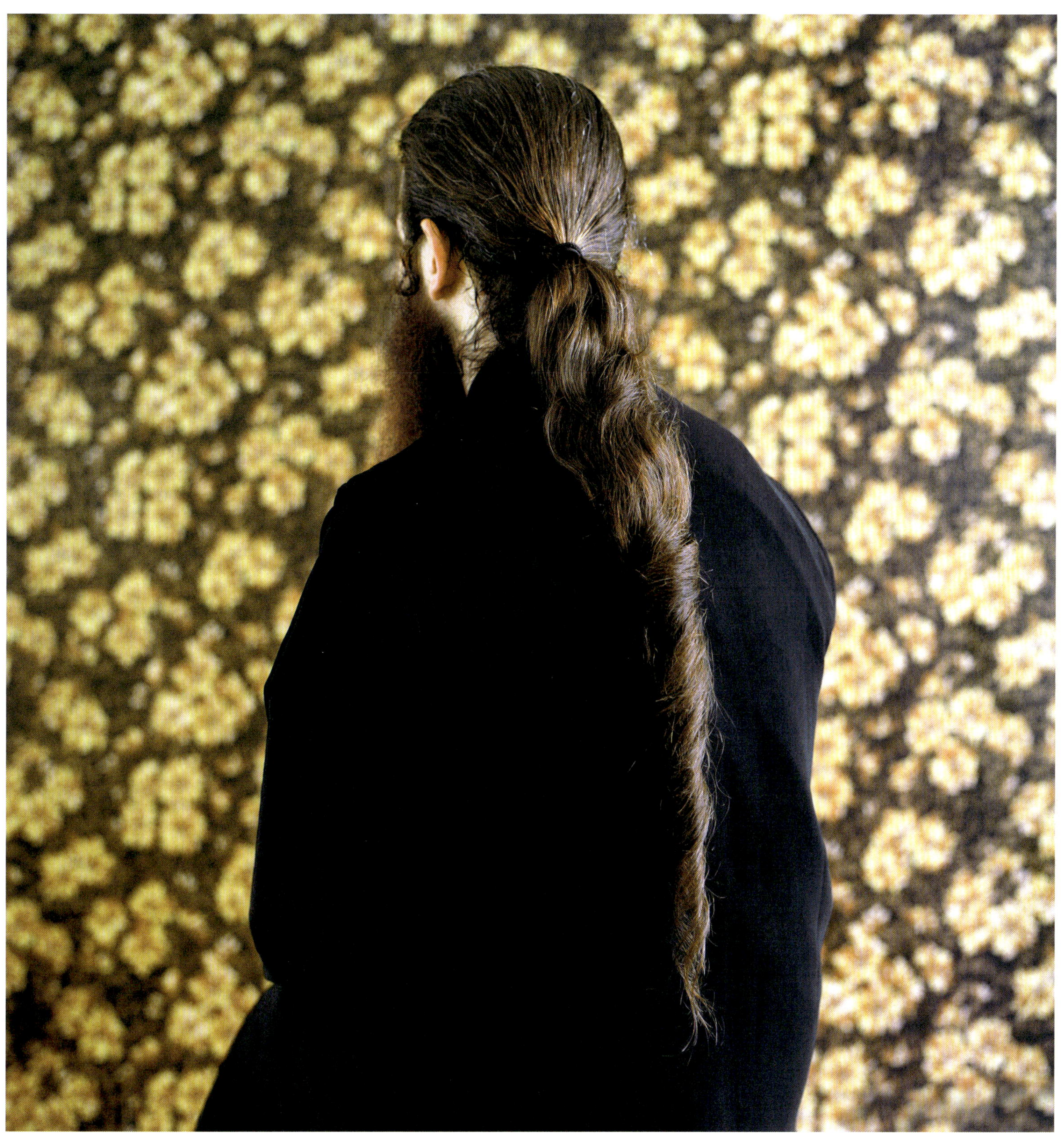

Stratos Kalafatis

Nikos Markou (born 1959, Greece)

Life Narratives

Nikos Markou places this project at the intersection between discourse and image. It is a contemporary photographic series based on an audiovisual work, which seems to engrave history: the portrait sits still as we listen to each person's life story, or an extract from it. In this juxtaposition between the flow of the story and the stillness of the face, there emerges a personal story that is part of the political and social life of Greece: glimpses from the crisis, from the life of immigrants, from the hardship that people have had to endure, ways of living, of loving, of getting married, of growing up. This is not a political piece, or was not meant to be. However, it seems as if the portraits dilate and become part of an image within an image: histories into history and faces into portraits. In this oscillation, the stories and the people matter for as long as the viewer is there to observe and participate. Then they fall into oblivion, just like the faces and the words of people one has never met, and probably never will meet. With *Life Narratives* (2012-14), Markou touches something very private - as if one is looking at a family album with him - and at the same time something extremely public, a great part of Greece itself.

VI

p. 119 (top)
02.03.2013, in 'Life Narratives', 2013.
Archival ink-jet print on fine art paper,
mounted on dibond, 119 × 148.5 cm

p. 119 (bottom)
15.11.2012, in 'Life Narratives', 2012.
Archival ink-jet print on fine art paper,
mounted on dibond, 119 × 148.5 cm

pp. 120–21
Life Narratives 2012-2014, 2014.
Video, 16′ 48″

Courtesy AD Gallery, Athens

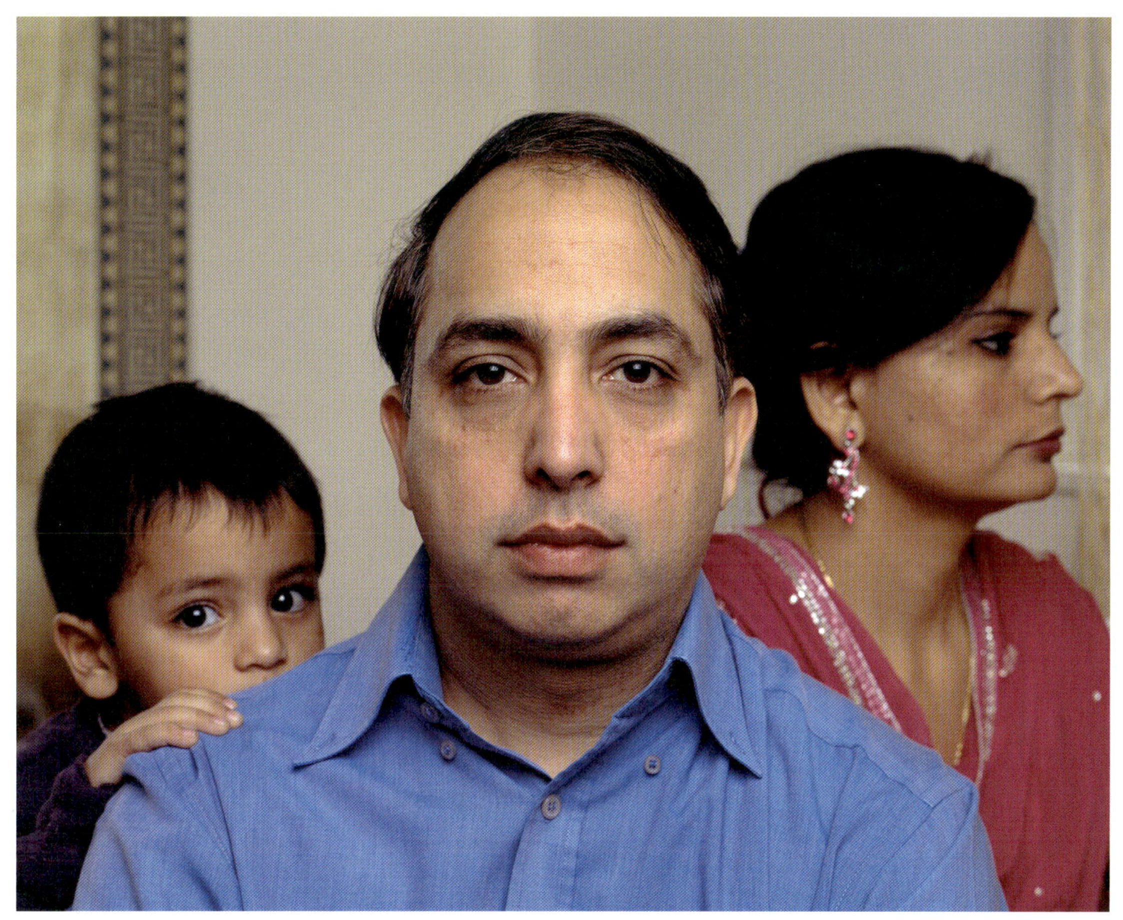

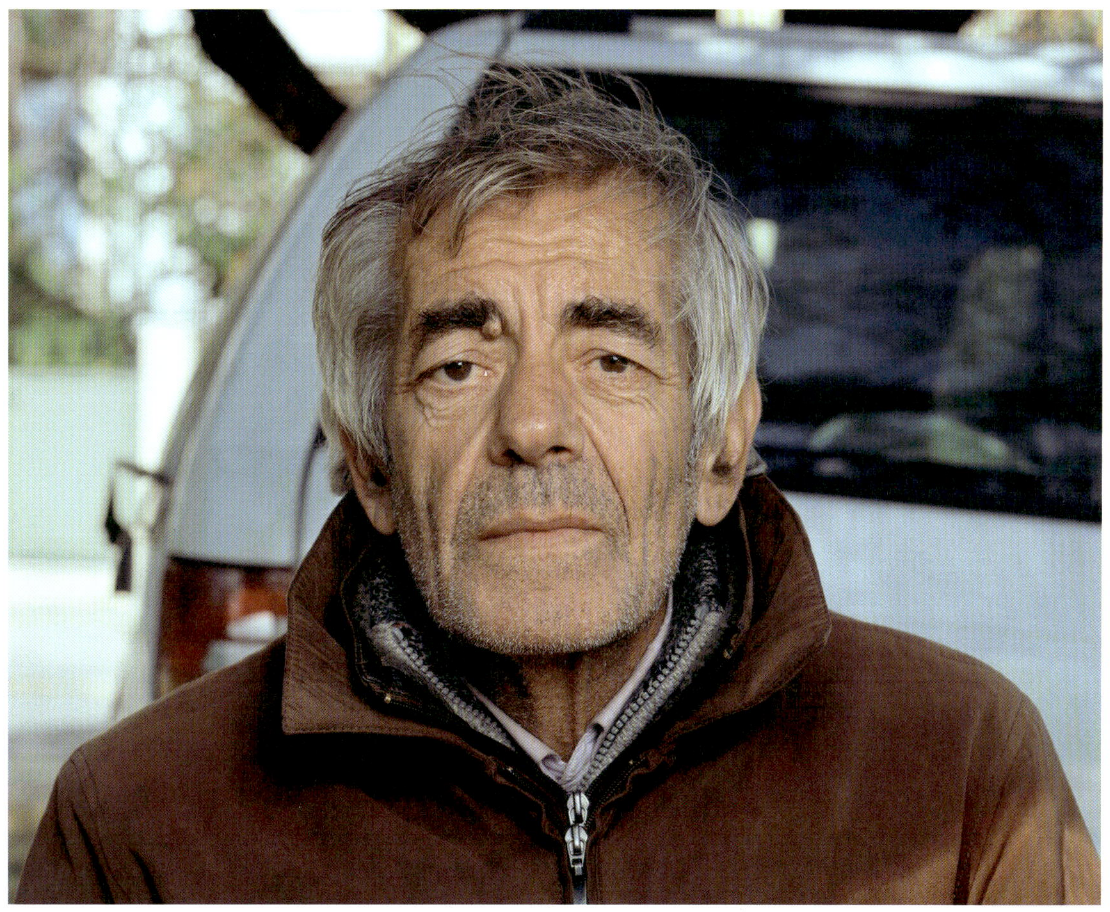

Nikos Markou

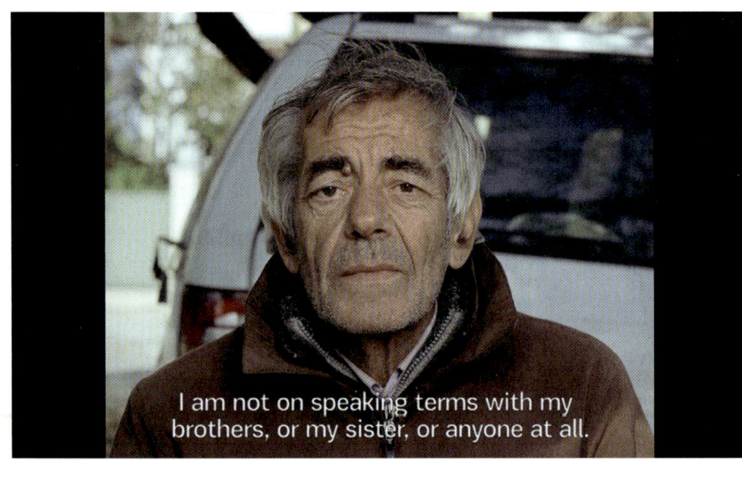
I am not on speaking terms with my
brothers, or my sister, or anyone at all.

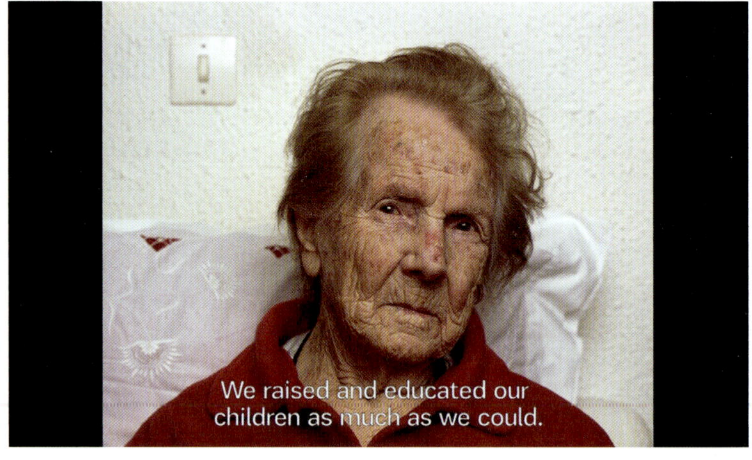
We raised and educated our
children as much as we could.

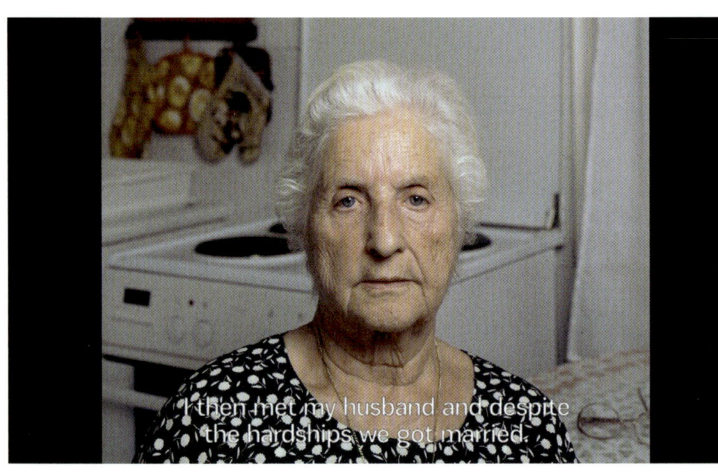
I then met my husband and despite
the hardships we got married.

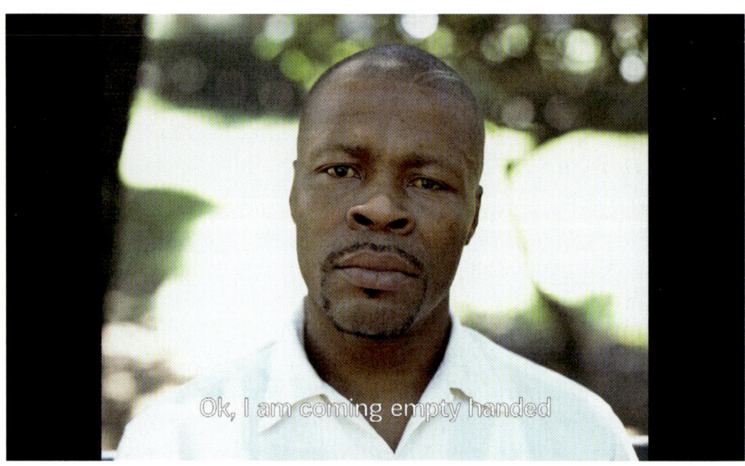
Ok, I am coming empty handed

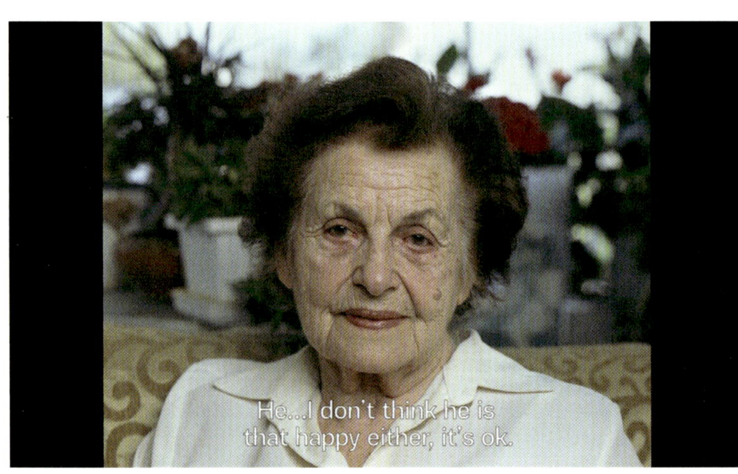
He...I don't think he is
that happy either, it's ok.

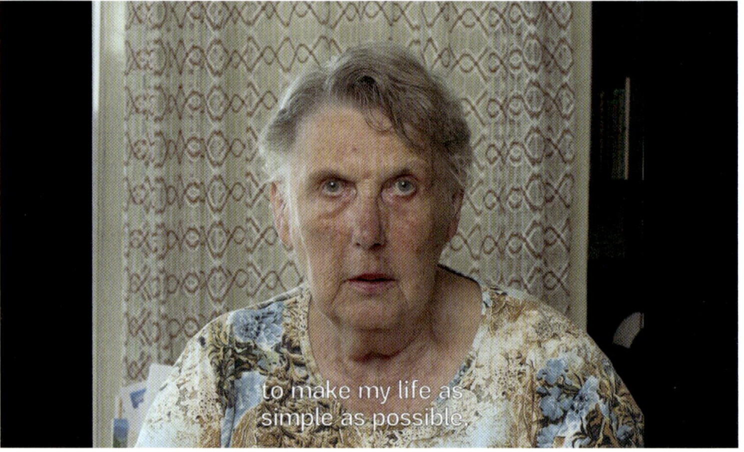
to make my life as
simple as possible.

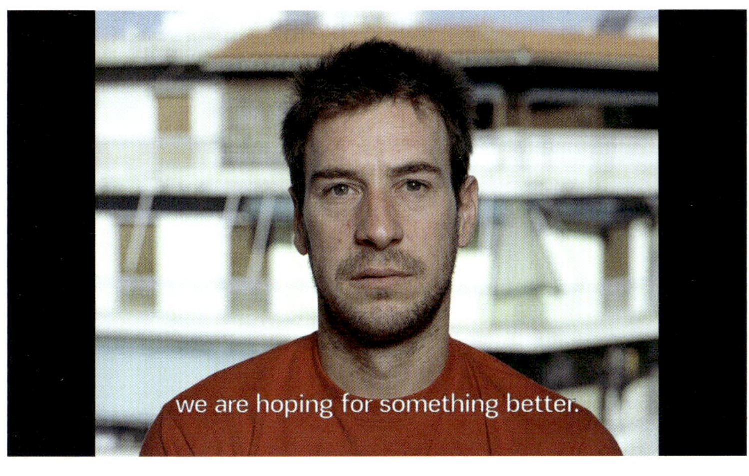

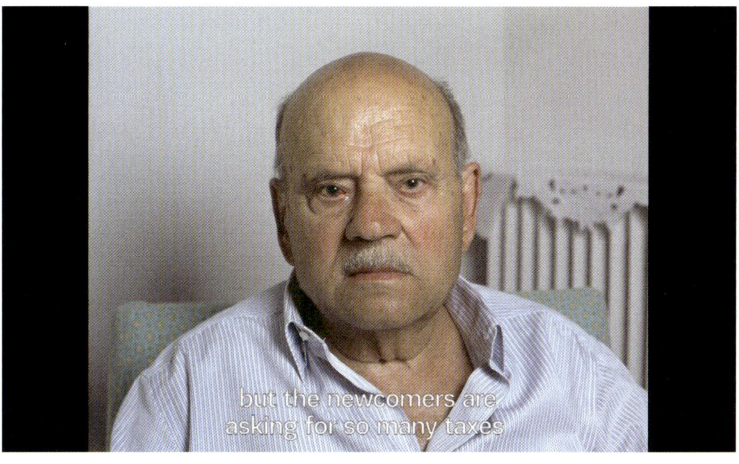

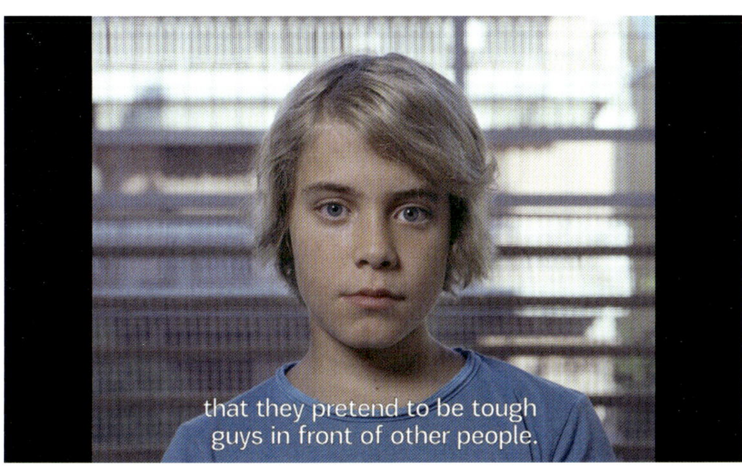

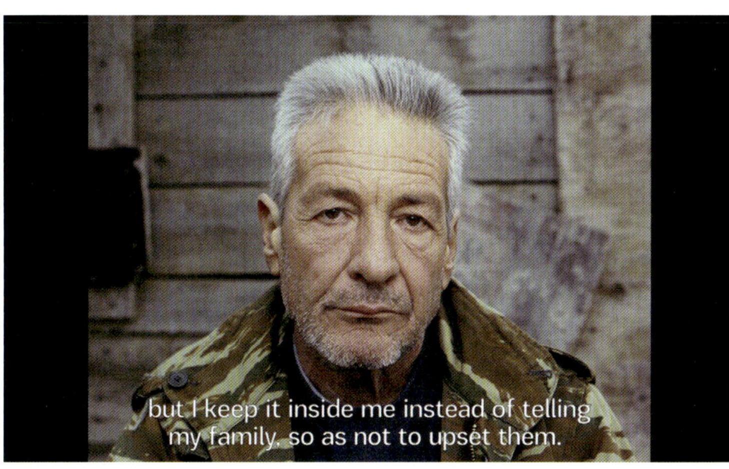

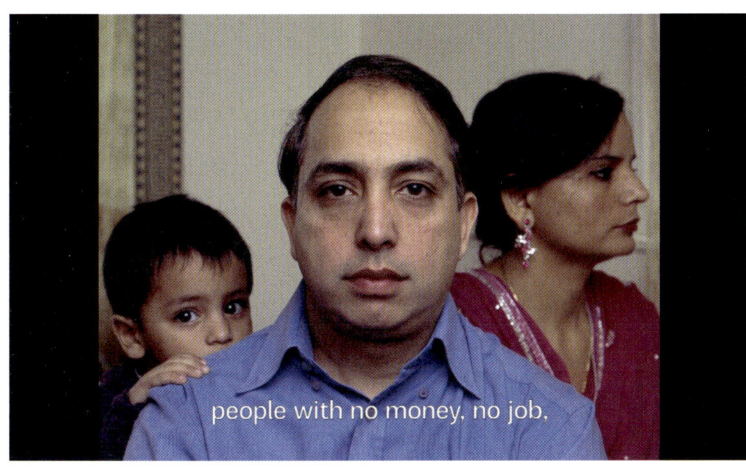

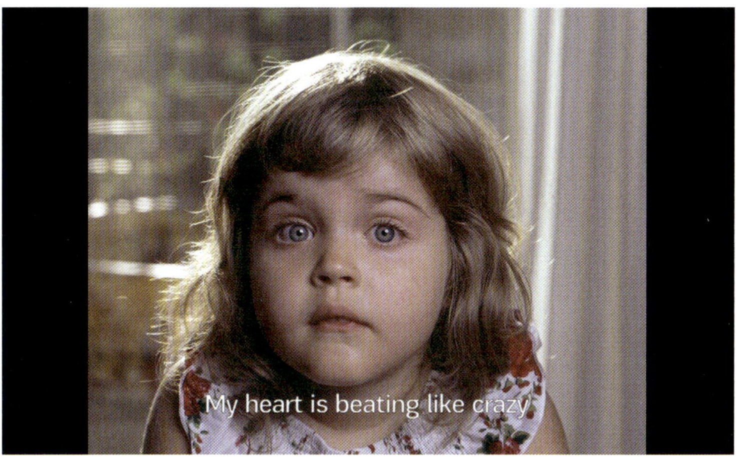

Nikos Markou

Boris Mikhailov (born 1938, Ukraine)

Case History

Boris Mikhailov was born in Kharkiv, in Ukraine, and worked there as an engineer for a company in the space travel industry. At the same time, he taught himself photography and developed a passion for it. For more than 35 years he portrayed the breakdown and eventual fall of the Soviet Union and its drastic consequences. In 1998, almost a decade after the collapse of the communist regimes in Eastern Europe, Mikhailov published his *Case History* series. In Kharkiv, he photographed vagrants, outcasts, tramps and alcoholics in exhibitionist poses that sometimes refer to historical scenes. The images are metaphors for the lives of these outcasts, who became victims of a rapidly changing economic system. The adventures of the individual within broader historical developments assume an important place in this work. Humour, lust, vulnerability, tragedy, physical decay and death are major connecting themes. As viewers look at the frightening images, they experience a sense of both revulsion and empathy.

CDJ

Courtesy the artist and Galerie Conrads, Düsseldorf

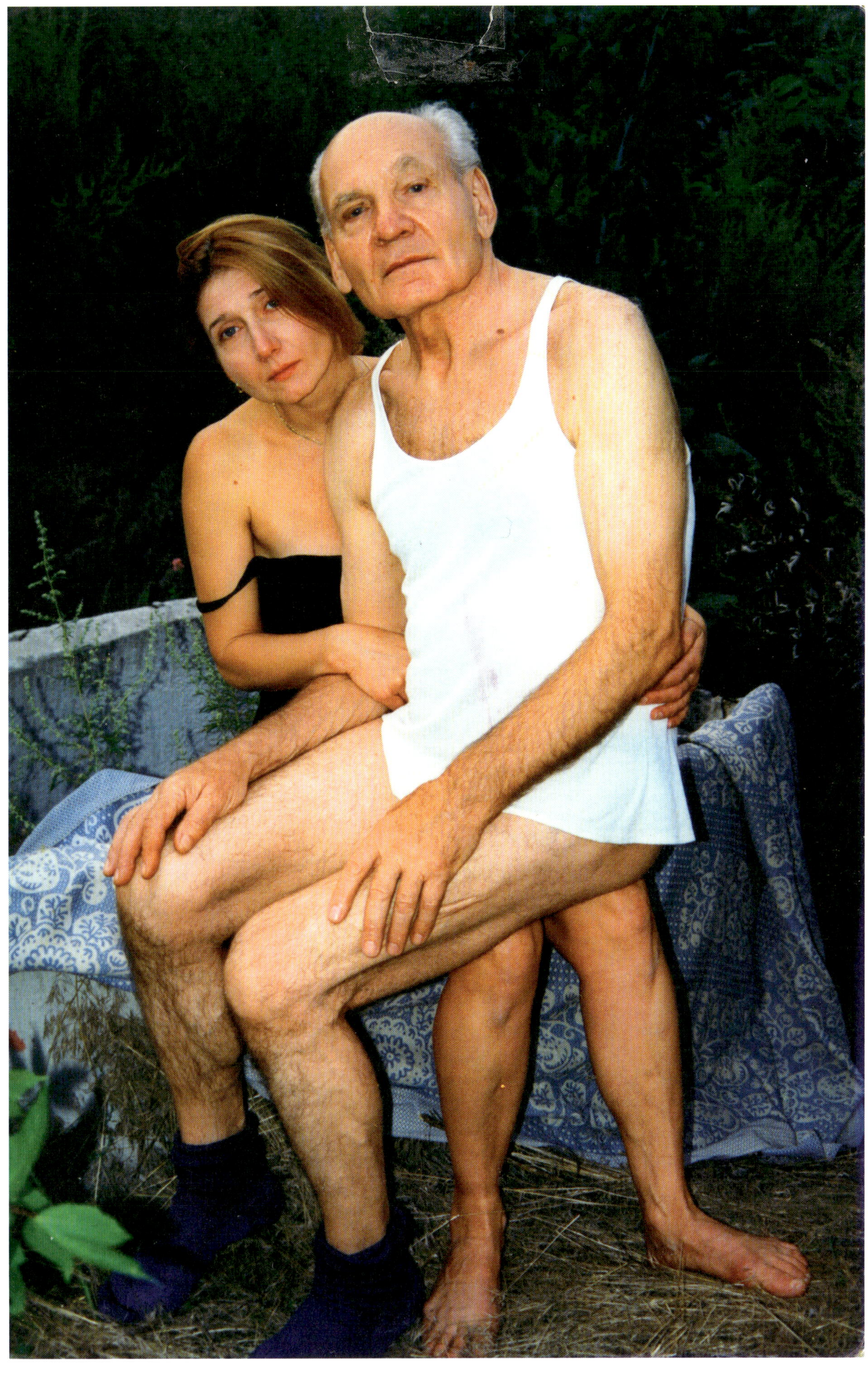

Boris Mikhailov

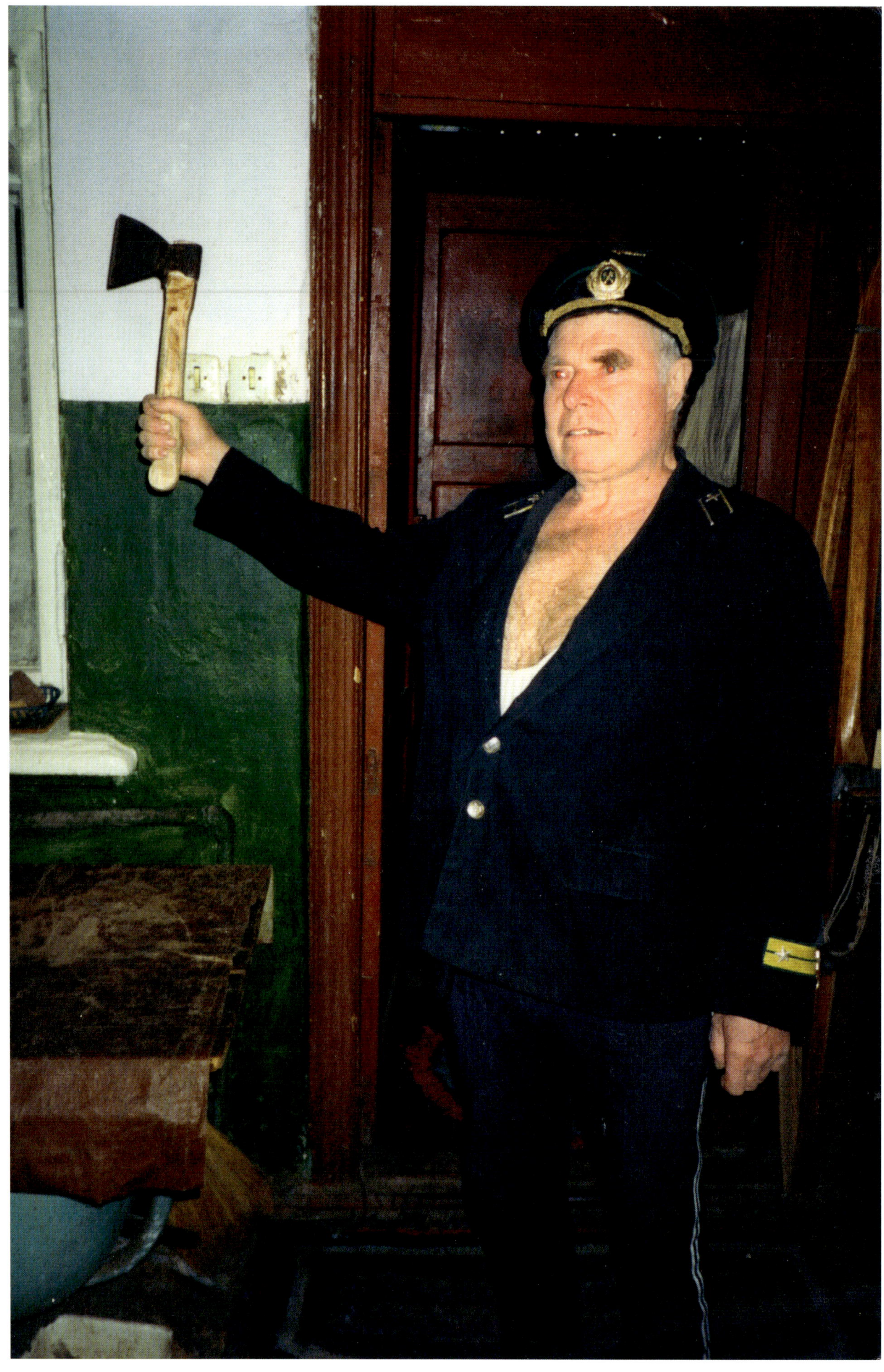

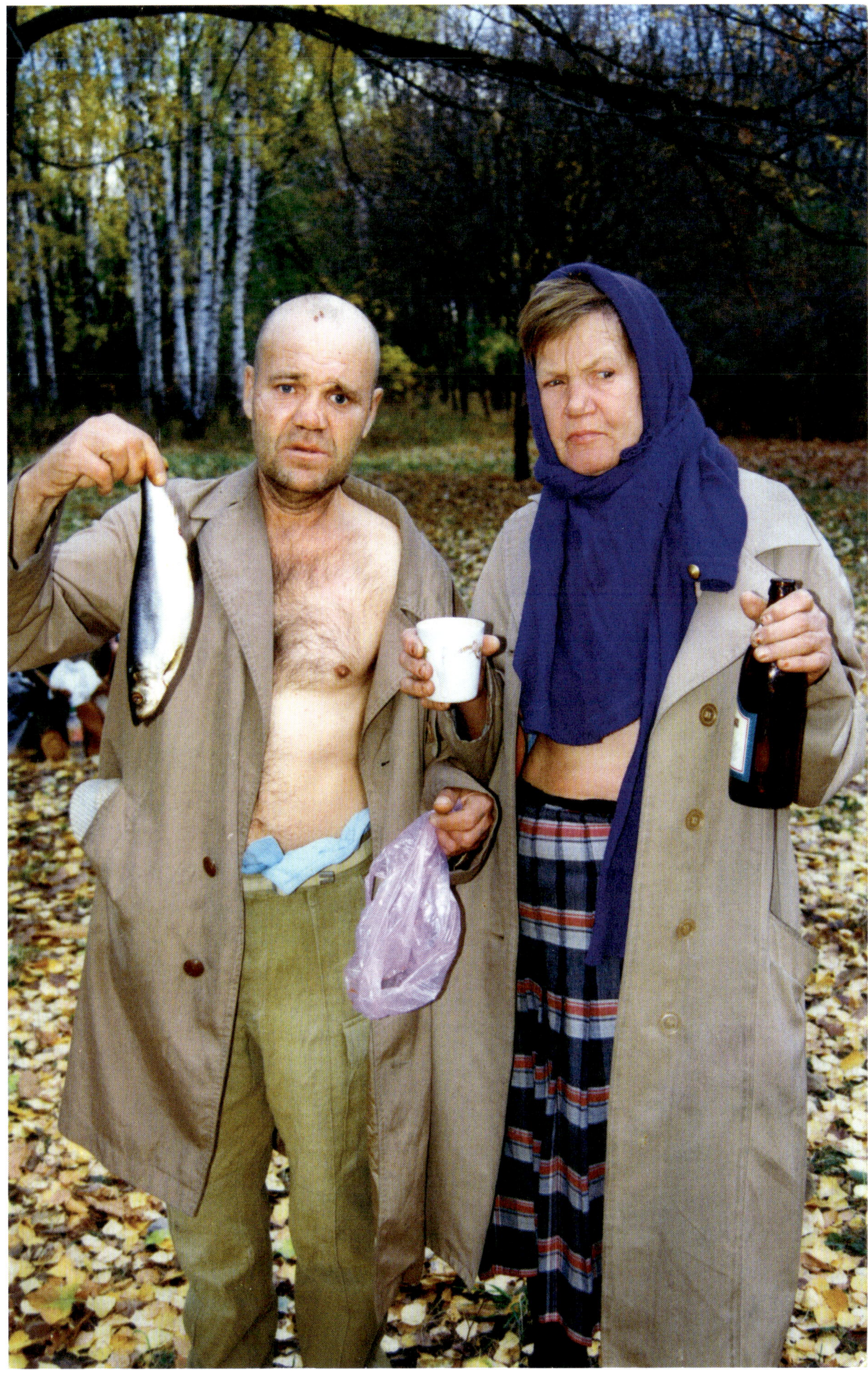

Boris Mikhailov

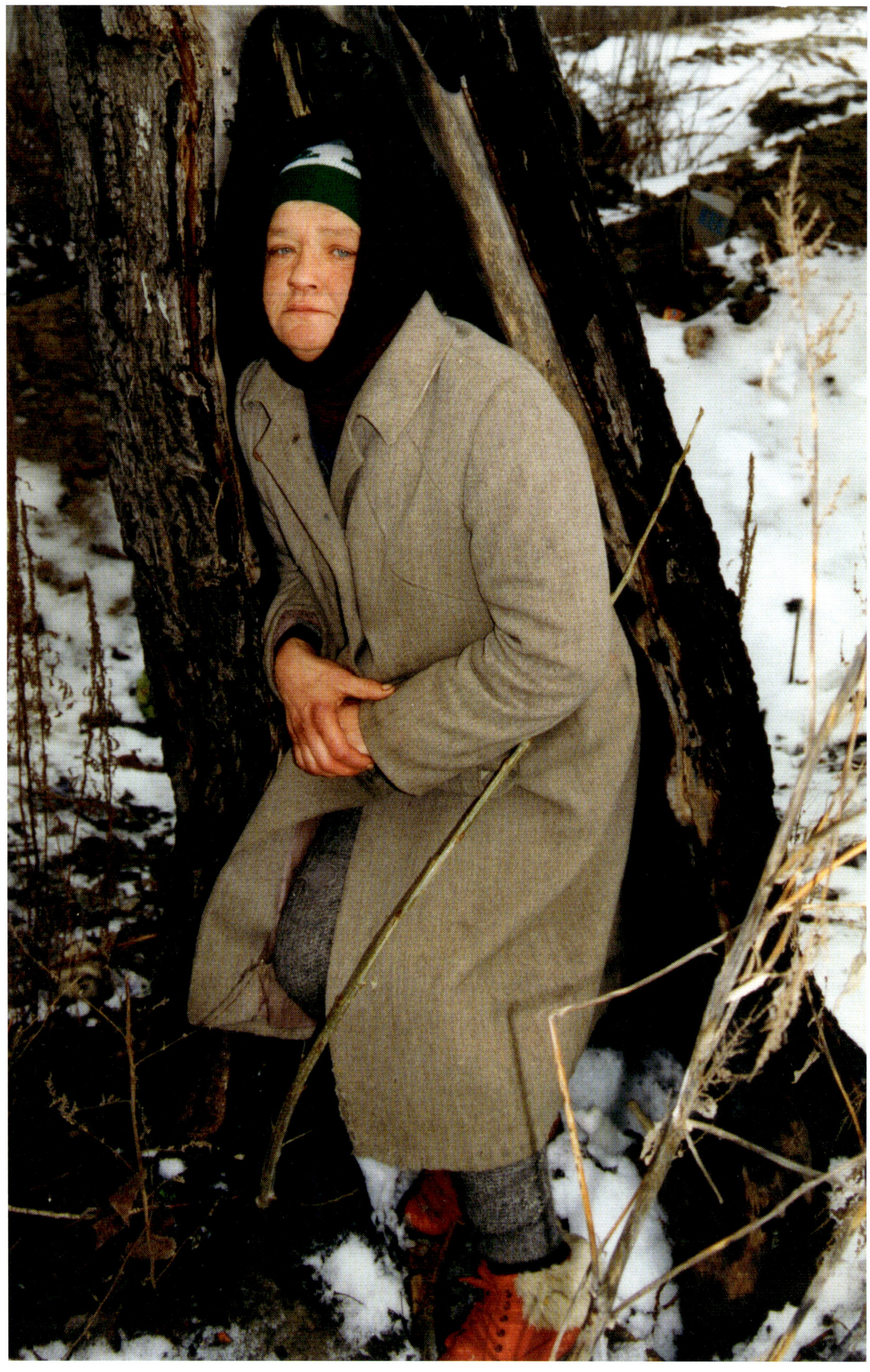

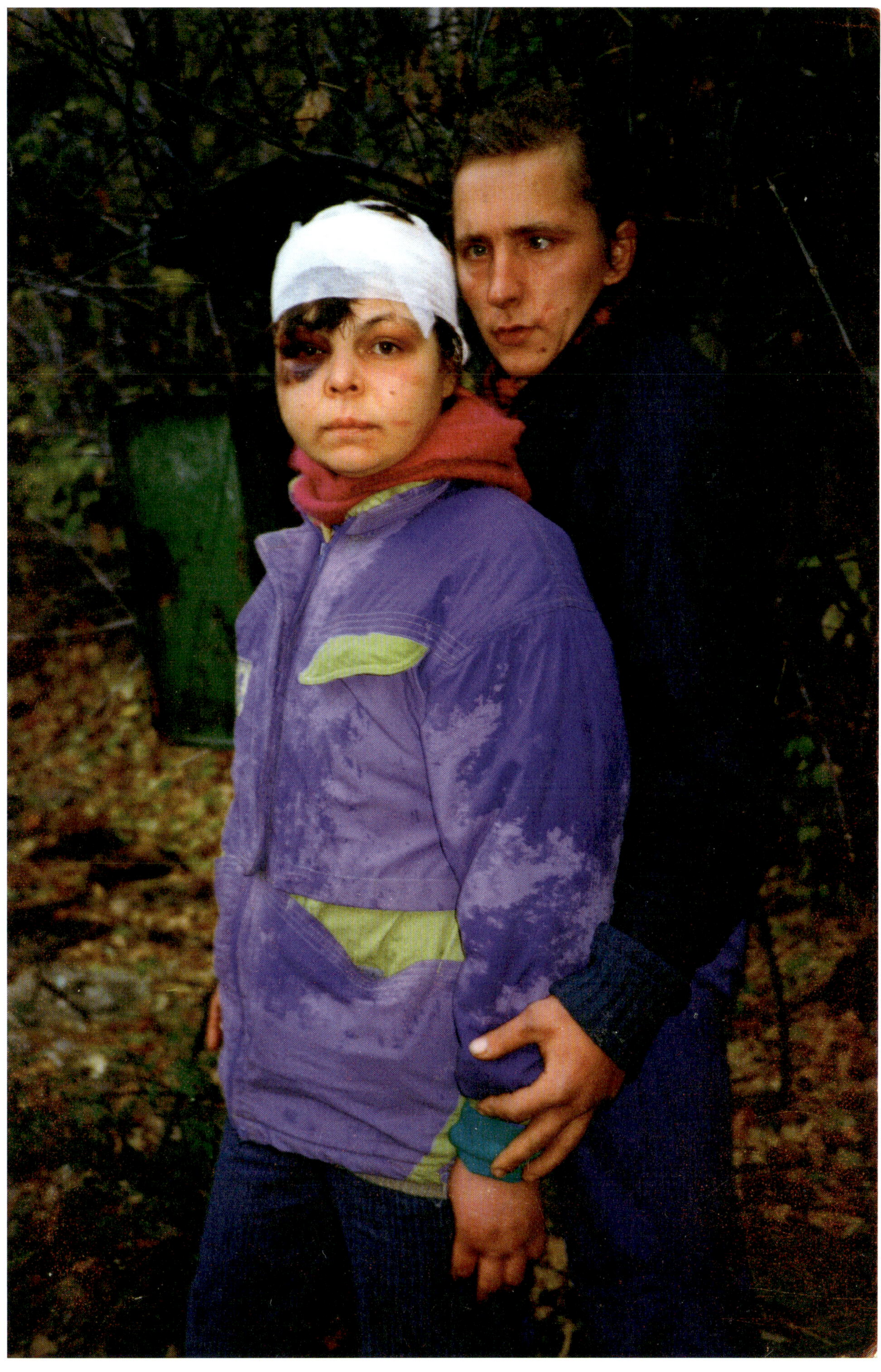

Boris Mikhailov

Jorge Molder (born 1947, Portugal)

pp. 129–31
Untitled, in 'The Scale of Mohs', 2012–13.
Digital pigment print on Arches paper 640 g/m²,
153 × 102 cm

Courtesy the artist

The Scale of Mohs

Jorge Molder uses the picture of his own body or face in what is
an expression of – or perhaps more a reflection on – a moment
when his identity is uncertain, between dreaming and waking
up, whenever space is created for a different 'I'. It is not entirely
coincidental that the philosopher and expressive artist Molder
has constructed a project 'about the interpretation of dreams',
a reference to Freud's famous book in which the subconscious
and dreams are related to the greater whole of culture and society. Molder is looking for his alter ego, 'the Other' within himself, even as an artist, while he opens himself up to influences
he has been exposed to during his life from literature, film,
expressive art, and philosophy, and which lie stored somewhere
in the recesses of his memory. For Molder, the face is where
interaction with the other takes place. And so his portraits are
not self-portraits, and he reflects not on his private existence
but on identity in the broader and more abstract sense of being
a person within a greater cultural and human context. He sees
the face also as a mask, an interface, and his work as part of a
process, maybe even of a struggle, hence the often cinematic
quality of his darker and sometimes disturbing, disorientating
series of portraits.

FG

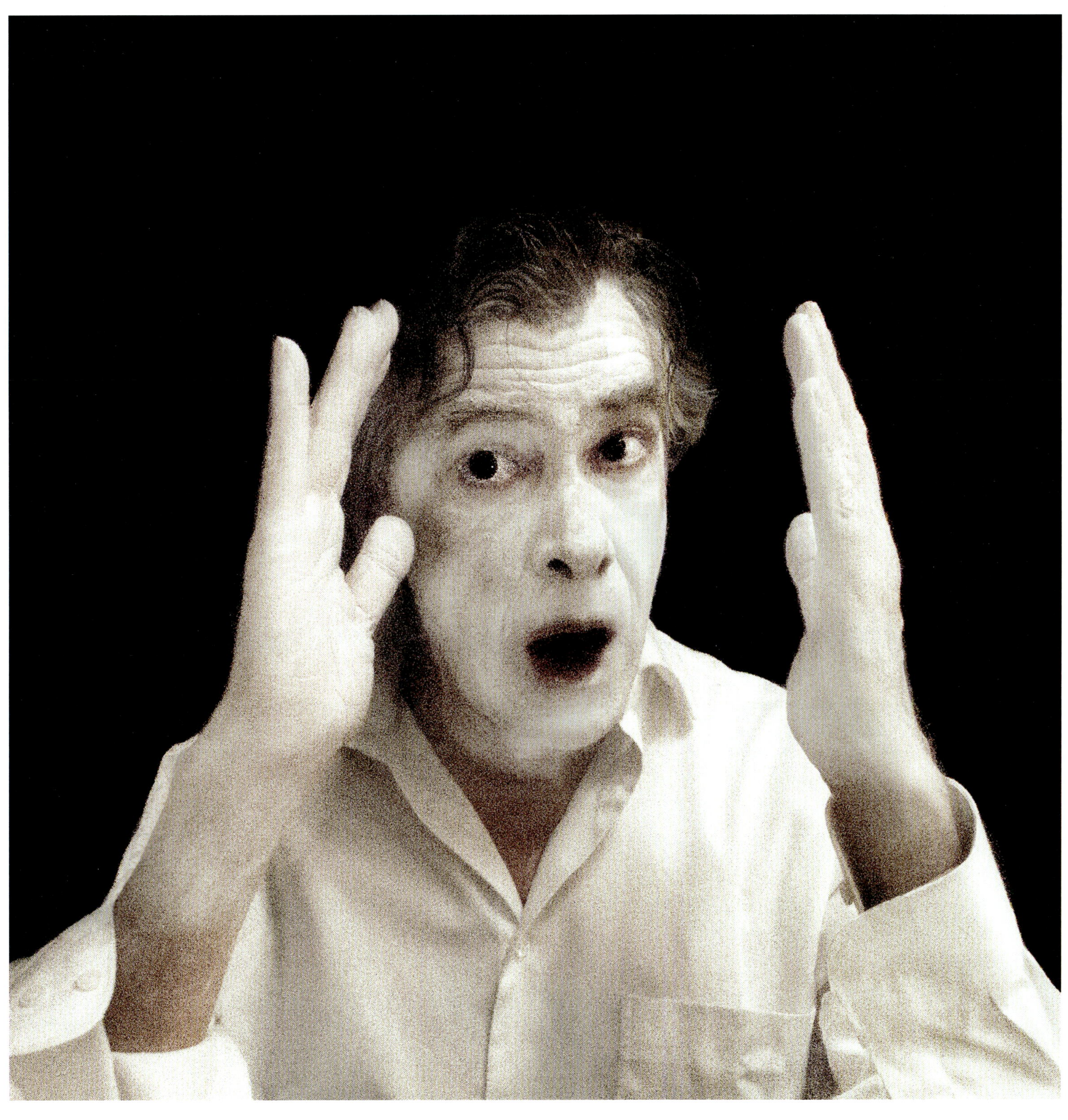

   Jorge Molder

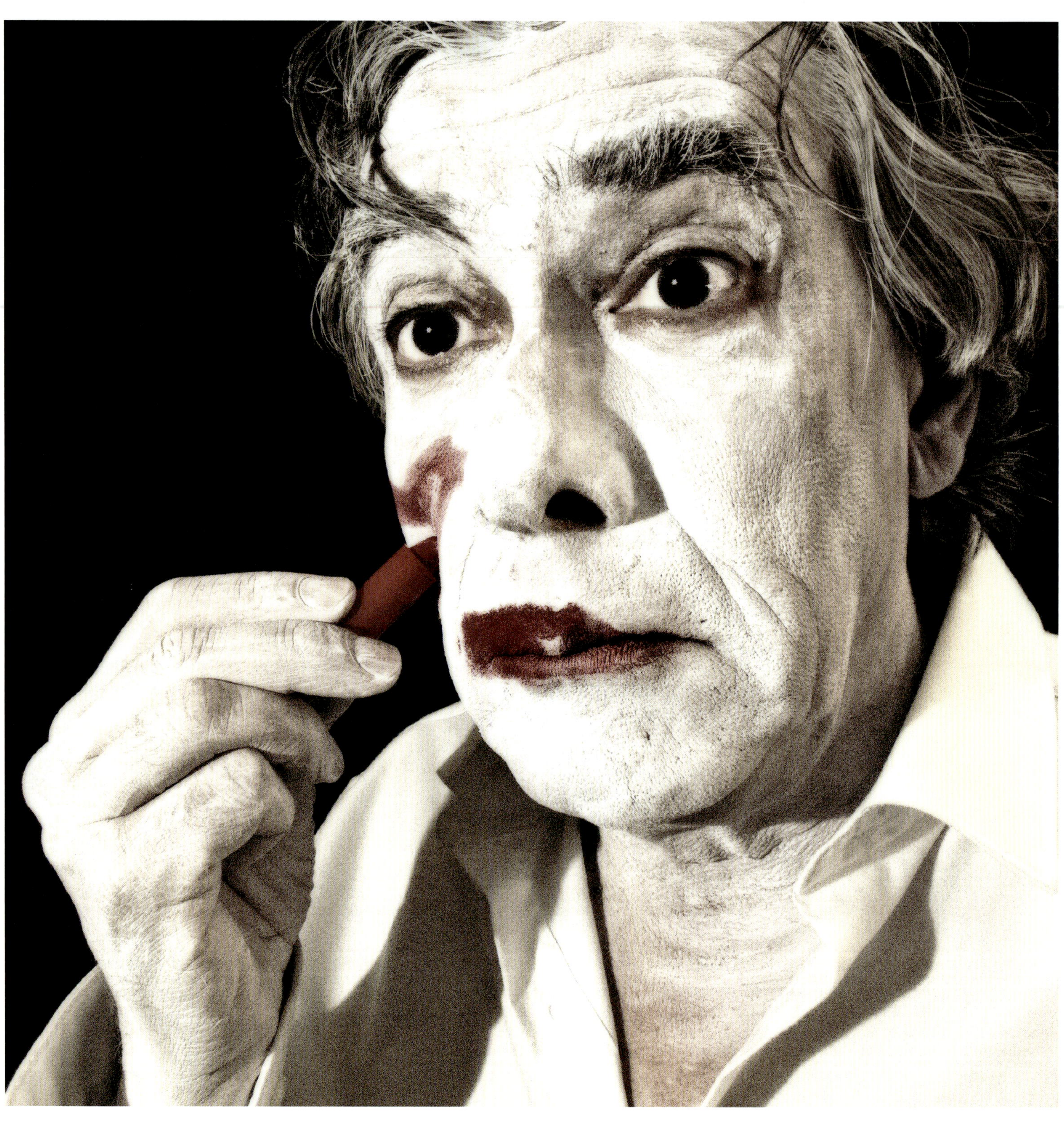

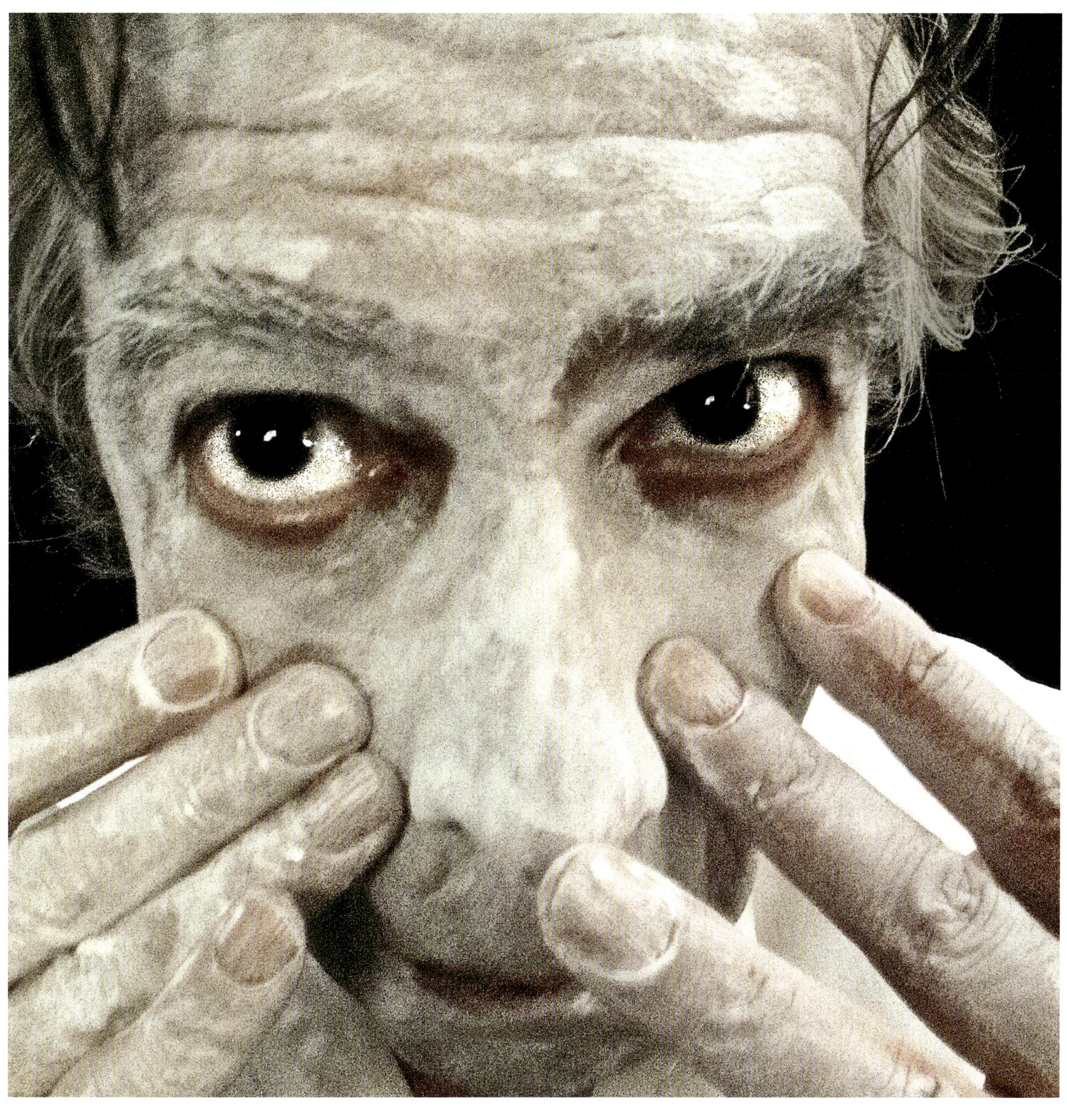

Jorge Molder

Lucia Nimcova (born 1977, Slovakia)

Unofficial

In her *Unofficial* series from 2006–08, Lucia Nimcova takes a
twofold approach in dealing with the face. She explores how
a face can become a sign, conforming to the norms and codes
of behaviour dictated by propaganda and culture, and at the
same time how this can be deconstructed. The project began
when Nimcova spent two years doing in-depth research into
the history of her home town, Humenné, in eastern Slovakia,
combing official archives and studying pictures by amateur
photographers. After scanning the archives of the photographer
Juraj Kammer, she started to take a closer look at specific photographs. Having appropriated much of the style of the archival
material, and after discovering that past events seemed to have
the same structure, she began documenting official events as a
regional reporter. What Nimcova shows is that the communist
mentality of passivity was immutable – even if the communities
themselves seemed to be changing façades. The project is deeply
humanistic and self-referential, showing that it is people who
constitute communities, while at the same time bringing to the
fore the power of the medium to play with memory and time,
in refabricating them in a sense. Nimcova's project does more
than just shed light on both the process of 'normalization' –
the ideological programme of social and political integration
designed to restore Communist Party control in Czechoslovakia
after 1968 – and its consequences. It also highlights the way this
process can be deconstructed once it is re-enacted. Façades are
transformed into faces, and by making copies of the surface, she
reveals the layers of masked faces that have created them. And in
a way calls off the show.

AA

p. 133
Competition, in 'Unofficial', 2007.
Archival ink-jet print, 80 × 60 cm (print),
60 × 45 cm (poster)

p. 134
Curator, in 'Unofficial', 2007.
Archival ink-jet print, 80 × 60 cm (print),
60 × 45 cm (poster)

p. 135
Discussion about Democracy, in 'Unofficial', 2007.
Archival ink-jet print, 80 × 60 cm (print),
60 × 45 cm (poster)

p. 136
Former Director, in 'Unofficial', 2007.
Archival ink-jet print, 80 × 60 cm (print),
60 × 45 cm (poster)

p. 137
Presentation of Cultural Institutions, in 'Unofficial',
2007. Archival ink-jet print, 80 × 60 cm (print),
60 × 45 cm (poster)

p. 138
Librarian, in 'Unofficial', 2007.
Archival ink-jet print, 80 × 60 cm (print),
60 × 45 cm (poster)

p. 139
International Women's Day, in 'Unofficial', 2007.
Archival ink-jet print, 80 × 60 cm (print),
60 × 45 cm (poster)

Courtesy the artist and Krokus Galéria, Bratislava

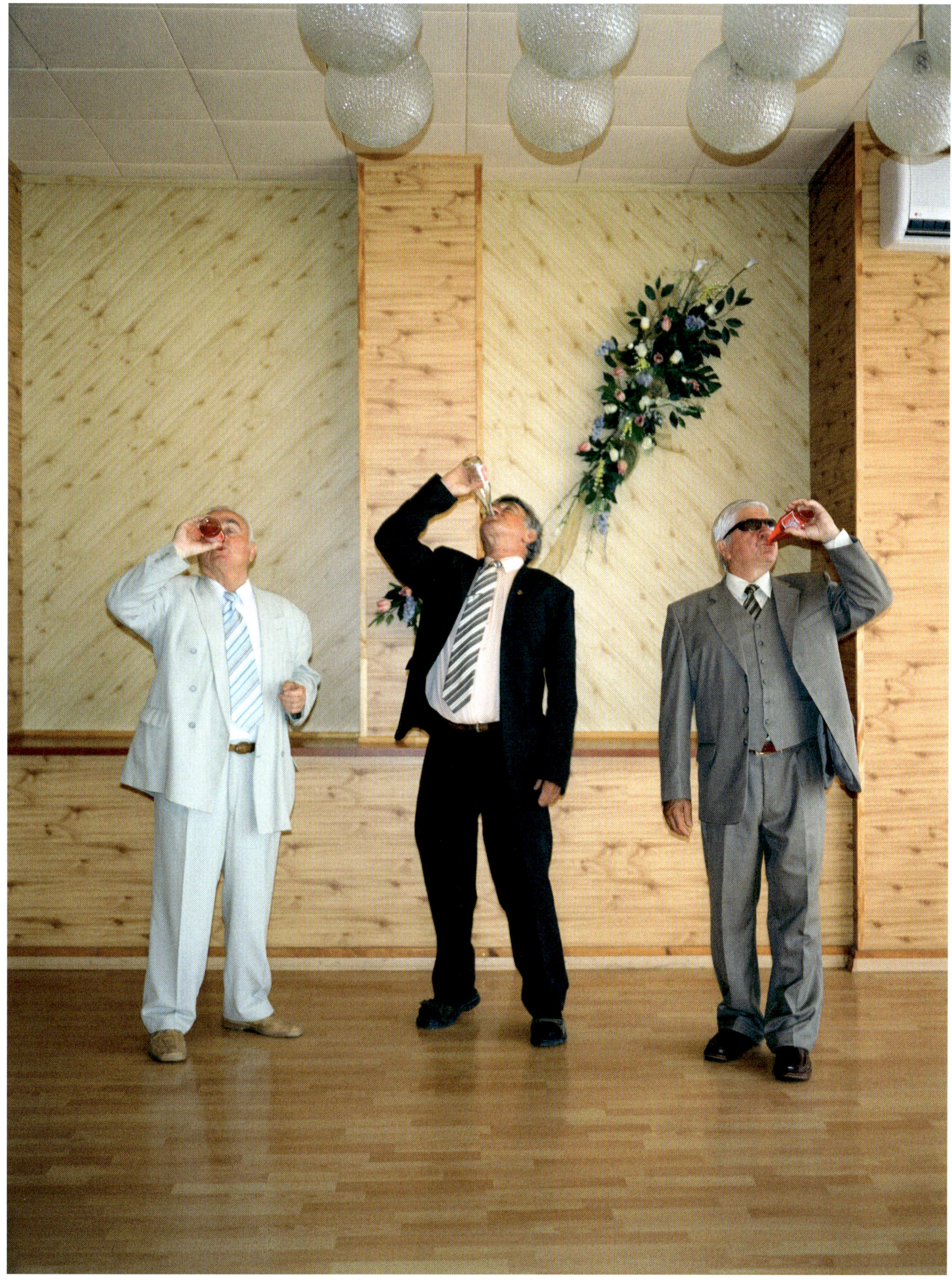

Lucia Nimcova

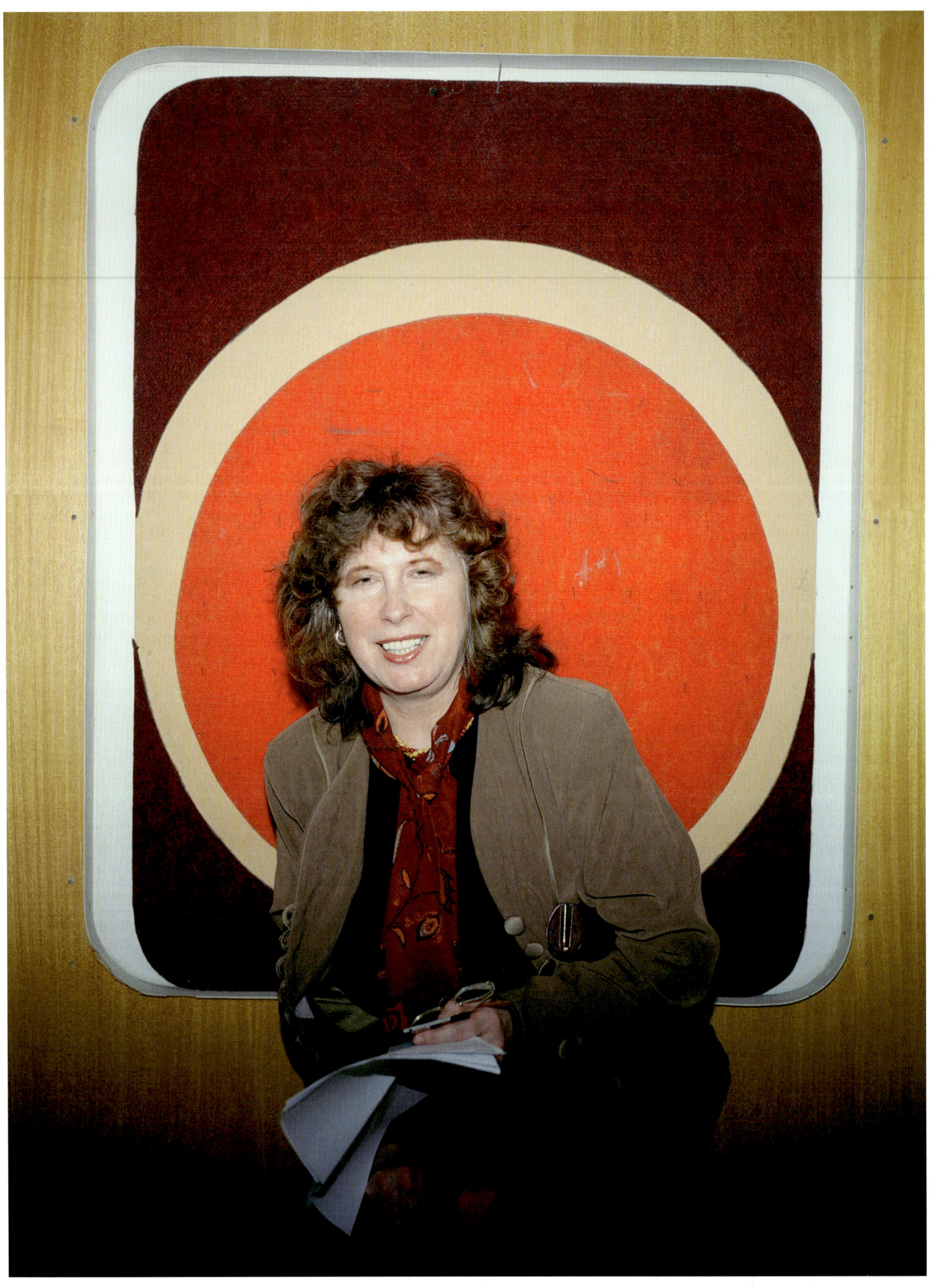

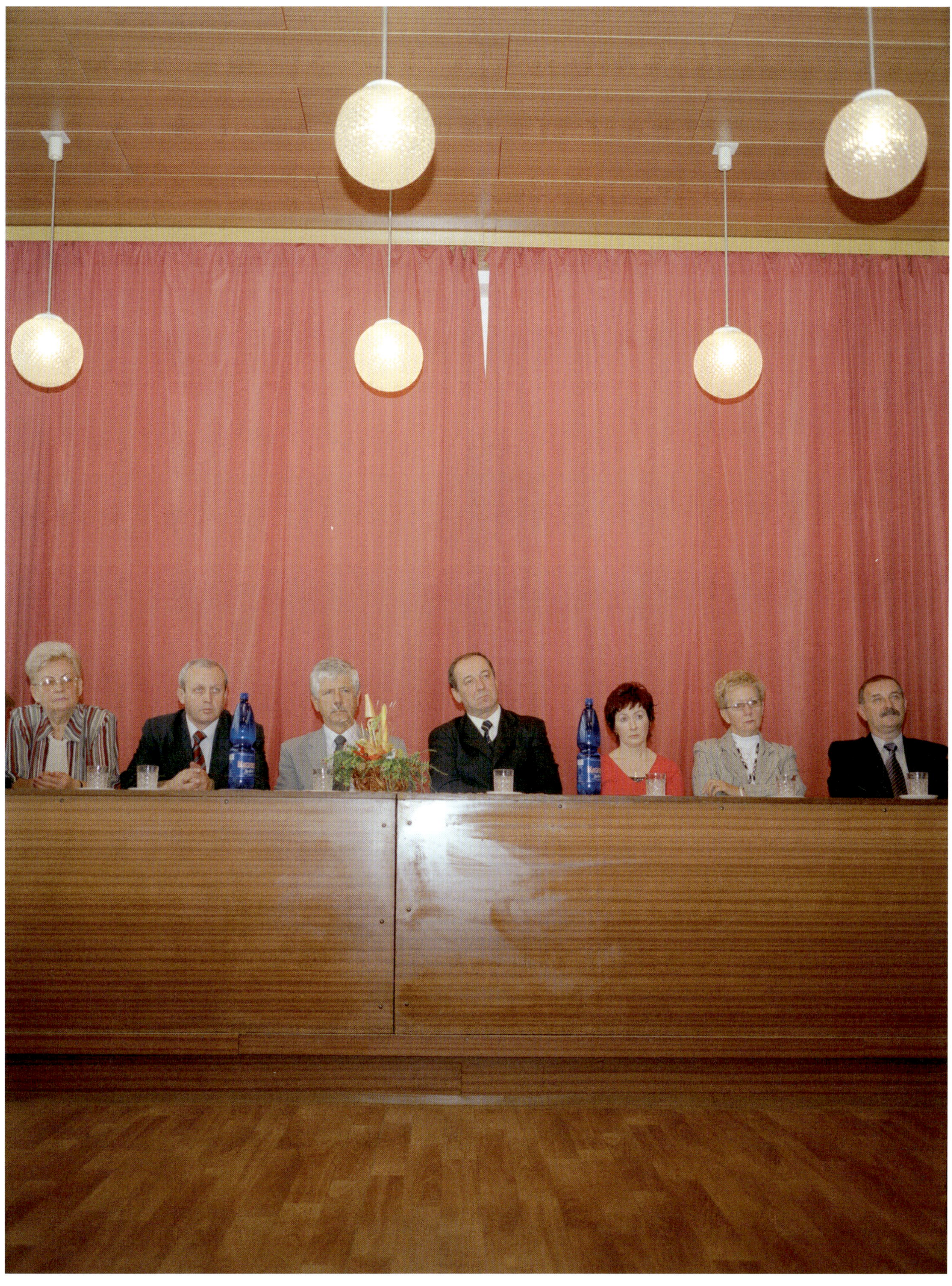

 Lucia Nimcova

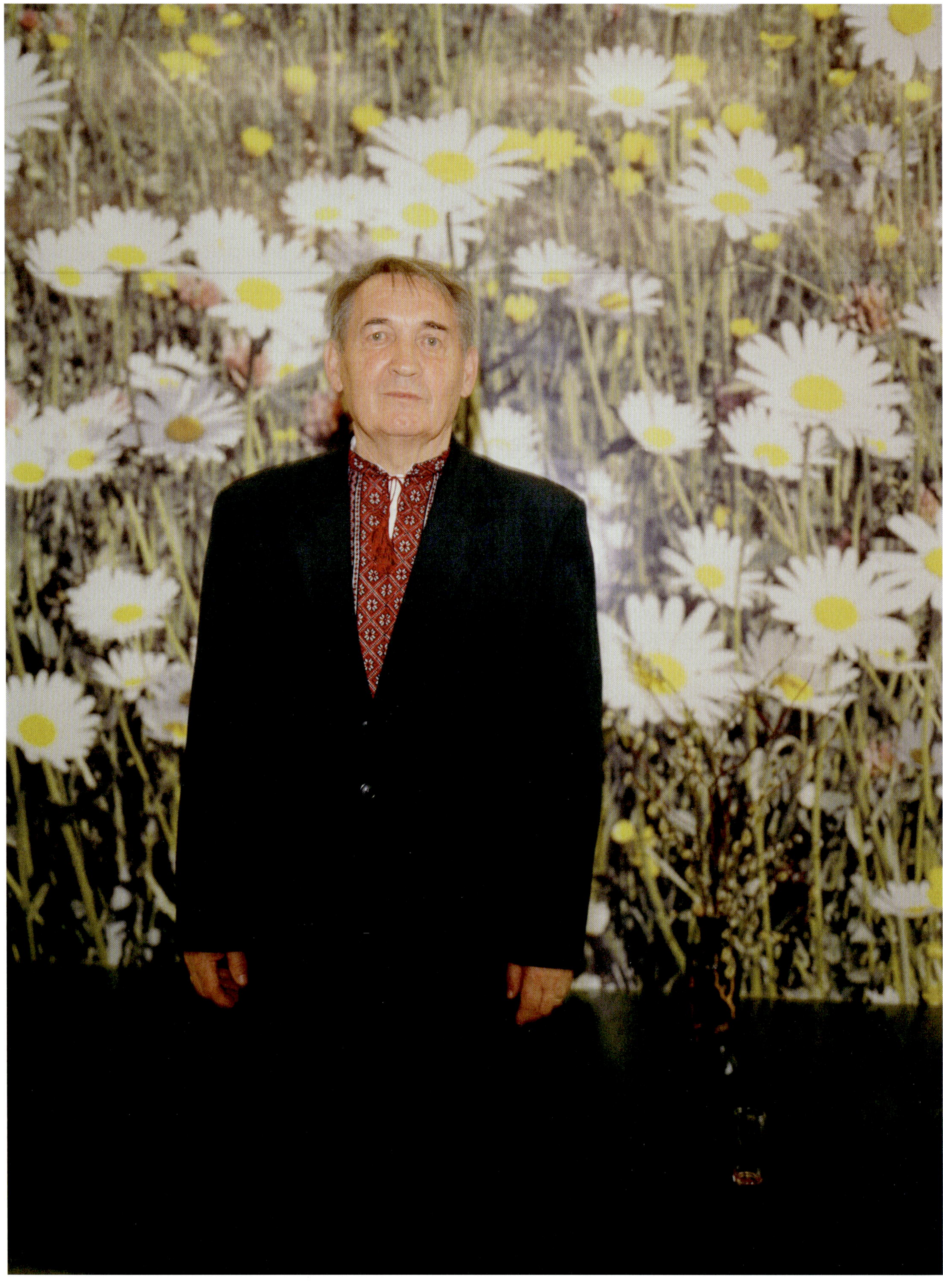

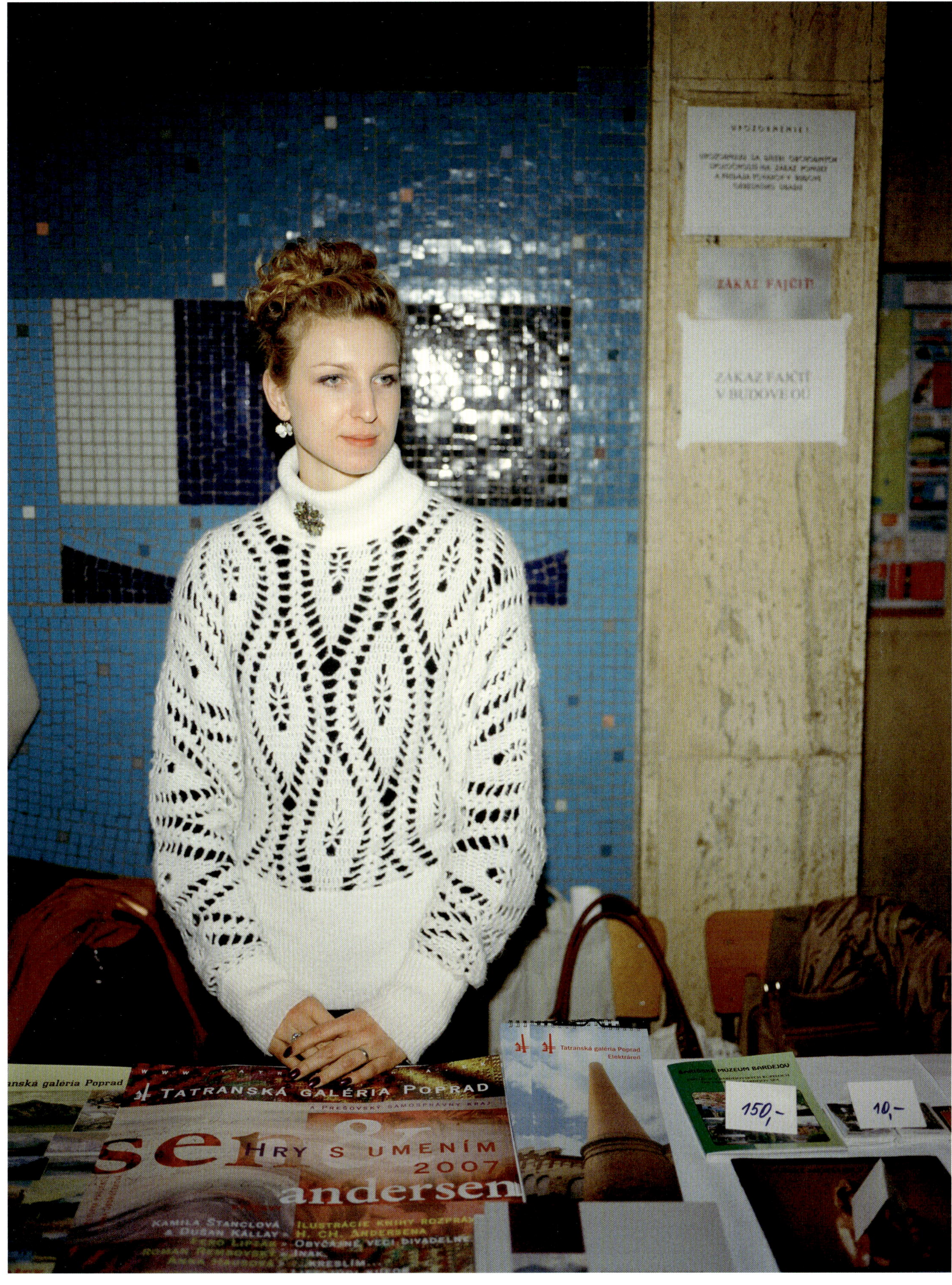

Lucia Nimcova

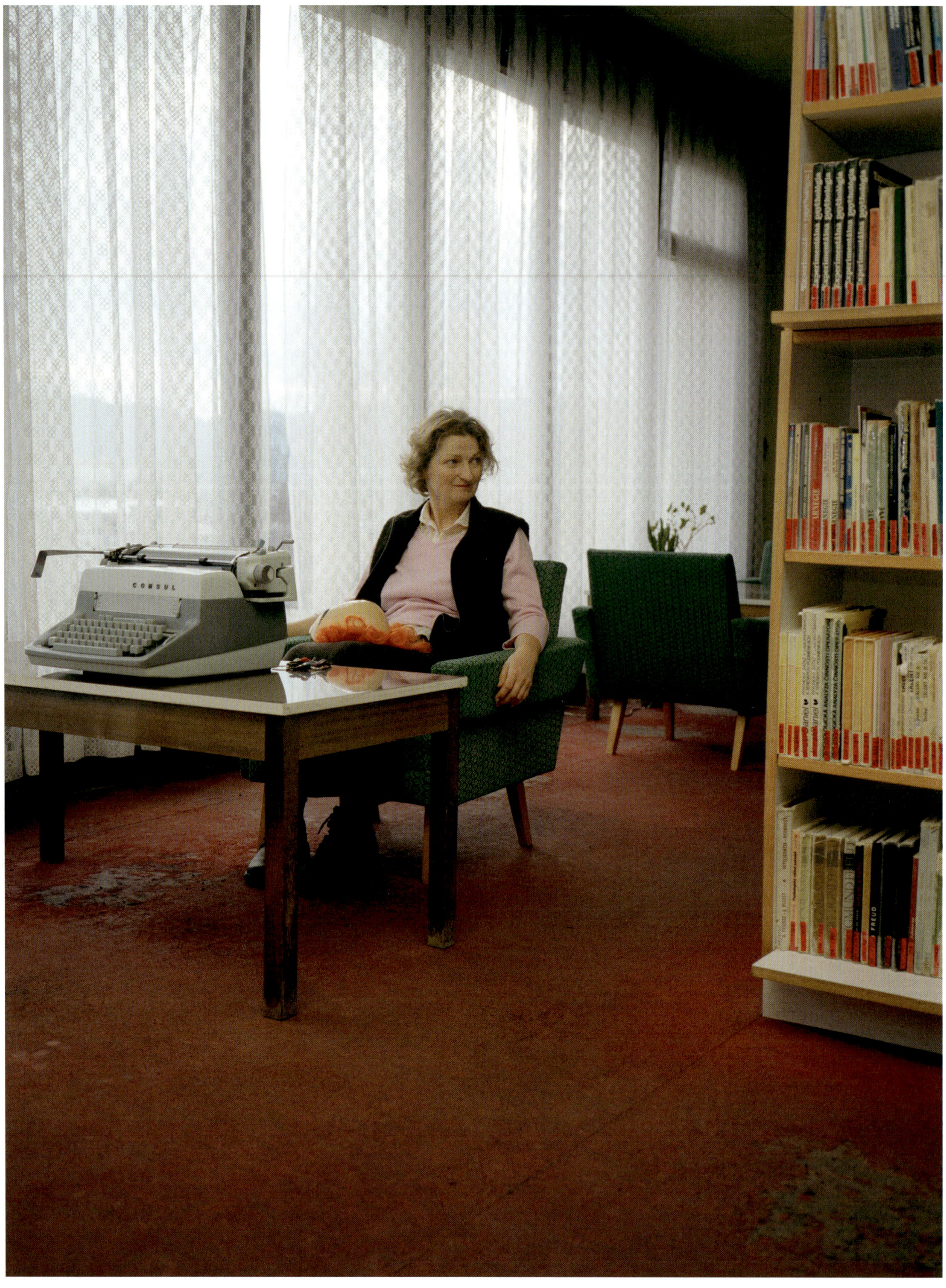

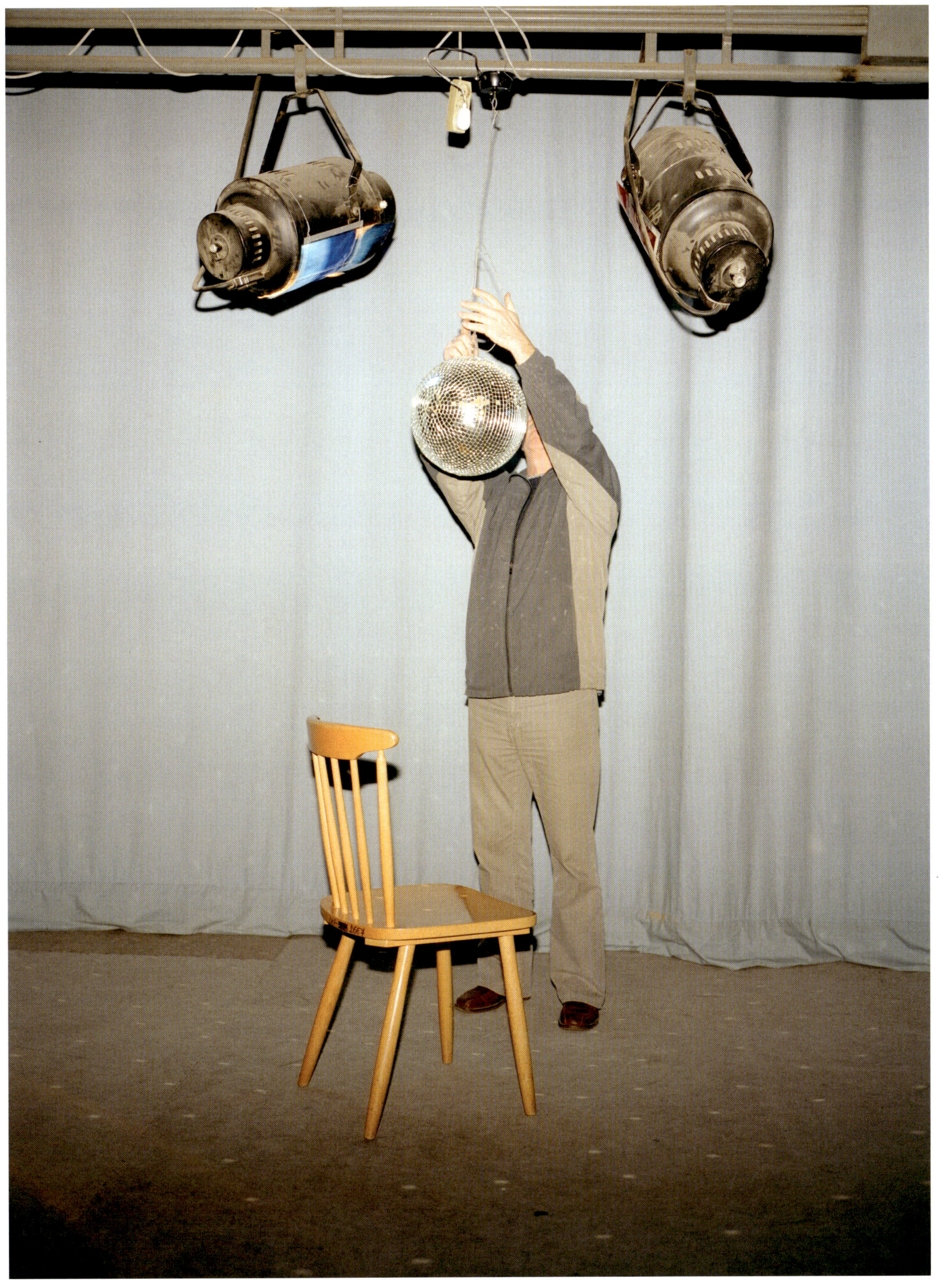

Lucia Nimcova

Adam Pańczuk (born 1978, Poland)

Karczeby

Karczeb is an old dialect spoken in the east of Adam Pańczuk's native Poland. Linguistically, it is a mix of Polish and Belorussian. The word Karczeb also refers to what is left in the ground once a tree has been cut down: a trunk with roots that simply refuse to budge. The inhabitants of the region concerned are called 'Karczebs' because they are so strongly rooted to the land of their birth. Not even Stalin and the forced relocations he instigated could make them move, and they paid for this with their freedom, sometimes even with their lives. When they die, Karczebs are buried in their native soil in order to become earth themselves. In the sometimes absurd-looking series of pictures that Pańczuk created in eastern Poland, tradition, myth, local culture and reality merge in inimitable fashion. Essentially, the story of the Karczebs can stand for that of countless rural communities, of which Europe has (or had) an abundance. The complex historical relationship between inhabitants and the land on which they live and which helps to determine their identity cannot be encapsulated in a simple portrait. Therefore, Pańczuk opted for the opposite of a realistic approach and decided instead to symbolize this relationship through his photographs, with or without the help of actors - like some sort of inverted anthropology that works not analytically but synthetically. He placed his models in the midst of the landscape and sometimes literally in the soil, or allowed them to be part of nature and taken up by it. By opting for black-and-white pictures, he has visually reinforced the hint of unity between mankind and landscape. Objects such as bread or an animal skin symbolize the connection with the land in different ways. The occasionally comical scenes suggest a wealth of stories, but Pańczuk does not provide any specific clues, leaving those who view the photographs - in most cases town dwellers - to work it out for themselves.

FG

p. 141
'Karczeby', 2009.
Archival ink-jet print, 90 × 90 cm

p. 142
'Karczeby', 2011.
Archival ink-jet print, 90 × 90 cm

pp. 143–47
'Karczeby', 2008.
Archival ink-jet prints, 90 × 90 cm

Courtesy the artist

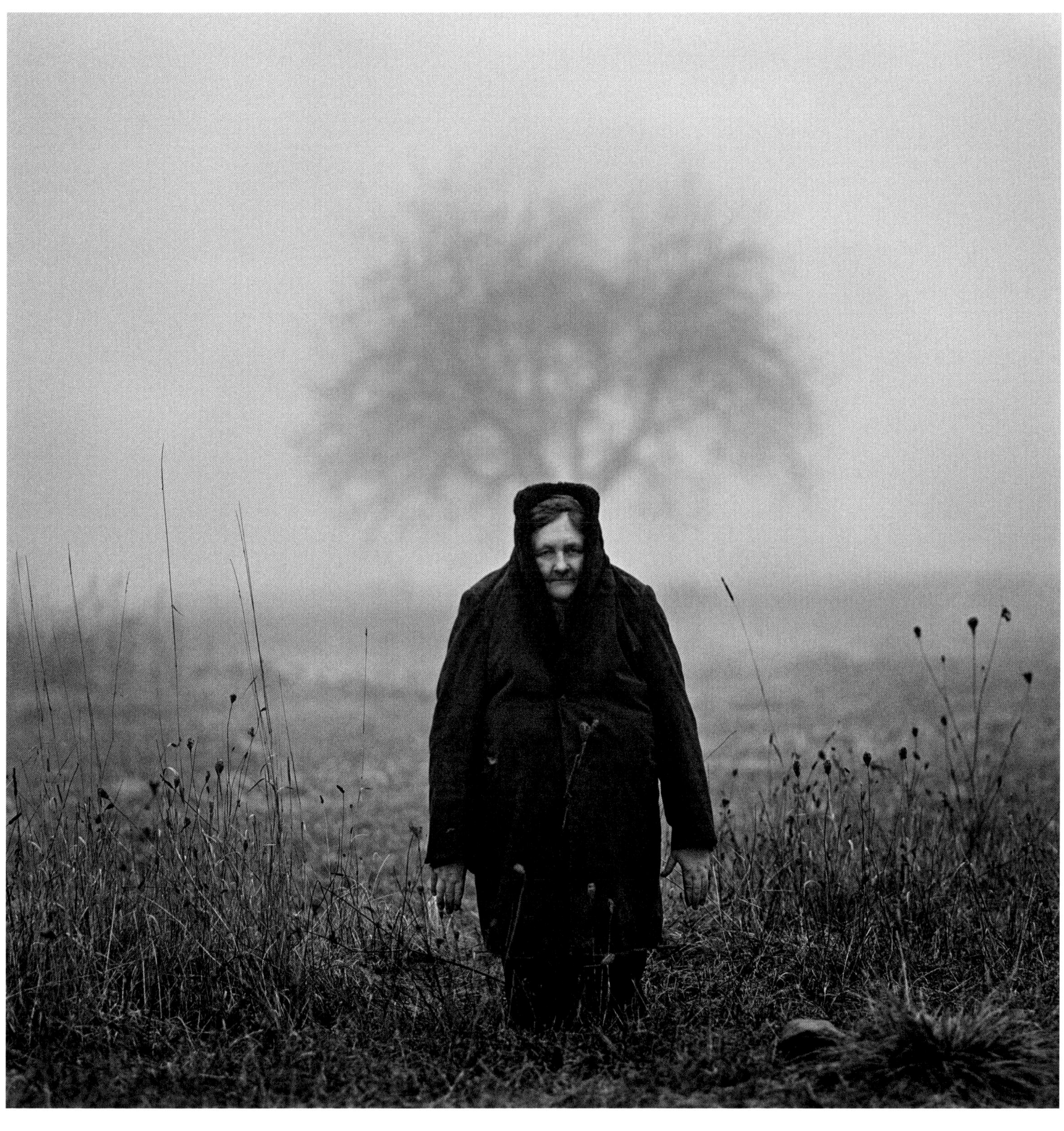

Adam Pańczuk

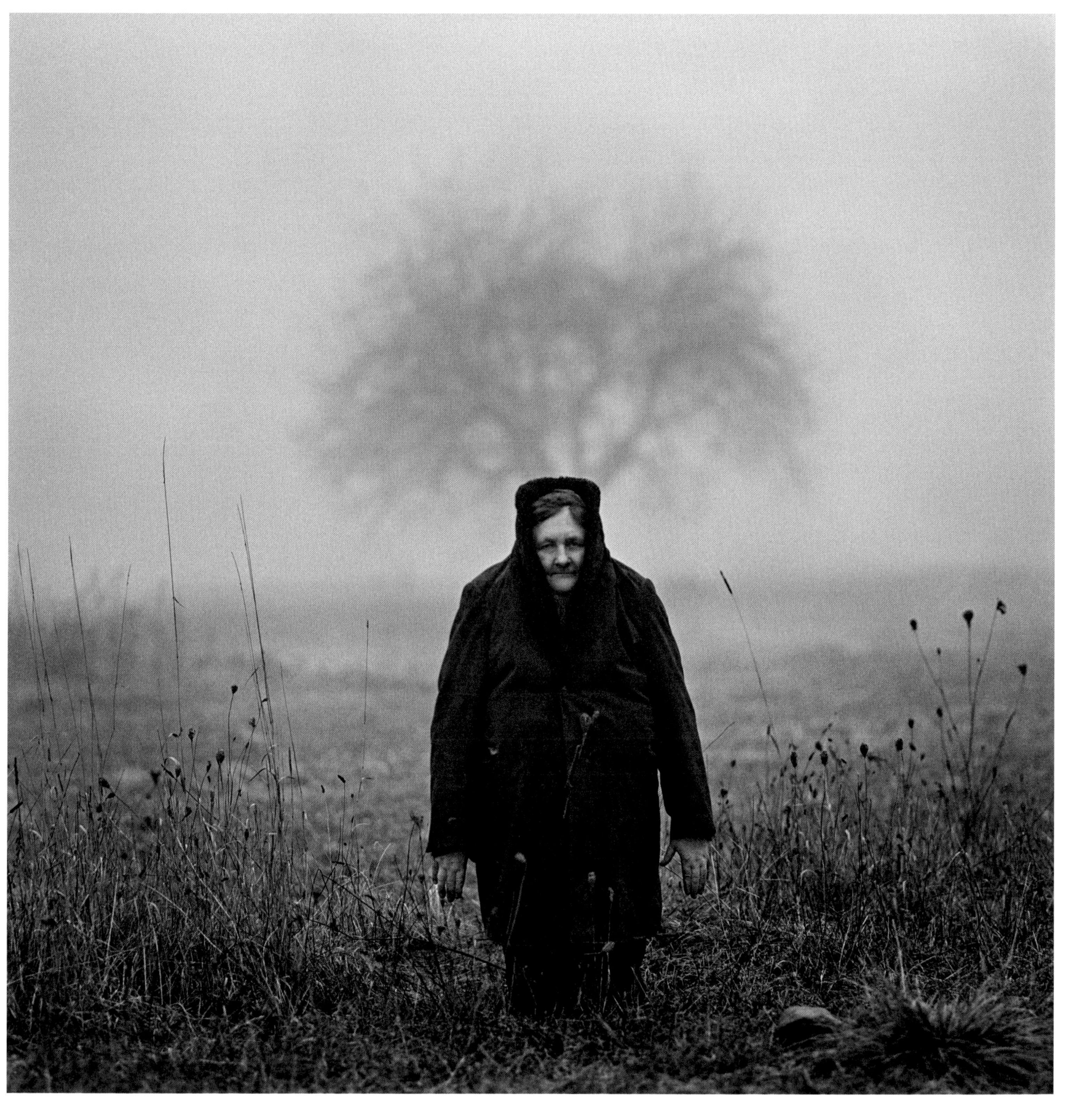

Adam Pańczuk

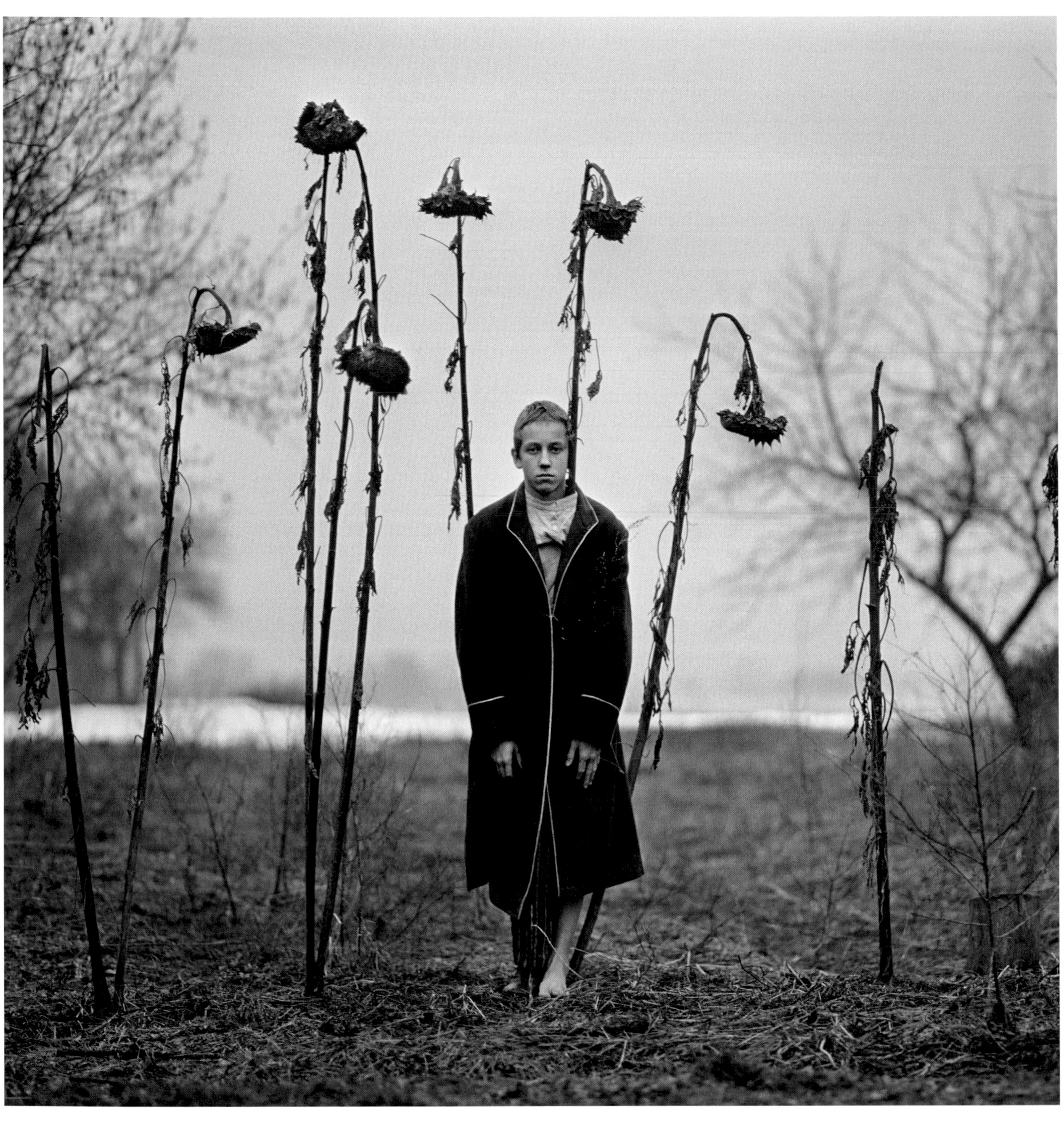

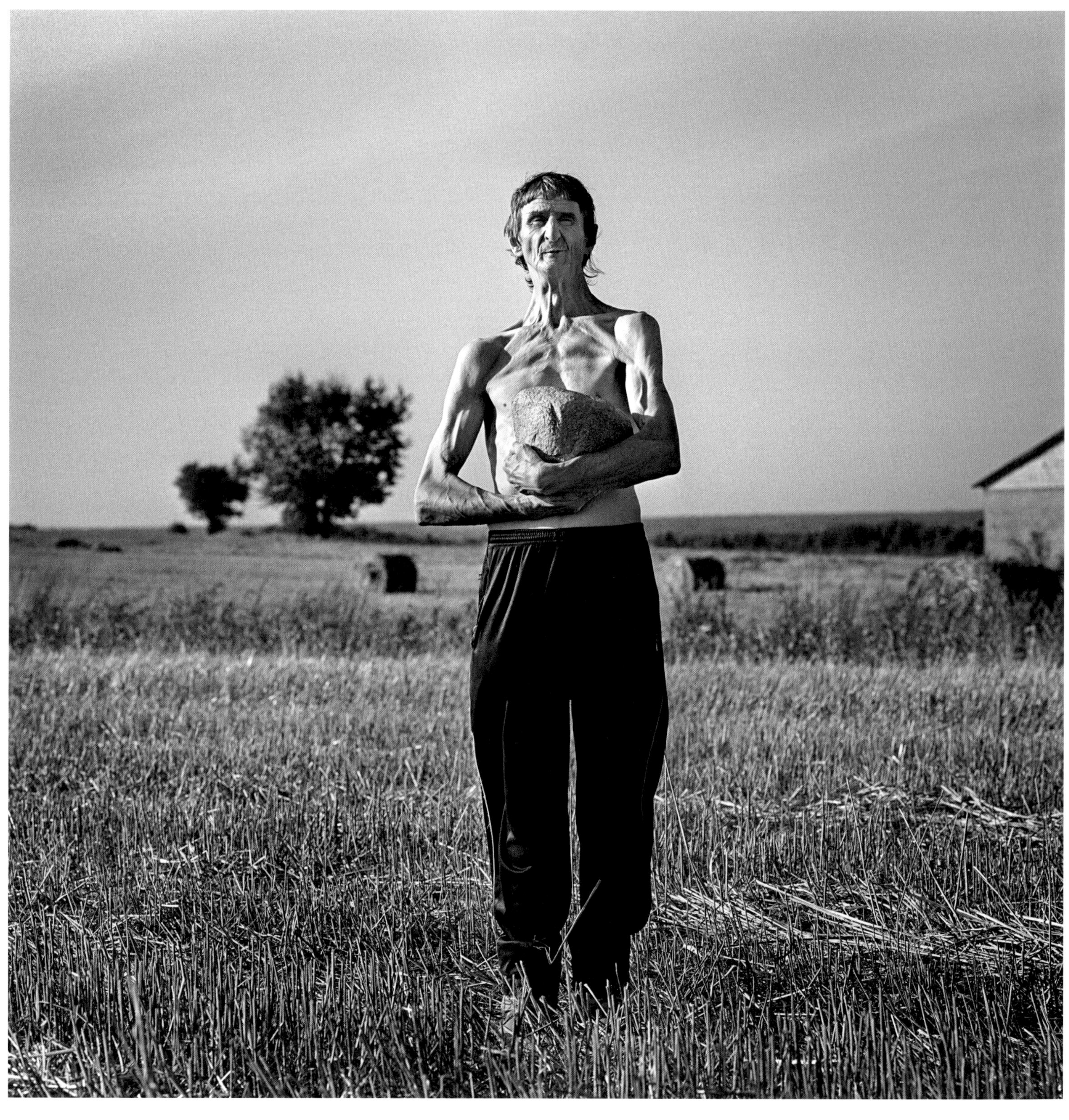

Adam Pańczuk

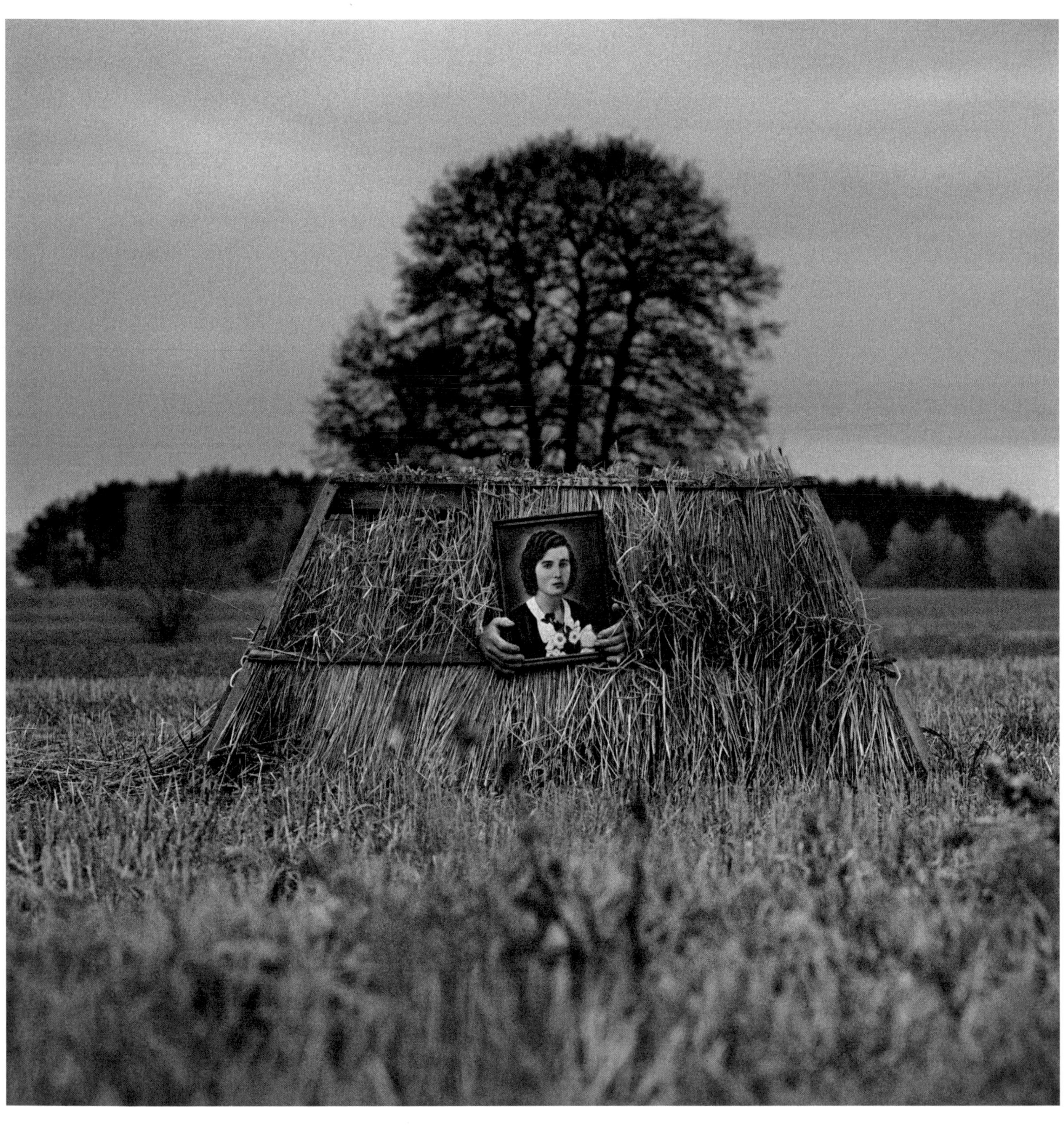

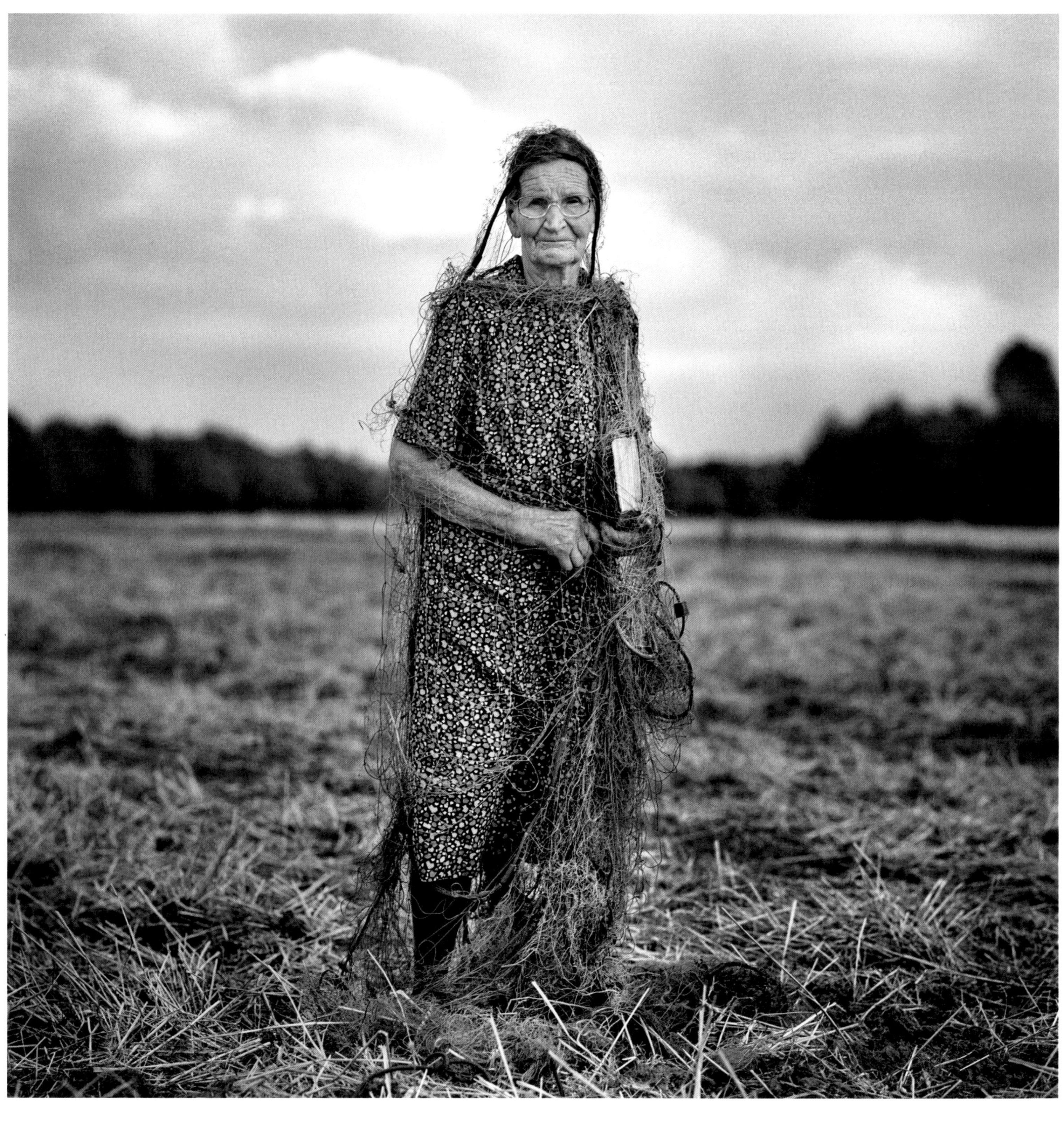

145

Adam Pańczuk

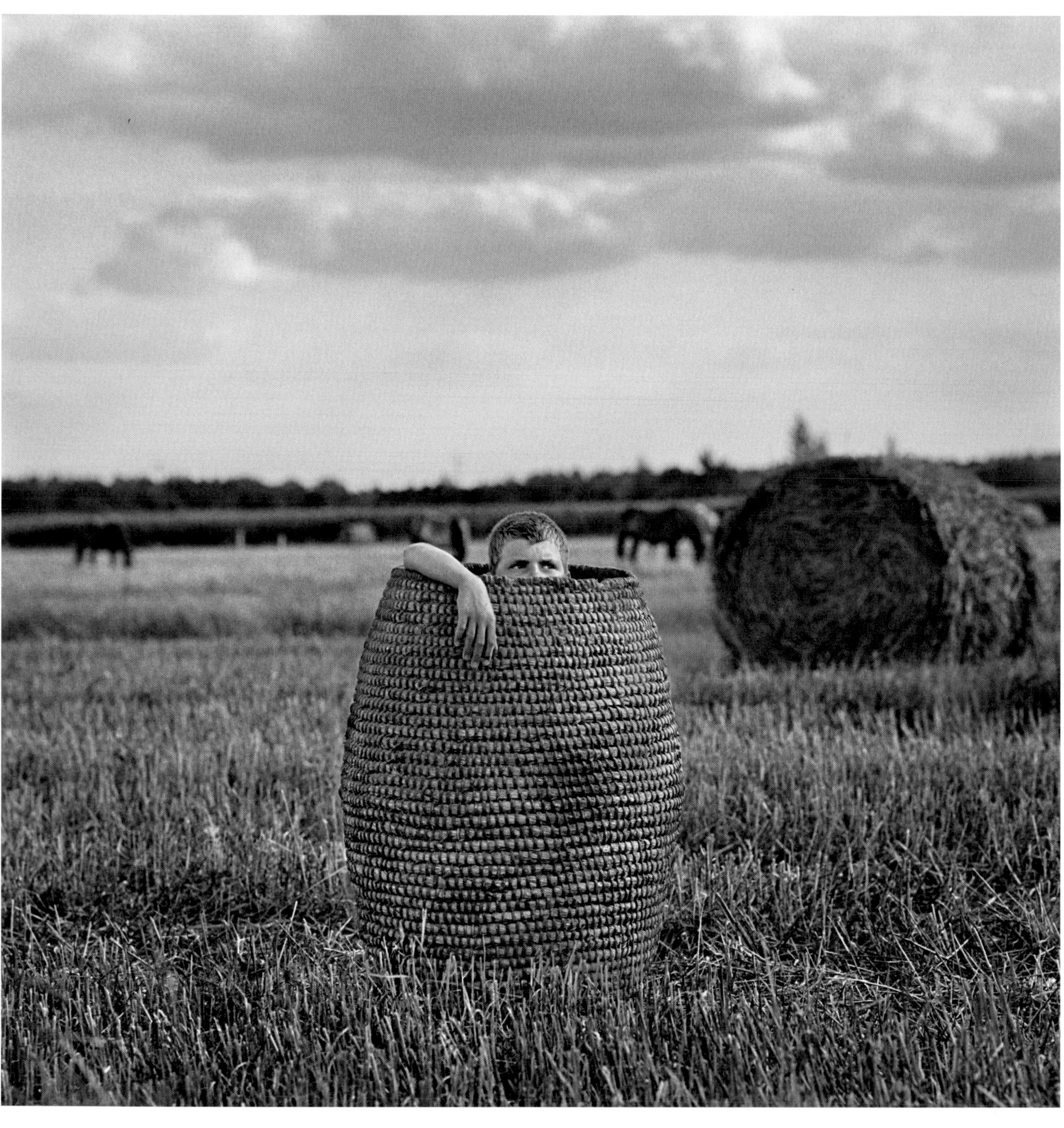

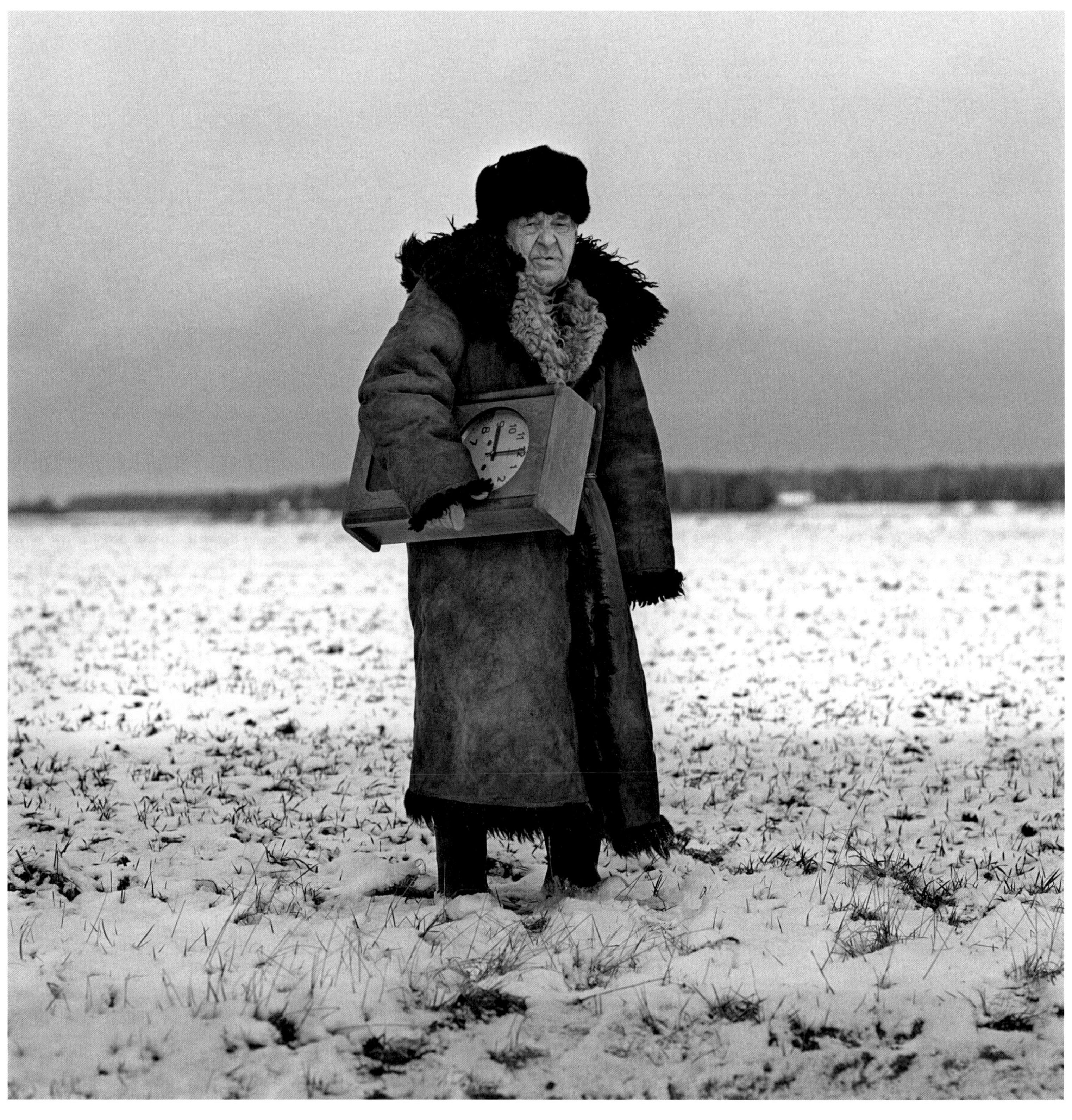

Adam Pańczuk

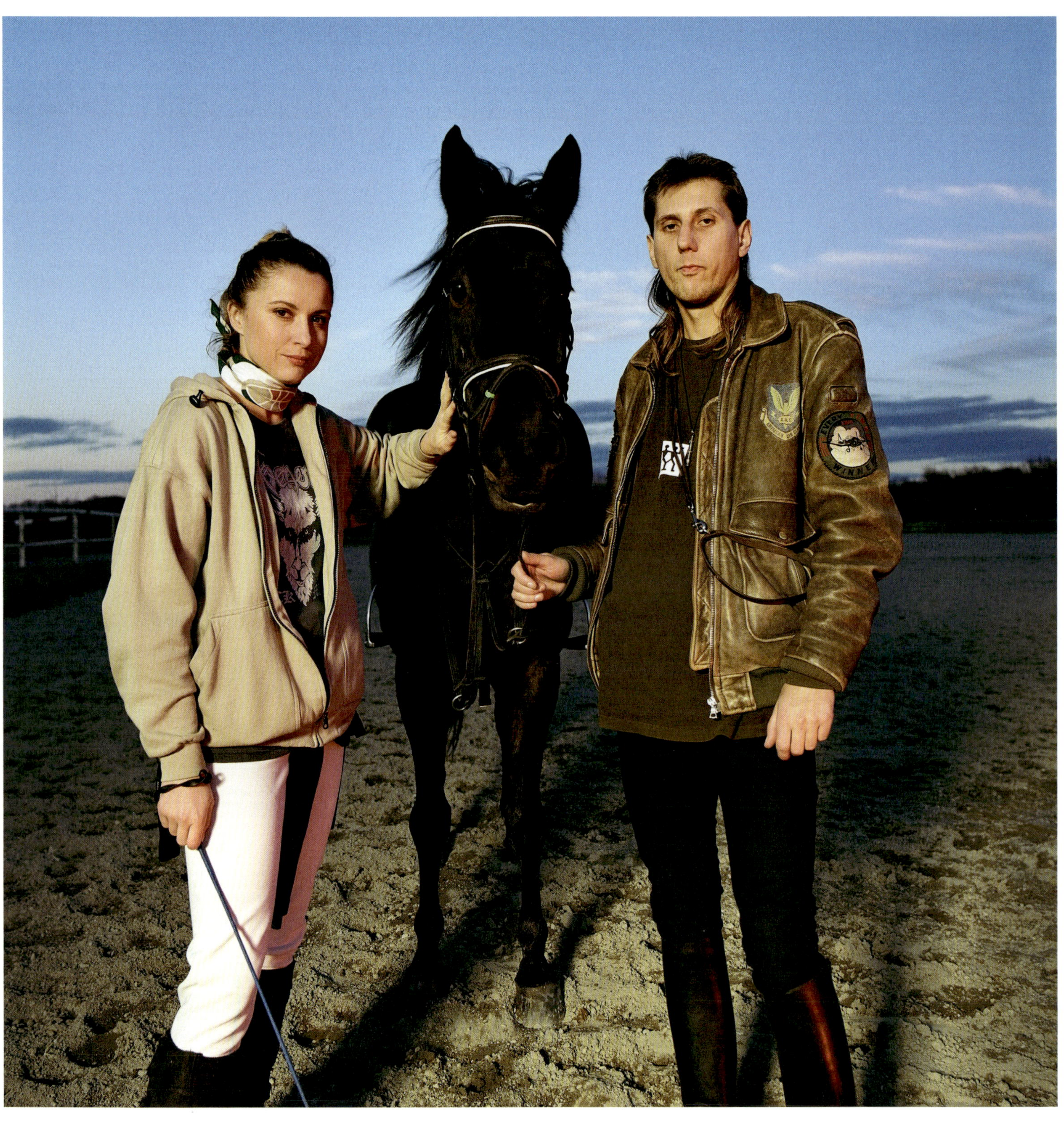

Dita Pepe (born 1973, Czech Republic)

Self-portraits with Men

How many lives can a person pack into a single lifetime? The project 'Self-portraits with Men' is an extension of Dita Pepe's famous 'Self-portraits', which began in 1999 – initially with Pepe taking pictures of herself standing in for other women in their own environments. In 2003, this developed into an ongoing project that shows Pepe partnered by different men she knew – again in their own social and cultural milieu and engaging in their hobbies or work. The next step was a matter of course: to photograph herself with strangers from various social strata. We are reminded of Cindy Sherman's autobiographical project, although Sherman's approach is different. Here, Pepe does not embody specific female identities, showing instead, with admirable chameleon-like ability, how we can adapt to different contexts, and how the faces we see may have the power to change our own face – or at least its image, unless these are regarded as one and the same thing. This can work synchronically and diachronically. That is to say, if the images are seen together, as a series, the first impression is that the image creates the face; seen individually, however, over an extended period of time, it becomes clear how it is possible to lead many different lives within a single life. In other words: be a different person just by changing the context. In this manner, the suffocation one may feel as we see Dita Pepe tirelessly changing roles, over and over again, can also be extremely liberating. Repetition, while underlining difference, alters the overall effect.

AA

p. 148
Milan, in 'Self-portraits with Men', 2002.
C-print, 43 × 43 cm

p. 150
Imraan, Ida, Ela, in 'Self-portraits with Men', 2011.
C-print, 43 × 43 cm

p. 151
Peta, in 'Self-portraits with Men', 2003.
C-print, 43 × 43 cm

p. 152
Jurgen, Ole, Cornelius, Ida, in 'Self-portraits with Men', 2011. C-print, 43 × 43 cm

Courtesy the artist

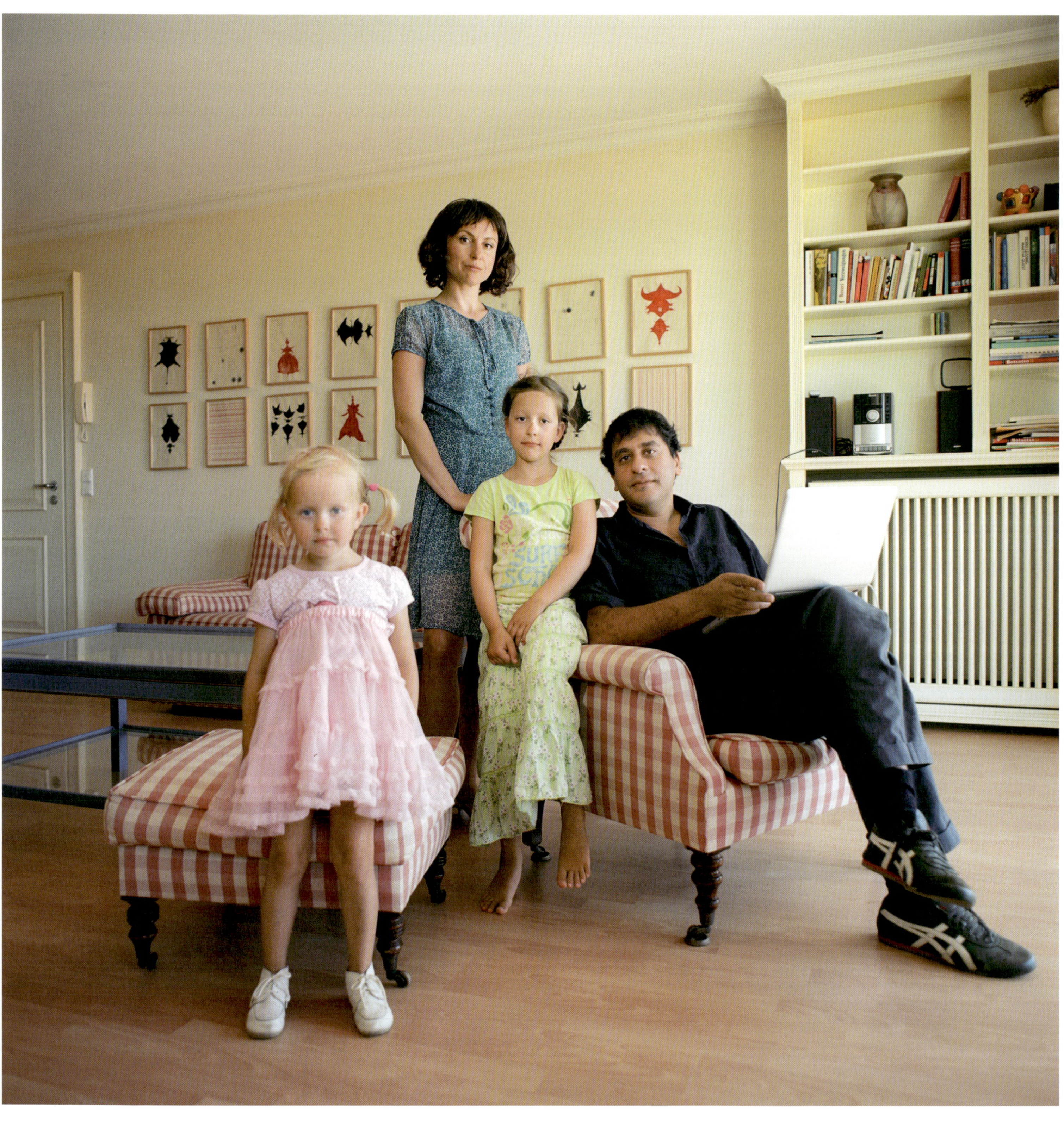

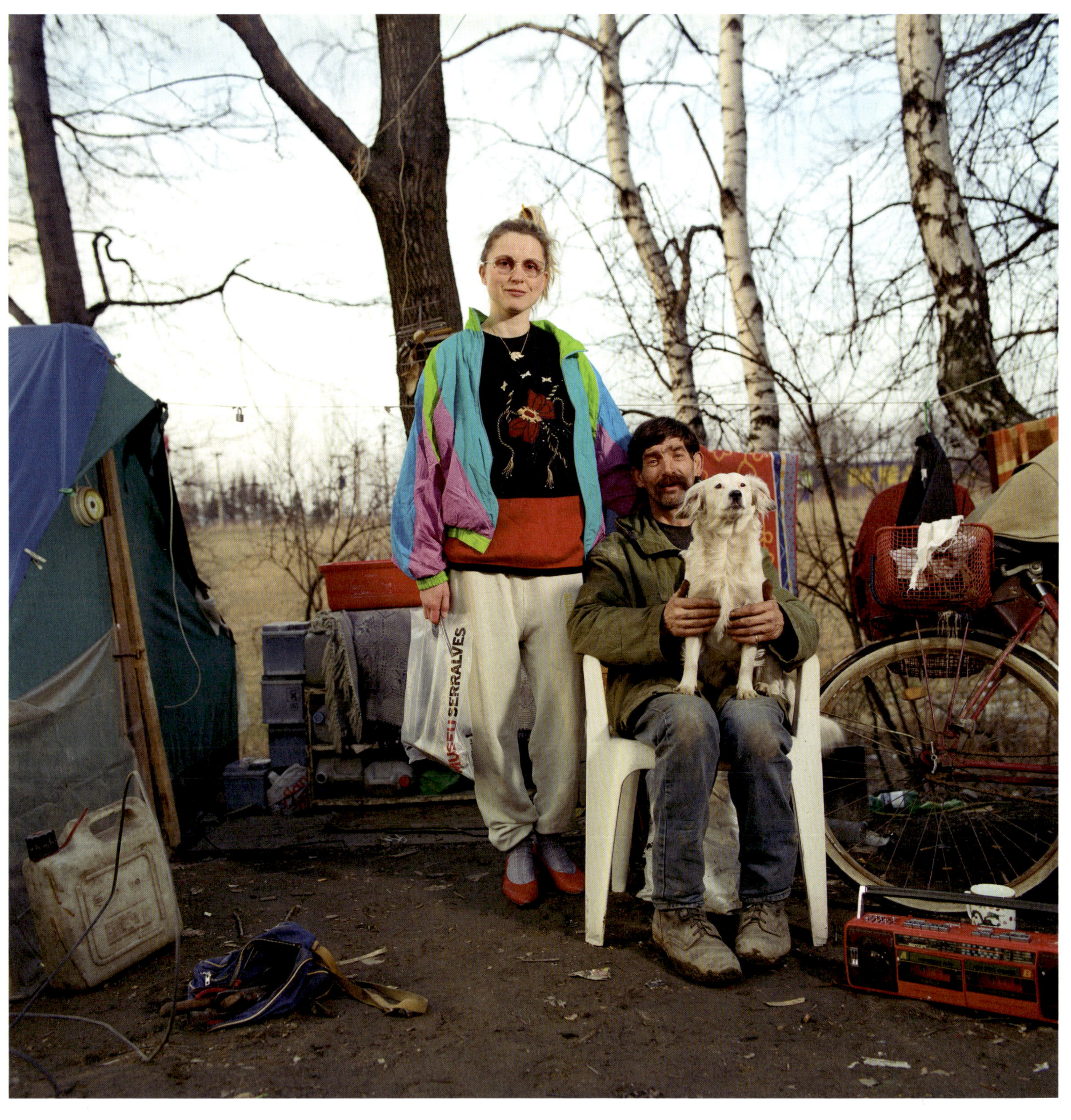

Dita Pepe

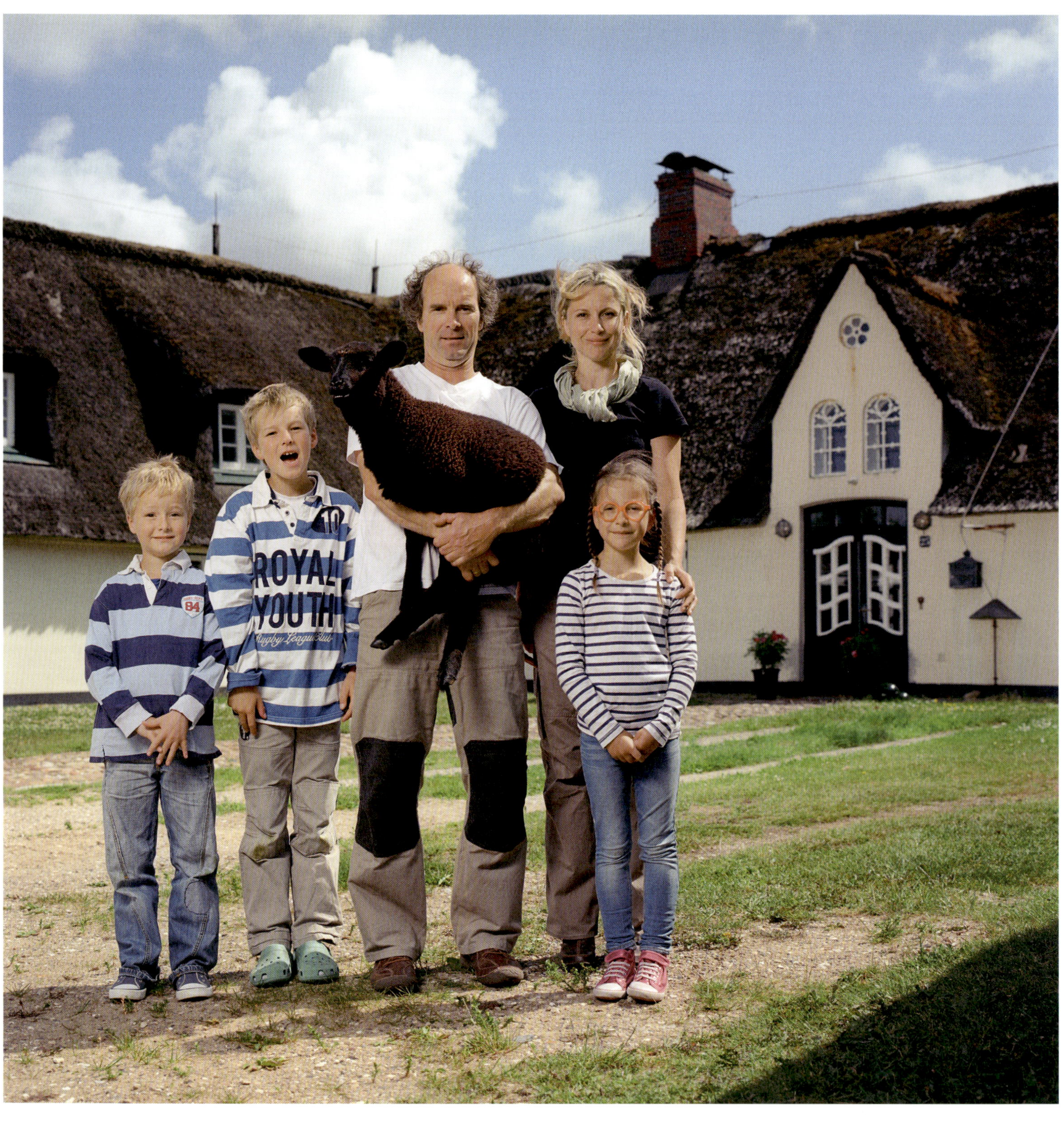

Anders Petersen (born 1944, Sweden)

Anders Petersen has been one of Europe's top photographers
ever since the 1970s, when he took his legendary rough and
intimate pictures in Café Lehmitz, a bar in Hamburg, Germany.
Actually, he regards the photography itself as secondary. What
matters to him is the encounter, immersing himself in different
realities and living with the people he portrays – regardless of
whether they are a motley crew at a sailors' pub in Hamburg,
prisoners, psychiatric patients or nursing home occupants.
Petersen has an intimate and personal documentary style in
black and white. He rarely used a flash during the first 30 years
of his career but now uses a camera with a built-in flash, which
he plays around with, as it were, by manipulating its duration
and scope with his finger. He does not slavishly follow any
particular method or style. He occasionally uses a Rolleiflex, a
'reflective camera with a slower process'. Petersen's series record
the human condition in all its chaos, mystery and loneliness,
but with an intense sensitivity that immediately demands attention for the way he portrays those on the margins of society. His
approach to the animal, the ugly and the banal creates a visual
dialogue. His pictures are encounters, often highly intimate and
close to his heart, and they say a great deal about the subject,
but also about the photographer. In addition to his exhibitions
and books, Petersen often conducts workshops, but claims not
to have a set technique. He says: 'I have no special method. You
have to be lucky and try to see where the light is and what is
about to happen before it happens.'

GP

p. 155
Rome 2005, 2005.
Digital fibre print, 90 × 60 cm

p. 155
Sunne / From Back Home 2009, 2009.
Digital fibre print, 90 × 60 cm

p. 155
Soho 2011, 2011.
Digital fibre print, 90 × 60 cm

p. 155
Stockholm 2001, 2001.
Digital fibre print, 90 × 60 cm

p. 156
St. Etienne 2005, 2005.
Digital fibre print, 90 × 60 cm

p. 157
Utrecht 2008, 2008.
Digital fibre print, 90 × 60 cm

p. 158
Copenhagen 2008, 2008.
Digital fibre print, 90 × 60 cm

p. 159
Rome 2005, 2005.
Digital fibre print, 90 × 60 cm

p. 160
Gap 2005, 2005.
Digital fibre print, 90 × 60 cm

p. 161
Soho 2011, 2011.
Digital fibre print, 90 × 60 cm

Courtesy Galerie VU, Paris

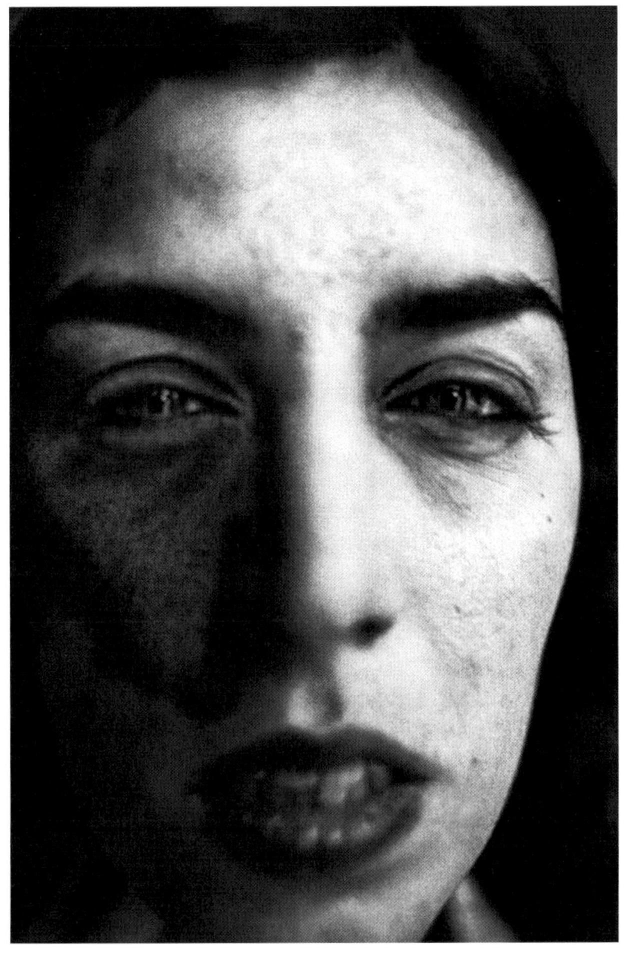
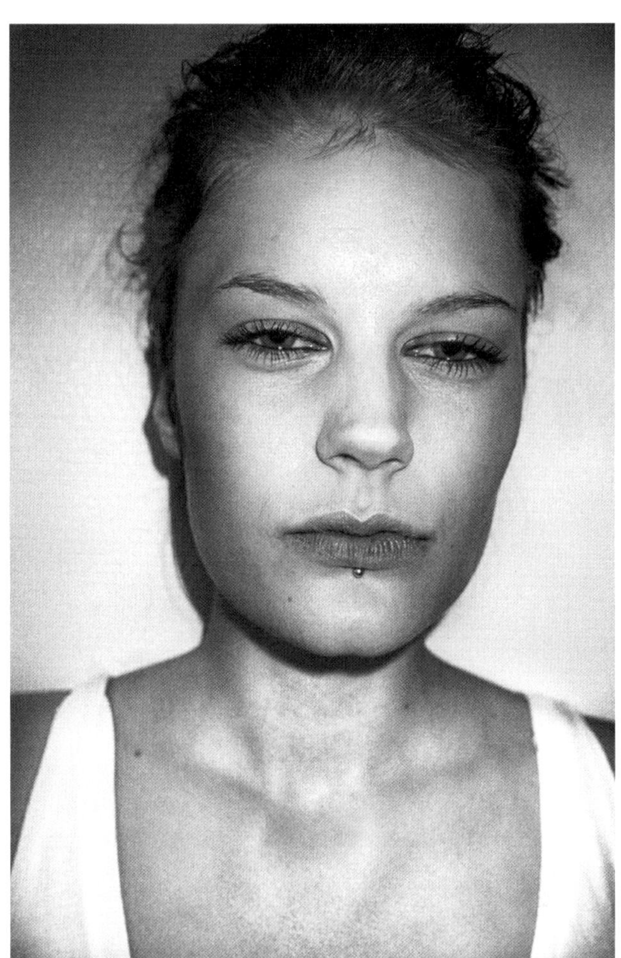
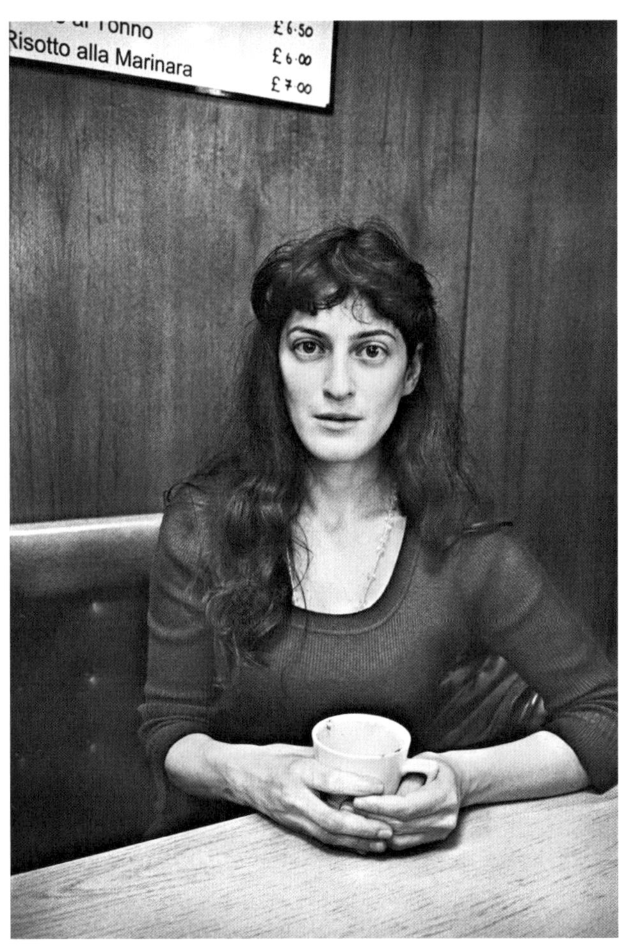

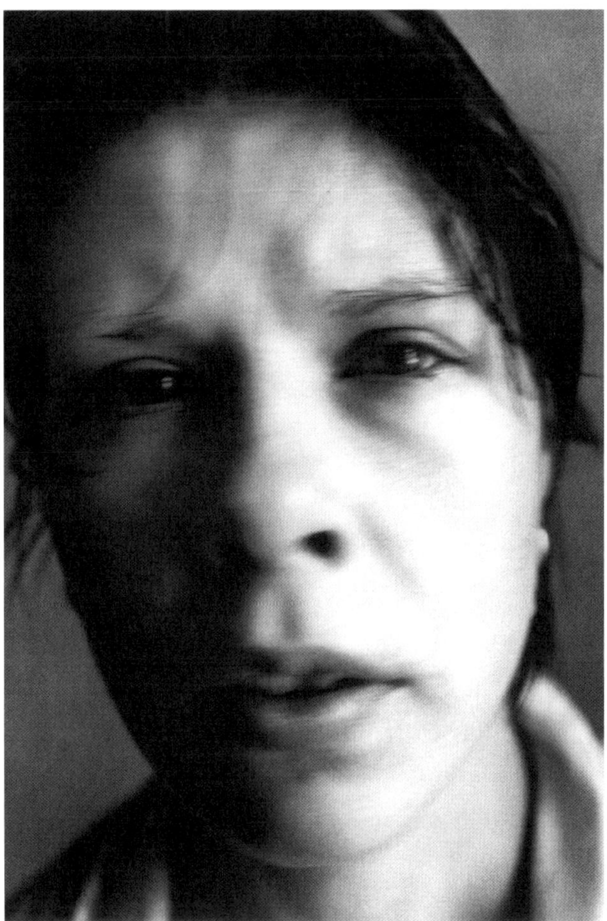

Anders Petersen

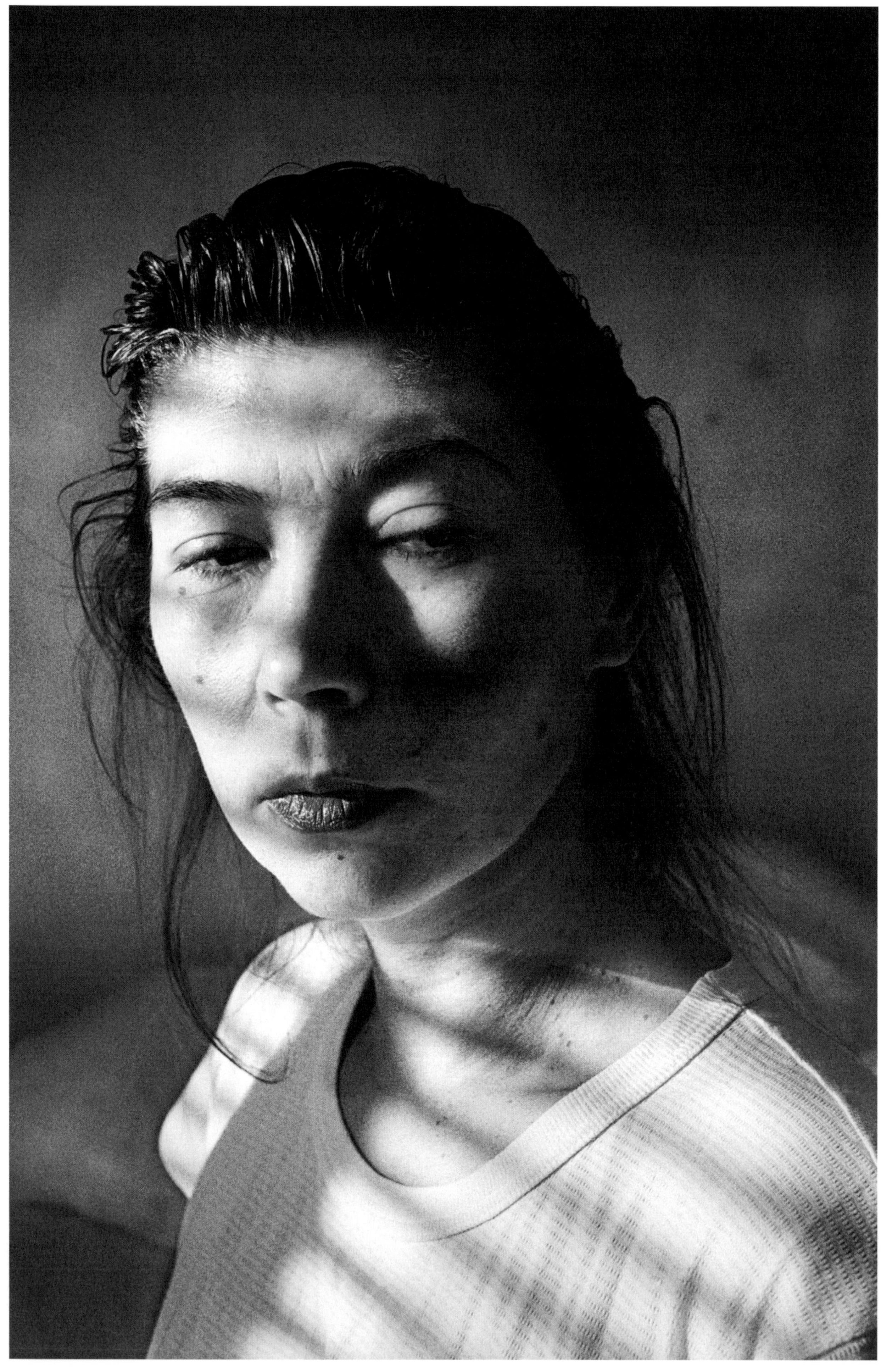

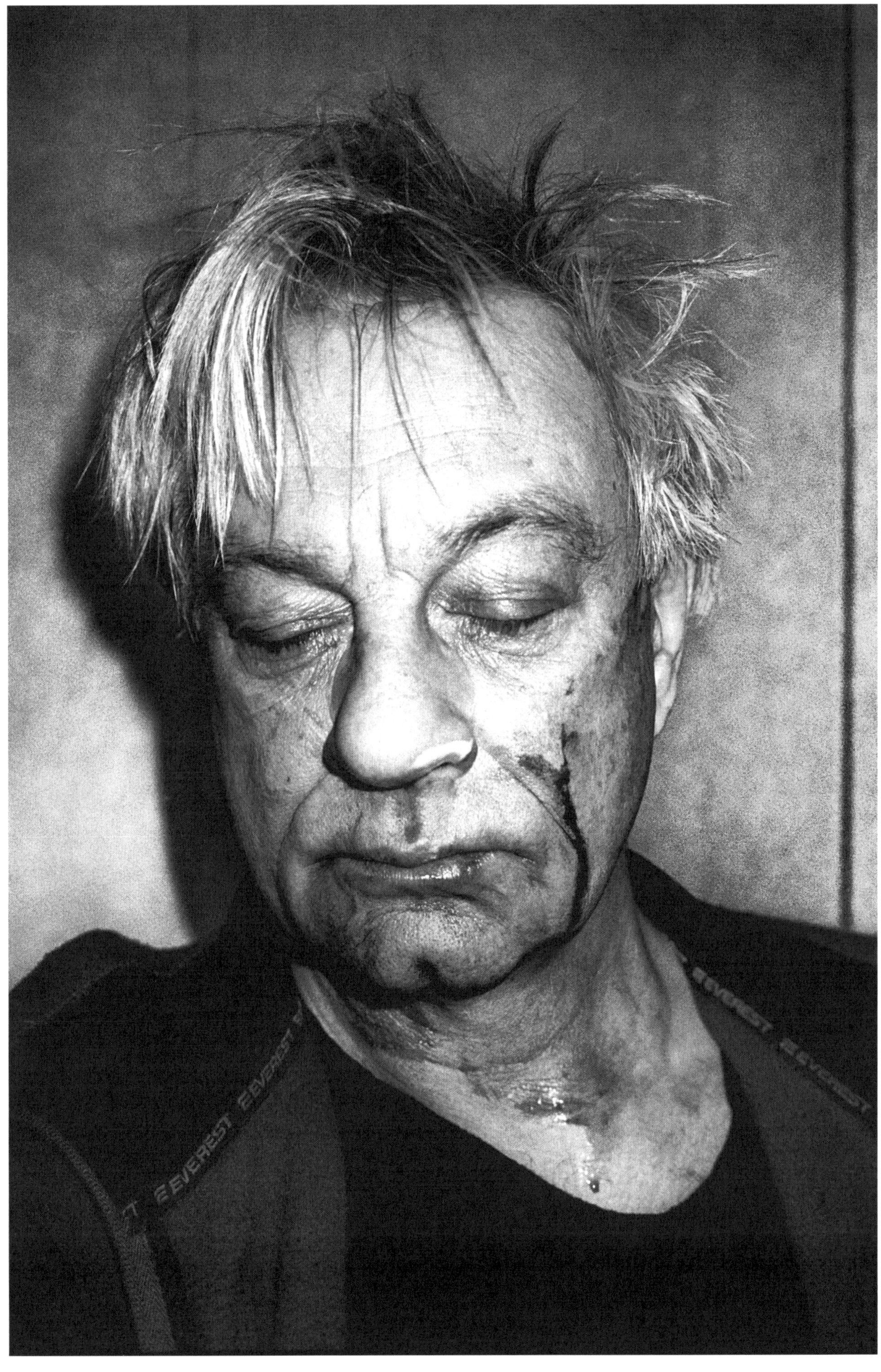

Anders Petersen

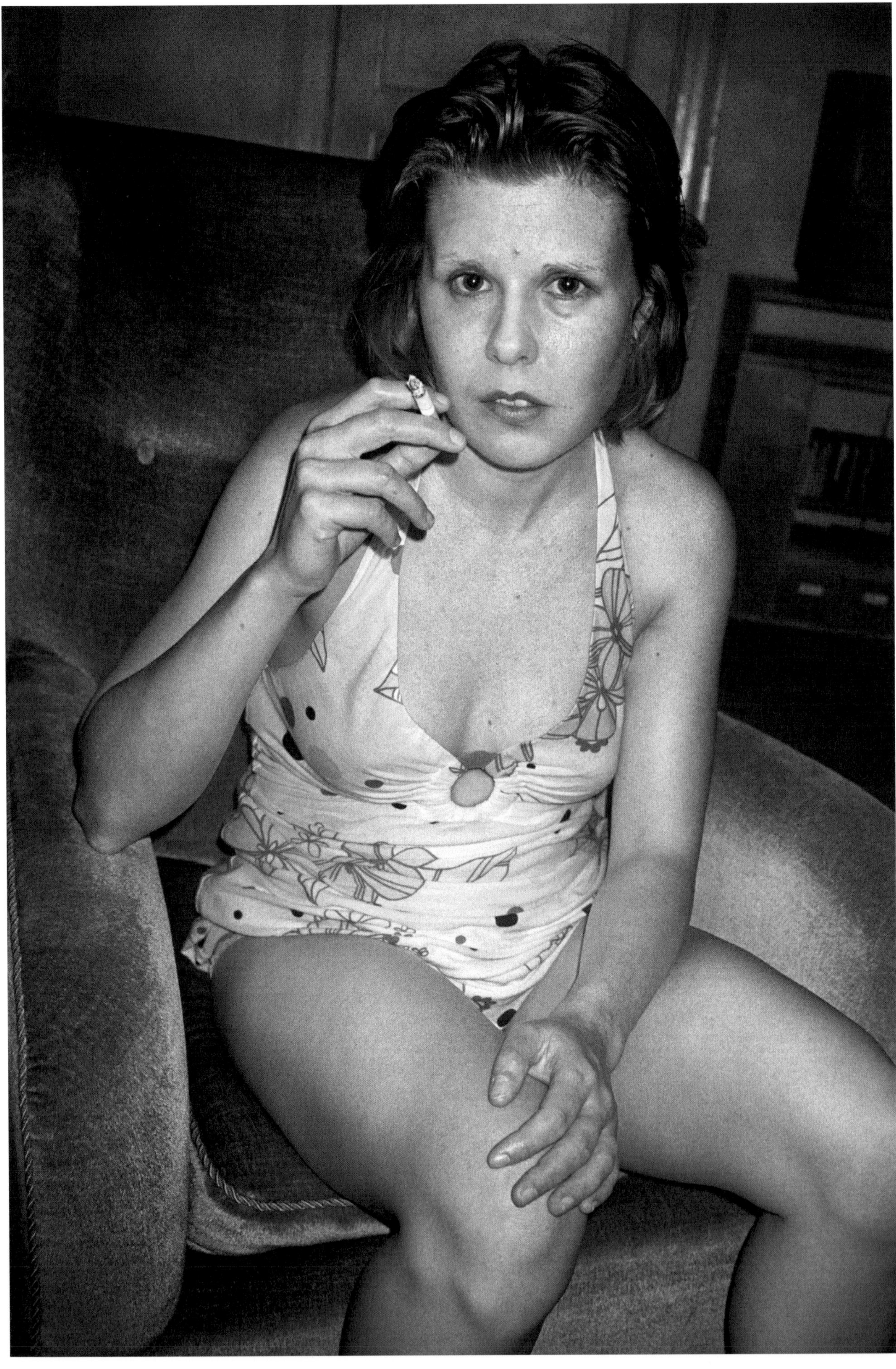

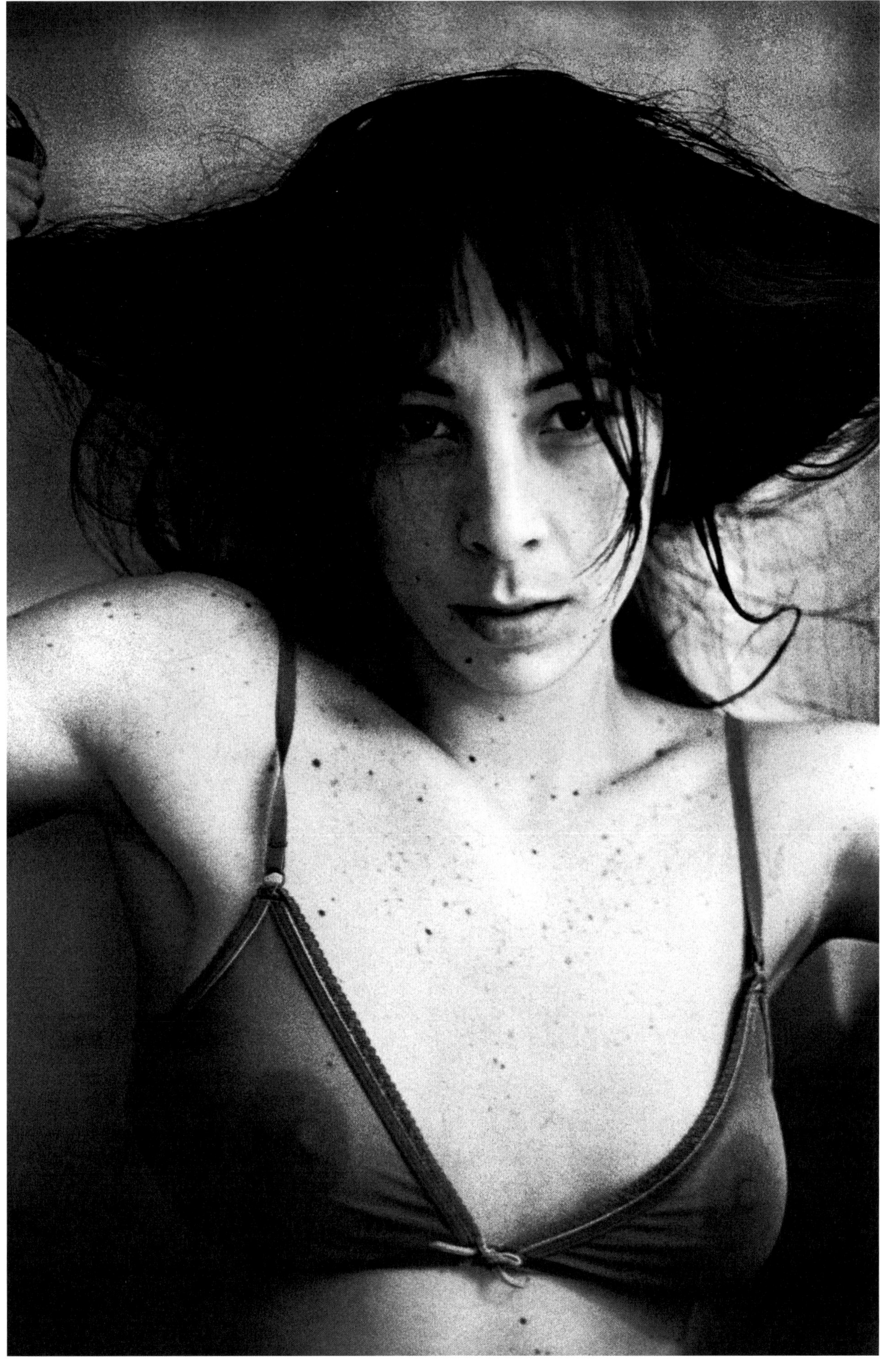

Anders Petersen

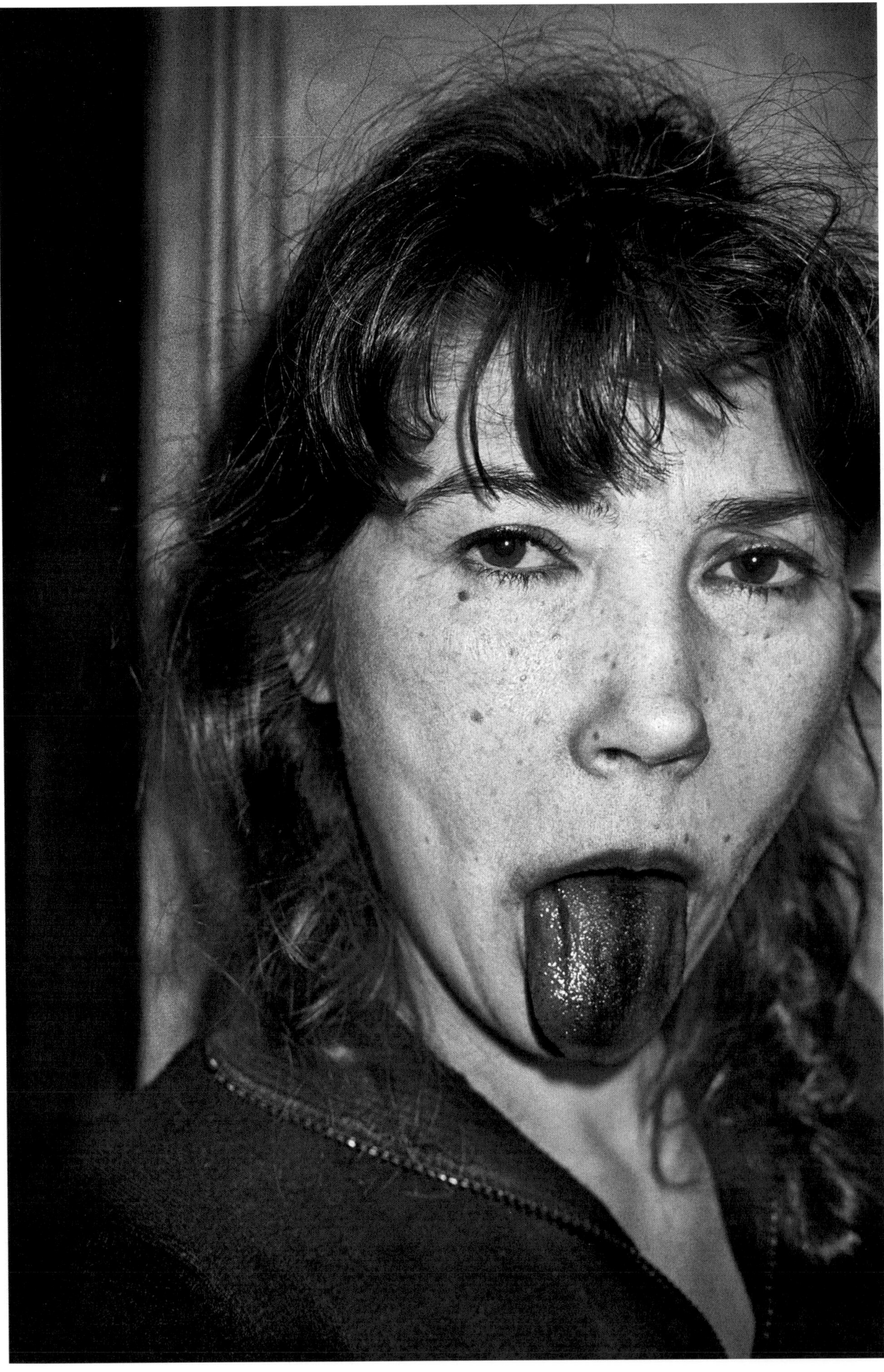

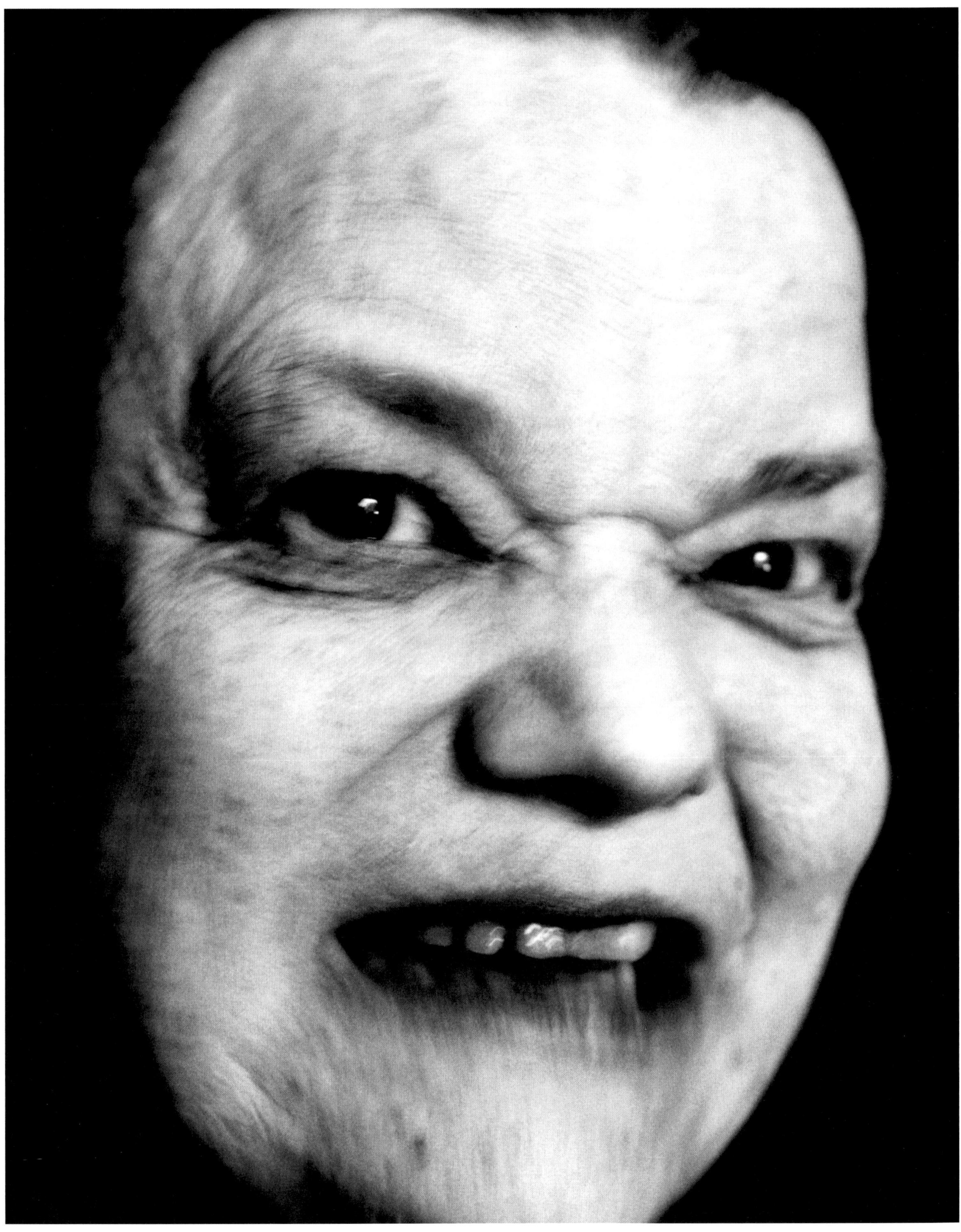

Anders Petersen

Jorma Puranen (born 1951, Finland)

Shadows, Reflections and All That Sort of Thing

There is a world of difference between painting and photography,
yet both media are part of the same Western pictorial tradition,
including the portrait genre. In the course of the 19th century,
what had previously been the preserve of the elite came within
the reach of ordinary citizens, namely an affordable and portrait likeness, albeit not produced by an artist but by a studio
photographer. Portrait photographers continued to embroider
on the artistic portrait tradition, which had taken shape at the
time of the Renaissance. Although 20th-century photographers
considerably extended the range of stylistic possibilities, each
portrait was and still is – partly as a result of the momentary
nature of photography – essentially the result of the relationship
between maker and model and between beholder and portrait
(and, indirectly, the person portrayed). However, in his series of
photographs *Shadows, Reflections and All That Sort of Thing*, Jorma
Puranen rides roughshod over this relationship by photographing, among other things, 17th-century painted portraits from
private museum collections. We see these paintings not only
reproduced as photographs, but also very 'subjectively' since
Puranen has intentionally transgressed all rules of 'correct' art
reproduction. In particular, the exposure with skimming light
ensures that we experience the paintings not as images but as
objects. The paint is clear matter, with a visible relief that stems
from the artist's brush strokes and the various layers of paint
applied to the canvas. Puranen has photographed the portraits
in a manner that also leaves the portrayed figure visible. In
many cases, there is 'eye contact' as the sitter looks at us straight
through the haze of the oblique incidence of daylight. Oddly
enough, despite that, or precisely because of it, the visual power
of the painting stays intact, possibly because the veil of light,
with its own aesthetic effects, is even more eye-catching. The art
of painting and the photography, the painting and the photograph remain visibly present and in focus as an image medium
and as an object; they do not disappear behind the illusionistic
nature of the picture. Puranen thus raises our awareness of the
intricate relationships that inevitably unfold via the chosen
medium between the makers, the viewers and those being
portrayed.

FG

p. 163
Shadows, Reflections and All That Sort of Thing 53, 2010.
Digital C-print, Diasec, 125 × 100 cm

p. 164
Shadows, Reflections and All That Sort of Thing 58, 2010.
Digital C-print, Diasec, 98 × 78 cm

p. 165
Shadows, Reflections and All That Sort of Thing 86, 2009.
Digital C-print, Diasec, 98 × 78 cm

p. 166
Shadows, Reflections and All That Sort of Thing 80, 2010.
Digital C-print, Diasec, 98 × 78 cm

p. 167
Shadows, Reflections and All That Sort of Thing 84, 2010.
Digital C-print, Diasec, 125 × 100 cm

Courtesy the artist

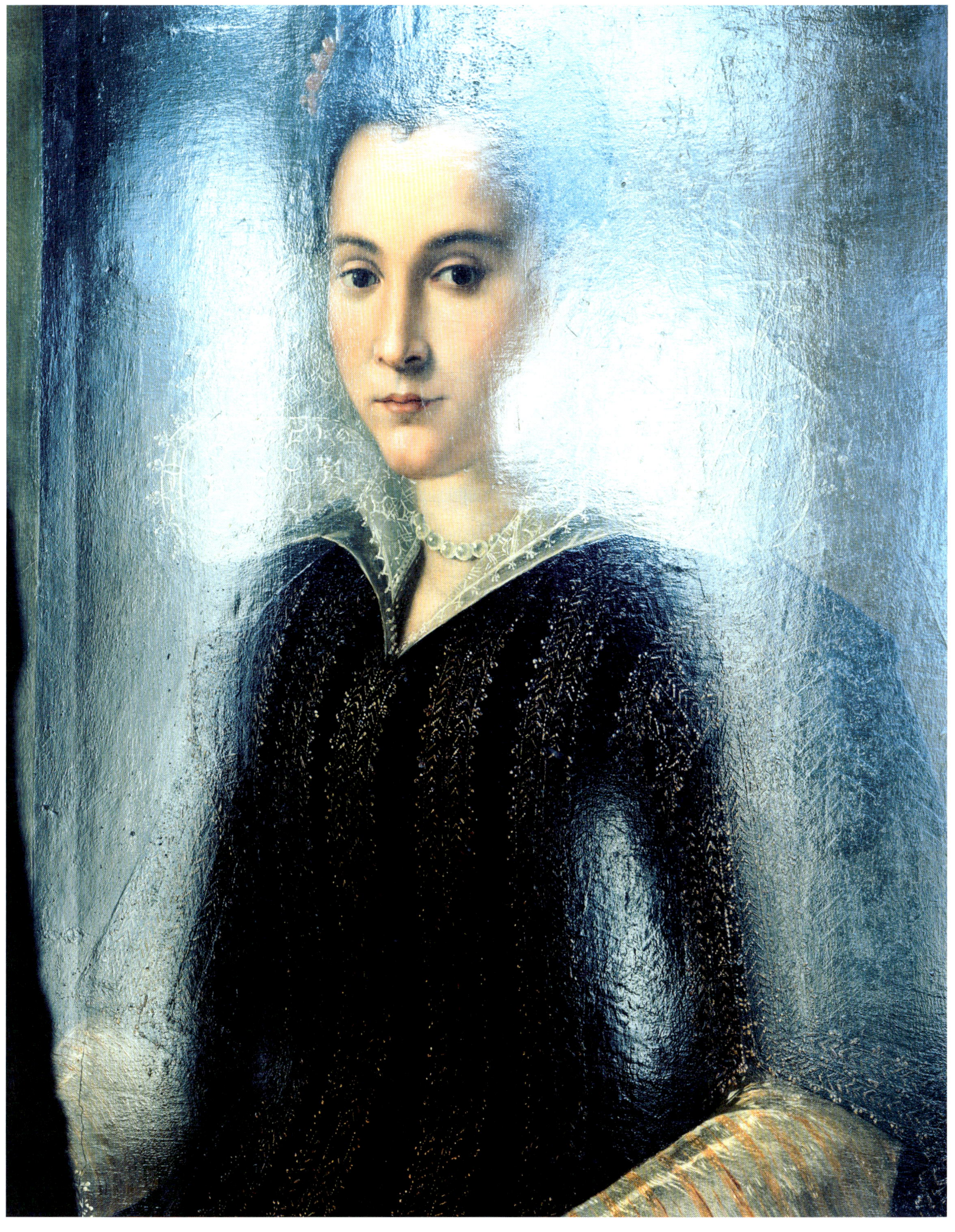

Jorma Puranen

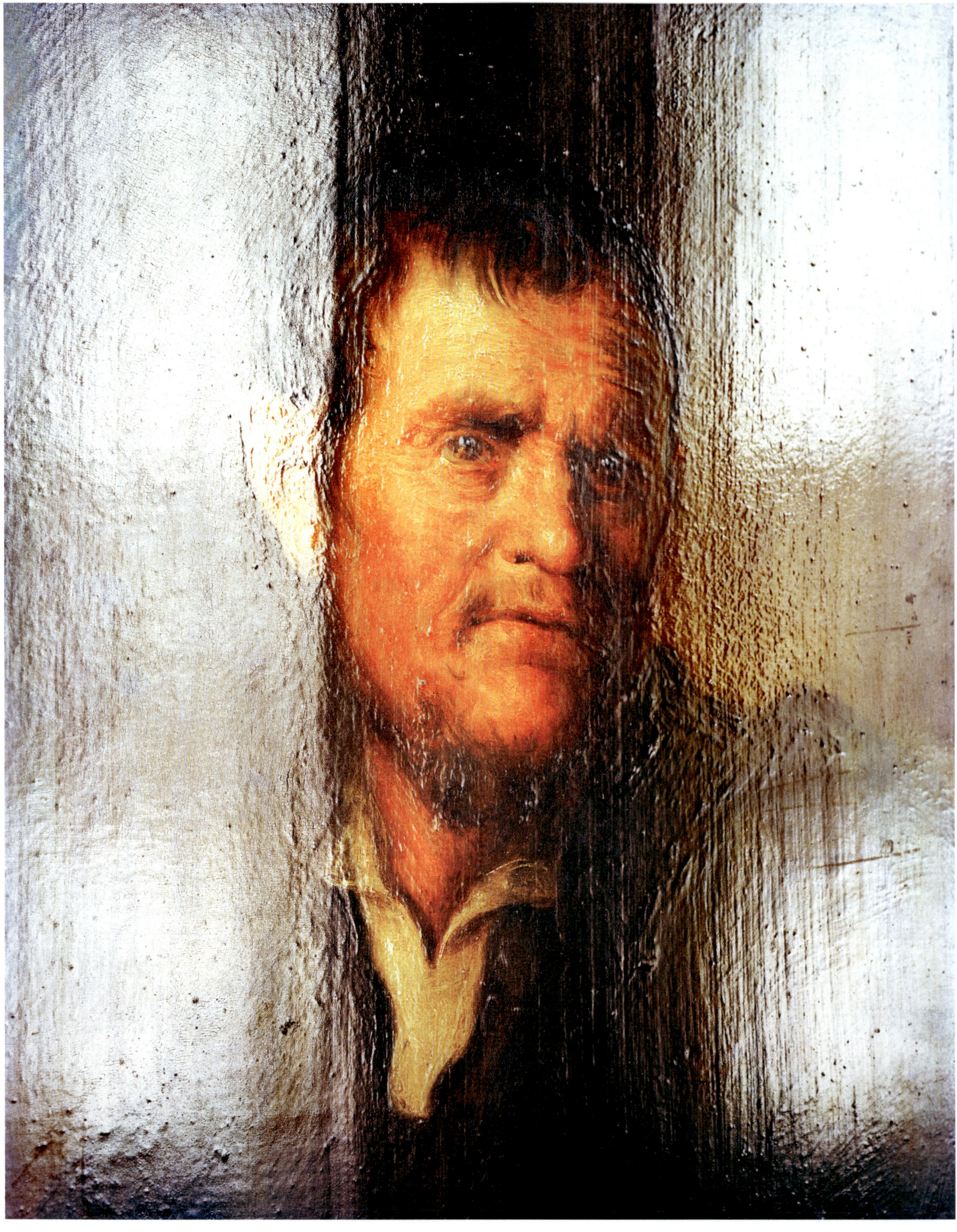

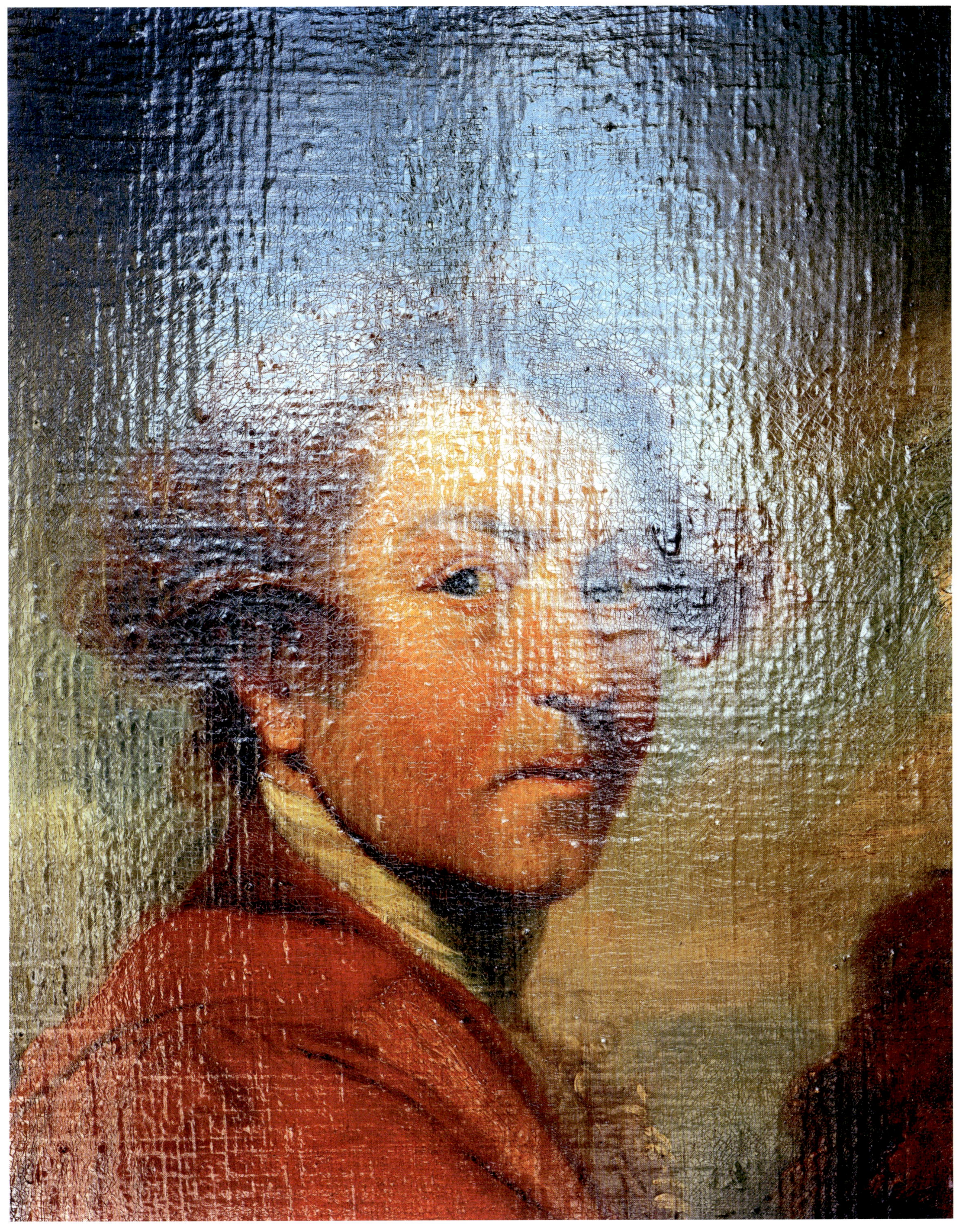

Jorma Puranen

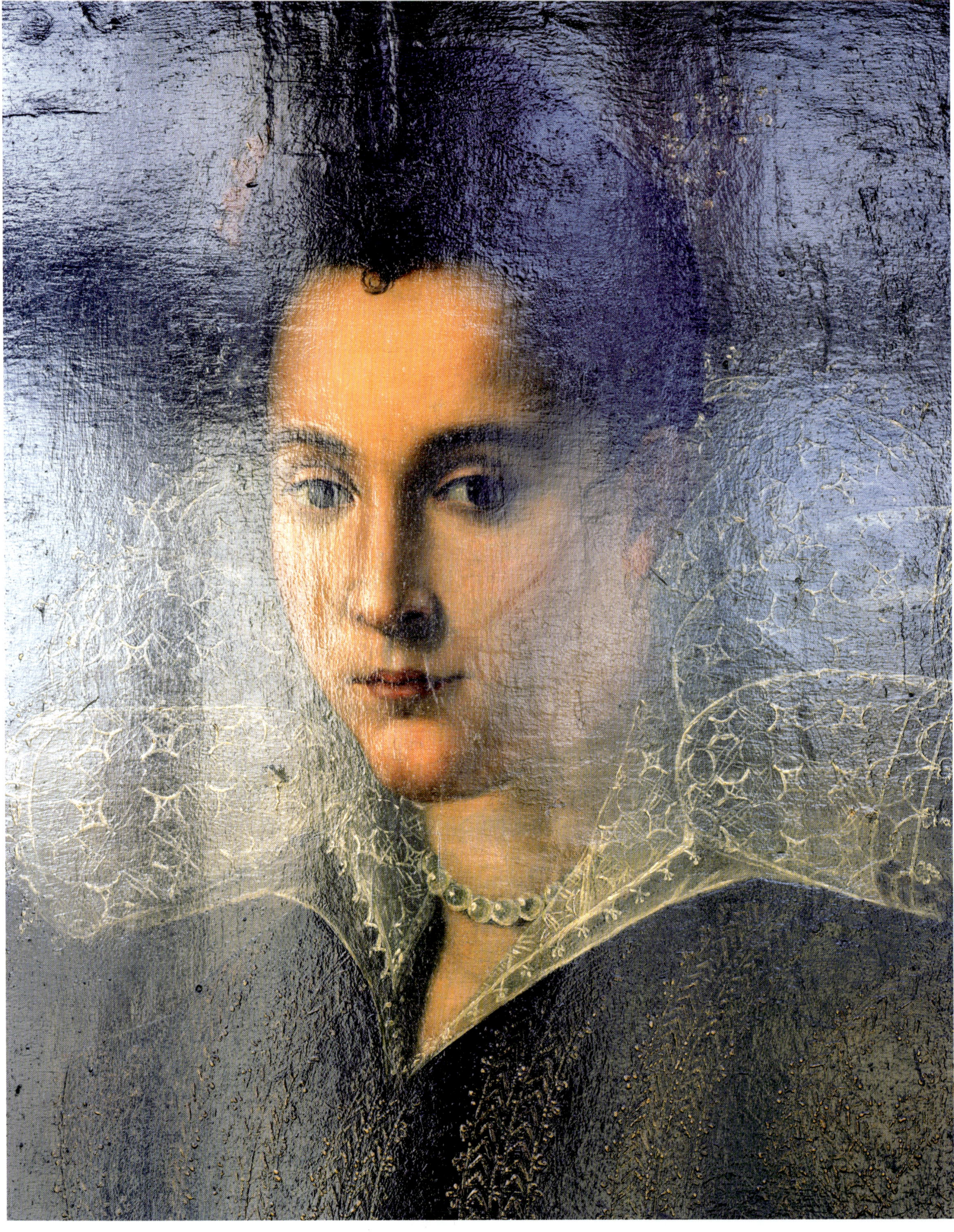

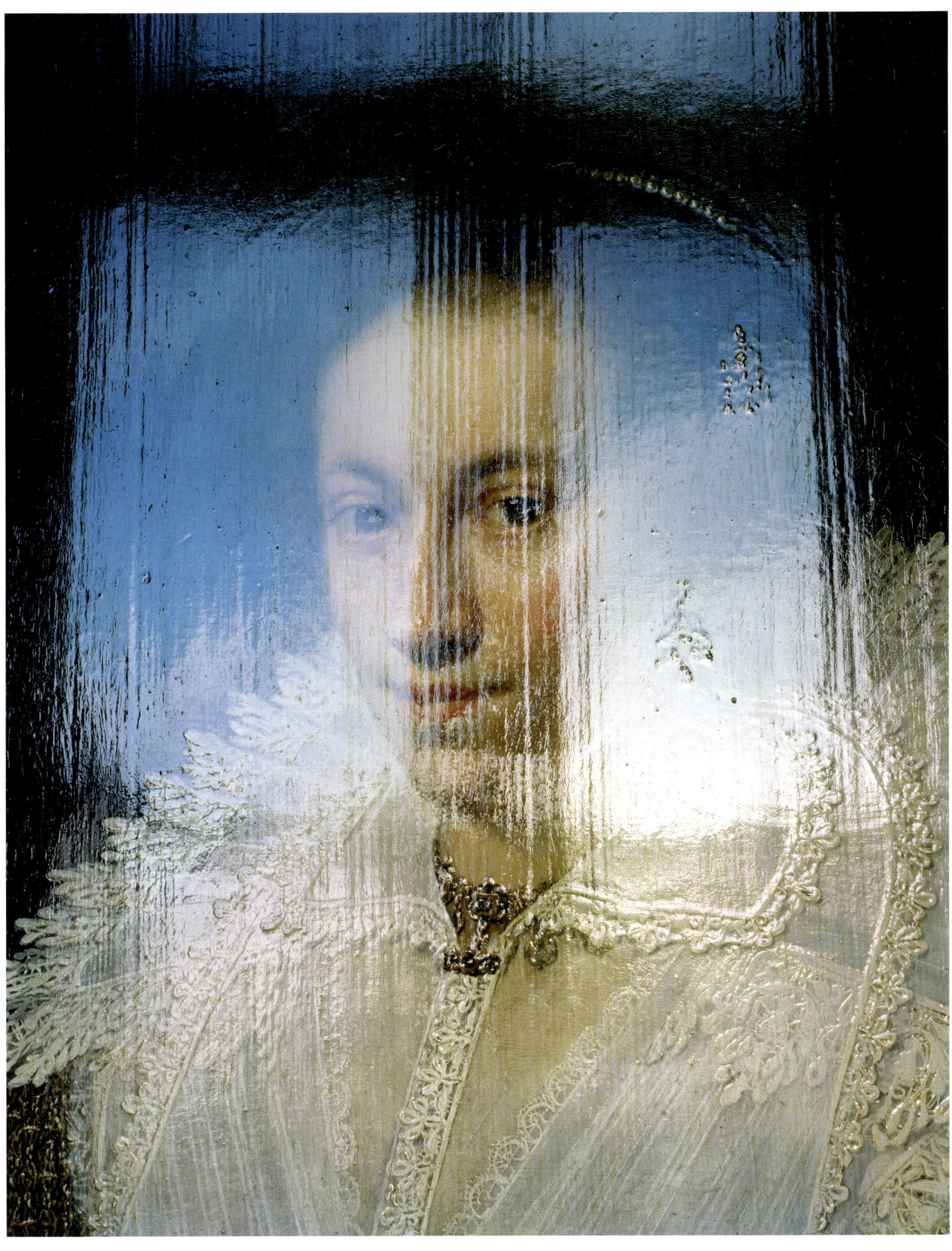

Jorma Puranen

Thomas Ruff (born 1958, Germany)

Thomas Ruff studied photography from 1977 to 1985 at the Düsseldorf Art Academy under the renowned photography couple Bernd and Hilla Becher. Andreas Gursky, Thomas Struth and Candida Höfer were fellow students at the time. In his student days, Ruff worked as an art director for a post-punk band, so the band members became the models for his first photographic experiments. At that time, he also worked on his renowned series of portraits. He researched the history of portraiture by experimenting with composition and framing. Ruff usually photographed his friends, all aged between 20 and 35. He asked them to show no facial expression or feeling and to be dressed in ordinary clothes as they sat down facing the camera against a neutral background, as if for passport photographs. The result was revolutionary. In 1986, Ruff decided to print these photographs in large size. The monumental images bring the viewer close to the real physical attributes of those portrayed; the pores, wrinkles and marks on their faces are all clearly visible. Whereas traditional portraiture would have us believe that we are standing face to face with the model, these images leave no doubt that each picture is explicitly a *photograph* of the person, a chemically treated sheet of paper with an image on it. With this series, Ruff stresses the objective and purely registration function of photography. From this point of view, any interpretations of the character or inner life of the person are 'merely' suppositions on the part of the beholder.

CDJ

p. 169
Portrait (Anna Giese), 1989.
Chromogenic print, 205 × 160 cm

p. 170
Portrait (Andrea Kachold), 1987.
Chromogenic print, 205 × 160 cm

p. 171
Portrait (Rupert Huber), 1988.
Chromogenic print, 205 × 160 cm

Courtesy the artist

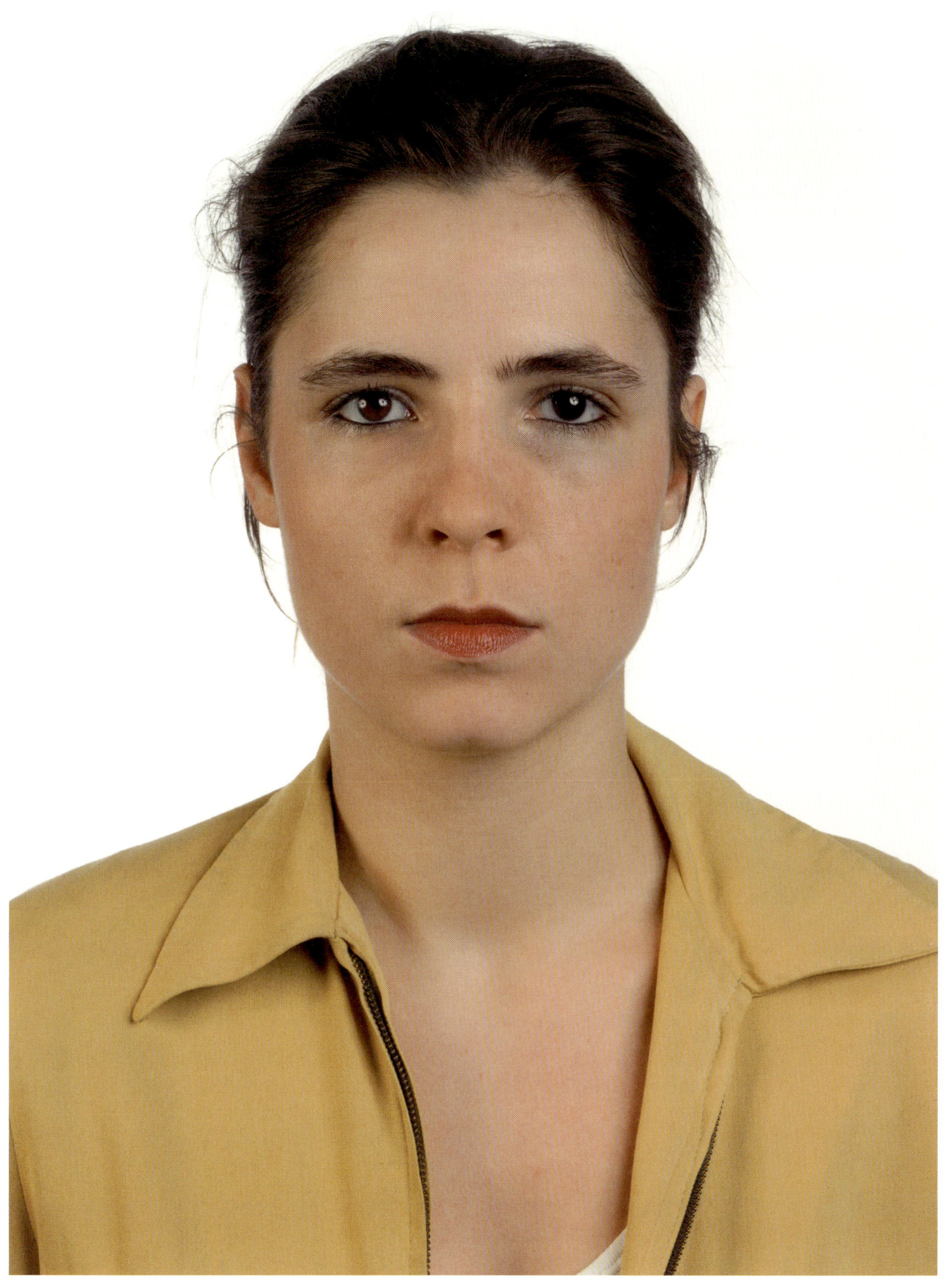

Thomas Ruff

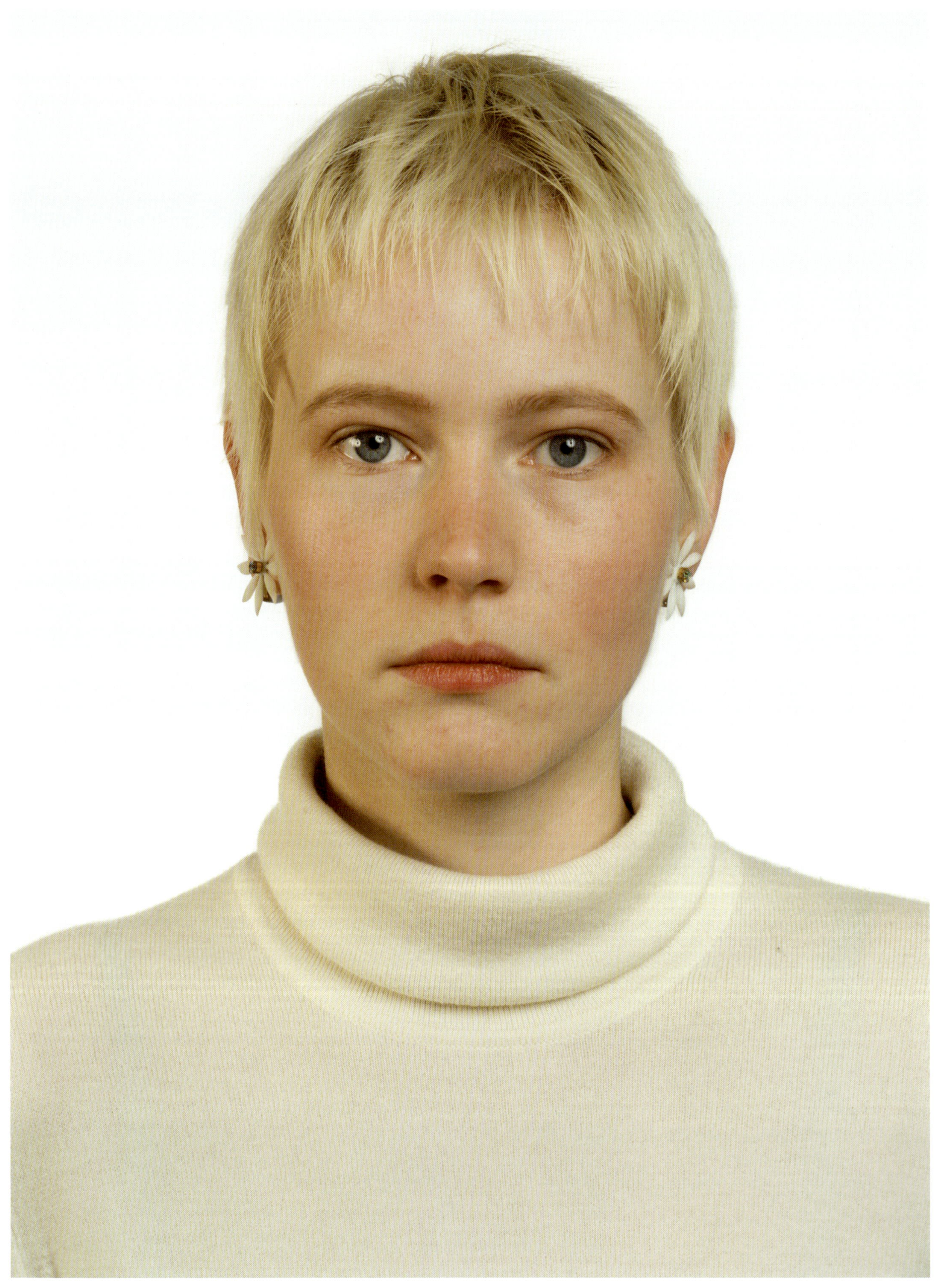

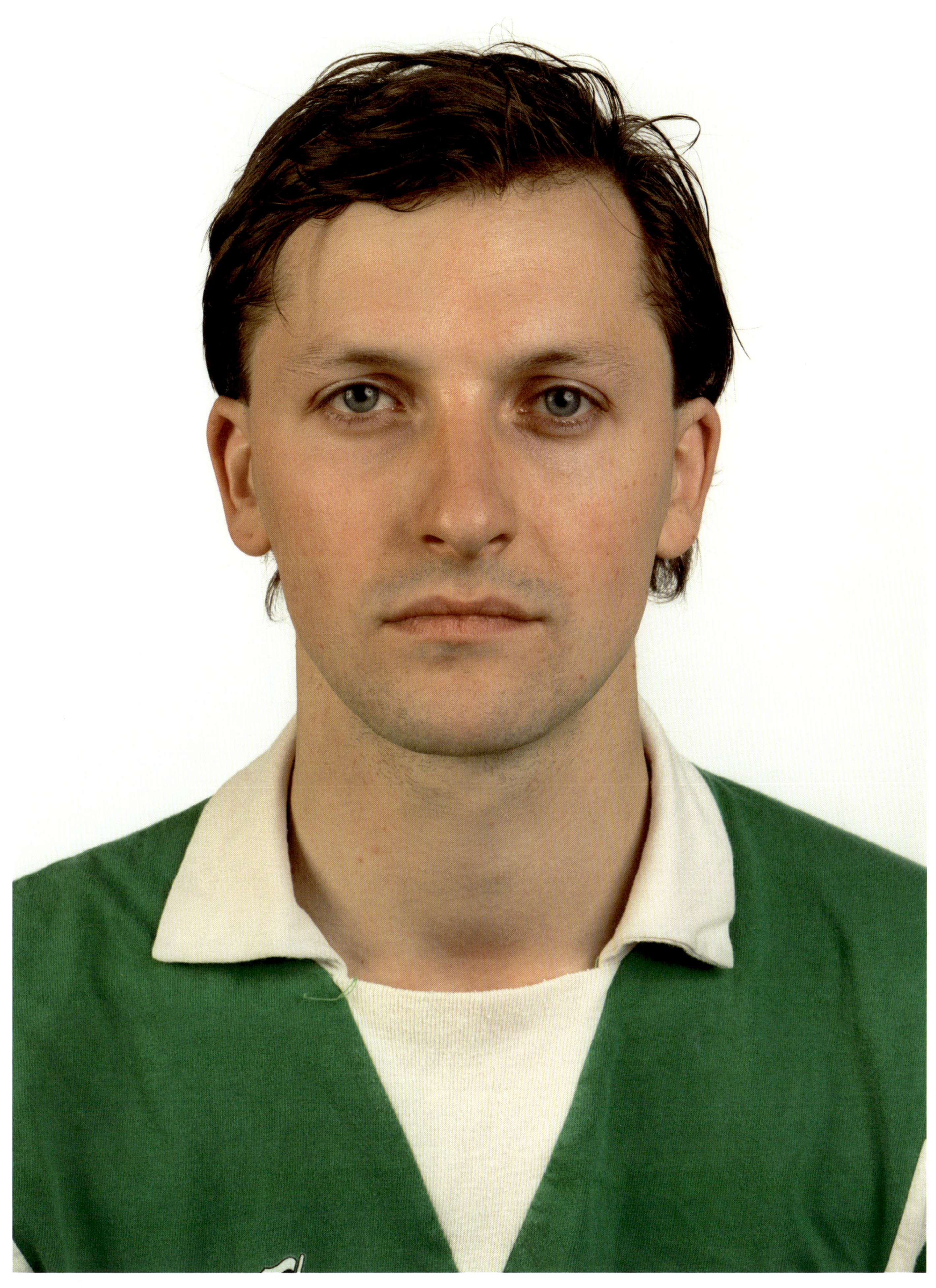

Thomas Ruff

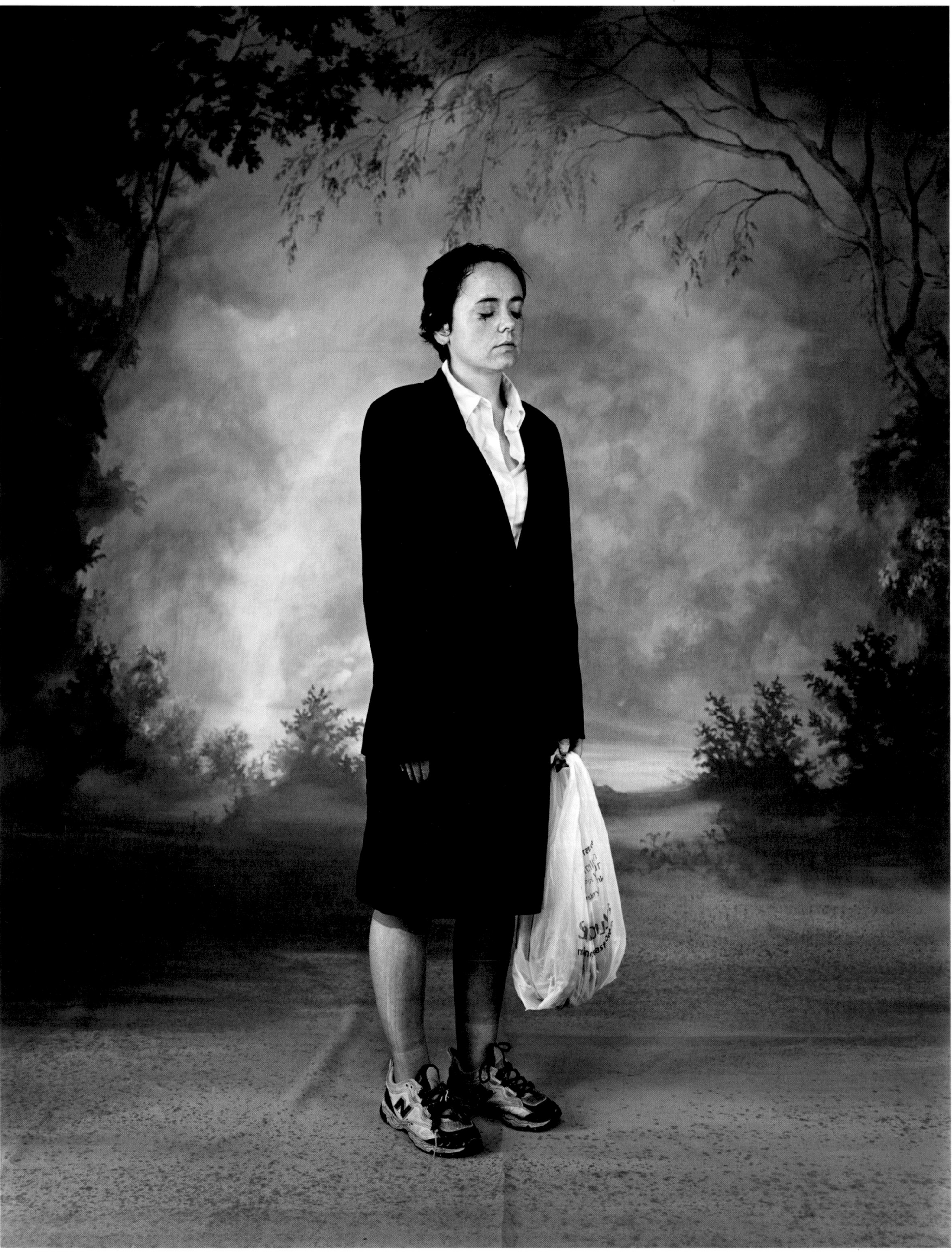

Clare Strand (born 1973, United Kingdom)

pp. 172–75
'Gone Astray Portraits', 2002–03.
Gelatin silver prints, 134.6 × 140.6 cm

Courtesy the artist and Camilla Gavin Gallery, London

Gone Astray Portraits

These pictures could be seen as the kind of mental images that
spring to mind when reading a Victorian novel, or rather, when
trying to direct a Victorian play in a contemporary manner, that
is to say, picturing situations and people from an earlier époque
into a modern context. People, or types of people, are more or
less the same in this 'theatre of the street where people collude'
– an idea from Dickens that inspired Clare Strand for her *Gone
Astray Portraits* (2002–03). Indeed, this project – which follows
her working practice and areas of interest, usually dealing with
death and frailty – has been formed out of her research (con-
ducted investigatively, out of curiosity and not necessarily aca-
demically), as well as literary references and her own writings.
Inspired by Clerkenwell, the southernmost part of the London
Borough of Islington, where Dickens set much of *Oliver Twist*,
Strand used material from city commentators and her own
personal diaries, also writing her own cryptic narrative, which
she and her partner would read to accompany the portraits.
Setting the date is the backdrop, which recalls a 19th-century
photographic studio featuring an Arcadian landscape. Repeated
throughout the entire series, it becomes neutral; the variety is
provided by the people portrayed. Or is it? These are people of
this day and age, but they bring with them something of the
weariness of an époque where even everydayness – trying to
make ends meet amid the squalor and poverty of life in the
streets of London – was a struggle. Is it perhaps still like that?
At times it seems that technology has indeed simplified life,
transportation, heating, hygiene – but not for all, and not at all
times. Are we still being Victorian, in the sense that we are being
hypocritical about our quality of life? And if we blur the 'then',
as indicated by the backdrop, and forget the 'now', as conveyed
by those portrayed, is it possible that what we are left with is an
atemporal despair? The title of the series interplays with the
works, leaving us to wonder whether we are the ones who have
'gone astray' or the portraits.

AA

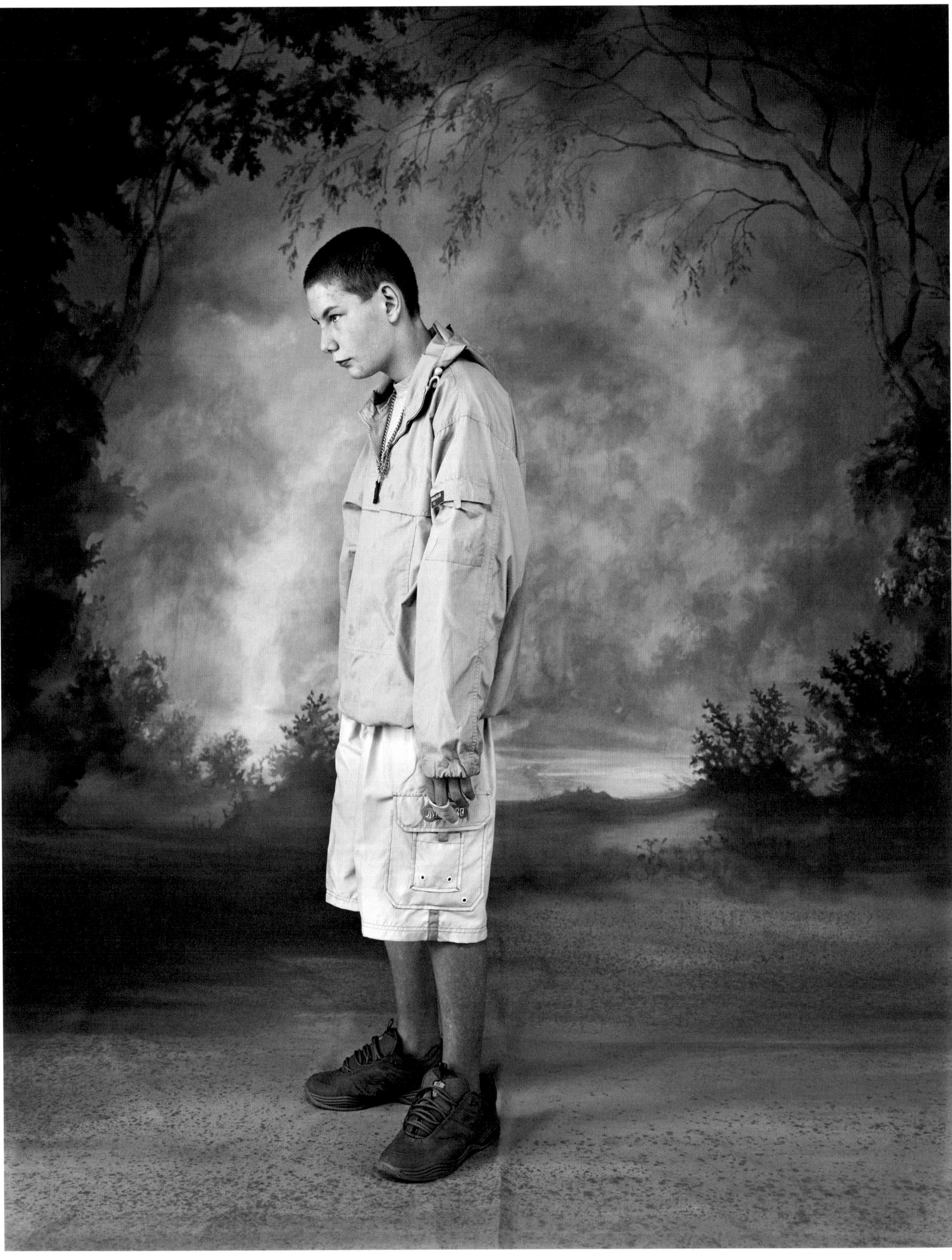

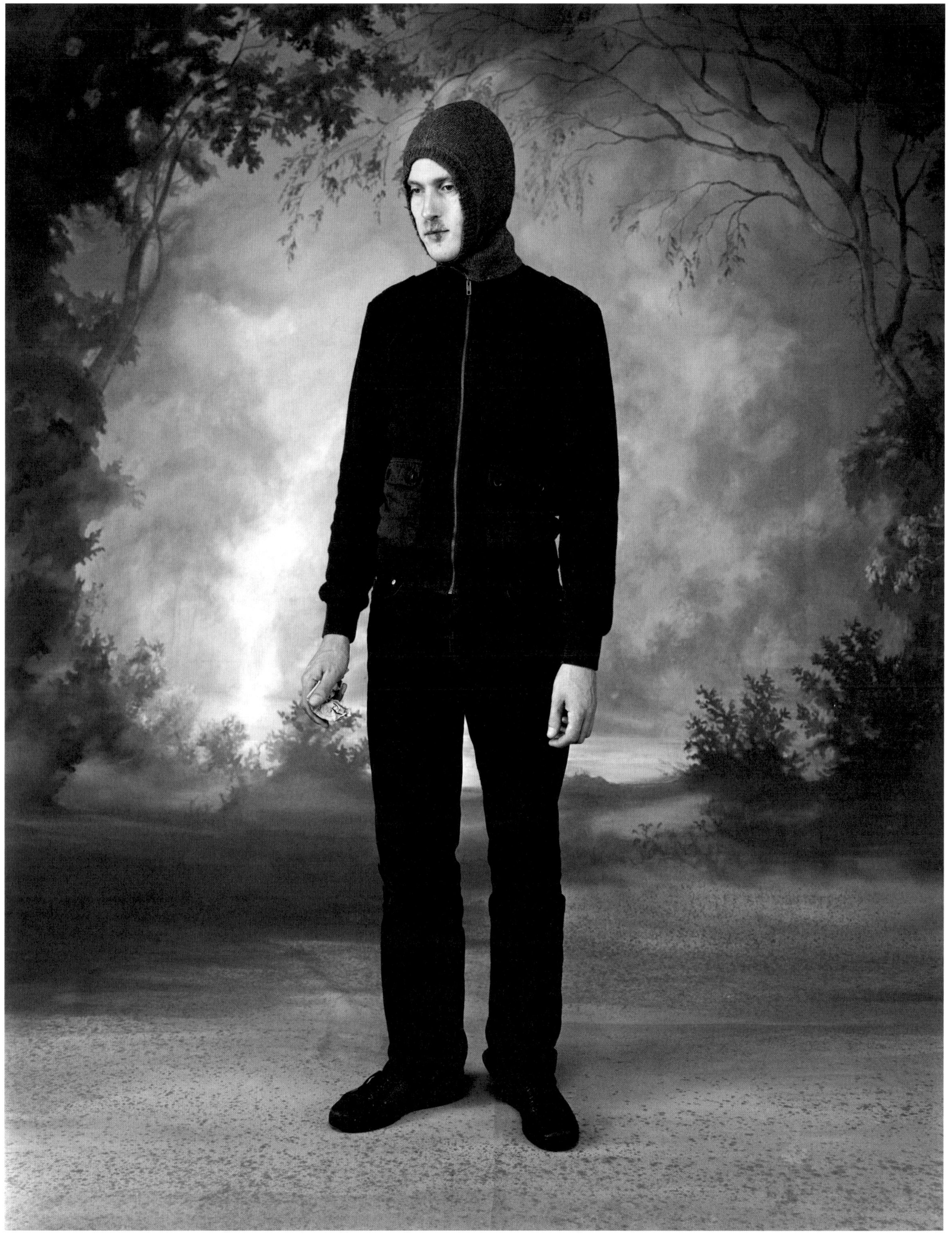

175   Clare Strand

Beat Streuli (born 1957, Switzerland)

pp. 177–79
'Bruxelles 05/06', 2007.
C-prints, mounted on Forex, 125 × 175 cm

Courtesy Galerie Conrads, Düsseldorf

Bruxelles 05/06

The heart of Beat Streuli's projects beats to the rhythm of life itself: portraits of everyday people on the street presented mostly as life-size images, or even larger, on billboards or in installations. That is the distinctive feature of his work, which sometimes encompasses a string of discussions about the relationship of photography to realism, to urban living and to cinema. The concept seems simple, yet in this simplicity lies all its strength: catching a glimpse of the particular, in this case a man or woman on the street of a metropolitan city, while alluding to the universal, to whatever is human, as expressed by each and every one of us, unknowingly, in our faces. This allows diverse readings of each iconic image, in the same way that we get various impressions of the people we see in the street. The photographs are rich and multilayered and can reflect any aspect the viewer chooses to focus on – social, political, aesthetic – because the viewer is confronted with what appear to be mirror images. However, these photographs do not reflect those viewing them, but prompt instead to reflect upon themselves. These mirror images seem to be endowed – in an almost natural, albeit well-calculated way – with different perspectives that have become one, in a single stroke, with an anonymous face in the street. The universal rests on the particular, proving once again that there is more to photography than just the symptom of the image. Streuli's works thus manage to reveal the complexity of this paradoxical union, allowing, if only for a short while, the power of the photographic to triumph over the narrative.

VI

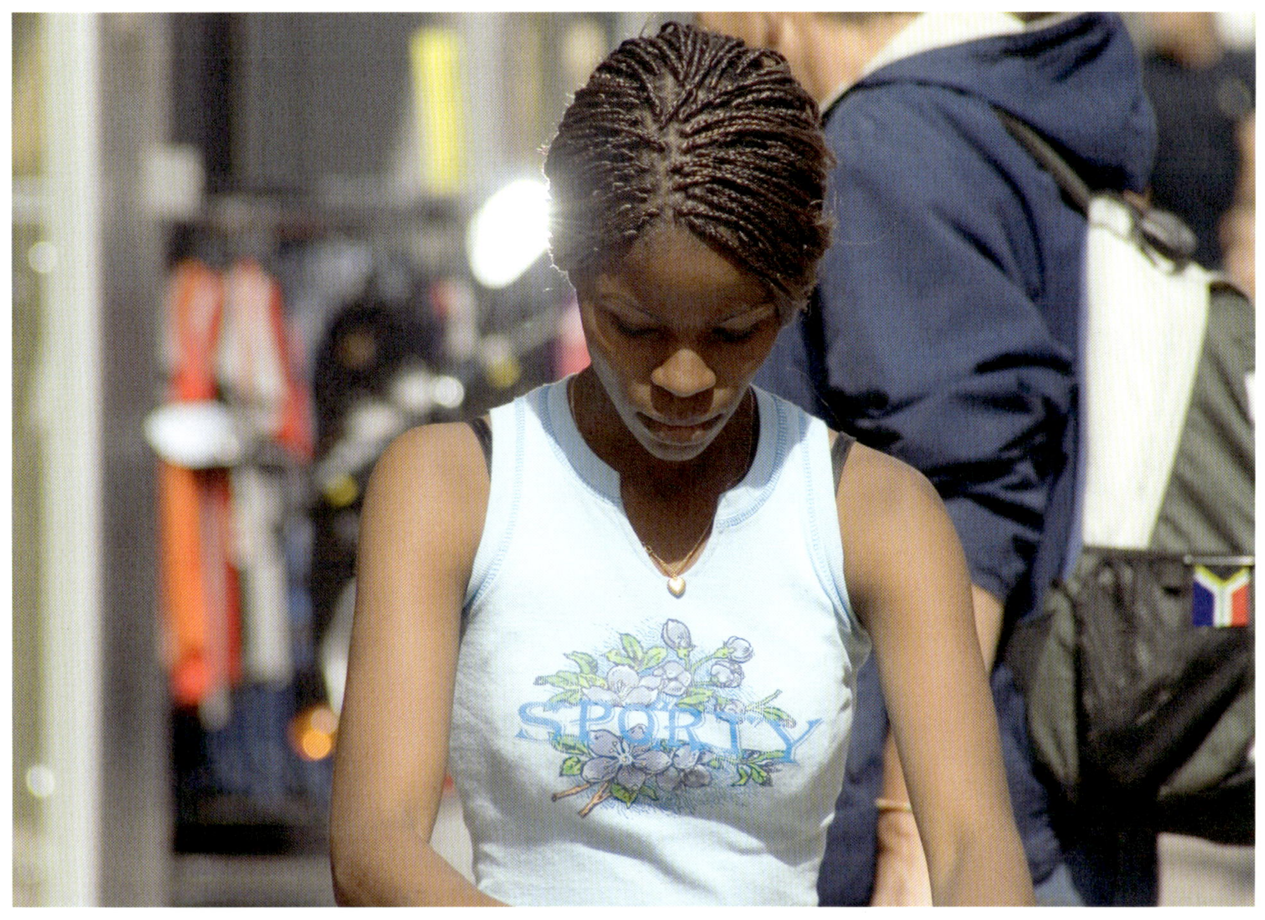

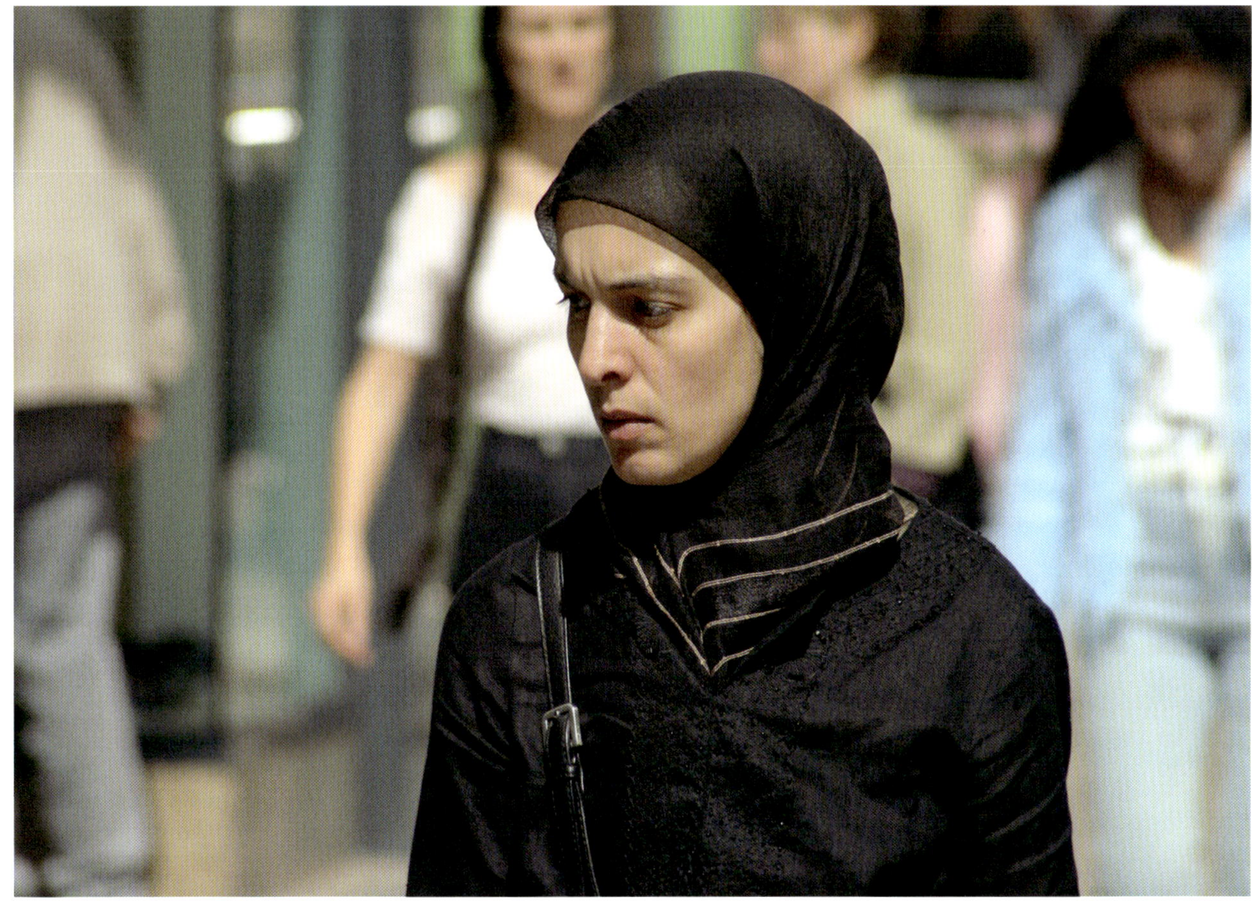

 Beat Streuli

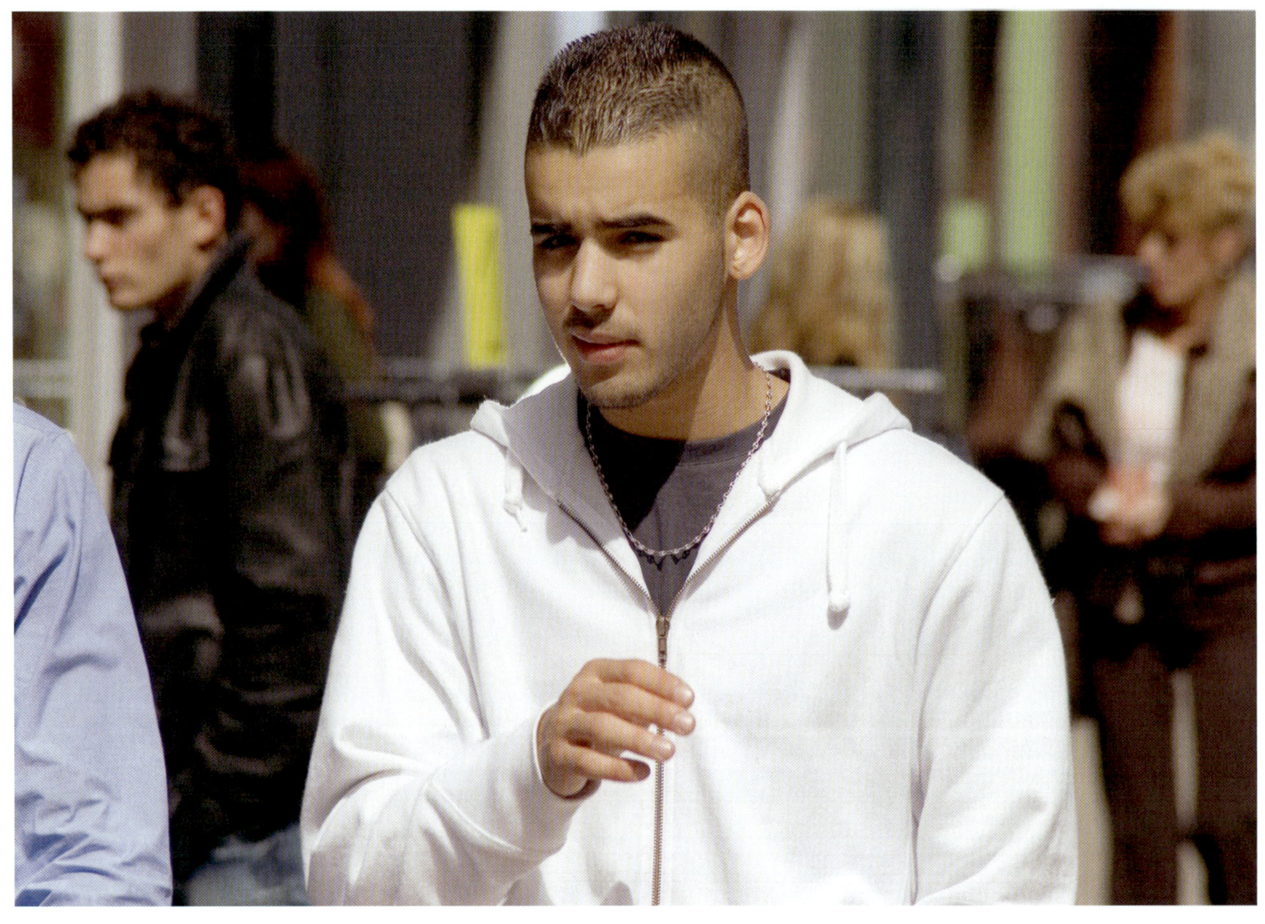

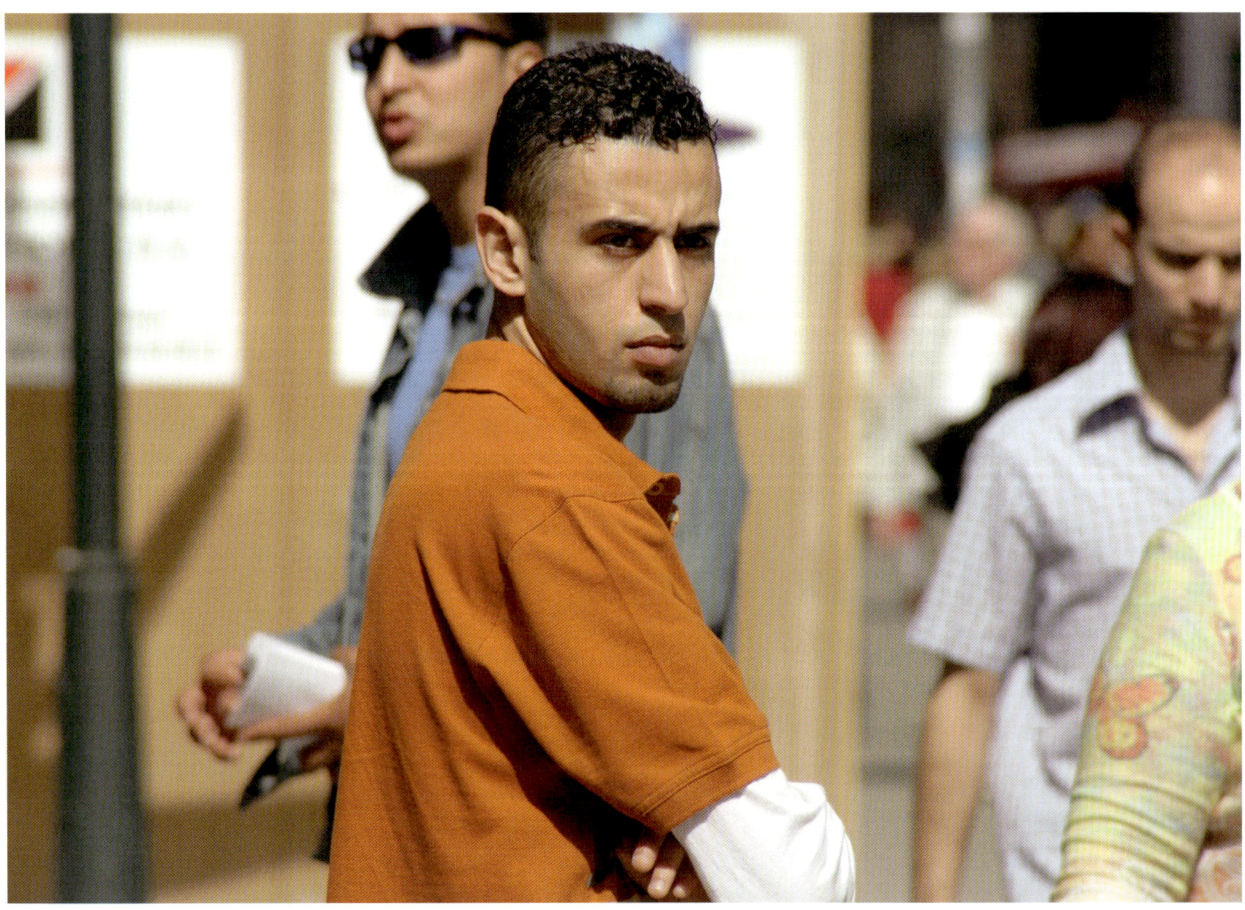

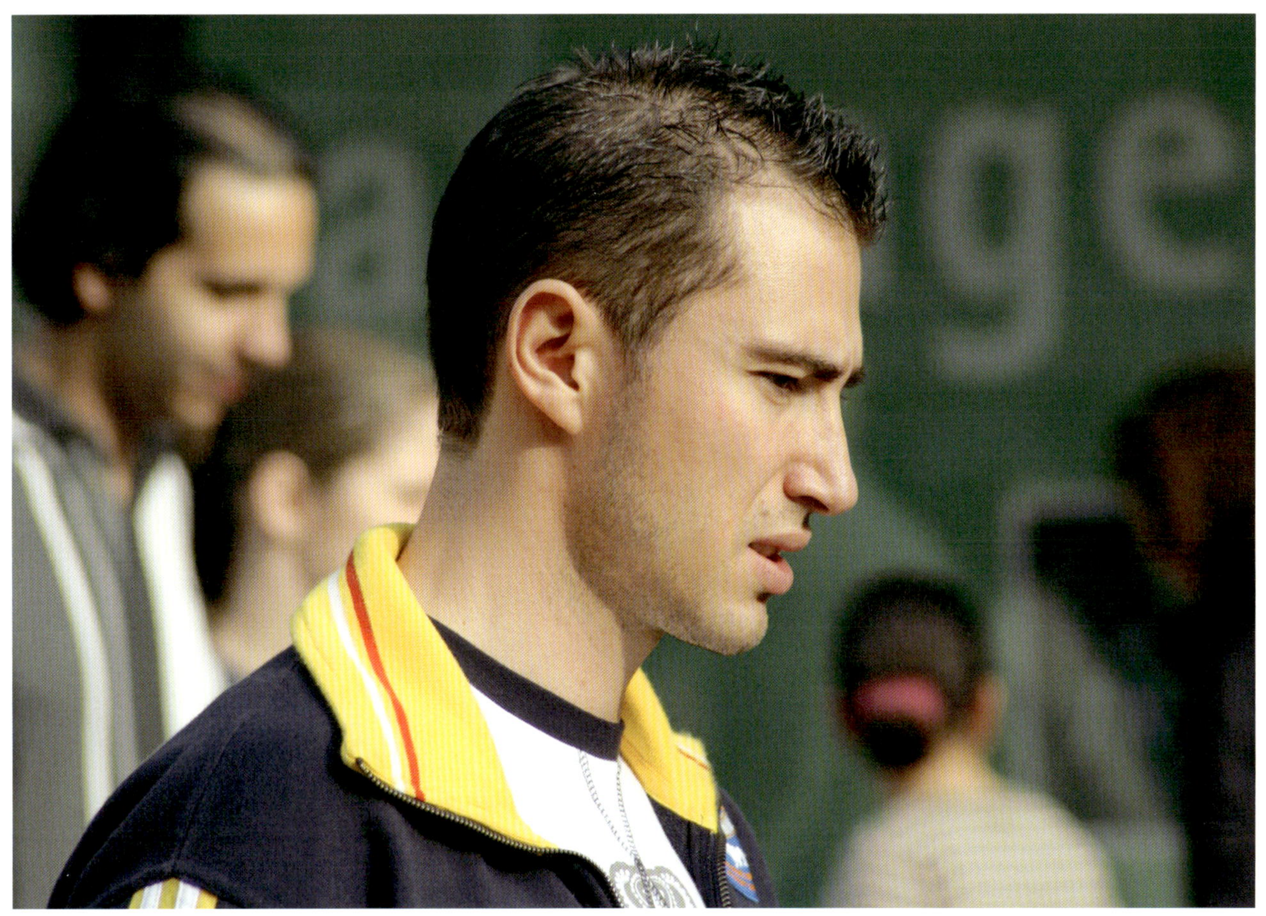

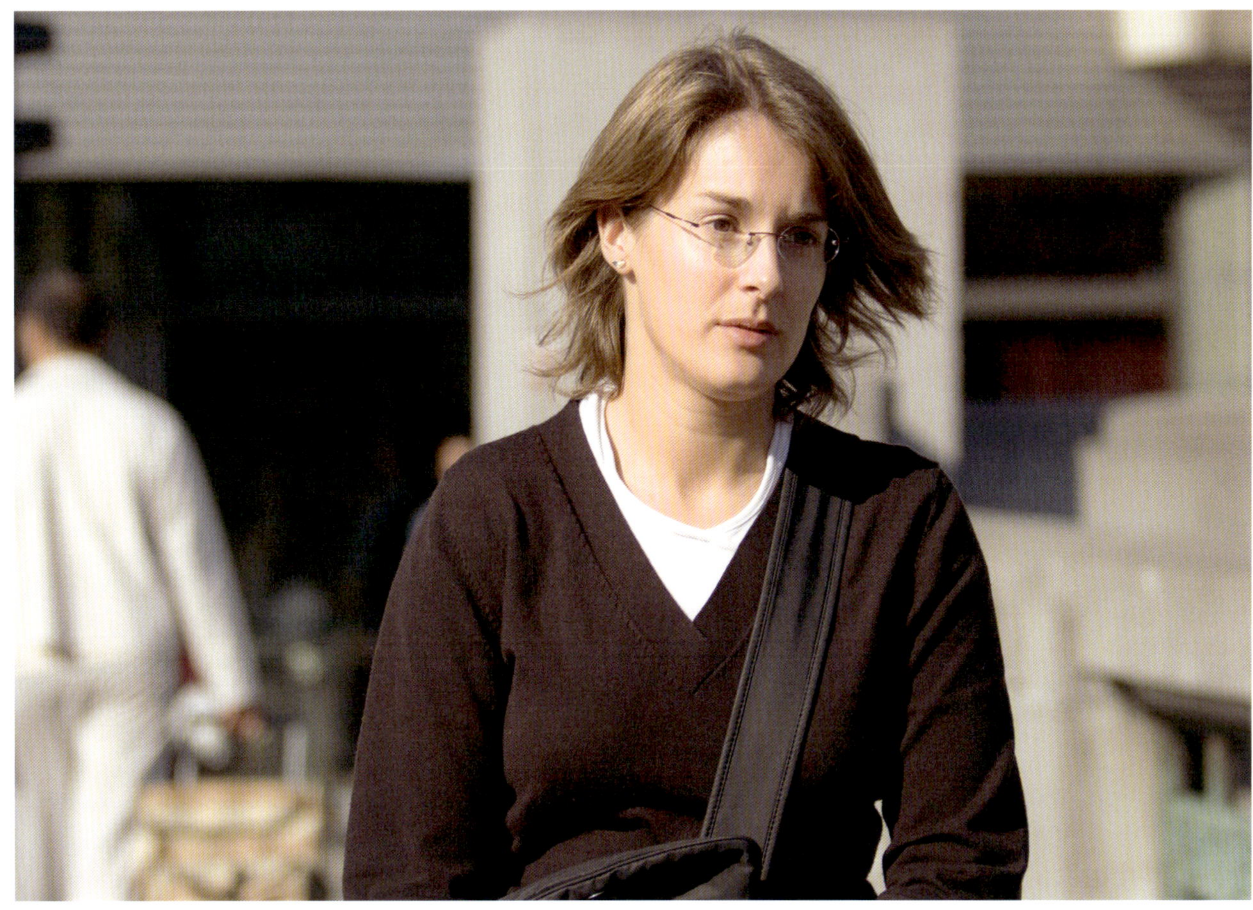

Beat Streuli

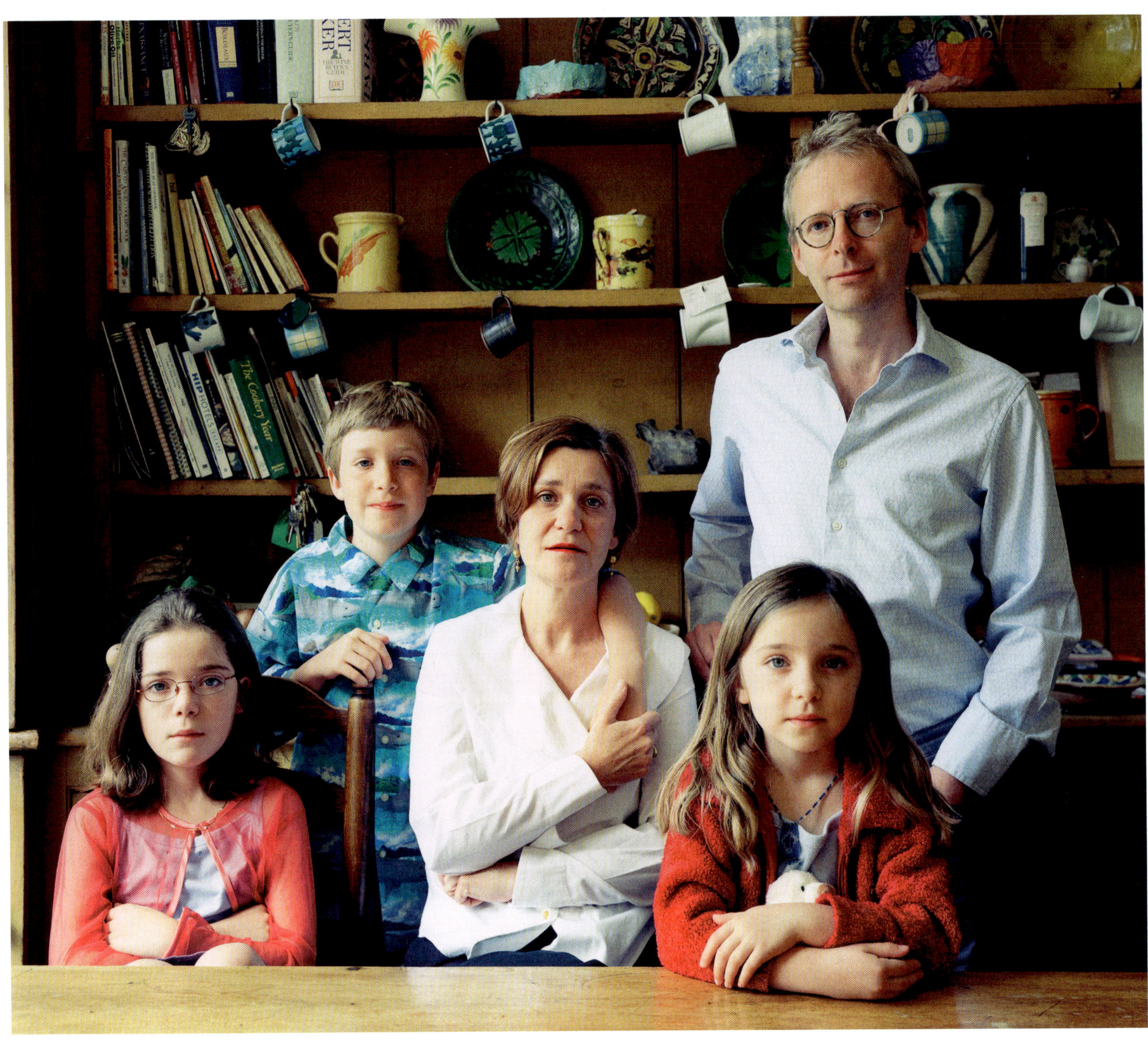

180

Thomas Struth (born 1954, Germany)

Thomas Struth studied photography in Germany under Bernd
and Hilla Becher, who are renowned for their typological series
of photographs of industrial monuments. His work is steeped
in their method of sharp and analytical observation and precise
registration. On that basis, Struth knows how to present the world
anew, namely as a fresh visual experience, and thereby almost
imperceptibly to raise existential questions about our being.

Apart from landscapes, cities, streets, modern technology
and museum visitors, he also photographs families in groups.
Struth uses a large-scale camera to capture in great detail both
the people photographed and their own daily surrounds. He
always composes his groups differently, depending on the setting, which is often a living room. He also uses the way in which
the people in the photographs, who know each other well or are
related, position themselves spontaneously in relation to each
other. For the rest, however, he retains precise control of all the
nuances of composition, incidence of light, and space. His style
of work together with the technique used suggest a certain neutral reservation, yet his photographs are never cold or impassive,
but rather leavened with a deep sense of intimacy and humanity. They radiate calmness and dignity in a subtle and balanced
manner. Those viewing the photographs get all the mental space
they need to look at the individuals, and to consider possible
personal relationships between them. The fact that these families originate from different parts of the world (from Japan to
Europe and the United States) adds another dimension. Is there
such a thing as a 'global family'? Struth presents the results
in large-scale (albeit diverse) sizes. In exhibitions, he mixes
up the various themes of his work to create deeper levels of
significance.

FG

p. 180
The Lingwood and Hamlyn Family, London, 2001.
Chromogenic print, 95 × 110.7 cm

pp. 182–83
The Däinghaus/Schwertlinger Family 1, Düsseldorf, 2012.
Chromogenic print, 141.6 × 192.8 cm

pp. 184–85
The Martin and Mason Family, Düsseldorf, 2001.
Chromogenic print, 97 × 125.2 cm

Courtesy the artist

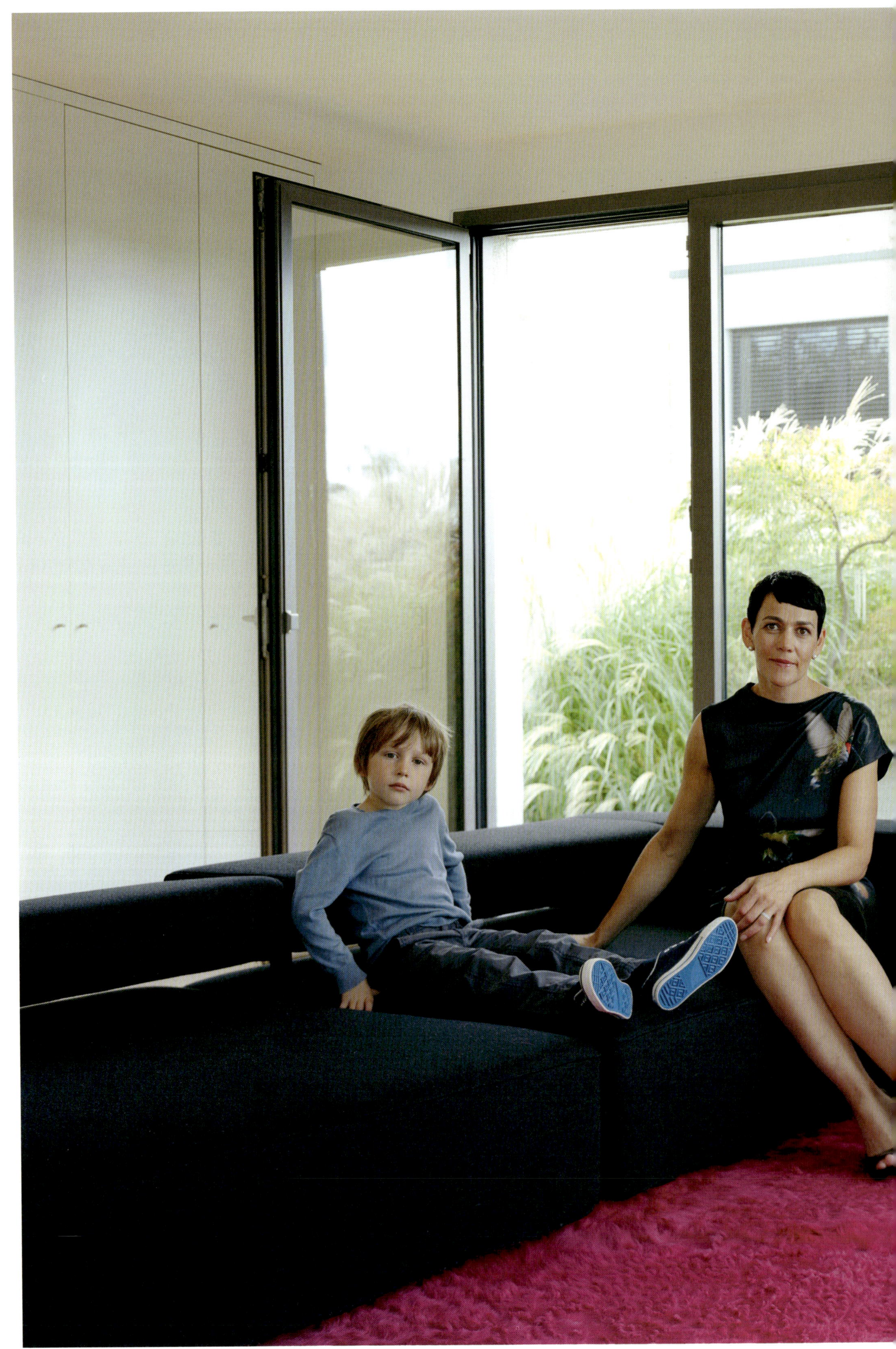

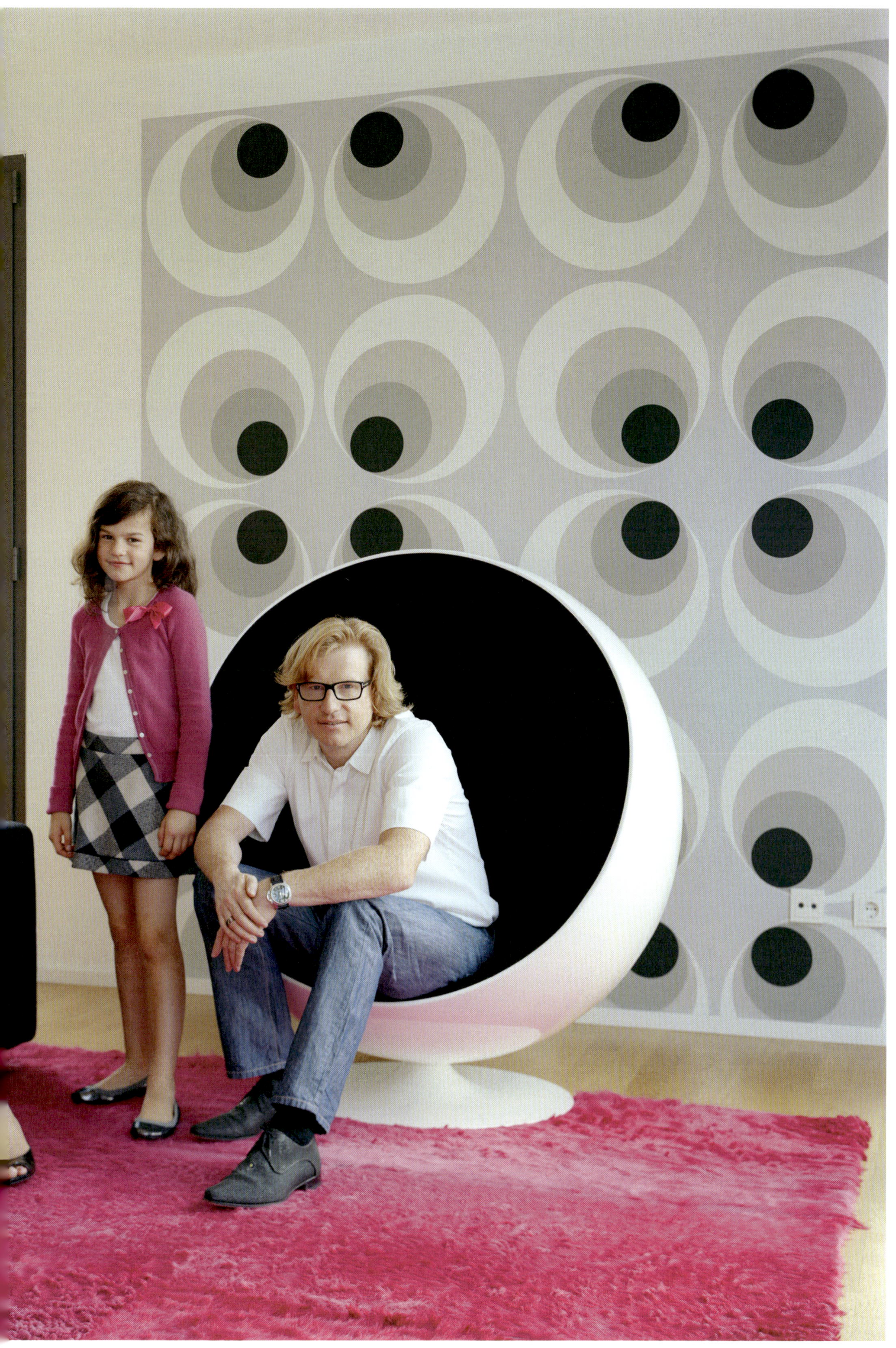

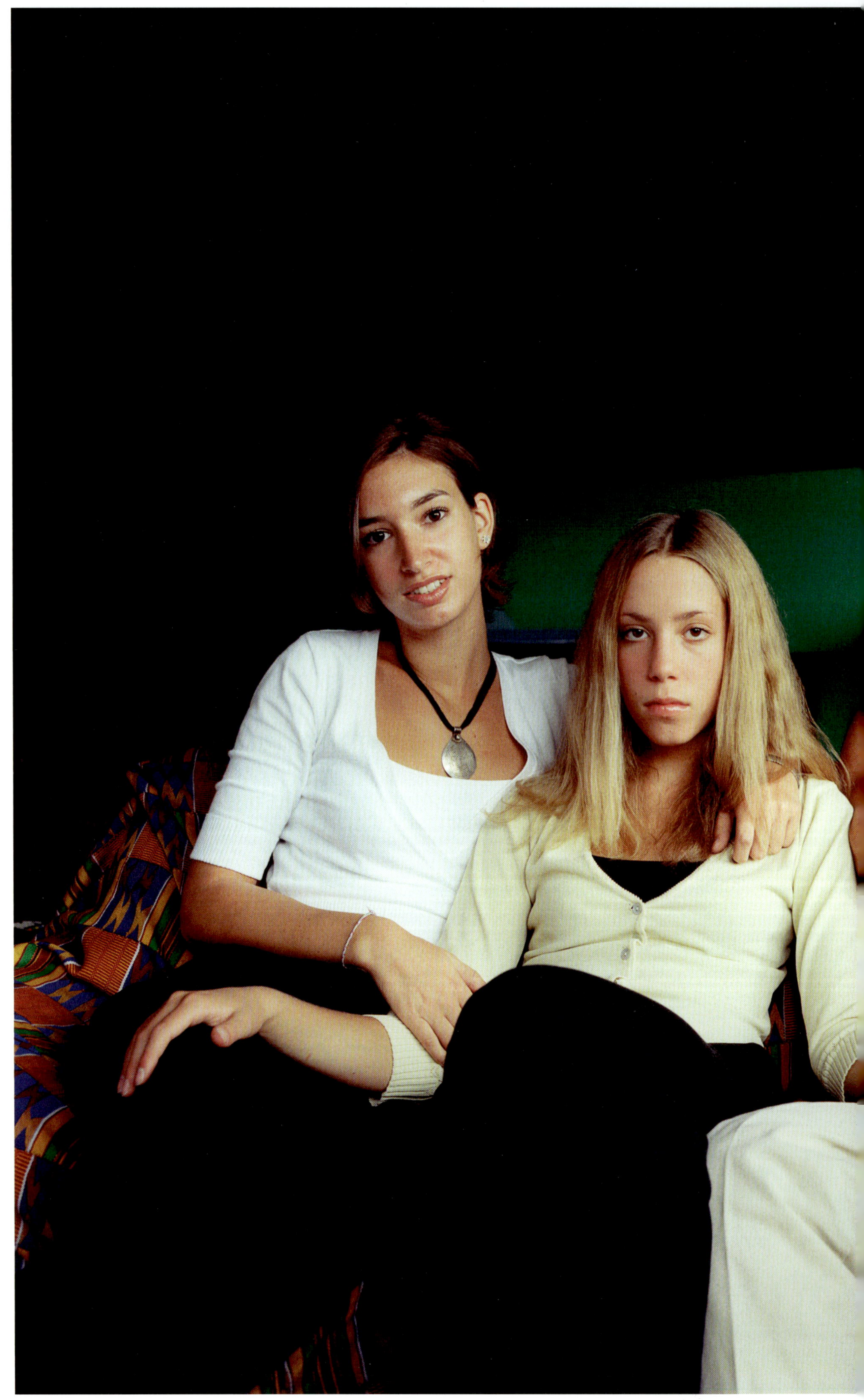

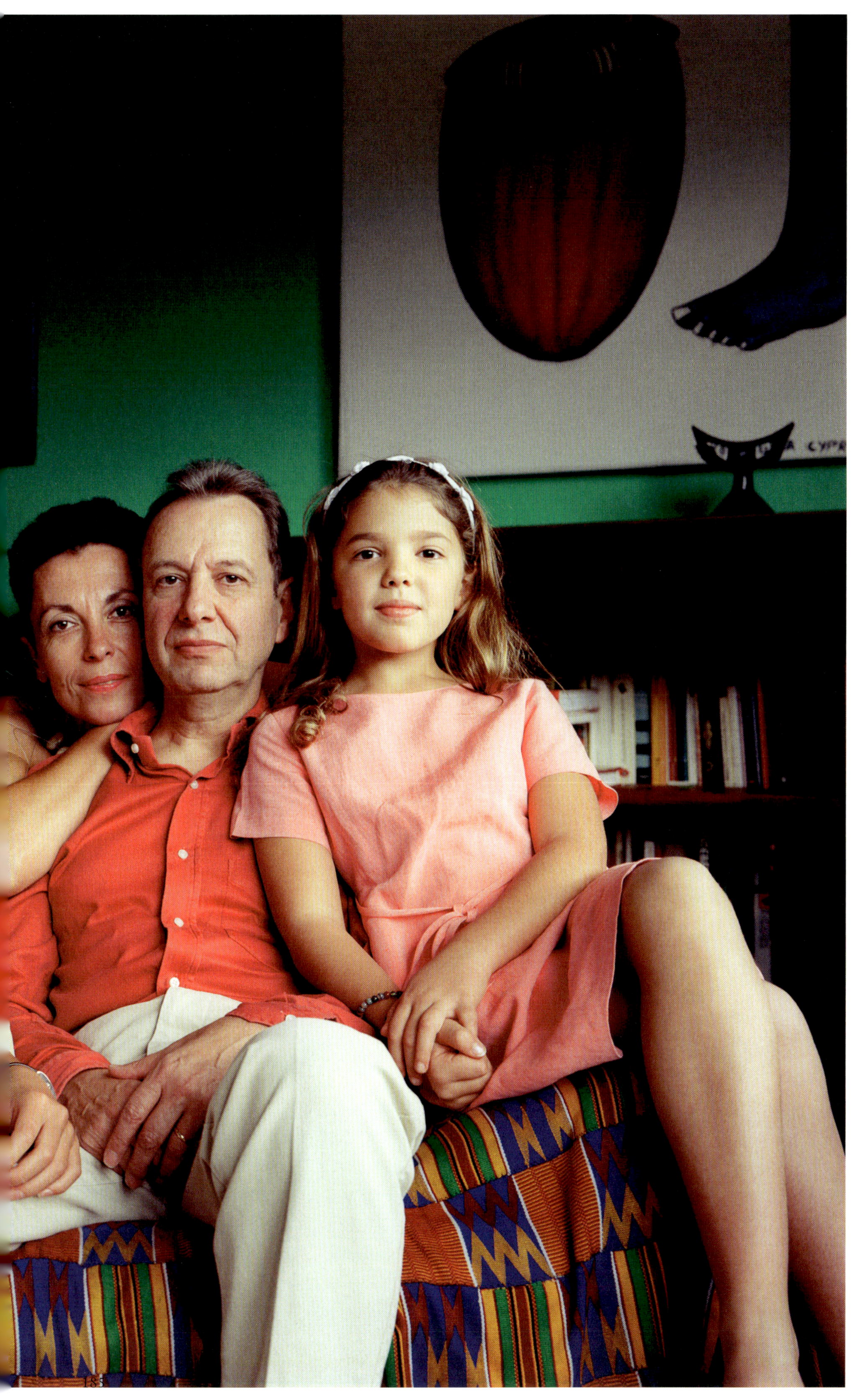

Juergen Teller (born 1964, Germany)

Go-Sees

Juergen Teller, who lives and works in Great Britain, started out in 1986 as a music and fashion photographer, the branch in which he acquired a reputation for his unconventional approach. Teller refuses to draw a distinction between commercial assignments and autobiographical pictures among close friends. His open, direct and often raucous style testifies to a dialogue between model and photographer, which challenges current expectations in that regard. He dares to show anti-glamorous snapshots and highlight the imperfections and human weakness of (top) models. He prefers to work in colour, using a Contax G2 camera with built-in flash, and regularly includes himself in his pictures. His 'amateurish' framing, which deliberately includes 'mistakes' such as the reflection of the flash or everyday objects in simple poses, contributes to a sort of aesthetic failure and imperfection that attracts attention because of its banality. At the same time, Teller makes it clear that his photographs are never coincidental, but the result of careful planning and precise staging. They distance themselves from polished fashion photography and conventional and stereotypical beauty. Despite the directness and 'straight photography', which conceals nothing, but strives for almost documentary realism and objectivity, his pictures nevertheless exude something fragile, a cosmopolitan complexity and sensitivity.

GP

p. 187
Alex Paton, London, 21st December 1998

p. 188
Lara, London, 4th March 1999
Tania Court, London, 3rd December 1998
Fiona, London, 1st April 1998
Keira, London, 30th March 1999
Mak, London, 9th October 1998
Carmel, London, 10th September 1998
Romilly, London, 14th January 1999
Jennifer Holmes, London, 19th February 1999
Lauren, London, 18th February 1999
Christie Foley, London, 20th October 1998
Sophie Dahl, London, 20th October 1998
Hayley Greer, London, 1998

p. 189
Desiree and Candice Neil, London, 22nd May 1998
Claire Bastin, London, 23rd March 1999
Charlotte Materne, London, 24th March 1999
Summer, London, 24th September 1998
Girl, London, 1998
Phoebe's mother, London, 24th September 1998
Jan Dunning, London, 24th September 1998
Helle, London, 24th September 1998
Christie Foley, London, 26th May 1998
Gemma, London, 29th March 1999
Domenique, London, 29th September 1998
Shona, London, 29th October 1998

in 'Go-Sees', 1995–1999. C-type prints, 30.5 × 25.4 cm

Courtesy the artist

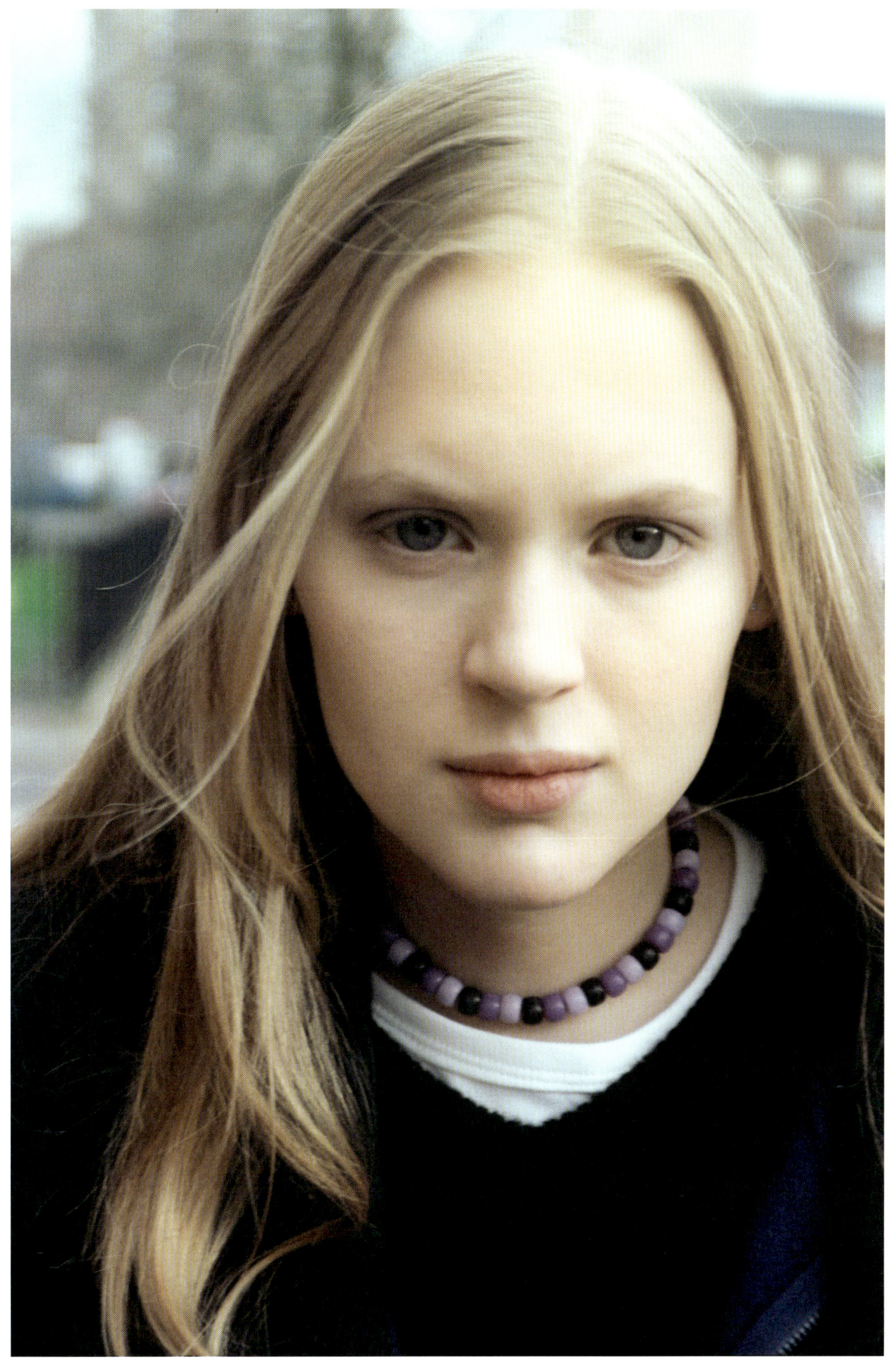

Juergen Teller

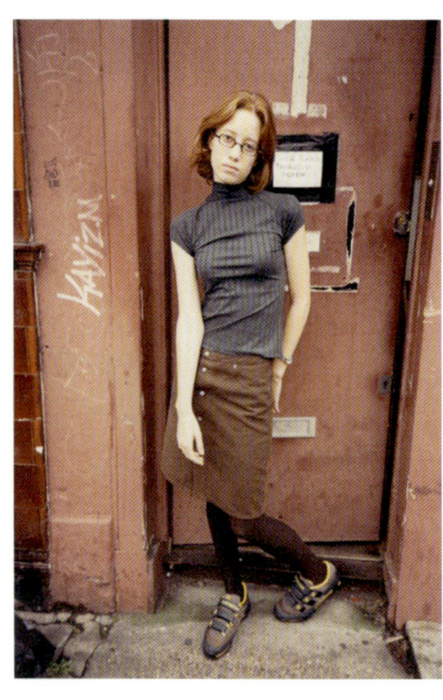
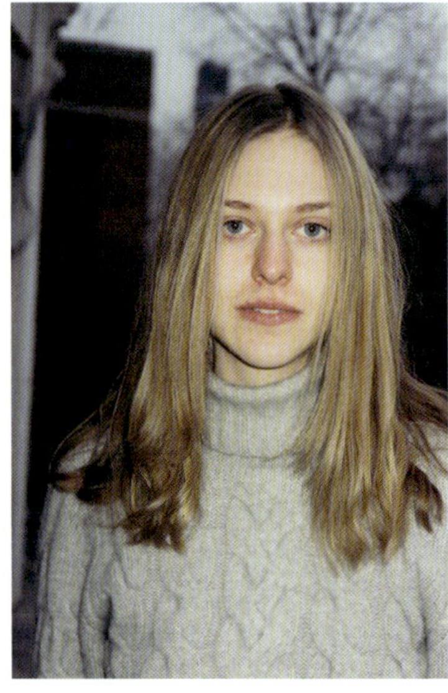
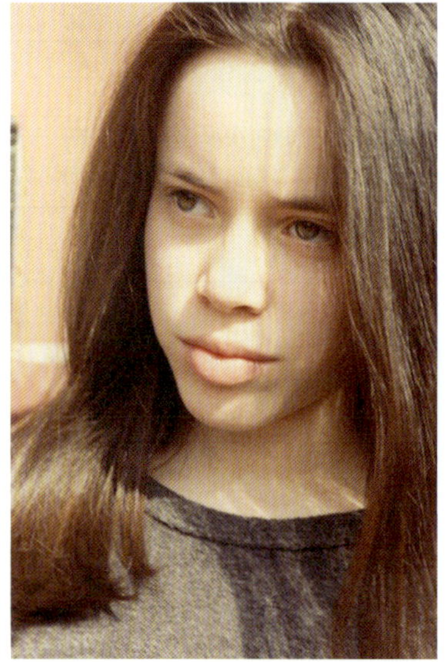
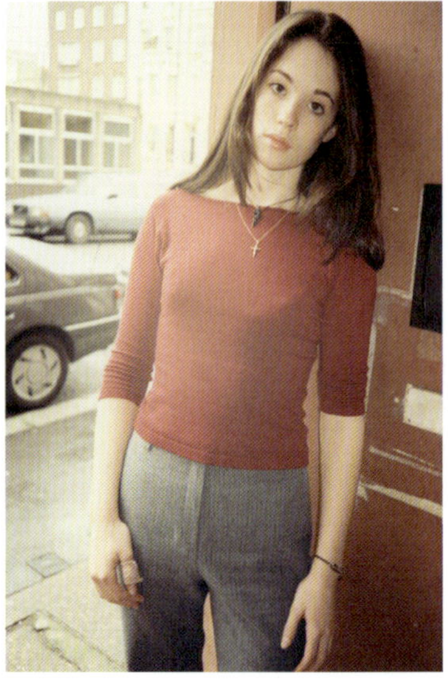
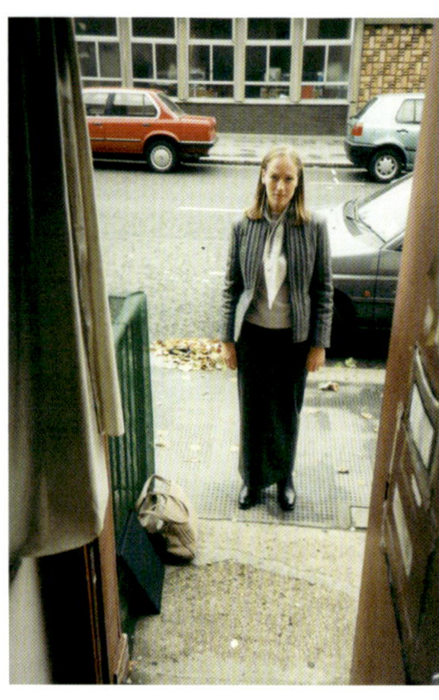
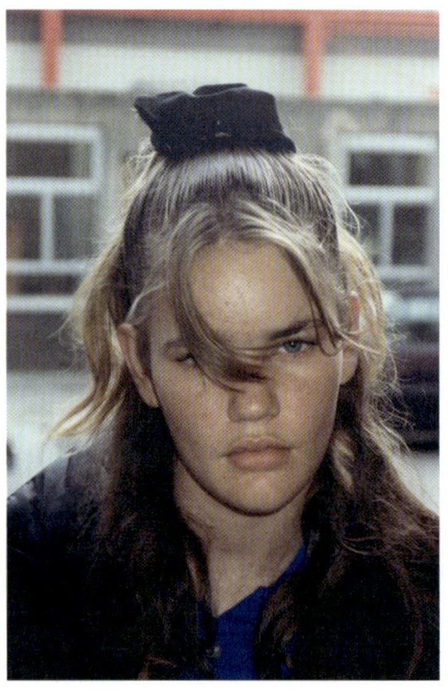
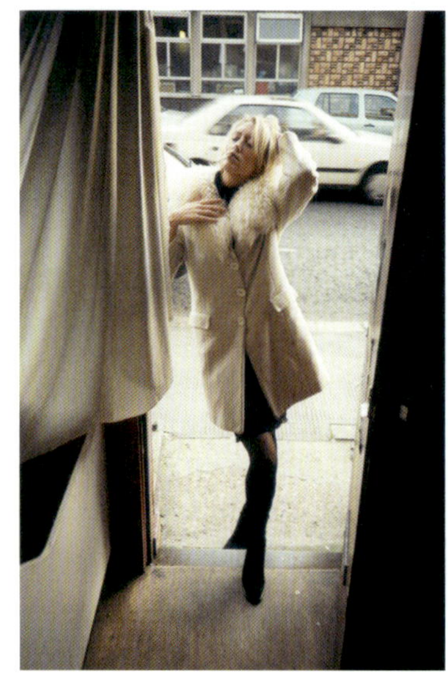
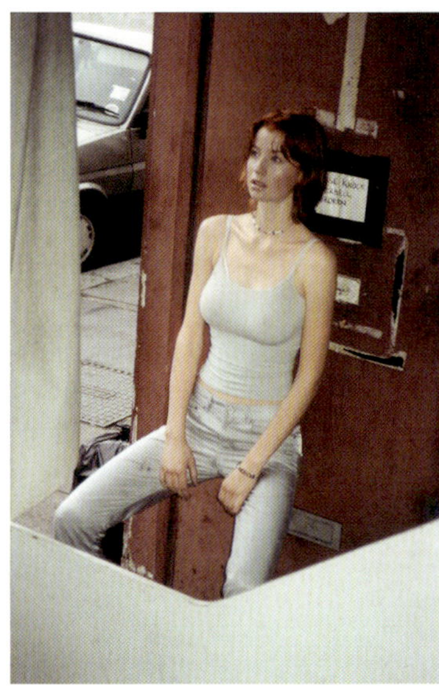
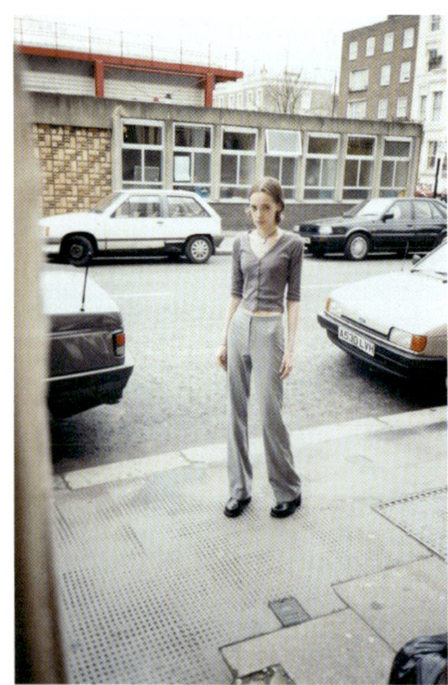
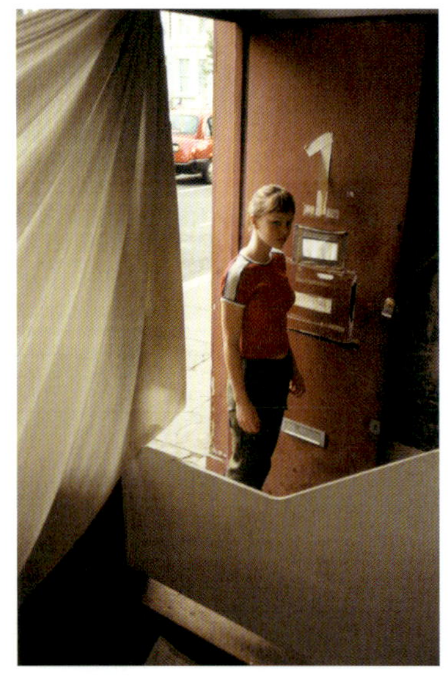
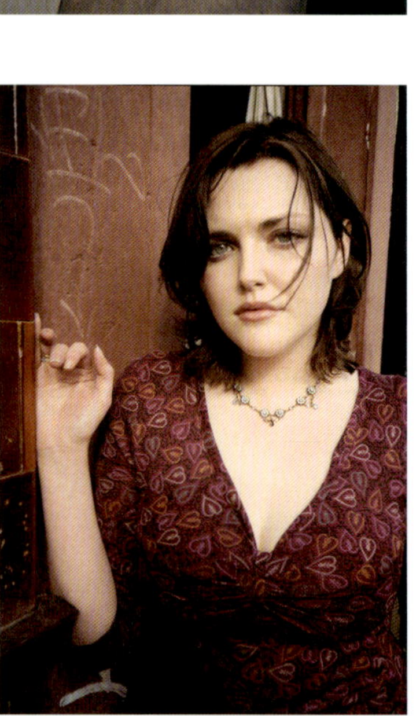
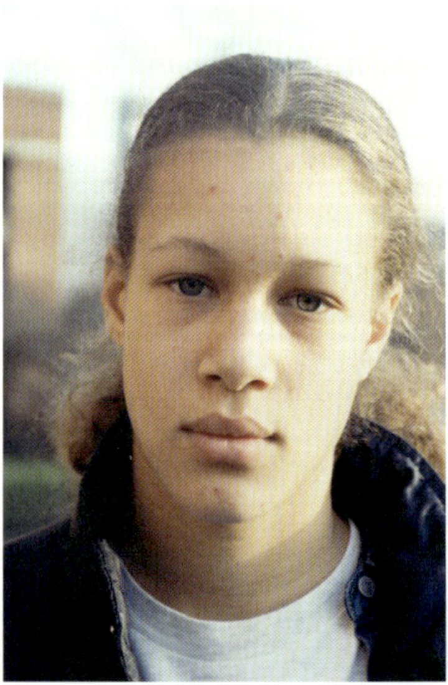

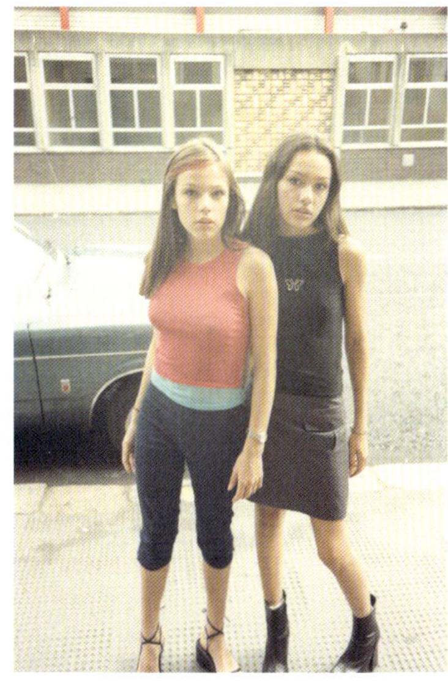 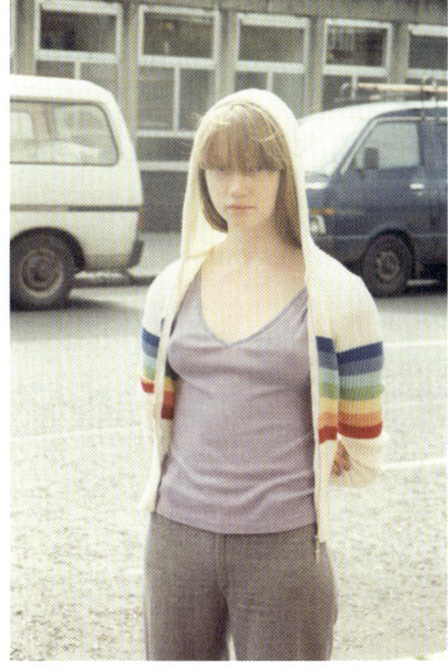 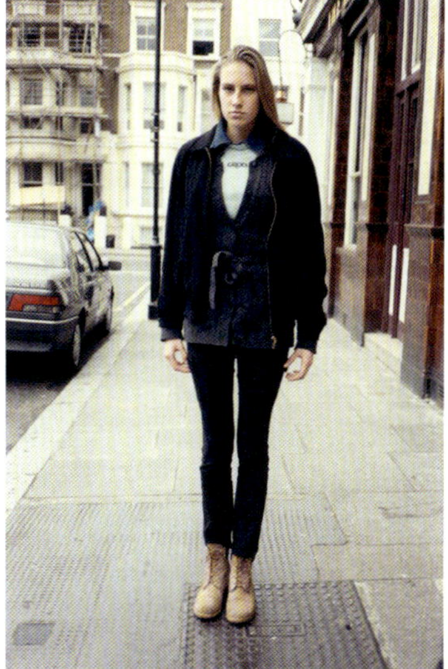 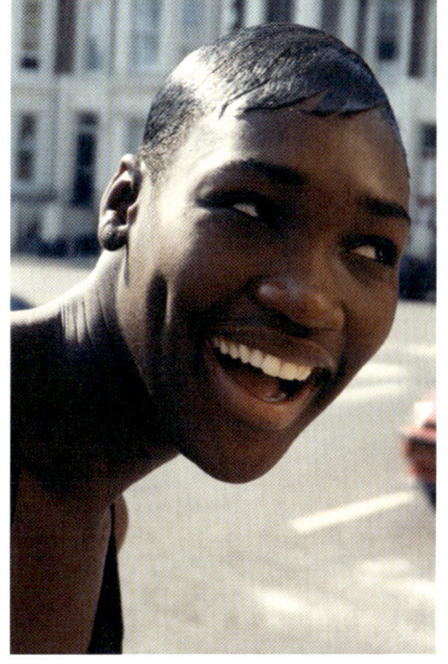

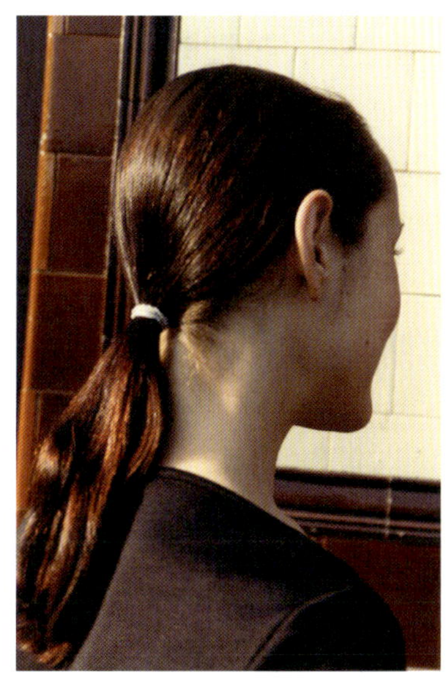 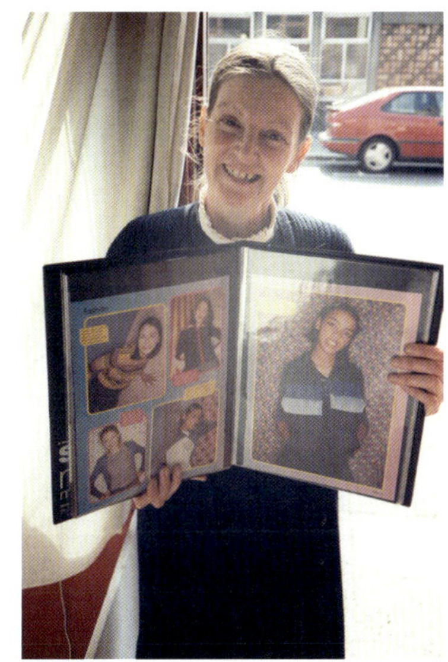 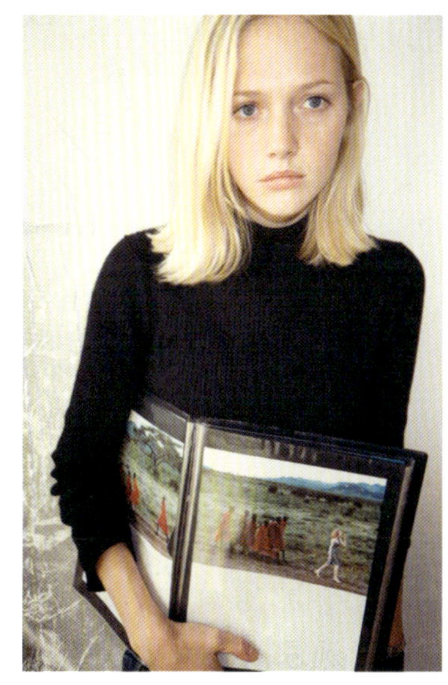 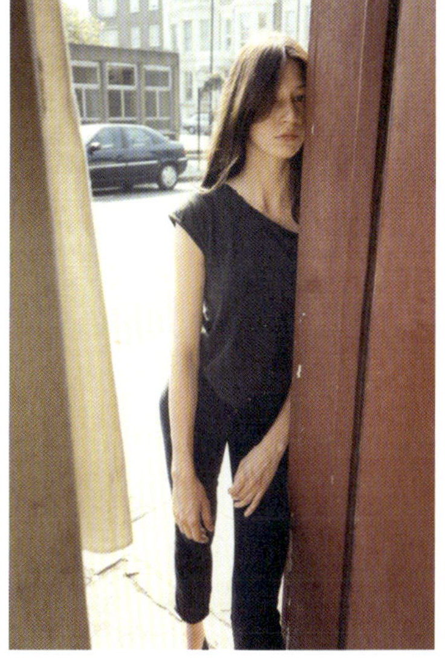

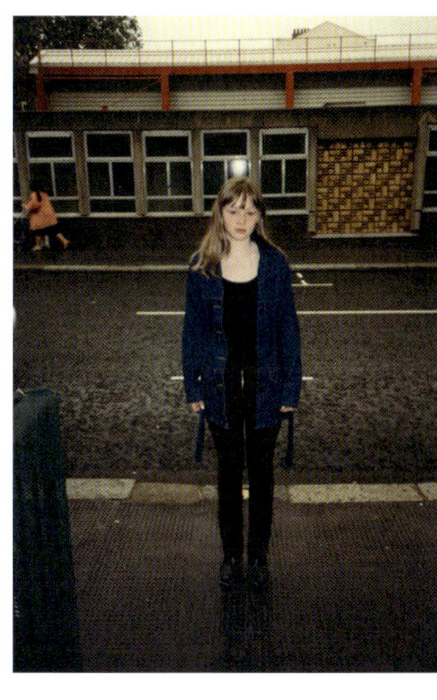 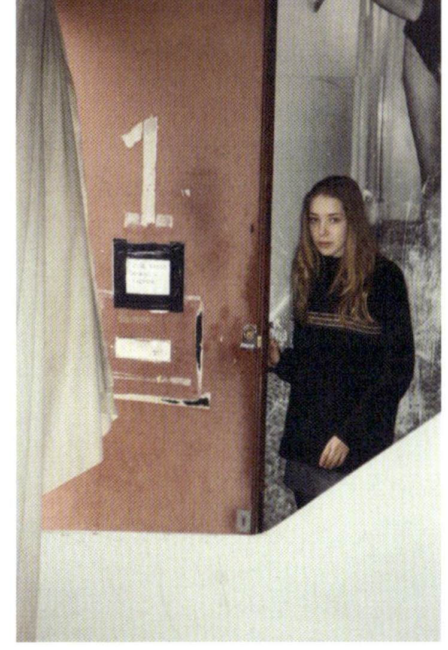 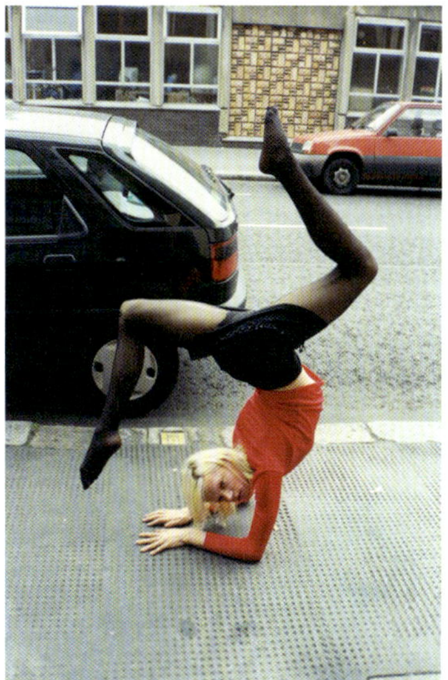 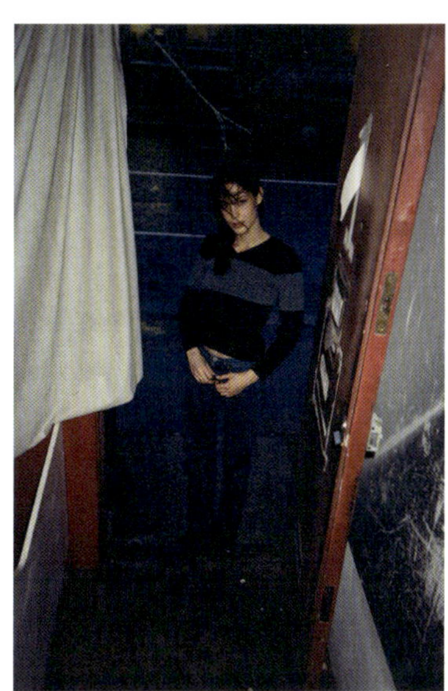

Juergen Teller

Stephan Vanfleteren (born 1969, Belgium)

Stephan Vanfleteren started out as a reporter-photographer
with a number of Belgian newspapers and magazines. He soon
developed his own style, always in black and white, typified by a
restraint and character photography that omits as much as possible. For him, it is never purely about aesthetics; he plays with
focus and major contrasts, which bring to light a sometimes
painful beauty. Recently, Vanfleteren has made the transition
from analogue to digital. His prize-winning book *Belgicum*
(2007) shows a country in its twilight and portrays those on
the fringes of society. Another of his books, *Portret 1989-2009*,
depicts Belgium's love for heroes great and small – from artists,
writers and musicians through sports personalities and actors
to politicians. They all have one thing in common, namely their
importance to Belgium around the turn of the century. The
portraits of his native land are very regional, but also universal.
Vanfleteren is a classic photographer who often takes pictures
to order, such as the award-winning portrait of Rem Koolhaas
or that of Stromae for *The New York Times*. Yet he also travels for
months, working for himself and searching for faces he has
to record before they disappear for good. The finiteness of life
comes out even more strongly in the portrait Vanfleteren did of
curator Jan Hoet – with his consent – shortly before Hoet passed
away. With this 'killing portrait', the photographer steps into
a long tradition of vanitas images, which began in the Middle
Ages and continued until well into the 20th century. Some vanitas portraits came about because no one had commissioned
them while the subjects were still alive (hence the relatively
large number of portraits of children who died at a young
age); at other times they were seen as a special mark of honour.
Killing portraits are often confrontational and intimate, for they
show that everything in this life is fleeting – even the viewer.

GP/FG

p. 191
Rem Koolhaas, 2012.
Ink-jet print on Hahnemühle fine art paper,
150 × 112 cm

p. 192
Jef, visser, 2006.
Ink-jet print on Hahnemühle fine art paper,
85 × 65 cm

pp. 192–93
Pontje, visser, 2004.
Ink-jet print on Hahnemühle fine art paper,
85 × 65 cm

p. 193
Bakelandt, visser, 2006.
Ink-jet print on Hahnemühle fine art paper,
85 × 65 cm

p. 194
Anoniem, 2003.
Ink-jet print on Hahnemühle fine art paper,
65 × 65 cm

p. 194
Regina, 2002.
Ink-jet print on Hahnemühle fine art paper,
65 × 65 cm

p. 194
Martine, 2002.
Ink-jet print on Hahnemühle fine art paper,
65 × 65 cm

p. 194
Anoniem, 2002.
Ink-jet print on Hahnemühle fine art paper,
65 × 65 cm

p. 195
René, 2004.
Ink-jet print on Hahnemühle fine art paper,
65 × 65 cm

p. 195
Colombo, 2005.
Ink-jet print on Hahnemühle fine art paper,
65 × 65 cm

p. 195
Marcelle-Josephine, 2004.
Ink-jet print on Hahnemühle fine art paper,
65 × 65 cm

p. 195
Moemoe, 2005.
Ink-jet print on Hahnemühle fine art paper,
65 × 65 cm

pp. 196–97
Jan Hoet, 2014.
Ink-jet print on Hahnemühle fine art paper,
112 × 150 cm

Courtesy the artist

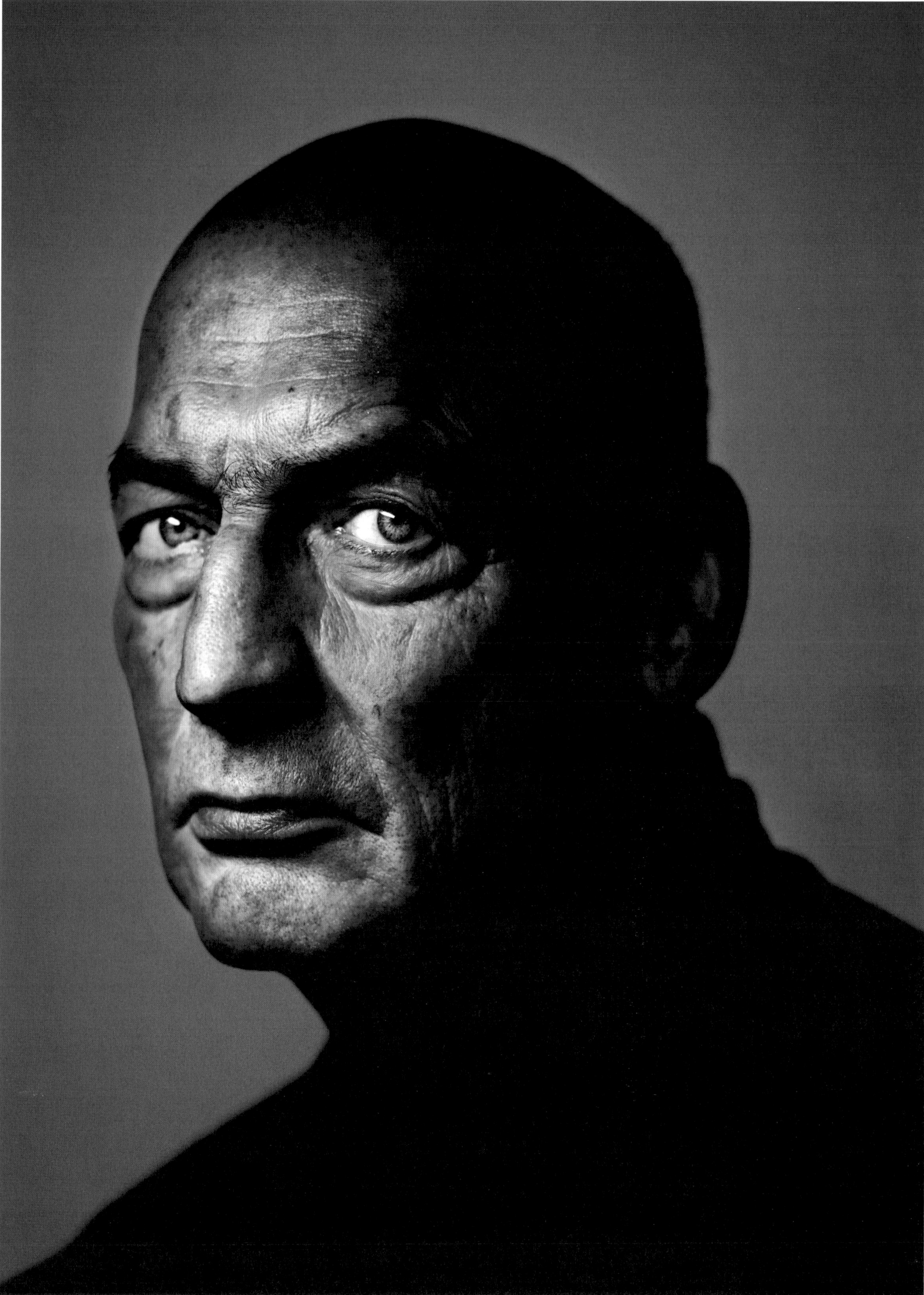

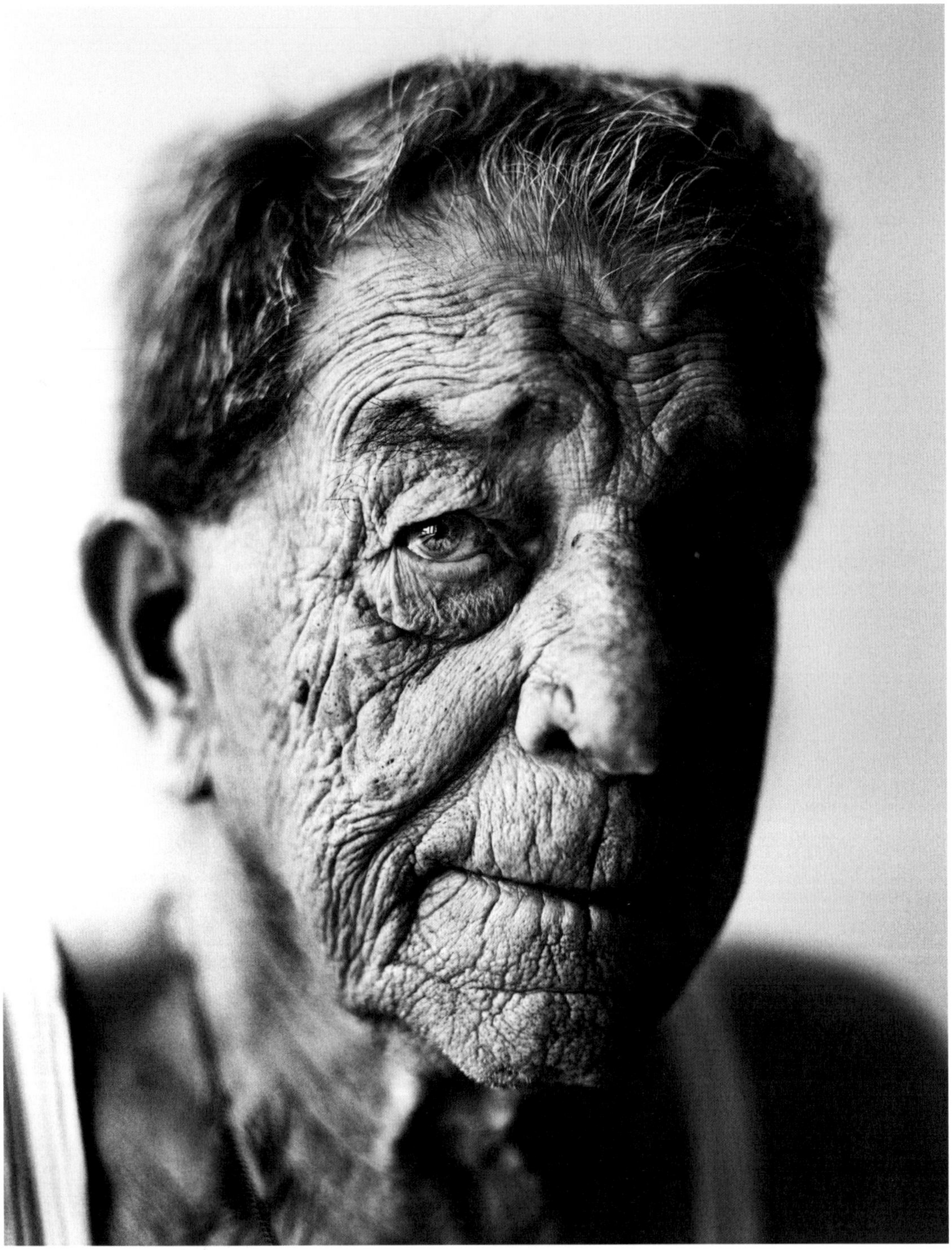

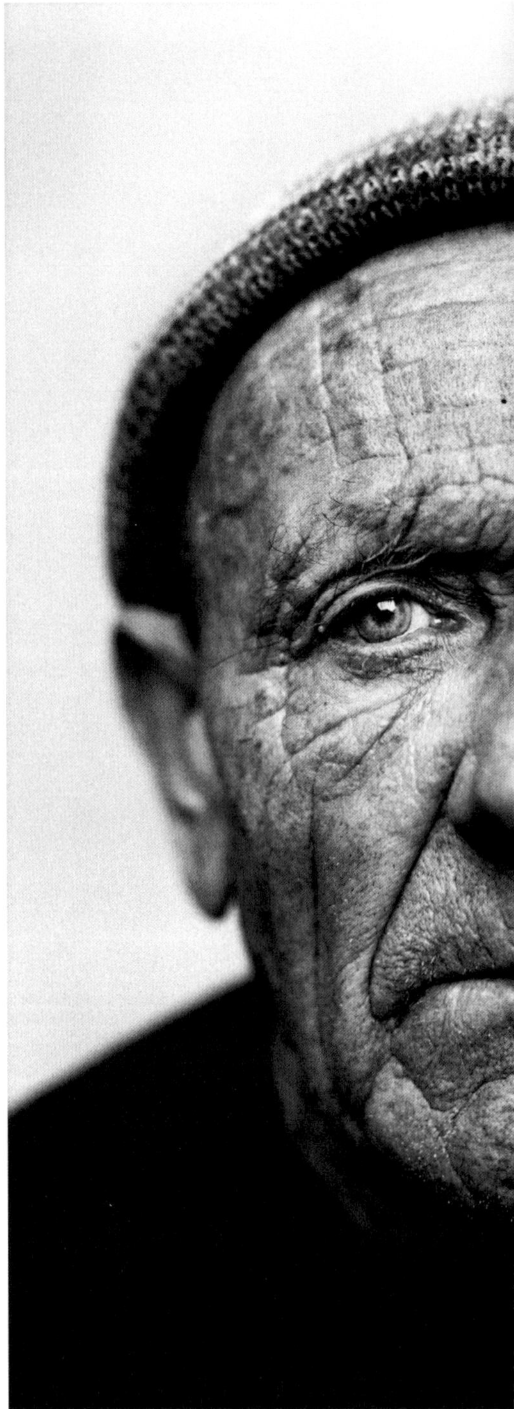

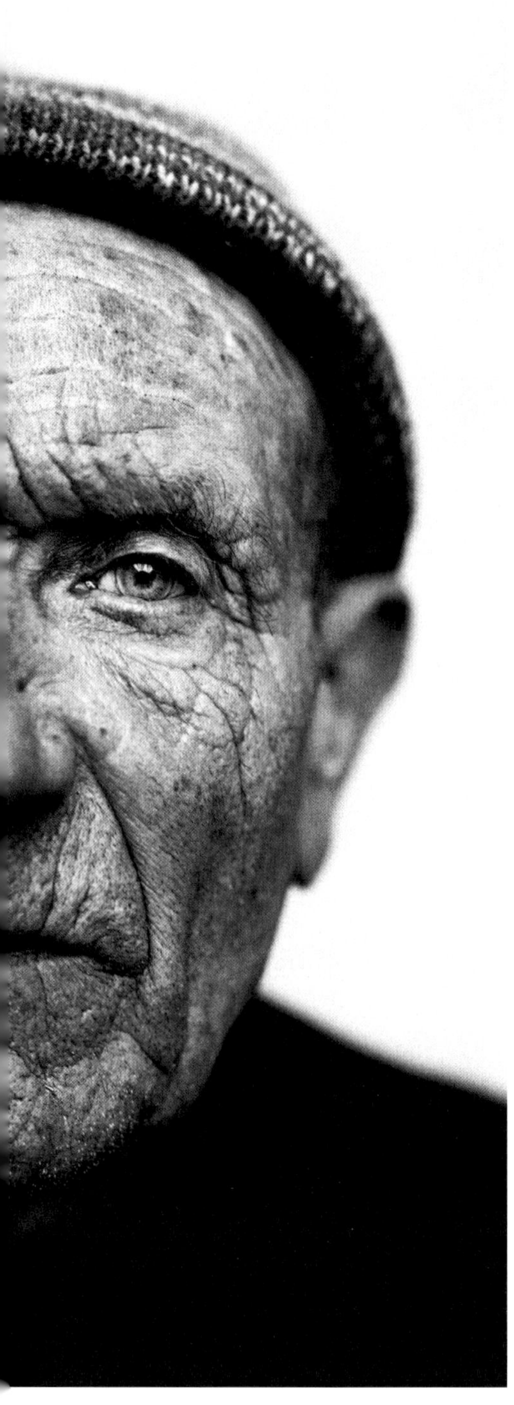

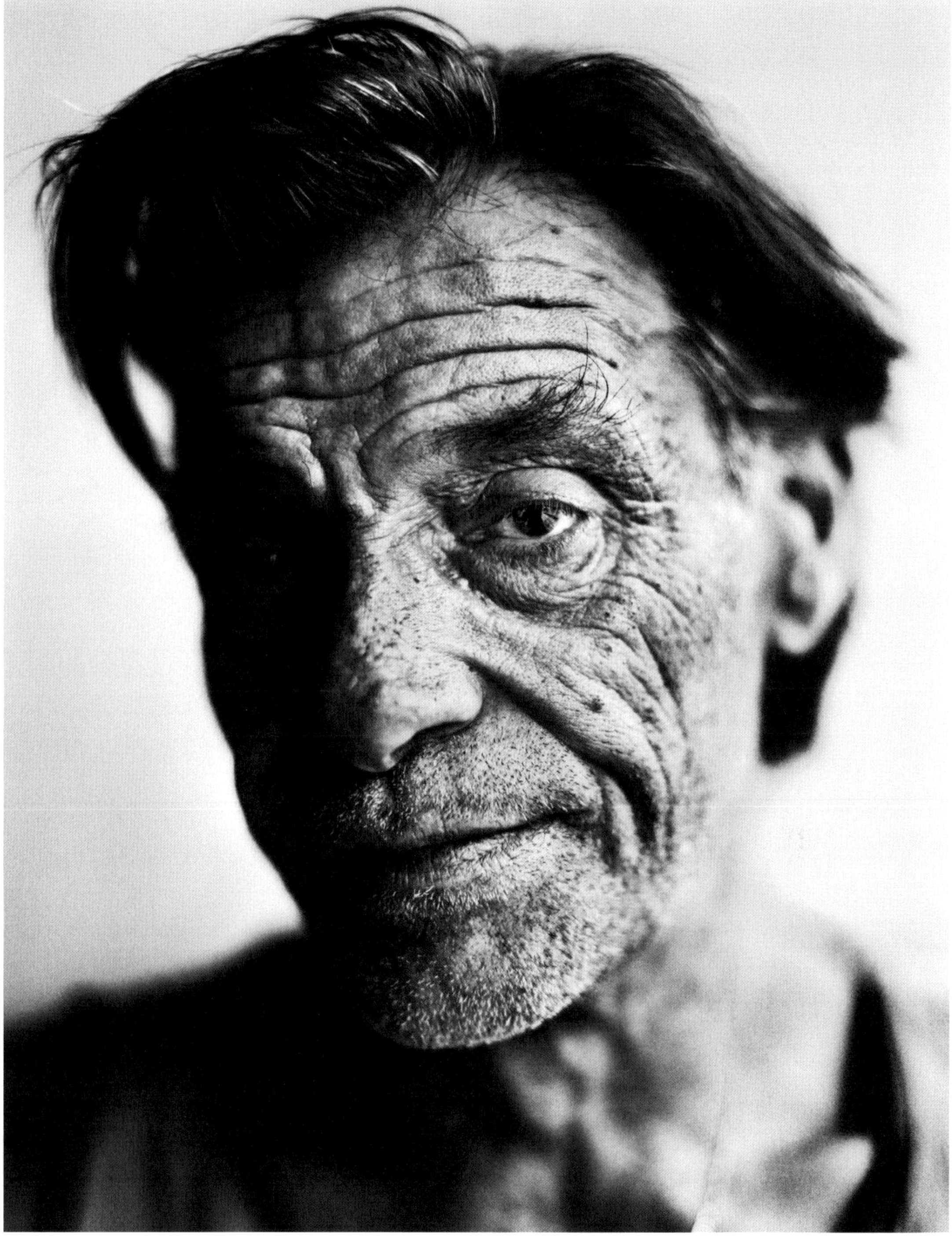

Stephan Vanfleteren

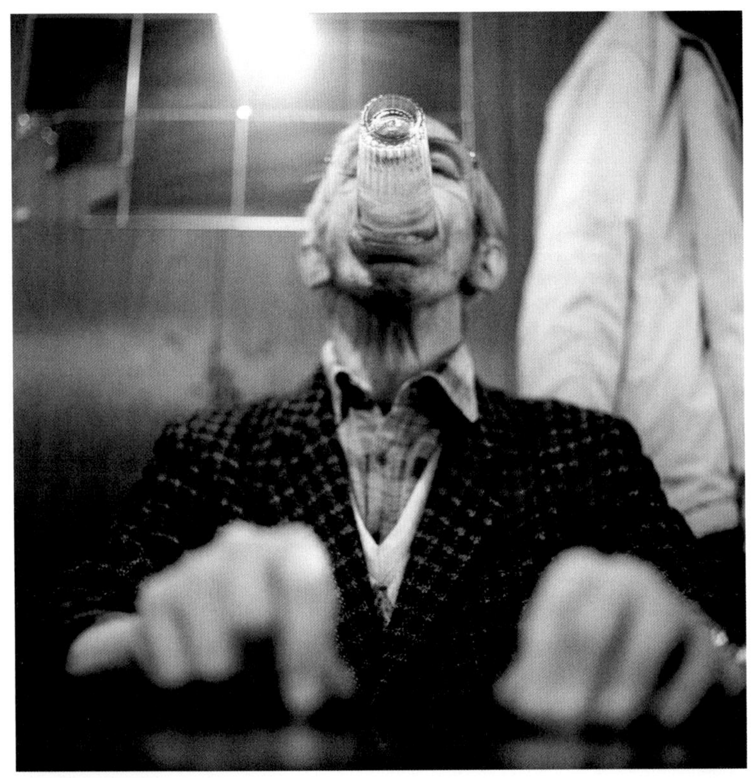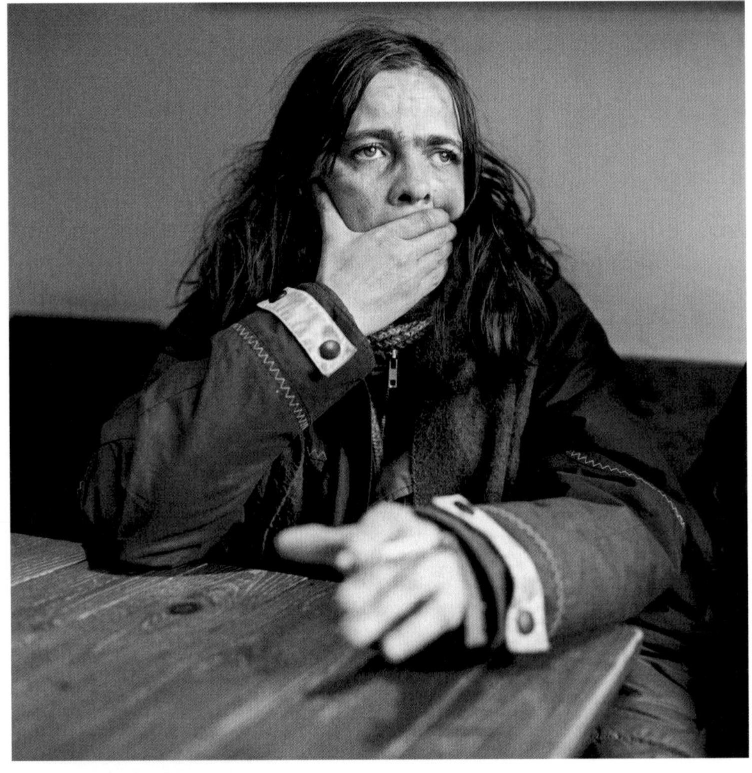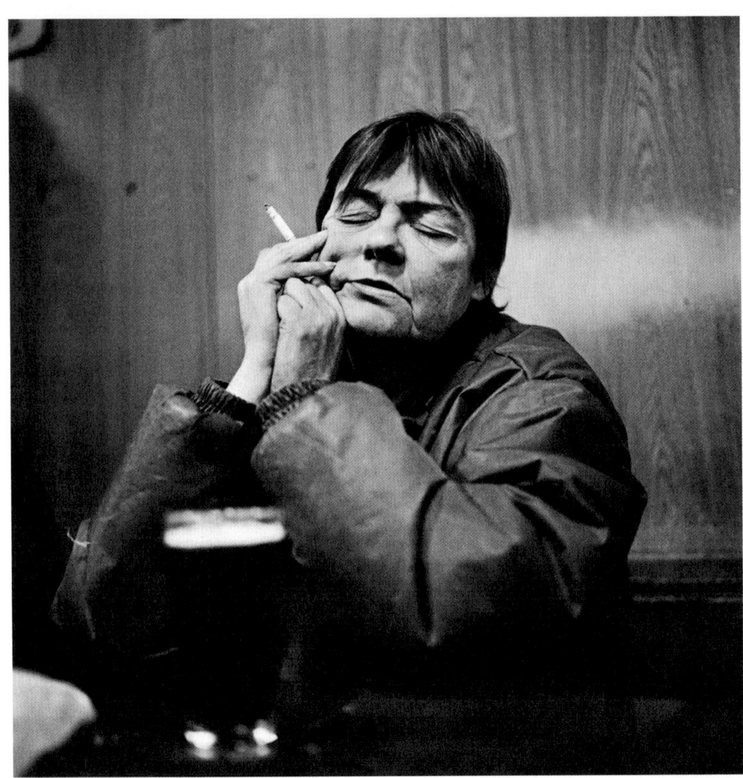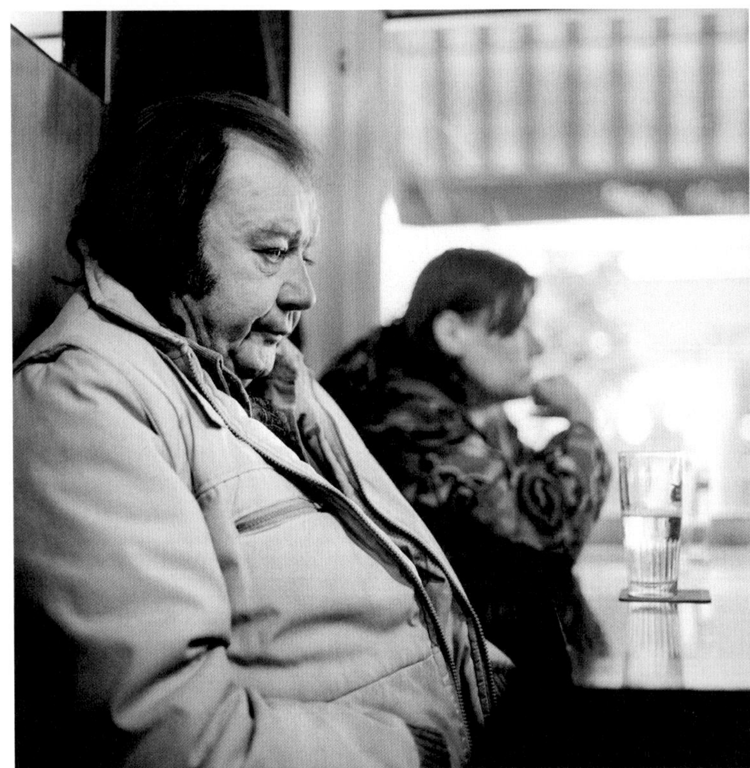

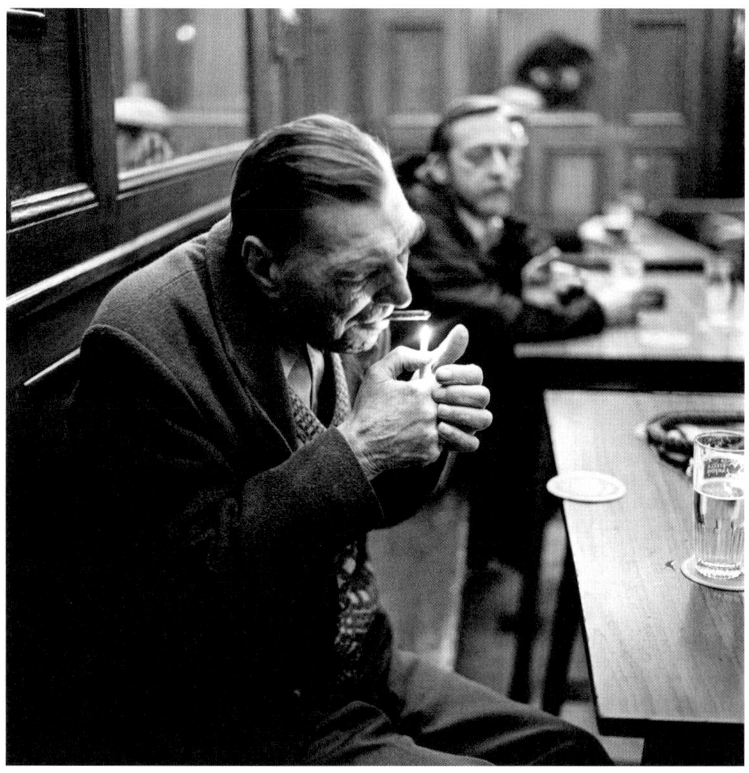
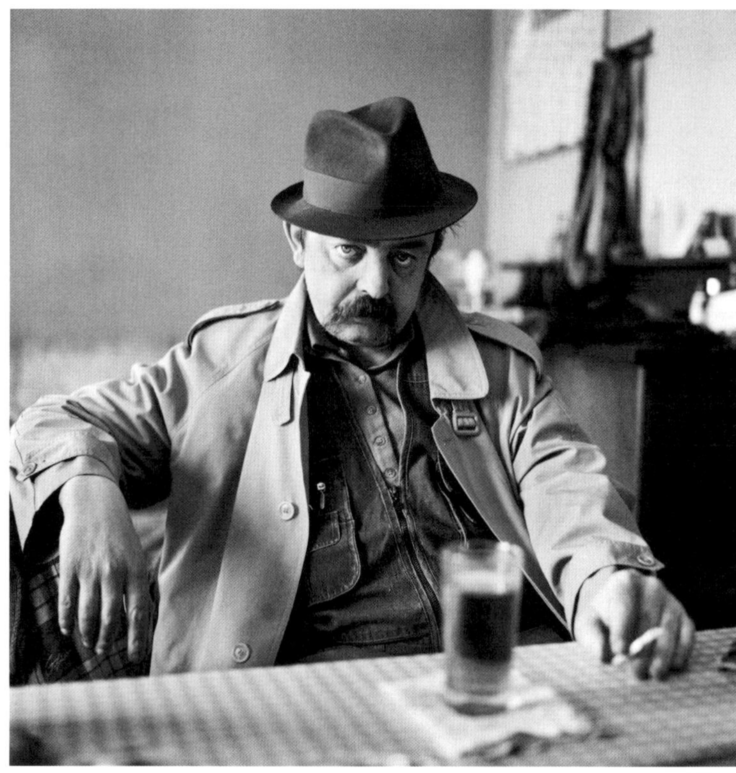
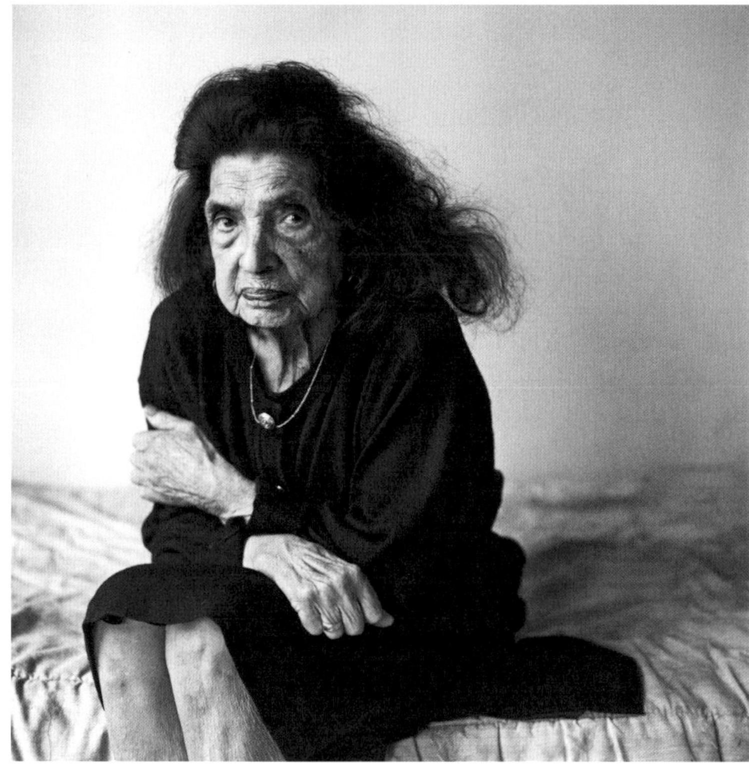
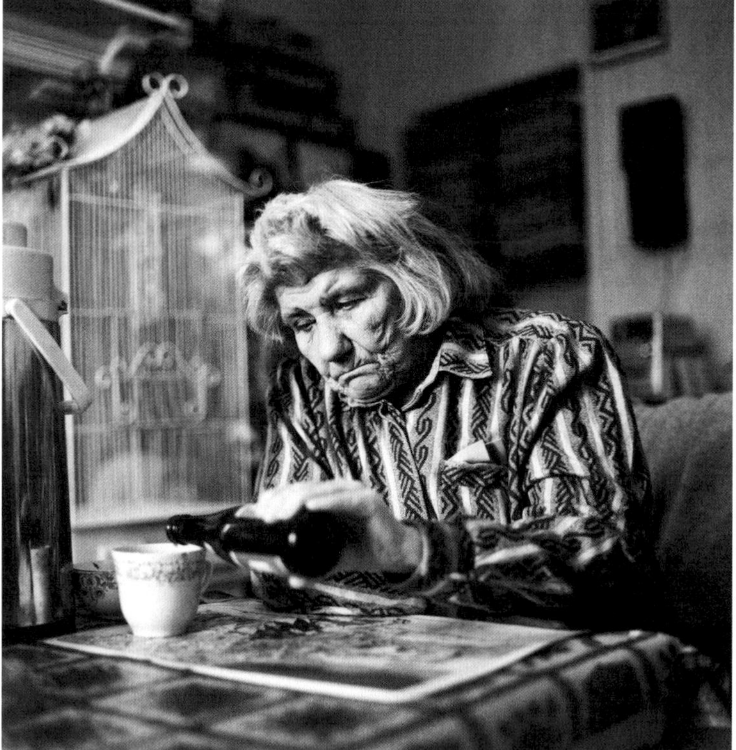

Stephan Vanfleteren

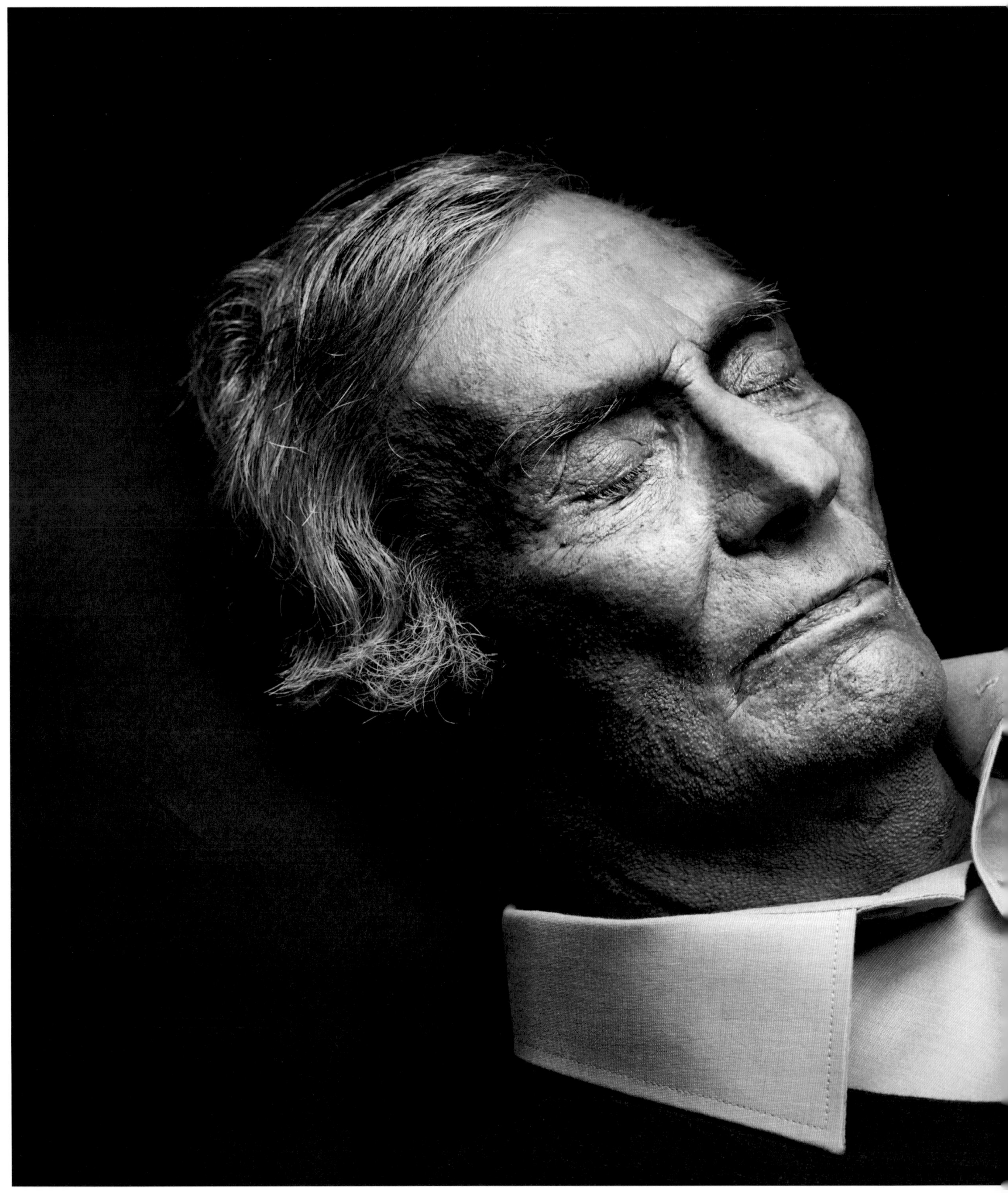

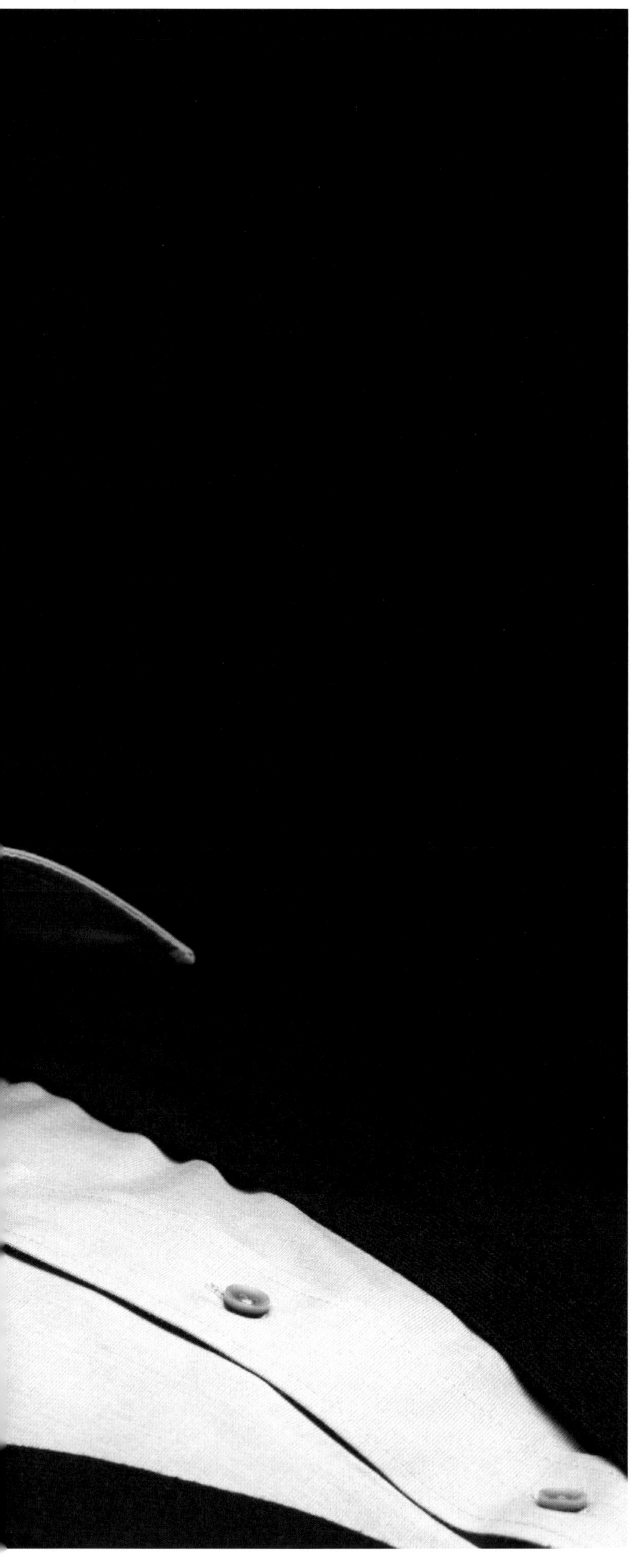

Stephan Vanfleteren

Hellen van Meene (born 1972, the Netherlands)

In Hellen van Meene's photographs of adolescent girls in the second half of the 1990s, the pose is often a striking and defining element. The somewhat strange manner in which the girls stand, lie or sit gives an initial impression of a spontaneous and random picture that is true to life. However, her photographs are definitely not snapshots, but carefully orchestrated pictures. They lend expression to the photographer's fascination for the mental and physical phase these girls are passing through in their transition from childhood to adulthood. On closer inspection, we also see that there is something awkward and imaginary about the poses. In some cases, the undercurrent is even surrealistic, such as with the girl in wet clothing or another girl who sits fully clothed in a tub of water. Their nudity is often only half-covered, an exposed shoulder or a budding breast revealed intentionally, but subtly. Yet the girls are too young, their bodies too shapeless to create an erotic effect from these poses. Van Meene tends to stress a sense of awkwardness and vulnerability. Their glances are usually sideways or inward-looking. The connection between the world of these growing girls and the outside world is simply not there yet. A child's mind and a child's body will make way in a relatively short time for the mind and body of the adolescent, accompanied naturally by a growing comprehension of the world, a knowledge of socially acceptable behaviour, and a loss of innocence.

FG

Courtesy the artist

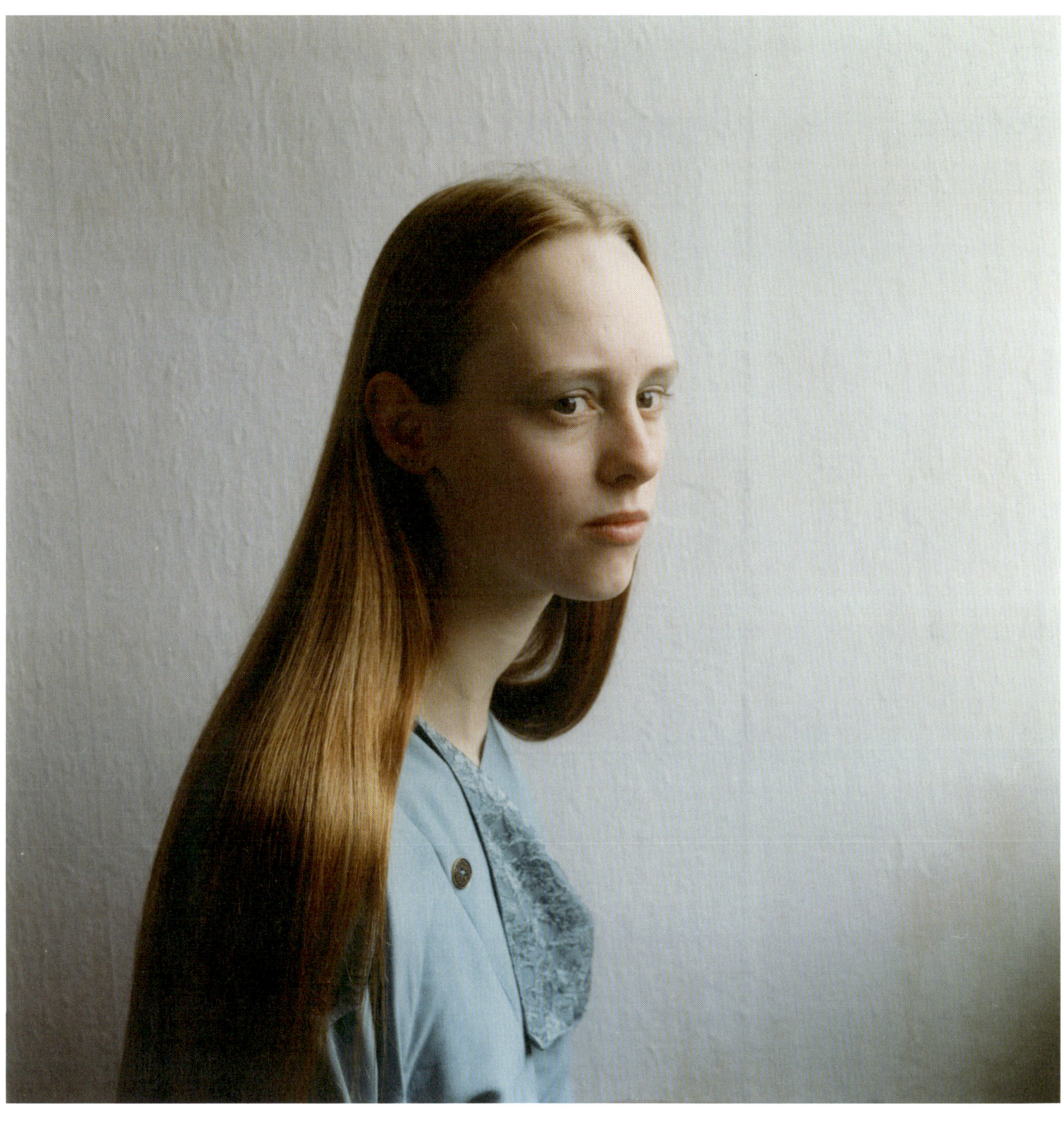

   Hellen van Meene

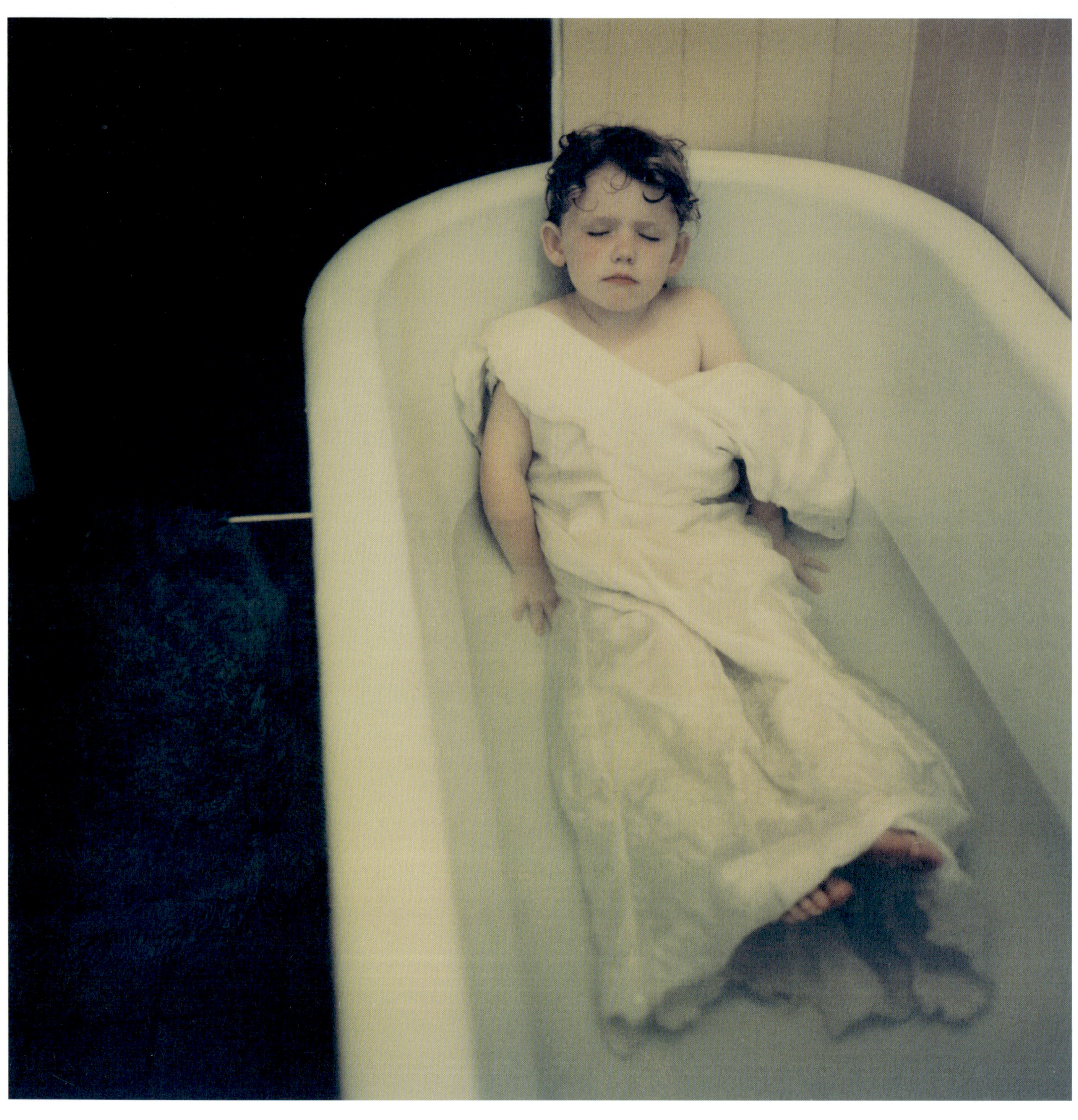

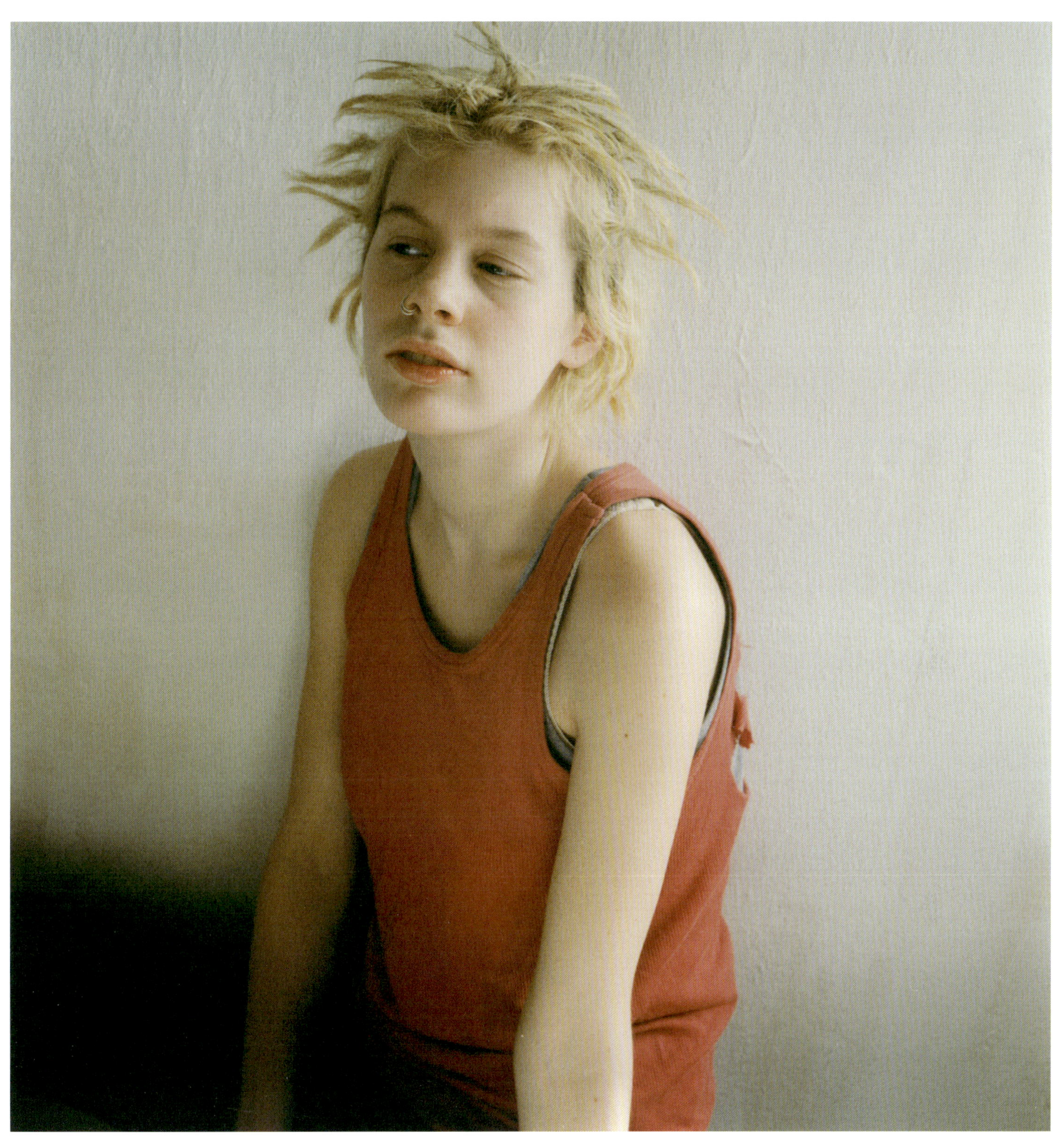

Hellen van Meene

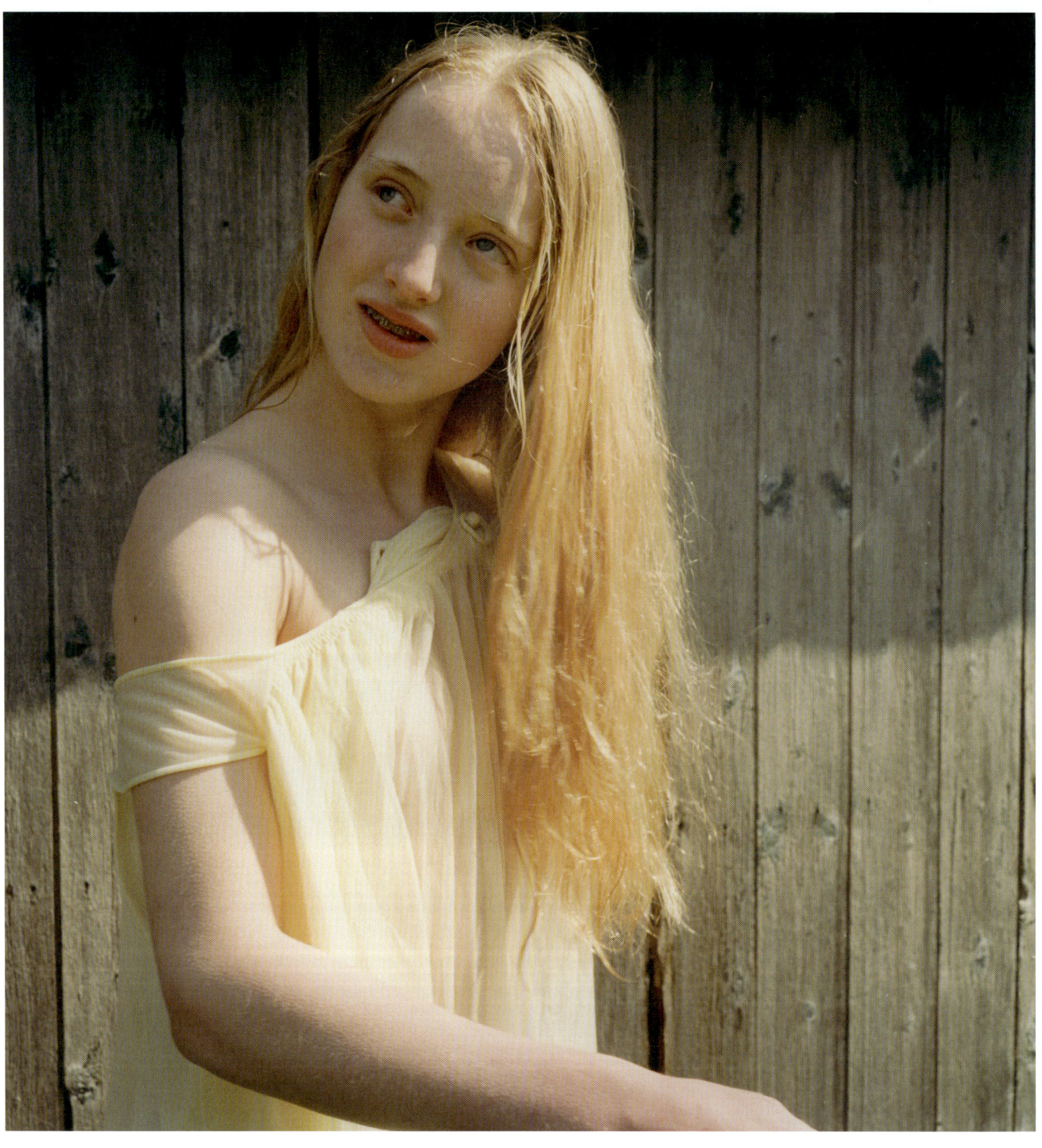

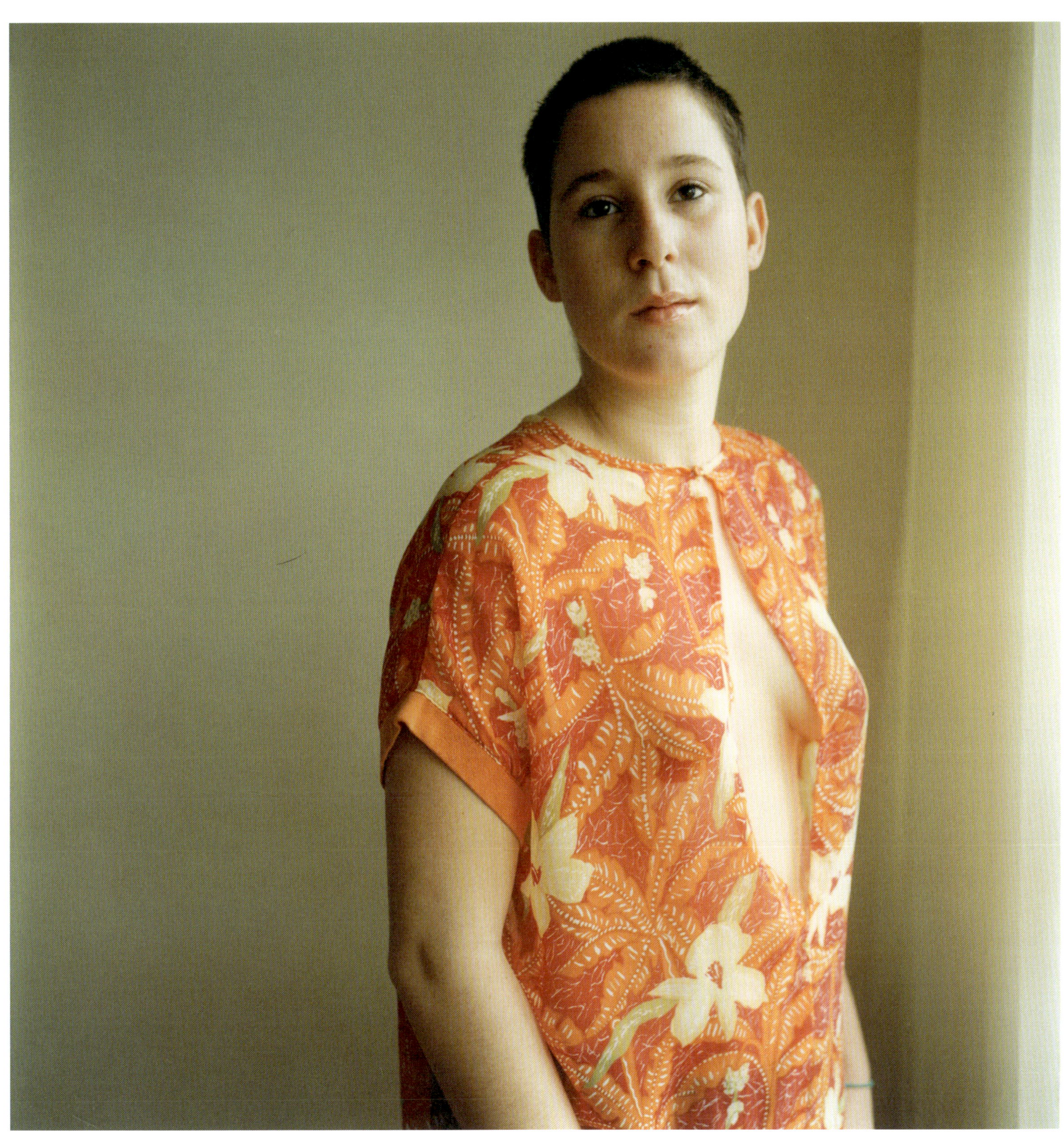

Hellen van Meene

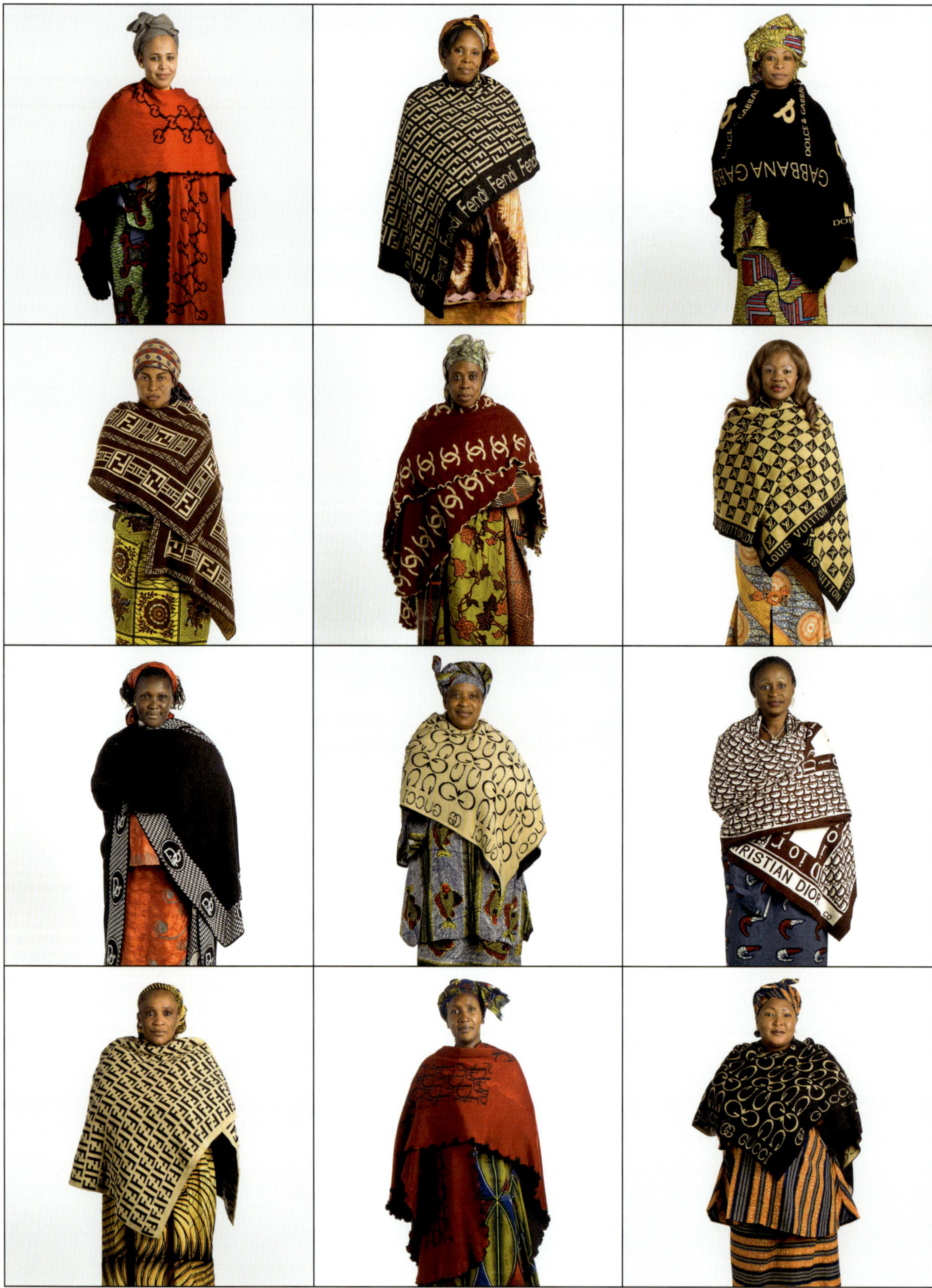

Ari Versluis (born 1961, the Netherlands)
& Ellie Uyttenbroek (born 1965, the Netherlands)

Inspired by the striking dress codes of various social groups, photographer Ari Versluis and stylist Ellie Uyttenbroek have systematically portrayed countless identities. They call this series *Exactitudes*, a contraction of the words exact and attitude. They look for and find most of their models in the street. Lookalikes are then collected in photographic grids of twelve pictures, which give each individual a place in a particular sub-group such as 'Young executives', 'Uomo Espresso', 'Gabbers', 'Tattoo Babes', 'Team Doppio', or 'Cappuccio Girls'. Bringing together people with the same dress codes makes clear how lacking they are in originality and how strongly certain tendencies or trends in society as a whole influence people in the expression of their individuality. Initially, Ari Versluis & Ellie Uyttenbroek did their work in Rotterdam, but later extended their sphere of activity to other cities, such as Amsterdam, Berlin, Luxembourg, Milan, London and Paris.

CDJ

p. 204
121. Boubou Logo – Evry, in 'Exactitudes', 2009.
High-gloss C-print, mounted on 2 mm aluminium, 135 × 100 cm

p. 206
138. Rebels – Rotterdam/Oslo, in 'Exactitudes', 2012.
High-gloss C-print, mounted on 2 mm aluminium, 135 × 100 cm

p. 207
112. Sapeurs – Paris, in 'Exactitudes', 2008.
High-gloss C-print, mounted on 2 mm aluminium, 135 × 100 cm

p. 208
135. Cappuccio Girls – Milano, in 'Exactitudes', 2011.
High-gloss C-print, mounted on 2 mm aluminium, 135 × 100 cm

p. 209
136. Uomo Espresso – Milano, in 'Exactitudes', 2011.
High-gloss C-print, mounted on 2 mm aluminium, 135 × 100 cm

Courtesy the artists

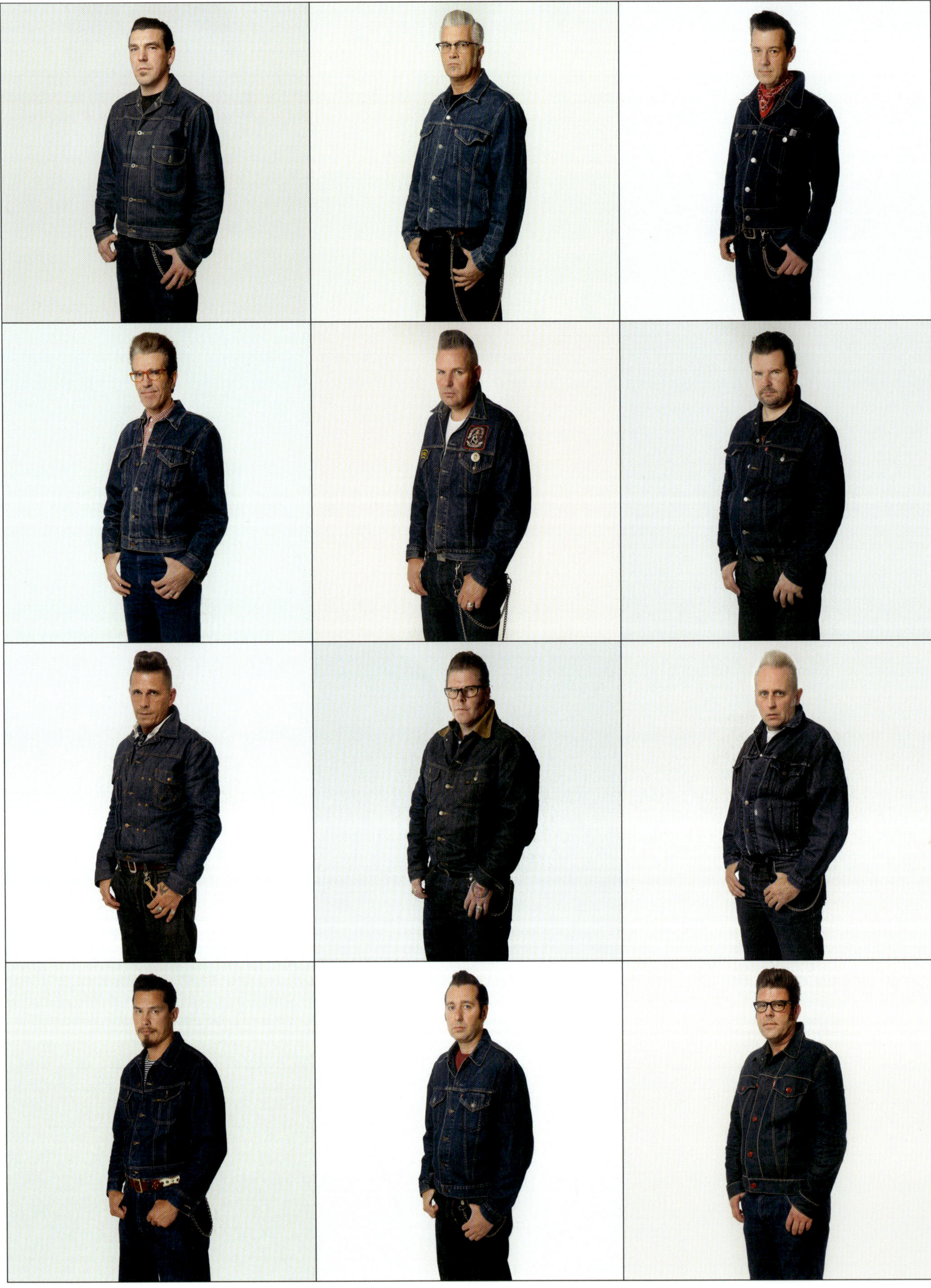

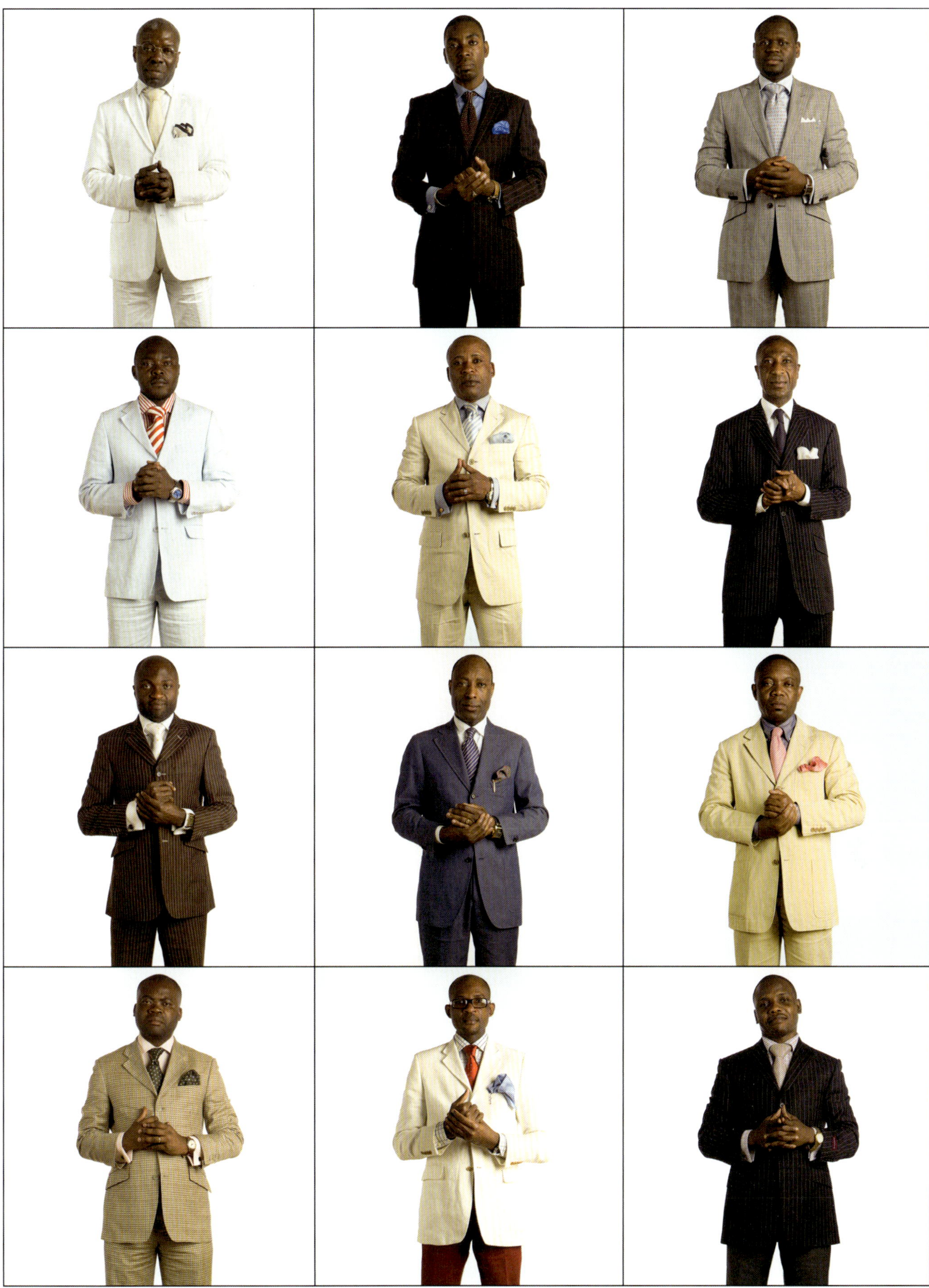

Ari Versluis & Ellie Uyttenbroek

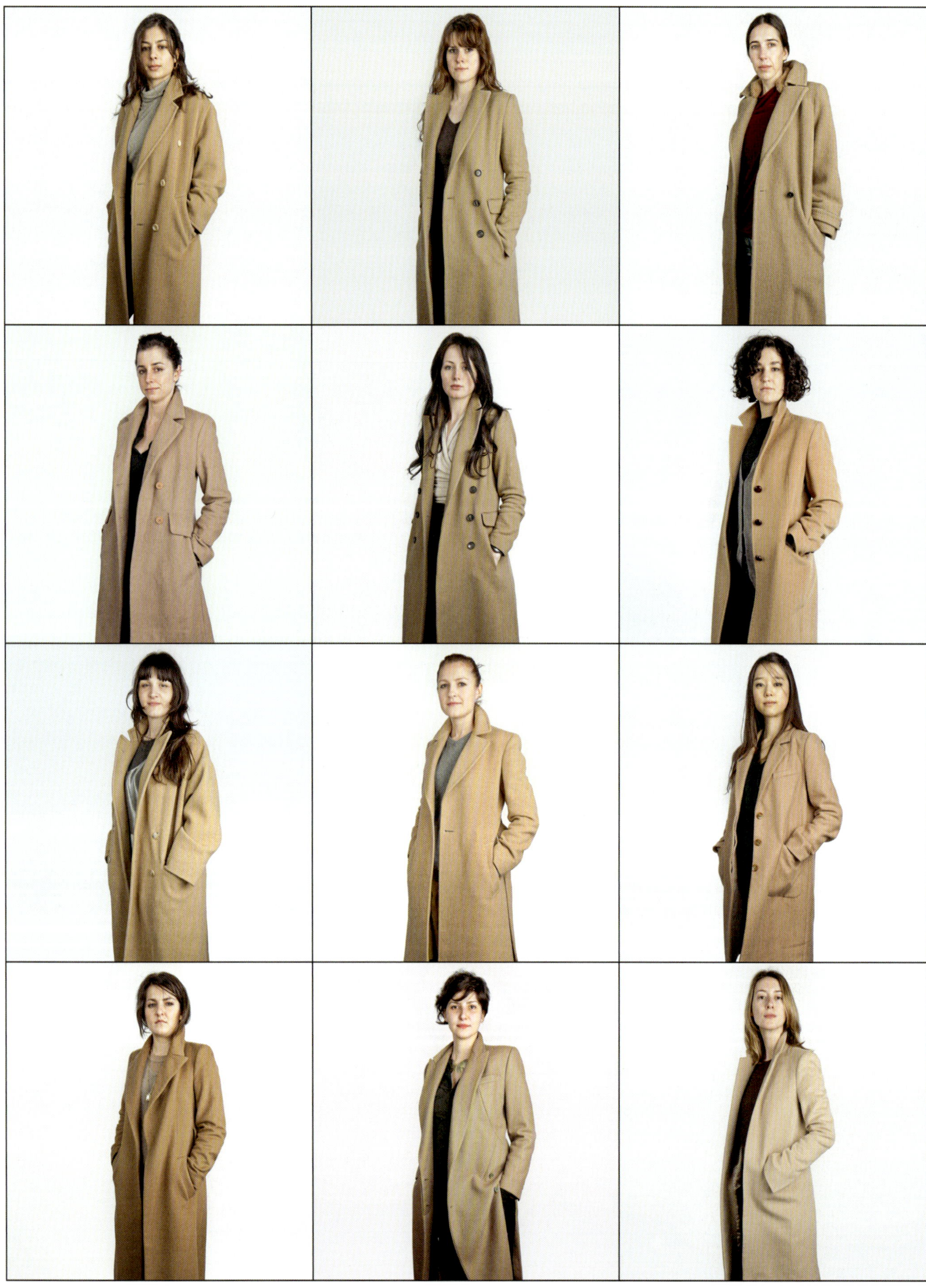

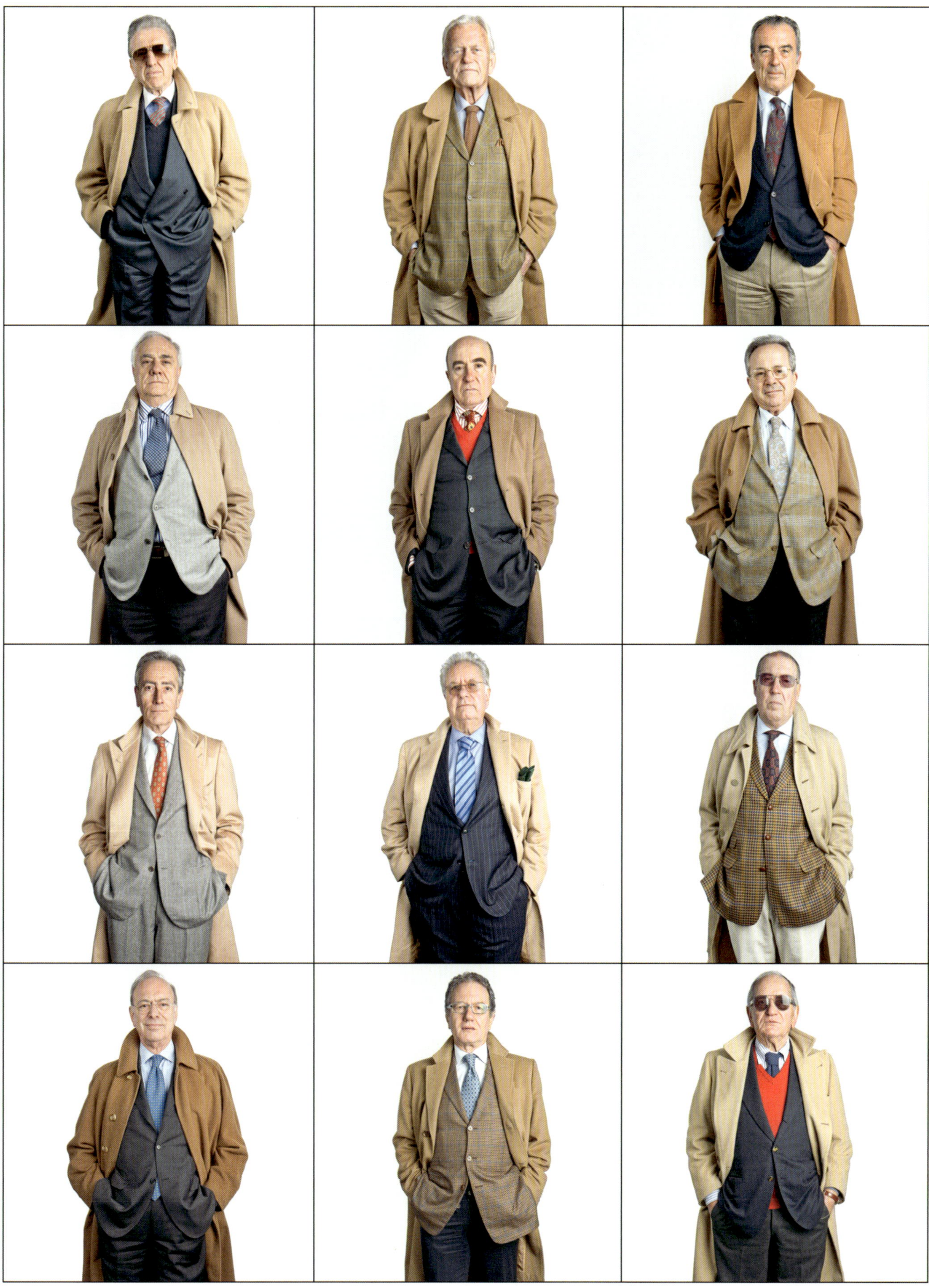

Ari Versluis & Ellie Uyttenbroek

Manfred Willmann (born 1952, Austria)

Das Land

In contrast to life in the city, life in the countryside usually proceeds in small, closely knit communities and in strong interaction with nature. The care for animals and crops imposes set daily routines, which rotate with the changing seasons throughout the year. Death and life, the slaughter and the resultant food, dwell visibly alongside each other. Local habits and customs are related to traditions, which in some cases can be centuries old. Often, religion, language (dialects) and eating habits or prepared dishes adopt a local flavour. Much more prominently than in the city, different generations blend into daily life and work. Inhabitants of these communities derive their identity and sense of belonging from the unique mix of these various aspects. Manfred Willmann's work reflects this reality. Between 1981 and 1993, Willmann regularly photographed scenes from daily life in a rural community in the Austrian province of Steiermark. The informal compositions and the use of flashlight initially make his photographs look like random snapshots, but Willmann uses his visual language quite deliberately to bring the photographed scenes closer to home and at the same time give them a light synthetic touch. This series did not come about through the documentary interest on the part of an outsider, but through participation. The photographer knows the community well, has been visiting it for years and even has a home there. The portraits are relaxed and spontaneous and always show part of the surrounds. In 2000, Willmann published this project in book form as *Das Land* (The Countryside).

FG

Courtesy Galerie Priska Pasquer, Cologne

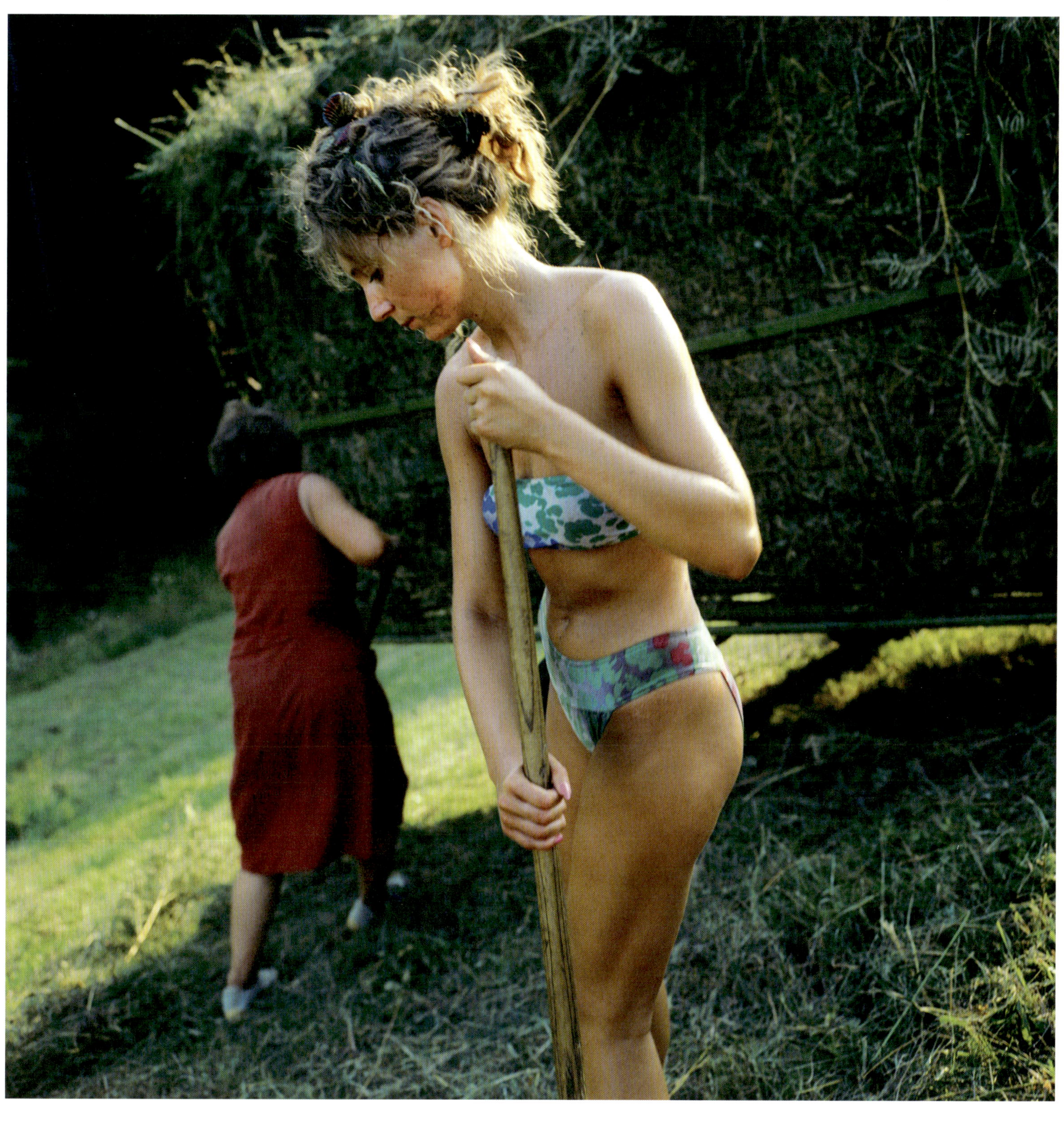

                                  Manfred Willmann

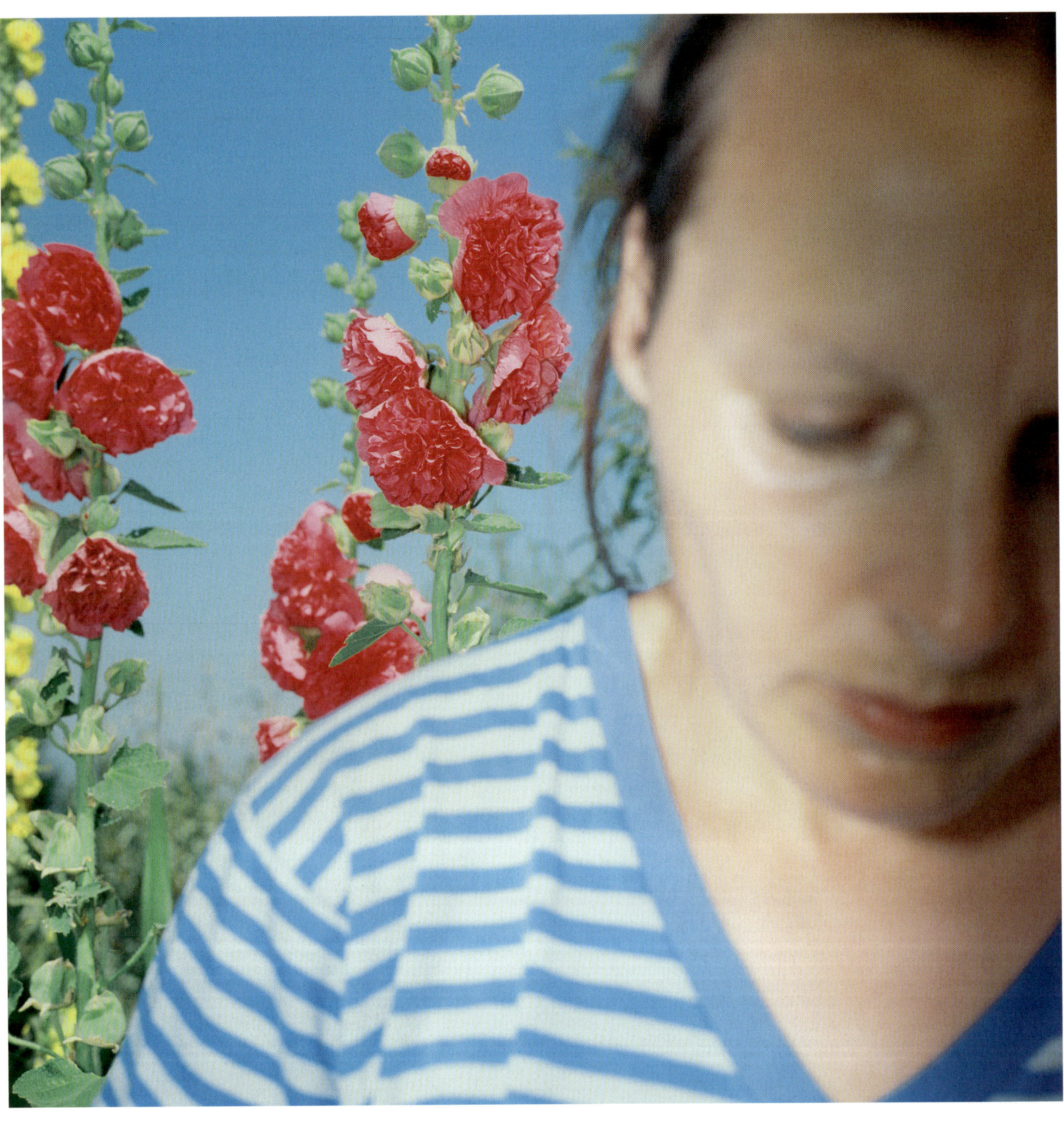

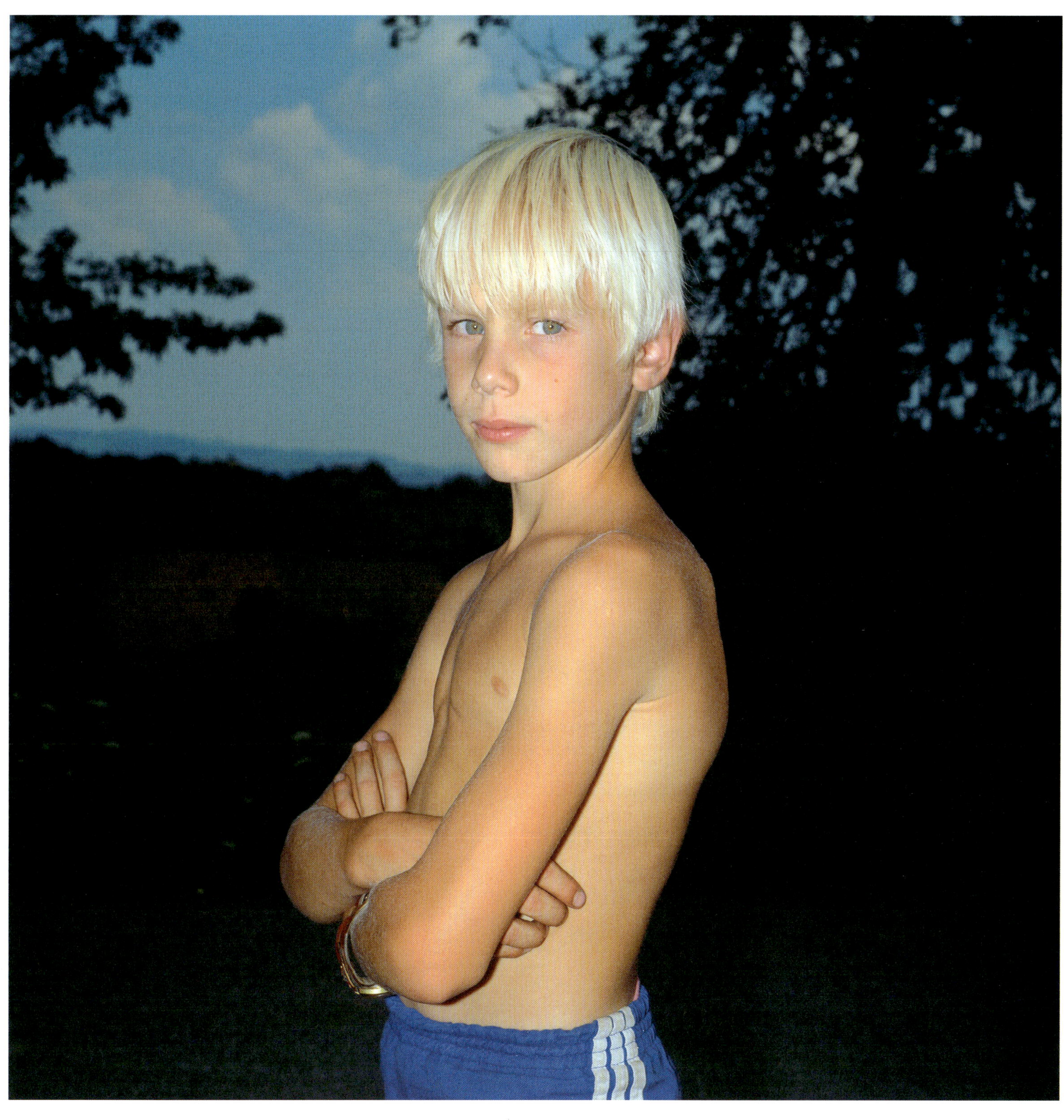

Manfred Willmann

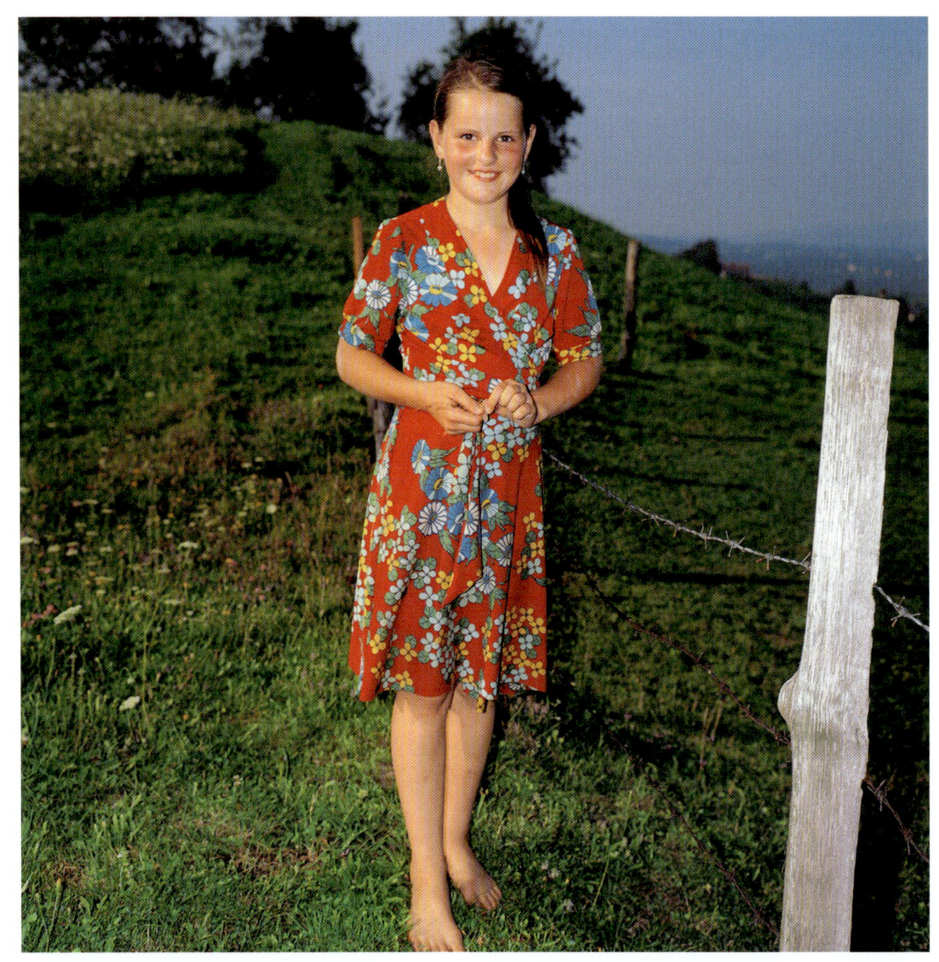

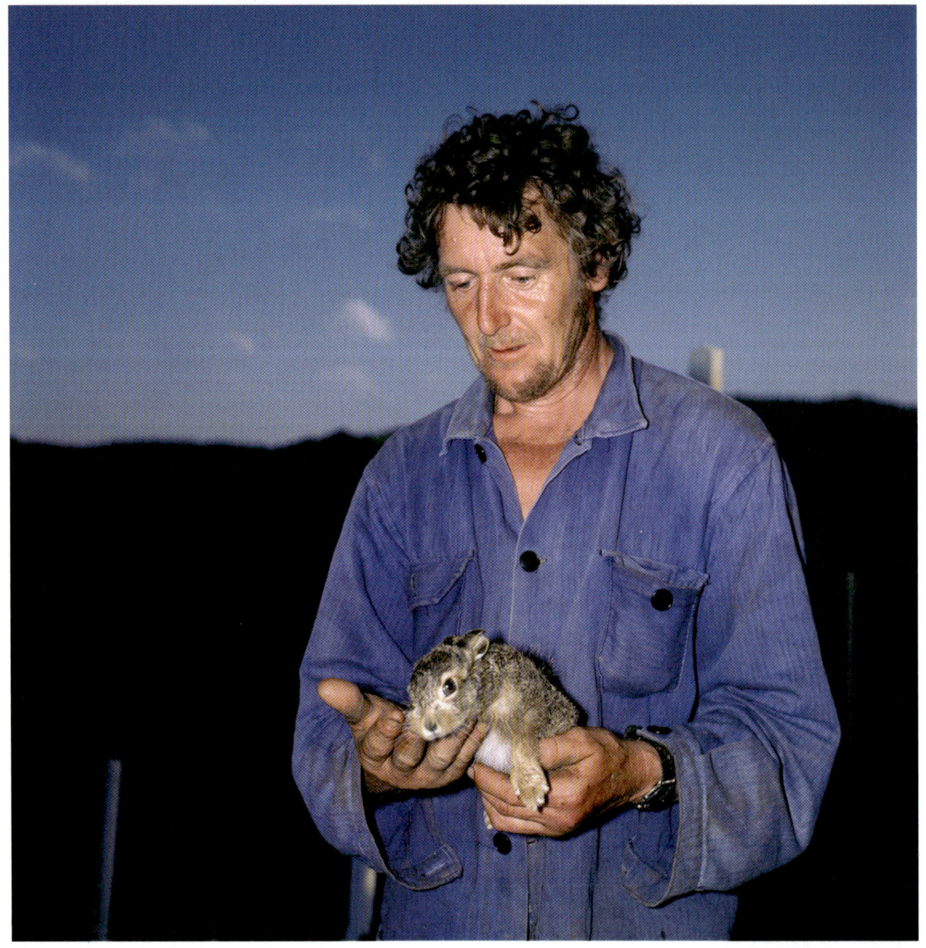

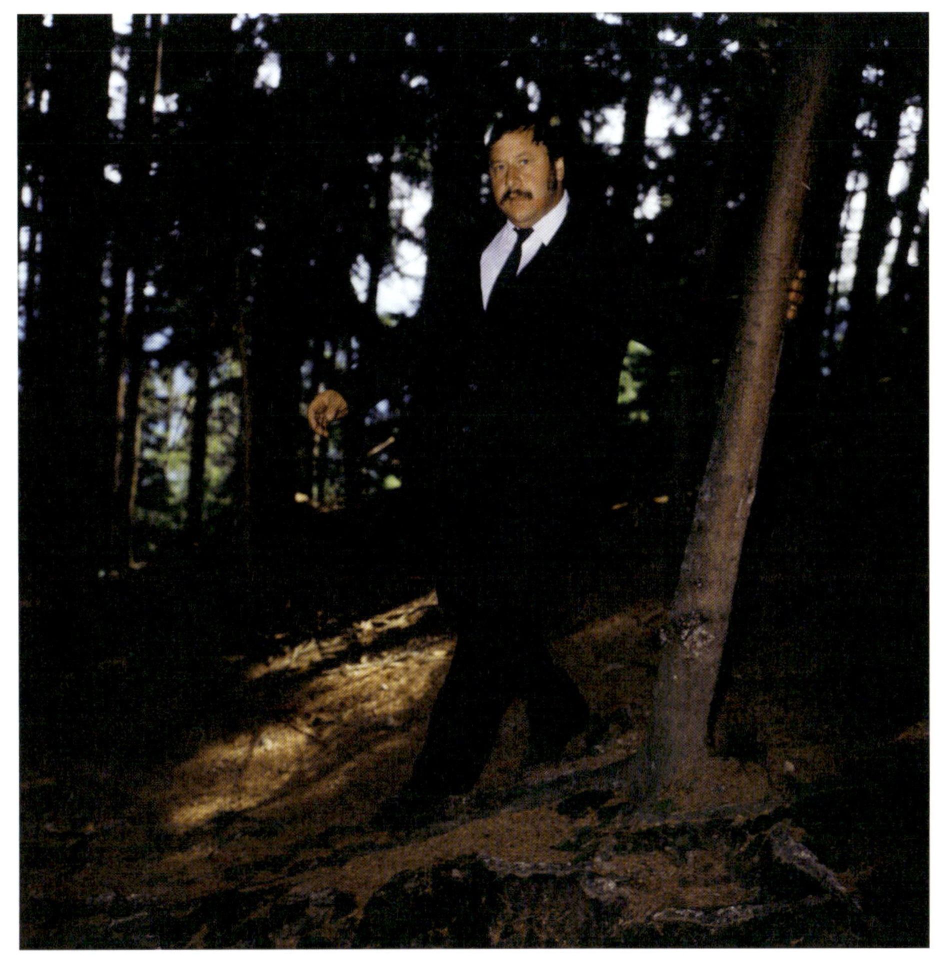

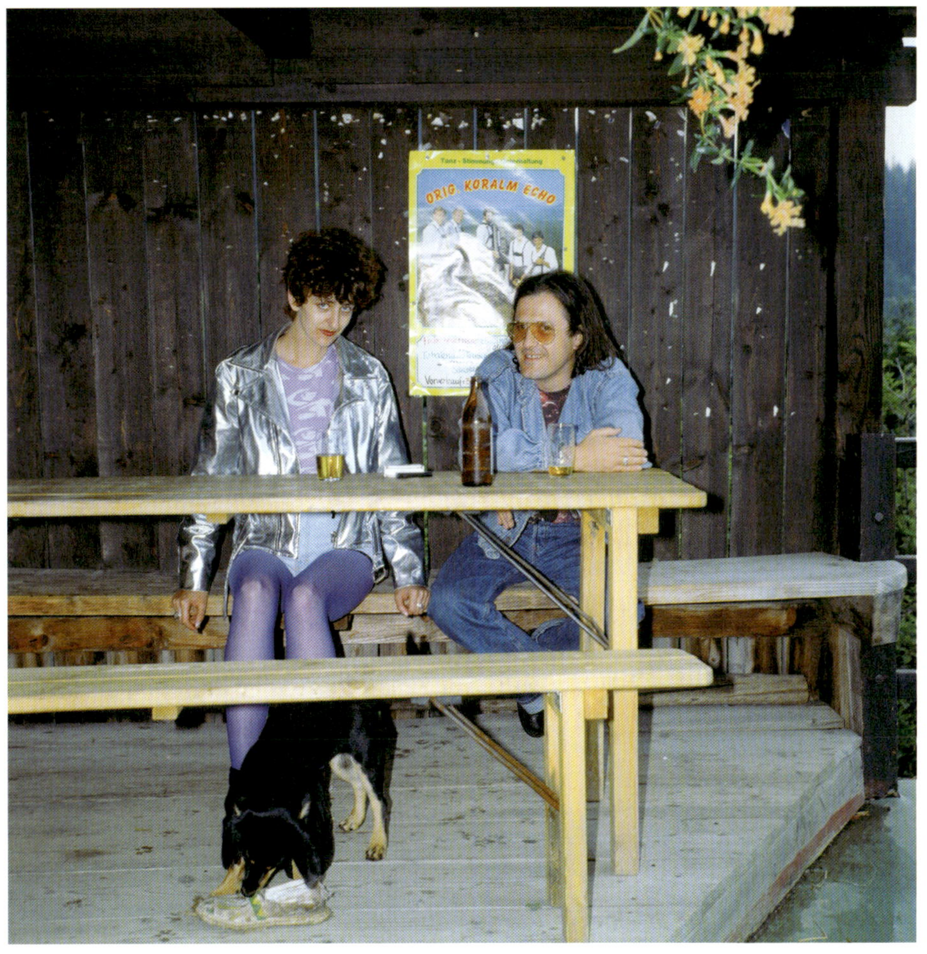

          Manfred Willmann

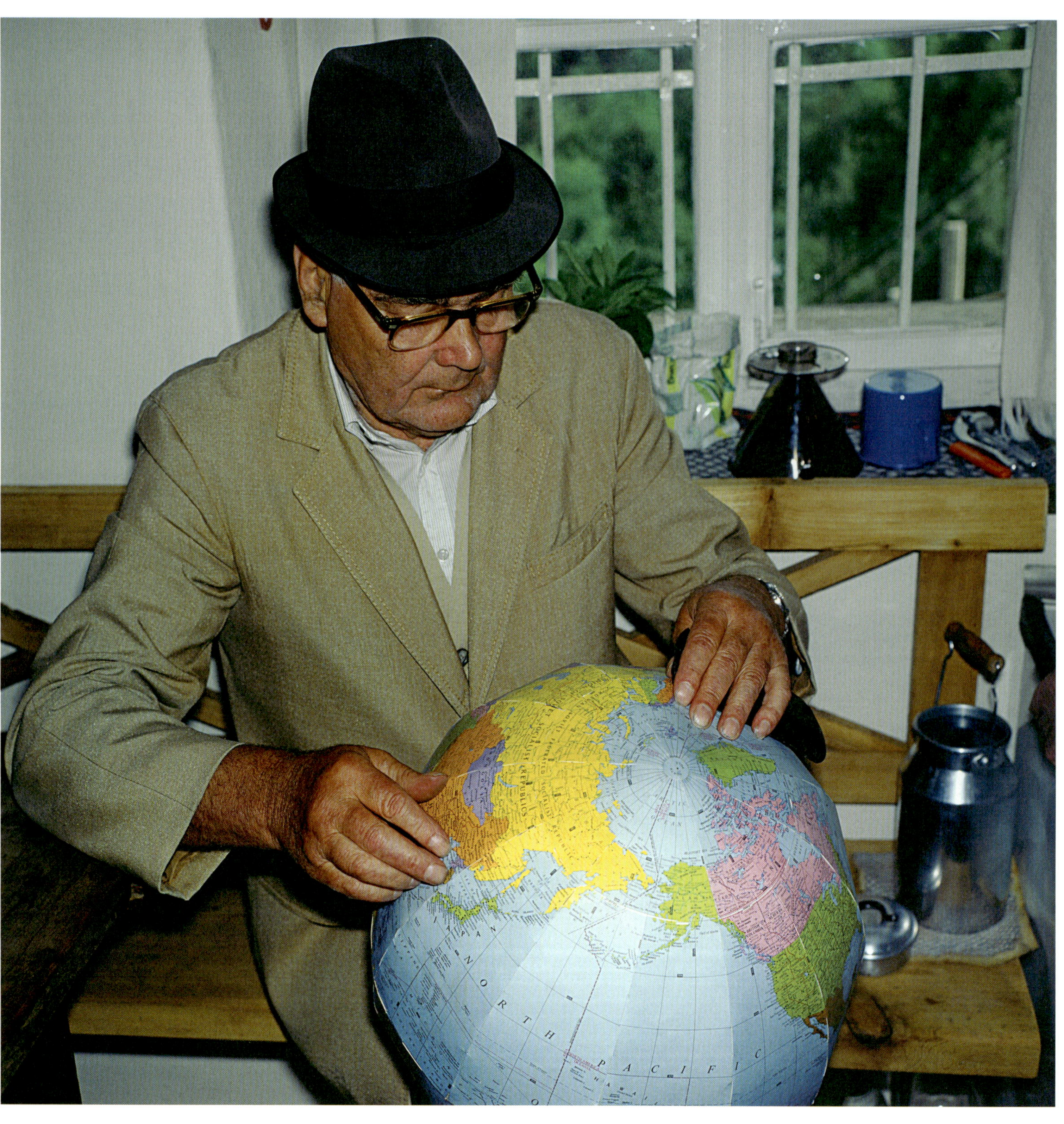

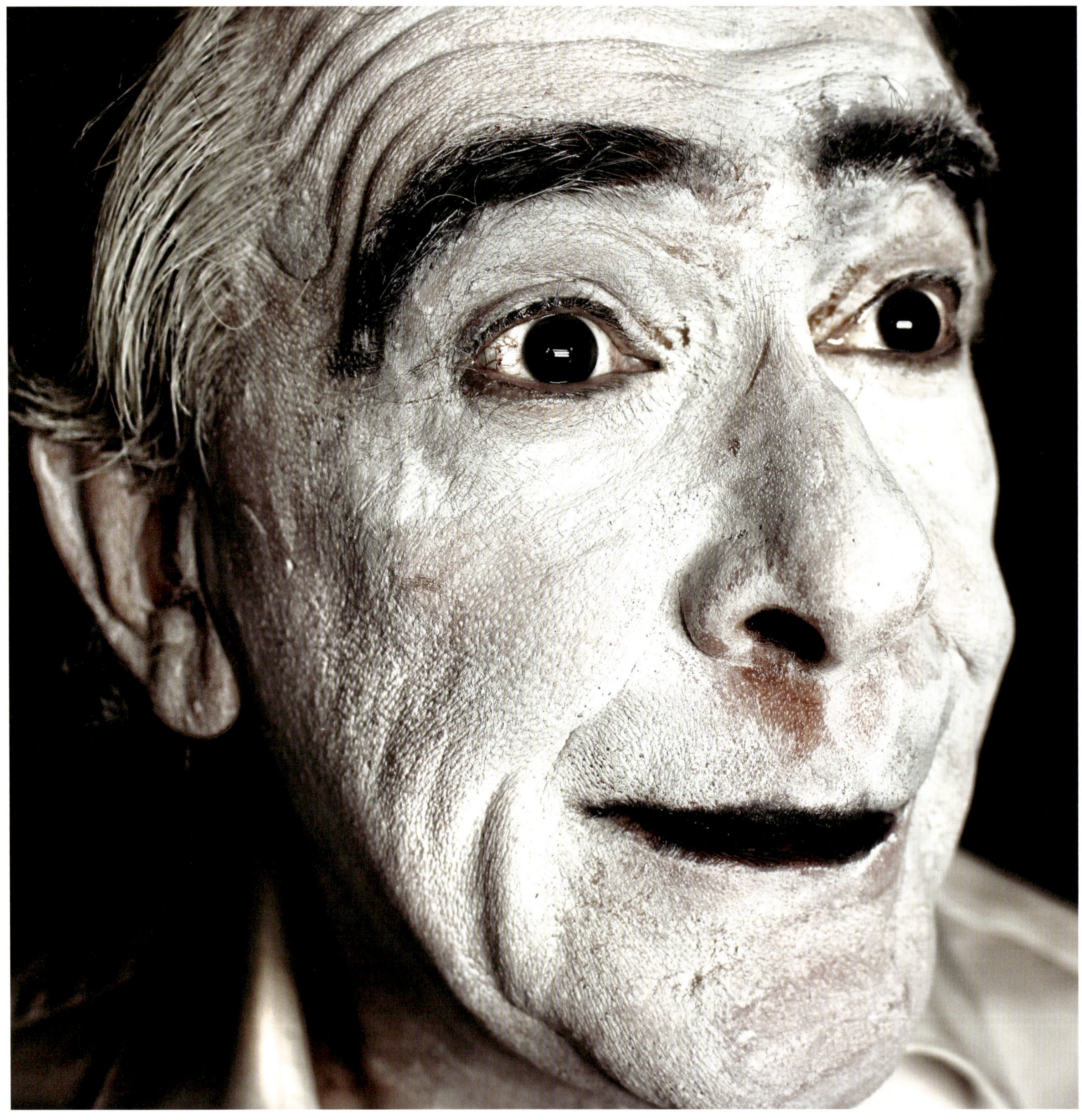

Jorge Molder, *Untitled*, in 'The Scale of Mohs', 2012–13. Digital pigment print on Arches paper, 640 g/m², 153 × 102 cm. Courtesy the artist

Round–table Discussion: Photography and the Renaissance of the Portrait

Paul Dujardin

In November 2014, the head curator of this photo exhibition - *European Portrait Photography since 1990* - and editor of this book, Frits Gierstberg (Nederlands Fotomuseum), sat down with the curators of the exhibition *FACES THEN: Renaissance Portraits from the Low Countries*, Till-Holger Borchert (Musea Brugge) and Koenraad Jonckheere (Ghent University). At BOZAR, the Centre for Fine Arts in Brussels, these two exhibitions are on the programme side by side. This provides the perfect opportunity to clarify a genre that is centuries old, yet still current, and to consider the features, functions and development of the portrait.

Paul Dujardin, Artistic Director of BOZAR, has been involved in this dual project from the very beginning and also sat at the table with them.

Why a dual project?

Paul Dujardin - The different trails came together quite naturally. We soon felt that the two exhibitions, which were originally scheduled for different times, had too much in common to be shown separately. They don't merely reflect a genre, but also show, between all the images, a stratified identity, namely European. That's important, certainly in the light of BOZAR's long-term vision and the question of where the individual fits into a group?

Till-Holger Borchert - We're delighted to have both exhibitions and books alongside each other. They complement each other and blend together seamlessly, even though they both have their individual characteristics. You see that, too, in this book. By combining the two exhibitions, and therefore also the books, you give the public an outstanding presentation of an entire pictorial genre.

PD - In fact, this spring, we're presenting a triptych about 'looking at other people': both portrait exhibitions build a bridge to our exhibition about the Renaissance and the Ottoman Empire: *The Sultan's World: the Ottoman Orient in Renaissance Art*. Together, the three exhibitions tell a stratified story about the construction of identities and the manipulation of perception. Highlights in *The Sultan's World* include portraits of Eastern rulers and Western merchants by Venetian masters such as Tintoretto, Veronese, Bellini and Titian.

Koenraad Jonckheere - Essentially, portrait photography is mainly a Western subject. You won't encounter portraiture as we know it earlier than the 20th century in other parts of the world.

THB - The form of the portraits in the Ottoman exhibition has an affinity with what we know from the Middle Ages. For the most part, that disappeared during the Renaissance. What we show in the Renaissance exhibition is the birth of a genre, the portrait. In the 15th century, it was still the time to look for the *significance* of the portrait, but in the 16th century, the rules had more or less been set out. And those rules proved to be universal: much of what we see in modern portrait photography is based on lines of thought discovered in those days, both in terms of content and form.

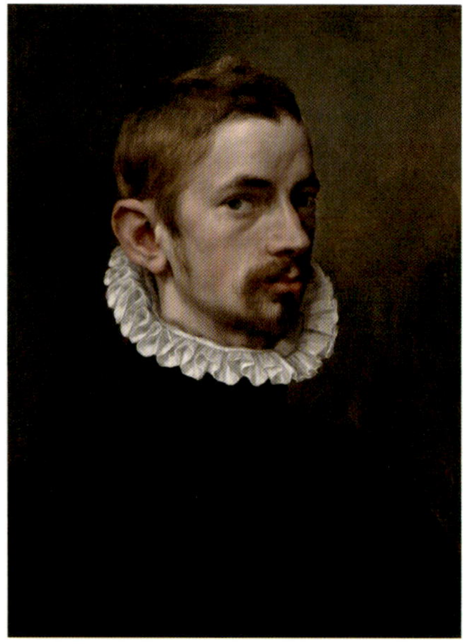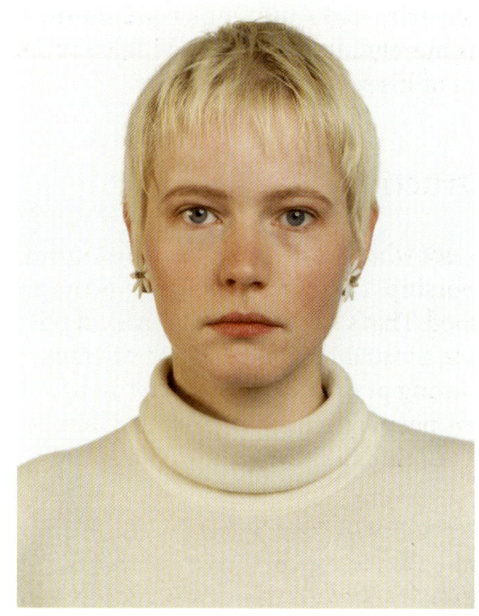

Anonymous, *Portrait of a Man*, c. 1575.
Oil on panel, 46.8 × 33.9 cm. The Art Institute
of Chicago, Samuel P. Avery Fund

Thomas Ruff, *Portrait (Andrea Kachold)*, 1987.
Chromogenic print, 205 × 160 cm.
Courtesy the artist

Frits Gierstberg – When you look at portraits of today, it's rather a complex story. That's partly
due to the abundance of portraits in our society. The situation was entirely different during the
Renaissance, when a portrait was something unique. That also brings about a different version of
the genre. Don't forget there's also a clear, or sometimes less clear, divide between journalism or
the single use of a portrait and what I like to call 'art', which is intended to be looked at for longer.
At the same time, we now also have that awareness of the significance of a picture and its tradition.
This photography exhibition includes several photographers whose portraits are quite consciously
rooted in that tradition. They're familiar with the history of art and make use of certain effects,
such as light, space and composition from the world of painting. They let it play the *trade*.

Construction (or reconstruction)

KJ – What I find so fascinating about the confrontation between both selections is that it becomes
clear that the portrait is always a *construction*. This confronts intuition, which tells us that a portrait reflects reality. When we choose portraits, for instance, we always go for the photograph we
think suits us, whereas there are other photographs we don't select, yet they also portray us. People
have an image of themselves and they want to project it. Artists will always construct. They look
at someone, see certain features, and will focus on those features when they make a portrait. The
big difference with the Renaissance is that in those days it cost time and energy to make a portrait.
That's obviously the nature of the trade. Nowadays, it's the other way round: you prepare the portrait, you study it, you construct a scene, and you can even manipulate it later, but, unlike painting,
taking a photograph lasts a mere fraction of a second.

FG – You certainly see with someone like Thomas Ruff that he invests a lot of time in advance in
his *form*.

THB – You also have to consider the *function* of that time investment. You could interpret the time
invested in a Renaissance portrait as literally indicating the level of esteem with which the person
being portrayed was held. By way of background: in artistic antiquity, people wondered whether
expressive art or literature was the medium best suited to conveying reality – *Ut pictura poesis*
(As is painting, so is poetry). The discourse in the 15th and 16th centuries, with the Reformation
and Counter-Reformation (and let's not forget Erasmus of Rotterdam), then moves towards the
belief that art can certainly portray the face, but not the soul. We also see that some (but not all)

photography tries to do just that by attempting to fathom the personality. At first sight, Thomas Ruff seems merely intent on taking highly spontaneous photographs, but he also tries to approach the essence of his subject's personality.

Deconstruction

FG – That's not what I see with Ruff. He has examined the post-war tradition of photography with its celebrity worship. The subjects in those pictures have a history: they've achieved something and are distinguished. That's not an inherent part of photography, but the camera doesn't detract from it at all. It's a *style*, a visual language. And so the image portrays a sort of drama, which suggests that someone has a strong personality, or perhaps not. Ruff tries to put an end to all that. In the years of post-modernism, people deconstructed everything. Ruff does that too. He empties the image, and makes sure it has nothing to do with the depicted person so that people will have another look at it later.

THB – A dissection of decorum …

KJ – Ruff transfers the search for the soul from the artist to the spectator.

FG – Or he says to the spectator: You're the one looking for the soul, but you won't find it in the picture. In fact, the picture says nothing.

KJ – What's fascinating about it all is that he uses old stereotypes. In portraiture, you have three major types: profile, three-quarter profile and frontal. These are also related to values. The profile portrait is ideal for emperors and kings; the frontal portrait is essentially a Christian type used to depict not only Christ, but also saints; and the three-quarter profile is usually for the middle classes. Generally speaking, those are the classic patterns. And Ruff also plays around with them.

FG – He also plays around with police photographs, identity photographs, which ought to be neutral and objective. Obviously, that's not possible.

THB – Biometric?

FG – Certainly, also biometric. Typological photography from the 19th century, vertex photography. It's all there. When this work was first published in the late 1980s, the lifelessness of portraiture was highly innovative, but also very surprising. Nowadays, by contrast, there's perhaps a glimmer of what you could call a 'soul'. It seems you can't detach that element completely.

Covering up to make a portrait

FG – The photography on show here includes work by some photographers who have consciously carried out research into the 'face as a mask'. Jorge Molder, for example, who also refers to the theatre, to poses, and the act of doing as if.

KJ – There was also a rhetorical tradition in the Renaissance.

THB – But we haven't included that in our selection because it remains exceptional. The portrait of the court jester Gonella by Jean Fouquet, for example, or *The Ugly Duchess* by Quentin Metsys – those are really freak shows.

KJ – There's also the woman with the beard, Marguerite Halscher, by Willem Key. But that doesn't matter. My impression is that those sorts of images are exceptions in your selection?

FG – Ultimately, yes, but they're not exceptions when you look at contemporary art. It's quite common to cover the face or render it unrecognizable. Look at Michaël Borremans, for instance.

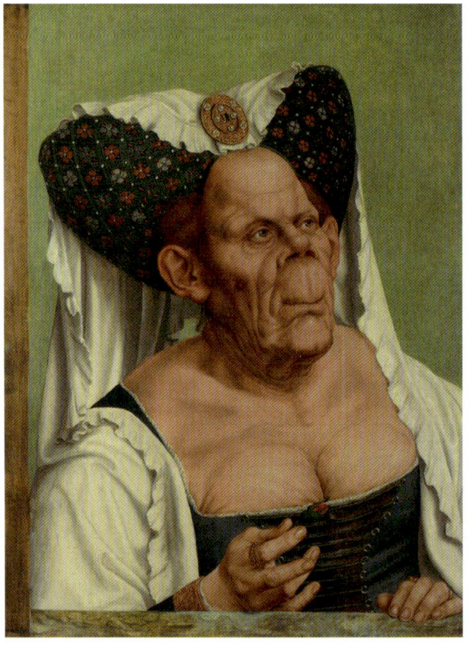

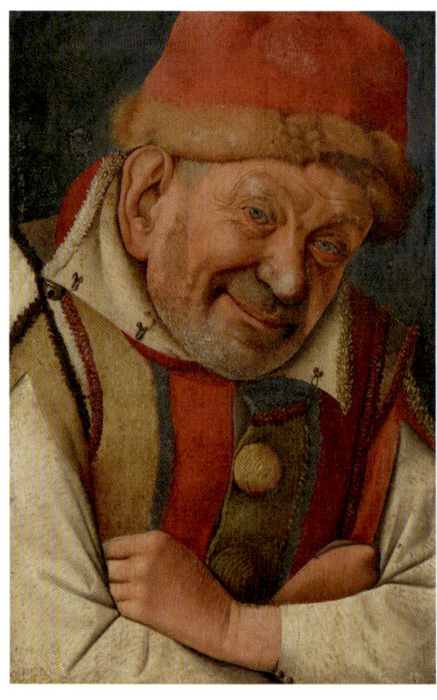

Quentin Metsys, *An Old Woman ('The Ugly Duchess')*,
c. 1513. Oil on panel, 64.2 × 45.5 cm.
National Gallery, London

Jean Fouquet, *Portrait of the Court Jester Gonella*,
c. 1445. Oil on panel, 36.1 × 23.8 cm.
Kunsthistorisches Museum Wien, Vienna

KJ – Yet this method also goes back a long way. Think of Timanthes. He had to portray the grief of
Agamemnon at the loss of his daughter Iphigenia, but he didn't know how. And so, he painted him
with a veil over his face, leaving beholders to imagine the king's grief for themselves. It's a real
topos from antiquity. Rubens painted it on the front of his house, while Bruegel has been compared to Timanthes: covering up to make a portrait is a centuries-old idea. Darzacq's 'helmets'
also work like that. They get the viewers' brains working by making them ask who, what and how?

PD – Does portraying divergence – the way Denis Darzacq does, for instance – have a different
purpose now compared with then?

FG – I don't think that Darzacq wants to photograph divergence for its own sake, but he's mainly
concerned with confronting viewers with the question of what divergence is.

THB – Obviously, that line of reasoning didn't arise during the Renaissance, when the 'freak' was
simply portrayed as such. Because it was a peculiarity, a rarity and, moreover, a punishment from
God. The circus monstrosity. In the case of Gonella by Fouquet, it should also be said that the
portrayed court jester was world-famous, so he could expect recognition. The Jay Leno of his day!

KJ – They also used such portraits as a mirror. No one wanted to look like that, so your own beauty
was confirmed, as it were. Mind you, people still register such curiosities today. We're quick to
photograph spectacular people or events. In those days, the only way to do that was by painting.
Artists would pluck people from the street for their attractive faces – and they still do so today.
Da Vinci did it, as did Fellini.

The psychoanalytical gaze and the selfie

FG – Just now, you all said that Renaissance portraits are realistic, or at least they're meant to be,
but that if you look at them a little longer, you find a sort of lower limit. That can't be deliberate,
surely, or can it?

THB – During the Renaissance, there weren't any artists who deliberately went off in search of themselves or others. The psychoanalytical gaze in particular has been one of the major developments in modern photography. That gaze wasn't part of the Renaissance. Self-portraits, for example, are conceptual, but they always involve people who are looking for themselves. Rubens and Rembrandt both have that gaze, but Rembrandt has it much more than Rubens, who plays with it more formally. It's still commission art, which is also linked to the idea of *portrait worthiness*. Not everyone in the Renaissance was worthy of a portrait. Albrecht Dürer once did a portrait of an old gentleman as a model for St Hieronymus, but that really was most unconventional. Dürer really should have appeared before the art inquisition for such a breach of decorum!

FG – From the 1990s onwards everyone was suddenly worthy of a portrait in photography …

THB – King Client!

FG – … and now, if no one makes a portrait of you, you do it yourself!

KJ – If you're not in the picture, you don't exist. Just look at Facebook, which is essentially a glorification of the portrait. The selfie is a product of it.

FG – You could also turn the question on its head. Are there certain features in the image of a face that turn it into a portrait?

THB – I think that with the selfie, the portrait now has undergone a revolution, while serving different purposes, as was the case back in the 15th century. The portrait has been hauled out of its museum context.

FG – Those new purposes are easy to summarize, namely profiling, in social media, but also in society. There are also form requirements, otherwise, you don't exist in certain environments or among your contemporaries. It's the construction of a self-portrait, and an indication of how you relate to society.
  It's also crazy that there's no such thing as a bad selfie.

KJ – The big difference between now and previous centuries is the repetitiveness. You can make as many portraits as you like nowadays, and reproduce them infinitely. Portraits have become a disposable product. This is totally different from the frequency of portraiture before the days of Polaroid. Photography used to be expensive, and you only did it once or twice, unless you were an emperor or king. That repetitiveness makes it much easier to construct an identity now than in the past, when you would record something once, but the idea was to give it eternal value. For example: if you were to ask people to tear up the wallet photos of their mothers or daughters, they would all say 'No!' But deleting digital pictures, which come in their hundreds, is apparently not so bad. The portrait as an 'object' makes a difference here. As soon as something becomes tangible, we attach greater importance to it. We need a sort of materialization to give it some magic.

FG – Moreover, the size of that materialization, at least in photography, will also create a different effect.

Universal values and archetypes

KJ – Renaissance portraits aren't huge in size. Most of them are full scale, but you also see miniatures. Depending on the way they were framed, you see busts, tronies and semi-anatomy – formats that are all related to social class. The king was portrayed full length, but citizens never were, at least not until the very end of the 16th century. In the mid-16th century, a certain type of citizen would be portrayed seated on a chair, with a degree of authority.

THB – We're focusing on the Low Countries at the moment, but we mustn't forget that all this is an international phenomenon. Those standards also apply to the Italian and German Renaissance.

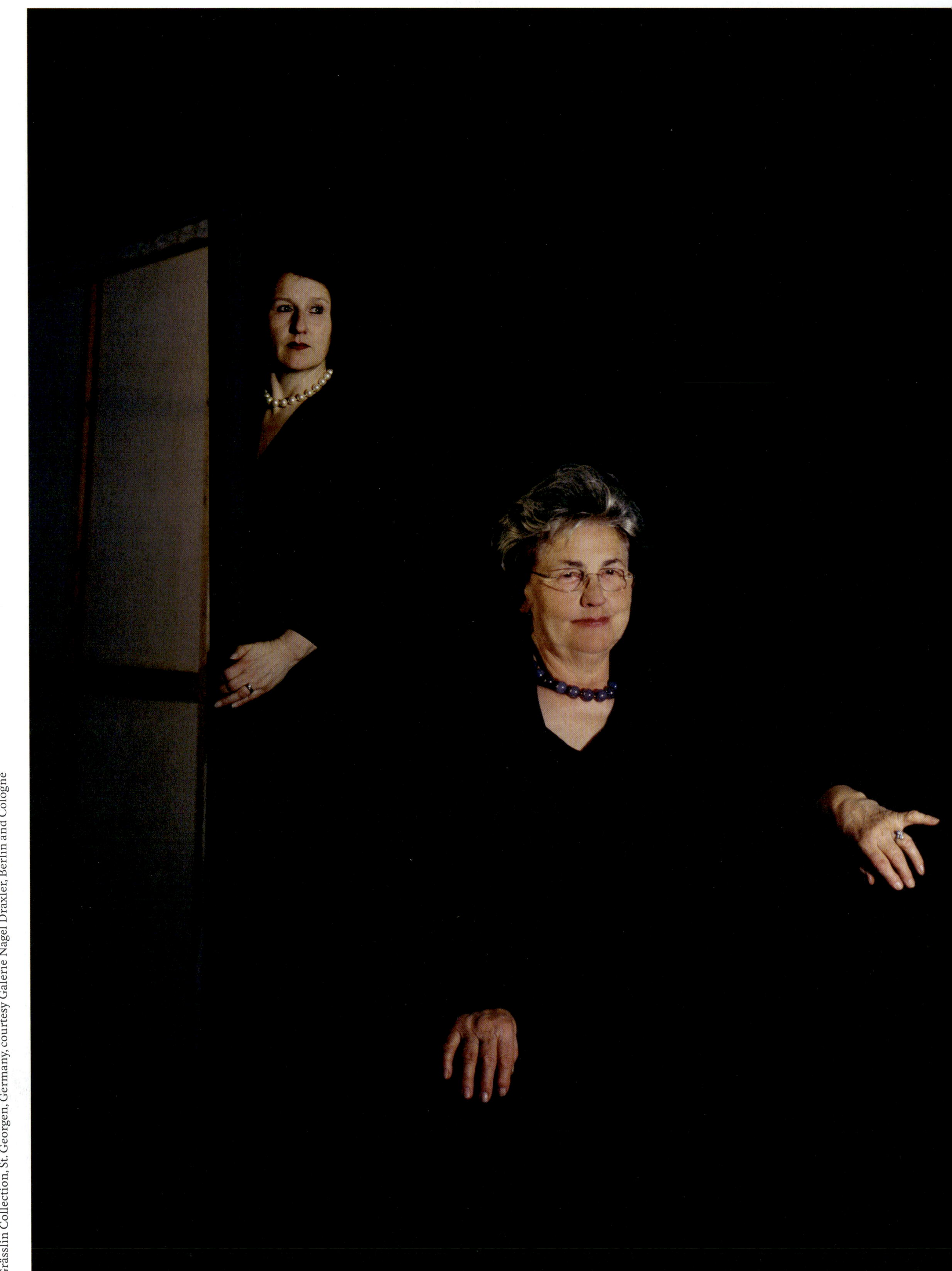

Clegg & Guttmann, *The Art Collectors*, 2008. Lambda print, 187 × 318 cm. Grässlin Collection, St. Georgen, Germany, courtesy Galerie Nagel Draxler, Berlin and Cologne

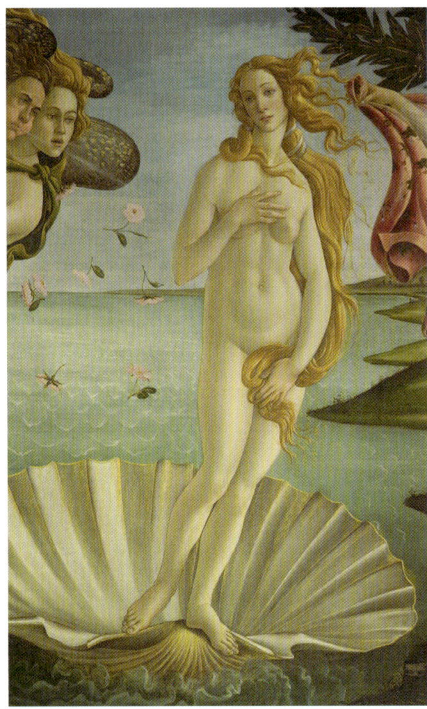

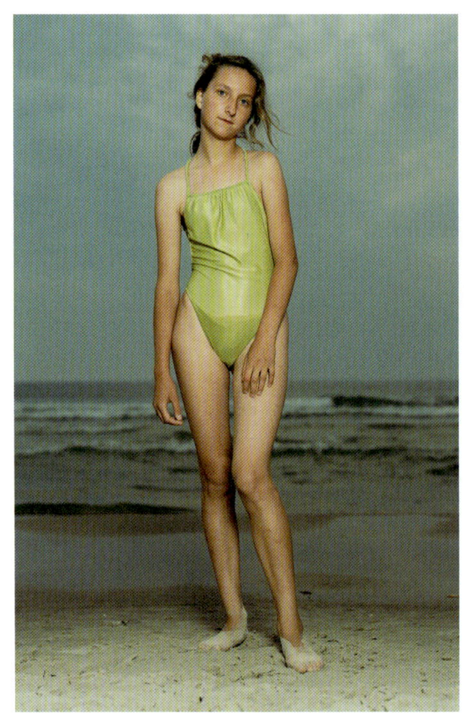

Sandro Botticelli, *The Birth of Venus* (detail), 1482/85. Tempera on canvas, 172.5 × 278.5 cm. Galleria degli Uffizi, Florence

Rineke Dijkstra, *Kolobrzeg, Poland, July 26, 1992*, 1992. C-print, 128 × 100 cm. Courtesy the artist and Marian Goodman Gallery, New York, London and Paris

In some cases that does make it difficult to contextualize, to discern whether something is Dutch, German or Italian. There were unwritten rules that people more or less adhered to. But to some extent we *can* detect national trends in those portrait conventions. Artists in German-speaking areas, for example, would have been quicker to make full-length portraits of citizens, compared with their more hesitant counterparts in monarchist societies.

KJ – In the Netherlands, you see that those conventions changed very quickly as soon as the monarchist structure disappeared in the 17th century and the country was in practice ruled by governors and regents. Social relations changed and the new situation invited experiments. The portrait was also something of a visual weapon in the 16th and 17th centuries, its prime function being to show that you had the means to pay for it – and money has always implied a certain power.

FG – Look at the photographs by Clegg & Guttmann. Even today, prominent people still have a portrait of themselves made – good examples in this book are Anton Corbijn, Konstantinos Ignatiadis and Stephan Vanfleteren. Corbijn's portrait of Luc Tuymans is a genre in itself, namely the artist and the studio.

KJ – Some portrait conventions and poses have become so universal that people continue to use them subconsciously. Take, for instance, the seated prominent figure with one leg under the chair and the other slightly further forward. That pose goes back to the Zeus of Olympus. Ever since then it has become the norm par excellence for portraying the mighty of the earth, something you also see today in portraits of world leaders. Note also certain hand positions or movements.

THB – It could be something neurological, but Carl Gustav Jung's archetypes could just as well be the reason. Obviously, you also have to take account of the conditioning we've undergone over centuries with regard to images. For example, it seems impossible to me to look at Rineke Dijkstra's beach portraits and not think of Botticelli's *Birth of Venus*. That's not a neurological phenomenon, but simply conditioning – on the part of the photographer, but perhaps also the depicted girl, who enjoys being depicted in this way because she's subconsciously aware of the effect that pose will have. Botticelli's

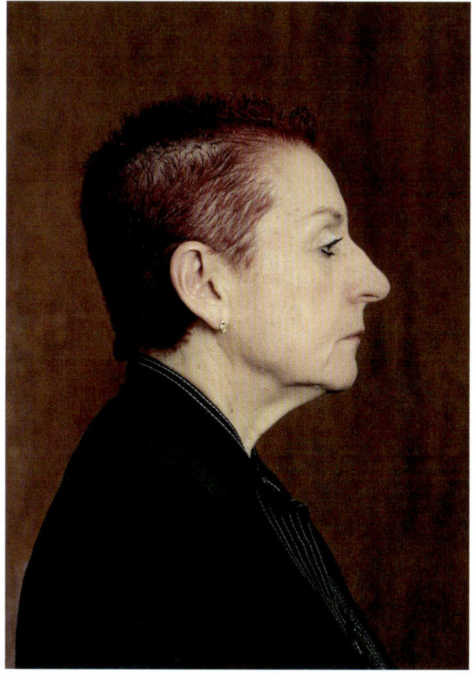 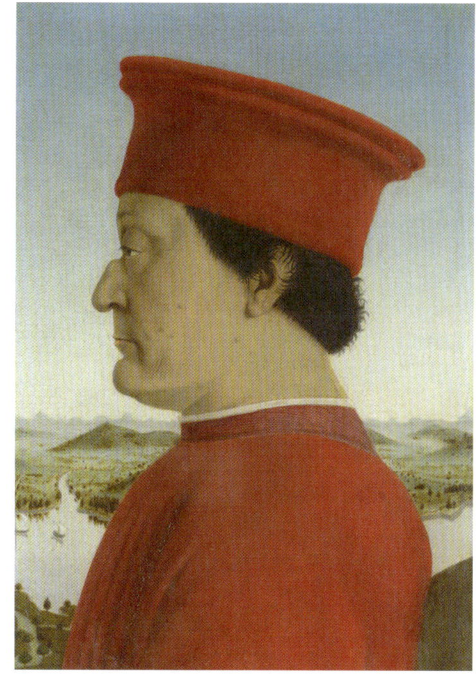

Jitka Hanzlová, *Untitled (Conca)*, in 'There is something I don't know', 2011. Archival pigment print on cotton, 52 × 37 cm. Courtesy the artist

Piero della Francesca, *Federico da Montefeltro* (right panel of a diptych), 1465/72. Oil on panel, 47 × 33 cm. Galleria degli Uffizi, Florence

Venus certainly had a conceptual dimension, and I can imagine that this is also the case with Dijkstra. Just from the way the hair turns out …

KJ – Botticelli's Venus herself also resembles the Venus pudica of the Medici family. Even more interesting than the question of whether or not the similarity is intentional is the tendency to associate all sorts of things with it. Of all the various photographs she took of this girl, Dijkstra may well have chosen this particular portrait subconsciously, that is to say, with Botticelli at the back of her mind.

FG – Although the main intention was to photograph ordinary girls on the beach, this extra layer, this extra interpretation that it could also be a girl from a painting, certainly adds value to the work.

KJ – There's a very common debate in our field about portrait history, in which portraits are put or integrated into the background of historical events. A guessing game often arises: is it that figure? Or the other one? But why does it have to be a yes-or-no question? When artists make a portrait of someone, they are, by definition, constructing an image. They can give those portraits a certain universality or neutrality, as someone like Da Vinci did. This tension is important. It struck me that few portrait photographs in the selection shown here go looking for that tension.

THB – You can also describe the minimal neutral element in the photographs of Rineke Dijkstra, for example, as 'very precise', and that's due to the more spontaneous procedure of making such an image. It goes without saying that this is precisely the reason – namely the differences in media – why such a portrait by Dijkstra simply couldn't have existed in the Renaissance.

PD – Are the profile portraits by Hanzlová subconsciously a reference to the portrait of Montefeltro by Piero della Francesca, just as that one beach portrait by Rineke Dijkstra reminds us of Botticelli's Venus?

THB – Those portraits refer to any sort of profile portrait in history. I see mainly a woman with a long nose.

KJ - According to Pliny, painting arose because someone once stood in profile in front of a wall, whereupon his shadow was cast on the wall and the first painter made the outline.

THB - I think it goes back even as far as Plato. And, of course, the ancient Egyptians. But apart from that, Della Francesca obviously plays a part. By means of the profile he tries to do two things: in the combination of the profile and the landscape, he shows his model (in this case Federico da Montefeltro) as Caesar, and at the same time as the sovereign ruler of the depicted landscape. That landscape is the property of the one portrayed, so the picture is definitely not neutral. Quentin Metsys' famous profile portrait, however, is also not unusual; it is found in sculpture, in illustrations and on coins.

KJ - Although the profile portrait in modern photography comes across less naturally or more artificially, it is also largely an artistic experiment. It's all about distance and vicinity.

The best of two worlds

PD - How would you view the pictures of Jorma Puranen as a link between modern photography and the Renaissance portrait? Is that maybe too obvious?

THB - It's neither one nor the other, but it does make handy use of both media and both periods.

FG - It's a new look at those paintings via photography. Details do emerge that the modern eye otherwise might not see. The photographic realism inherent in the medium gives the painted models a presence and brings them back to life. It makes both media visible, both photography and painting.

PD - I think that was also our objective, namely to show the cross-connections between two different media and two different periods. We wanted both the connecting theme and some progression, but also to show the universality in a particular iconographic genre. And I think we've clearly succeeded.

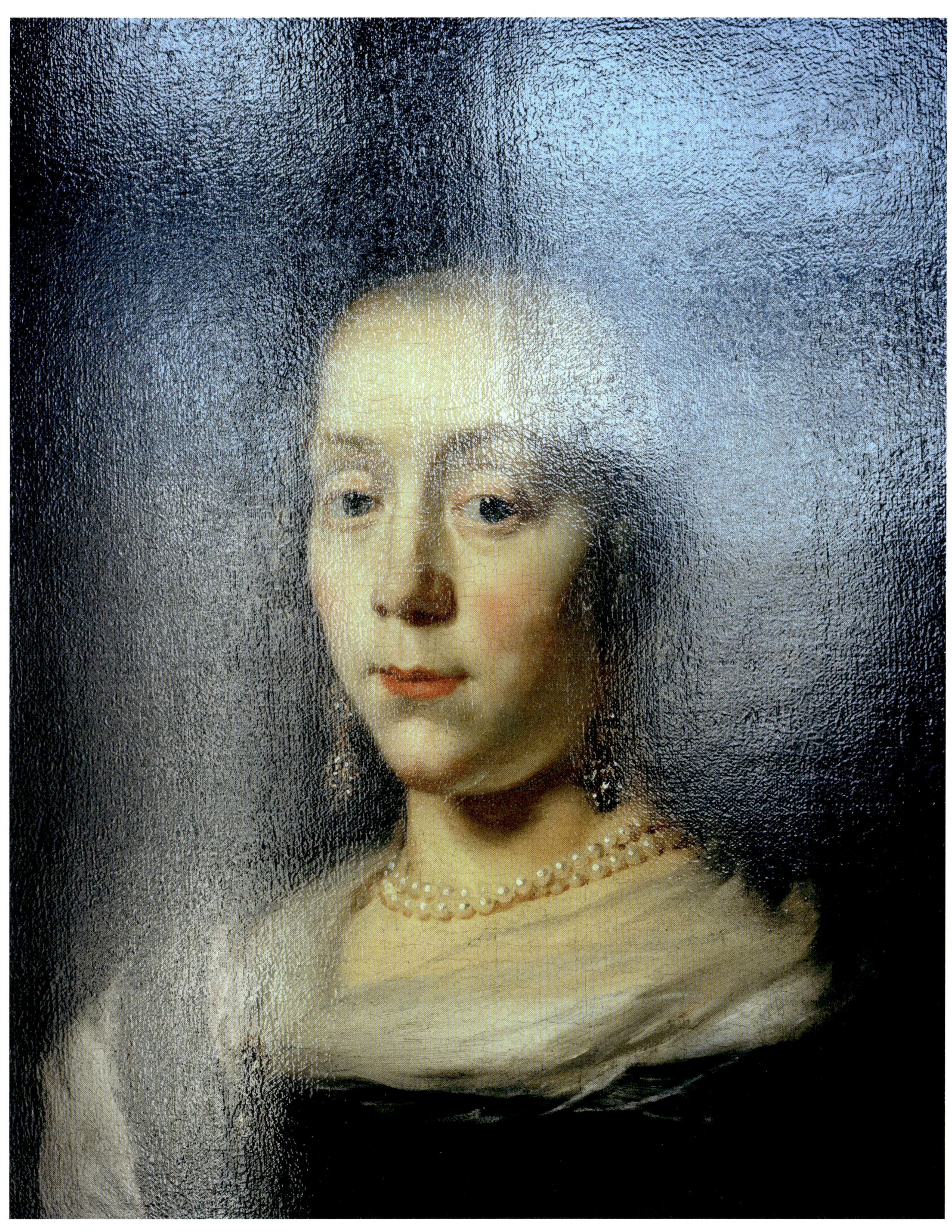

Jorma Puranen, *Shadows, Reflections and All That Sort of Thing 78*, 2010. Digital C-print, Diasec, 98 × 78 cm. Courtesy the artist

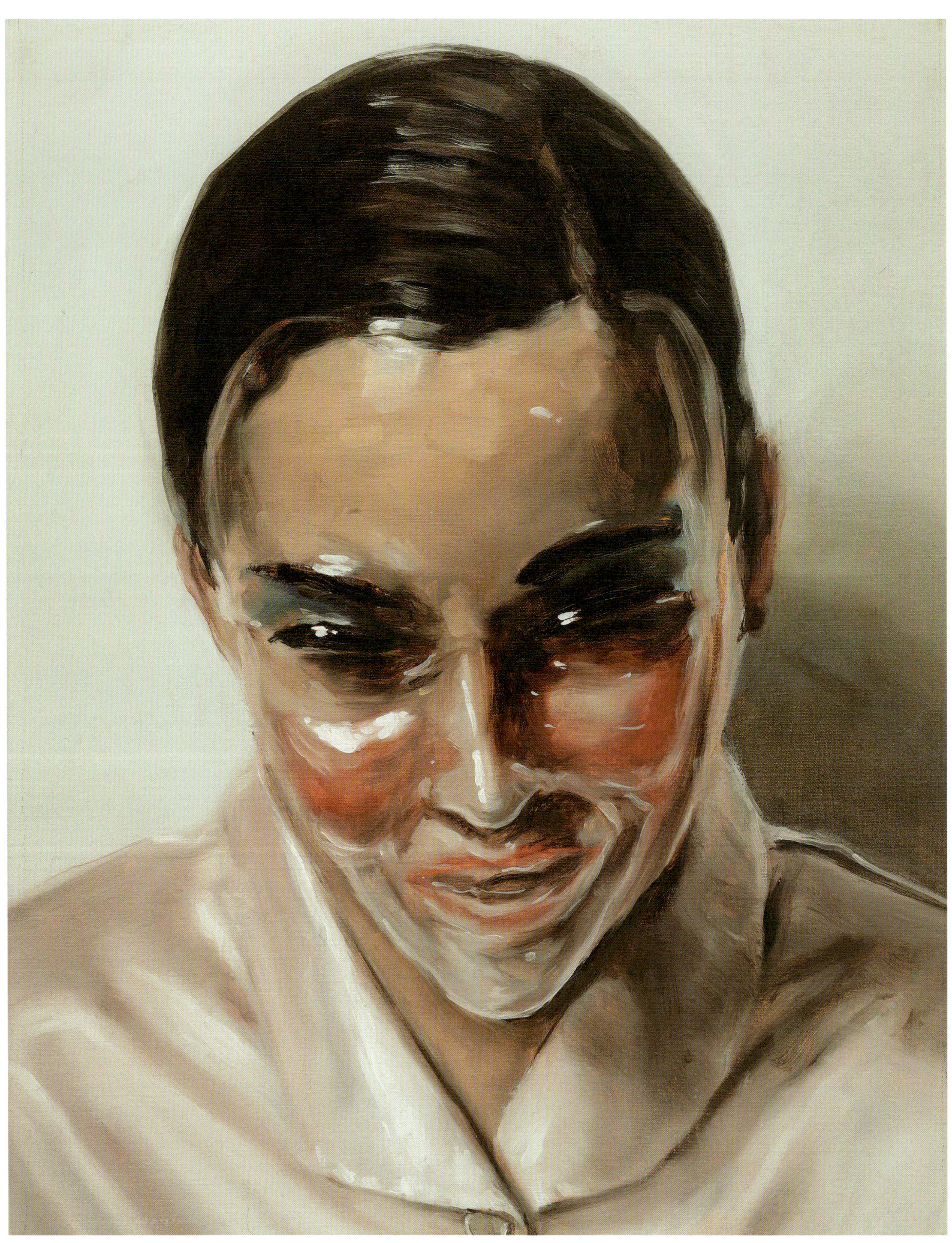

Michaël Borremans, *Mombakkes I*, 2007–08. Oil on canvas, 56.5 × 44.5 cm. Collection François Pinault Foundation, courtesy Zeno X Gallery, Antwerp

The Face of Europe:
Regarding European Identities

Alicja Gescinska

A face is a story that time tells

According to a popular saying, the eyes are the windows of the soul. But is it not the entire face that shines with the soul that looks from it? Our faces make our personalities and identities visible. The secrets of an entire life lie hidden in the folds of skin and wrinkles on our faces – and history, too, is silhouetted there.

Are we rich or poor, young or old, cheerful or tired, relaxed or anxious, healthy or ill? Has life scarred us, or do we feel blessed for having been spared the worst forms of misery? The answers to these questions are etched – completely or partially – into our faces. The human face is a story written by time, one that provides answers to the great questions of human life: What am I? Whence came I? Whither do I go?

The meaning, importance and complexity of the human face cannot be overestimated. The reason we gravitate towards faces lies in human evolution. Our ability to read faces and to communicate through them brought with it a tremendous evolutionary advantage.

Evolution and morality

The human brain can be likened to an information sponge constantly absorbing and processing information. This information often seeps away again, but in general, our brains try to interpret and process information as efficiently as possible. Throughout the ages and in the course of evolution, our brains have been trained to decode and interpret the information contained in faces. The better we were able to do this, the more likely it was that we would survive.

Imagine the disastrous consequences for our ancestors if they had been unable to judge from a person's face whether that person was in danger, seriously ill, furious, menacing, or gripped by fear and about to flee from an approaching predator. The capacity to interpret such signals was vital in order to avoid falling victim to, say, a contagious disease or an attack by a rage-filled human. But it was also crucial in recognizing an opportunity to indulge in sexual relations and thus pass on one's genes. Also, in the social context, it was a matter of knowing the right thing to do at the right time.

While some facial expressions will always prompt an instinctive 'run away' reaction, there are other occasions when a face will have the opposite effect, eliciting a moral obligation, as it were, to come closer – such as when a loved one or a neighbour shows signs of being in trouble, in distress and in need of help. In such cases, the facial information is converted into an inner command to go to the rescue of that person. The evolutionary advantage of that ability for people who live and work together is immense. The ability to read faces lies at the basis of human solidarity.

The entire oeuvre of the French-Jewish philosopher Emmanuel Levinas revolves around that particular idea. In Levinas's oeuvre, the other and the face of the other are pivotal concepts. The face of the other contains a moral call, which we cannot just evade. The face of the other – meeting the face of the other – is the beginning of philosophy and morality. When we see the face of the other, we feel the need to provide help, to give solace. In short: we feel the need to do good.

A face – even a particular look in the eyes – can therefore be extremely penetrating, something we remember all our lives. The Polish philosopher Leszek Kołakowski wrote of just such an experience. In an autobiographical note about his youth in inter-war Poland, he said he could clearly remember – even after about 70 years – the face of a beggar he had once seen somewhere in the 1930s. The inter-war period was a very turbulent time in Poland, a time marked by social, economic

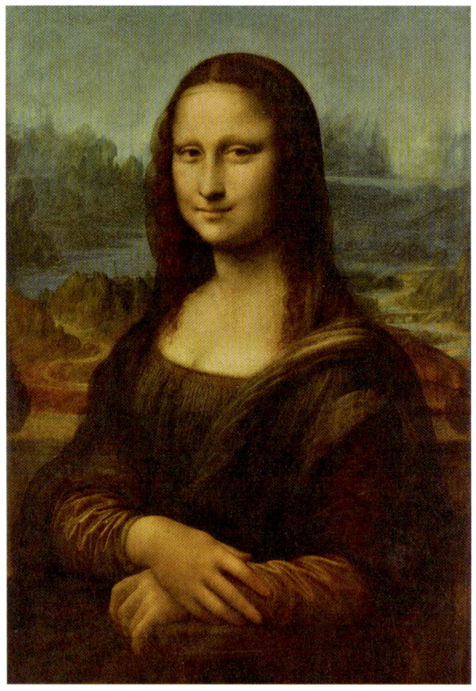

Leonardo da Vinci, *Mona Lisa*, c. 1500–1506.
Oil on panel, 33.6 × 23.7 cm. Musée du Louvre,
Département des Peintures, Paris

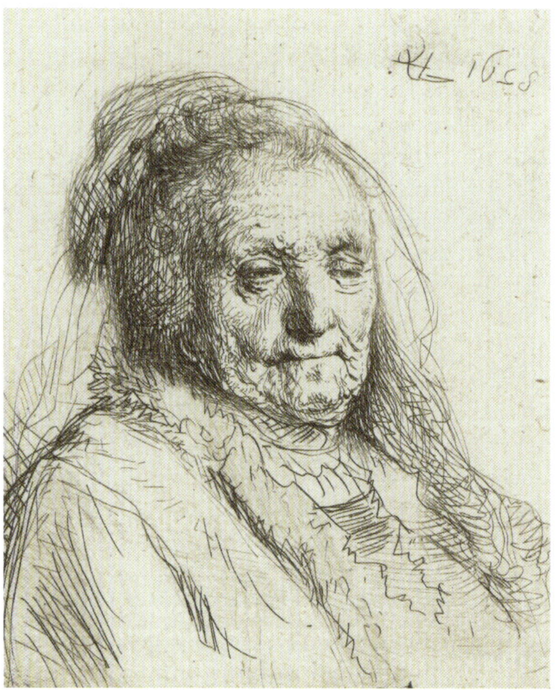

Rembrandt Harmensz van Rijn, *Rembrandt's mother: head
and bust*, 1628. Etching on paper, 6.6 × 6.3 cm. Rijksmuseum,
Amsterdam

and political upheaval. The face of that beggar revealed a deeply personal suffering and feelings of shame and failure, but it also expressed the turmoil and suffering of a nation. It was a face from which a penetrating moral call sprang: a cry for help – the disturbing echoes of which Kołakowski was still able to hear more than half a century later.

Do we not all have faces imprinted on our minds, faces we always carry around with us, like the pictures in our wallets or on our smartphones? The fact that we do reveals something fundamental about how our brains work, and about who we are as human beings: that for us, faces are souls.

When a face tells us nothing

All advanced forms of cooperation and coexistence, and the solidarity that these require, begin with the face. That is, beyond all cultural diversity, a universal phenomenon: an innate aspect of the human condition. It is, therefore, no coincidence that recent scientific research has shown that babies are able – at a very early stage already – to recognize the faces of their mother and father and are drawn towards faces and face-like figures. For the same reason, we often see faces and facial expressions in abstract and rather elementary shapes: a face in the clouds, or a joyful face in a smiley, which is basically nothing but an upward curling line beneath two small ovals. The area of the brain chiefly concerned with the task of identifying and reading faces is located deep in the brain, which tells us that face perception is an ability we acquired ages and ages ago.

Damage to and neurological deficiencies in that part of the brain can impair the ability to read faces, causing the patient to suffer from prosopagnosia: face blindness – a disorder that makes it difficult to deal with various practical matters that are part of everyday life. Many patients say that it is also a source of social embarrassment, since their inability to recognize faces or interpret facial expressions often results in reactions that seem rude and inappropriate.

A face that is concealed from us cannot be read and can therefore tell us nothing. It may not leave us indifferent, but it does make coexistence and cooperation difficult. As human beings, we encounter each other face to face, and that is how we live: face to face. So when people deliberately turn their faces away from us or hide them from view, this often provokes feelings of uncertainty and unease.

This discomfort may explain coulrophobia: the abnormal fear of clowns. A clown disguises his real face, leaving us unable to determine whether that person is young or old, happy or angry, gentle or dangerous. What we see is not a real face but a grotesque facsimile of a face, which is why people who suffer from coulrophobia feel uneasy and anxious in the presence of clowns. While most people do not experience this anxiety, the reasons behind it lie deep in our human existence: in our need to communicate through faces.

There are instances, though, when masked faces will cause no alarm whatsoever. Those encountered at a costumed ball, for example, are more likely to generate a sense of intrigue, even excitement, and a desire to find out who is hiding behind each mask, than any feelings of discomfort or dread.

The eternal topicality of portraiture

These reflections and facts on the importance of the human face and its personal, moral and social meaning help us to understand why portraiture is such a universal and timeless form of artistic creativity and expressiveness. In every epoch, in every culture, in every society, the representation of faces has been a crucial artistic activity. When we look today at portraits of Rembrandt's mother, we are able to read in her face the same things that Rembrandt's contemporaries would have read. Ages have passed, but the faces, the expressions and the meanings remain.

Evidently, there can be minimal yet significant differences in how we interpret a face. Sometimes a face is mysterious, an expression unclear, a look ambivalent. Eyes that look tired to one person may seem to express sadness to another. A frown may actually be a sign of trepidation, or merely indicate that the person is deep in thought. That we read faces is a universal fact, but what we read there varies, which is why, to this day, we are still puzzled by the Mona Lisa's enigmatic mouth. Is she smiling or not? And what does that smile mean, if it is a smile at all? It is generally acknowledged that a profoundly sad face will be perceived as such, and that a happy face will be understood as an expression of joy, regardless of any cultural differences. That is due in part to the fact that the information we deduce from a face is reinforced by other bearers of meaning. Our brains can, for example, distil information about a person's identity and personality from his or her posture or the setting and general context.

Faces and identities

Much of this comes to the fore in the portraits that have been collected here, a particularly interesting case in point being *The Europeans* – Tina Barney's series of portraits of wealthy European citizens. From their faces, clothing, posture and surroundings, we can easily infer that the subjects are affluent. Completely different yet similar is the work of Alberto García-Alix, who often depicts marginalized groups in disturbingly penetrating portraits. The work of both Barney and García-Alix show how a face and a portrait can tell us something about a person's history and background, both personal and socio-economic.

In her own unique way, Dita Pepe, too, depicts this most intimate and intrinsic relationship between the face and the life of a person. The Czech photographer has created an interesting series of self-portraits in which she places herself within different fictive families, standing next to a different man and sometimes different children in each photograph. It is always the same woman in every picture, and yet she is always someone else. Pepe places herself in marginalized groups of society, in average middle-class families, and among the upper class – resulting in portraits of different lives, different identities and, ultimately, different faces.

Portraits speak volumes (or do they?)

Denis Darzacq's *Casques de Thouars* series of photographs shows young people wearing motorcycle helmets, which serve as an expression of their identity. Yet those very helmets simultaneously hide an important aspect of that identity, and form a barrier between the wearer and the real world. This concealment and the resulting anonymity of those portrayed give rise to a certain uneasiness, for what are we to feel and think about a person whose face is hidden from us? On the other hand, the existential discomfort caused by these hidden faces may well reflect the often aggressive and incomprehensible world from which these youngsters are trying to set themselves apart.

Adam Pańczuk's portraits of the Karczeb people in eastern Poland are entirely different. The various pieces of information conveyed by these photographs tell us a great deal about these people. The portraits reveal a specific socio-historic background, a specific way of life, a specific identity, as well as a specific state of mind. Even if the identities of these people will remain unknown to us, their faces already tell us so much. For a face is worth a thousand words.

European faces

If faces do indeed reveal something about a person's history, personality and identity, then European faces - like the ones brought together for this exhibition - must surely also reveal something of a European identity. But that is a complex matter, for what exactly is a European identity? As the process of European political, economic and social integration proceeds, this question becomes increasingly important.

Some people doubt the existence of a European identity. Others recognize that there is something that constitutes the individuality of Europe, without, however, being able to point out what exactly that is. Looking at the faces and portraits that have been collected in this book, one cannot help but be struck by their enormous variety? What connection is there between Adam Pańczuk's impoverished Karczebs and the wealthy people portrayed by Tina Barney? What do the children photographed by Sergey Bratkov have in common with Christian Courrèges's European intellectuals?

If Europe does have its own face, it is a face composed of many faces. The face of Europe is a mosaic of the faces - and thus identities - of all Europeans. In much the same way that identity is a multi-layered concept (with possibly a core that cannot be grasped completely), so, too, is the European face multi-layered. This is definitely true of the physiognomy of the European face, which is the result of the ancient and more recent mingling of many peoples. A European face does not immediately reveal itself as European, at least not at first sight. *The* European does not exist, but many kinds of Europeans do.

If there is such a thing that can be called typically European in faces, it is not what they look like, but the way they look at the world: through open and inquiring eyes that meet the eyes of the other, and look for the other. An open gaze that reflects an open heart.

Is that not what we recognize in so much of our literature, as well as in the European tradition of portrait painting, which is unique in the annals of civilization? The recognition of the other self, and the openness to dialogue - that, surely, is the European face, which lends itself to photography because it is always part of its surroundings. A face is a mirror of a soul - sometimes a mirage too - but it always integrates into the world that surrounds it, however chaotic and sad that world might be, however encumbered with luxuries or worn thin by penury.

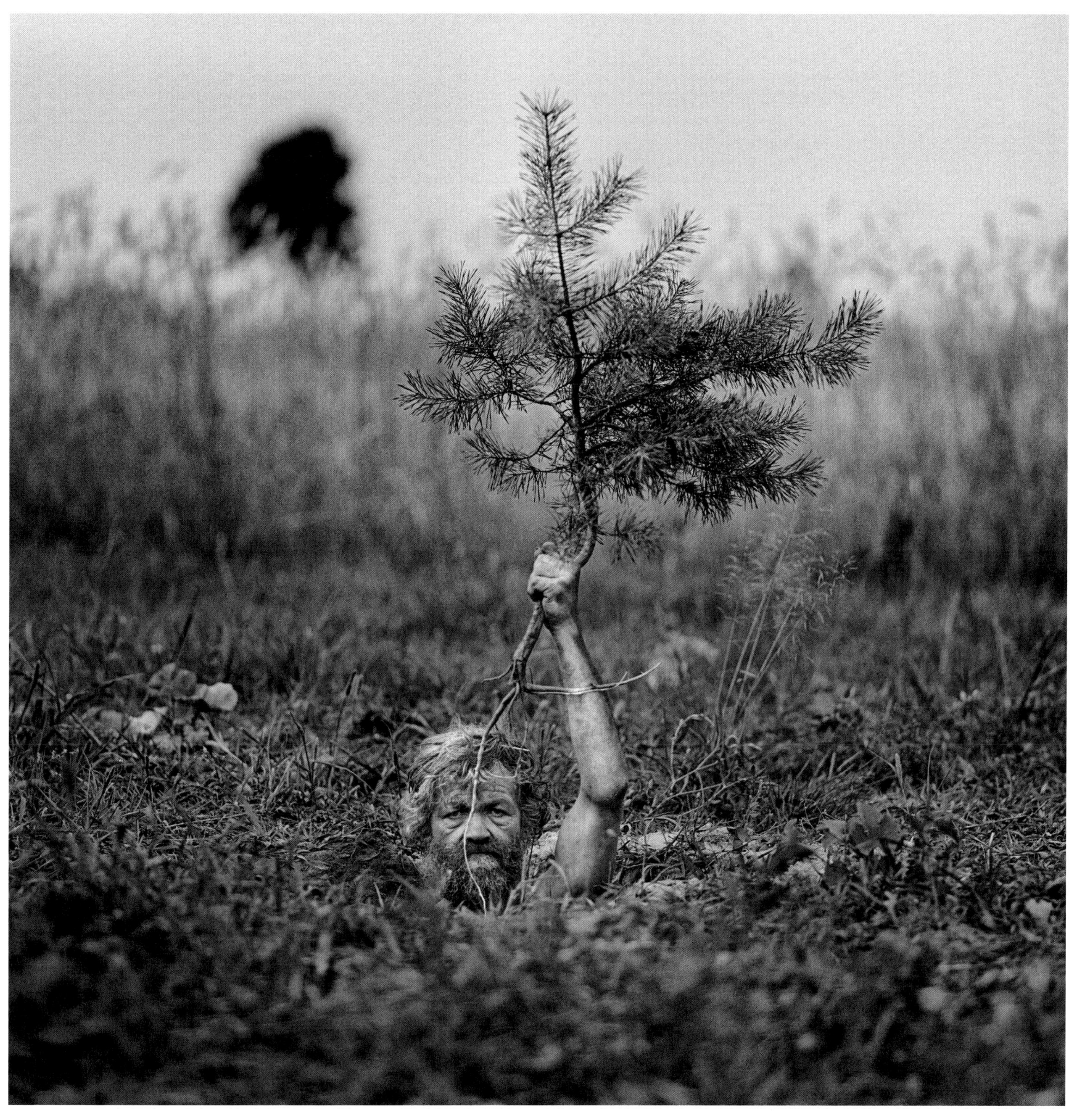

Adam Pańczuk, 'Karczeby', 2008. Archival ink-jet print, 90 × 90 cm. Courtesy the artist

*FACES NOW. European Portrait
Photography since 1990*
BOZAR, Centre for Fine Arts,
Brussels
6 February – 17 May 2015

*FACES. European Portrait
Photography since 1990*
Nederlands Fotomuseum, Rotterdam
30 May – 30 August 2015

*FACES. European Portrait
Photography since 1990*
Museum of Photography,
Thessaloniki
11 September 2015 –
28 February 2016

with the support of

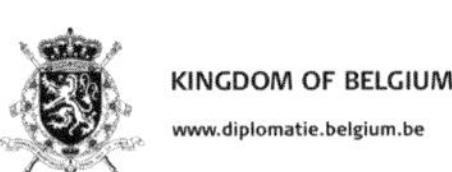

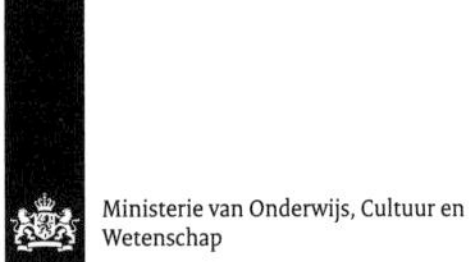

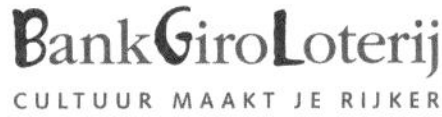

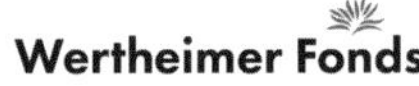

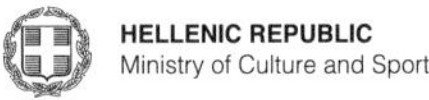

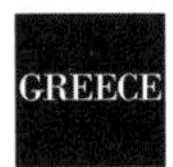

sponsors

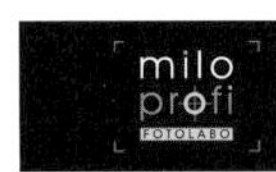

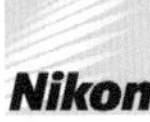

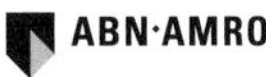

EXHIBITION

Artistic Director
Paul Dujardin

Deputy Director Exhibitions
Sophie Lauwers

Curator
Frits Gierstberg

Board of Advisors
Alexandra Athanasiadou
Christophe De Jaeger
Vangelis Ioakimidis
Gautier Platteau
Olga Sviblova

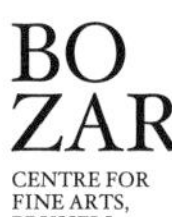

*Chief Executive Officer –
Artistic Director*
Paul Dujardin

Director Artistic Policy
Adinda Van Geystelen

BOZAR EXPO
Deputy Director Exhibitions
Sophie Lauwers

BOZAR MUSIC
Director
Ulrich Hauschild

BOZAR CINEMA
Head
Juliette Duret

BOZAR COM
*Director Marketing,
Communication & Sales*
Filip Stuer

BOZAR TECHNICS
*Director Technics, IT, Investments,
Safety and Security*
Stéphane Vanreppelen

BOZAR PRODUCTION & PLANNING
Director
Jean-François D'hondt

BOZAR FINANCES
Director
Jérémie Leroy

GENERAL ADMINISTRATION
Director
Didier Verboomen

HUMAN RESOURCES
Director
Marleen Spileers

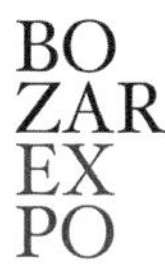

BO
ZAR
EX
PO

Axelle Ancion
Helena Bussers
Mieke De Bock
Christophe De Jaeger
Rocío del Casar Ximénez
Gunther De Wit
Ann Flas
Ann Geeraerts
Anne Judong
Vera Kotaji
Sophie Lauwers
Alberta Sessa
Maïté Smeyers
Christel Tsilibaris

Chief Executive Officer – Artistic Director
Paul Dujardin

Deputy Director Exhibitions
Sophie Lauwers

Exhibition Coordinator
Christophe De Jaeger
Intern
Ilse Raps
Technical Coordinator
Isabelle Speybrouck
Art Handling and Installation
BOZAR art handlers

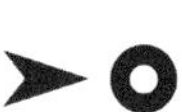

Director
Ruud Visschedijk
Curator
Frits Gierstberg
Head of Presentations
Marieke Wiegel
Project Management
Mandy Prins
Communication
Annemarie van den Eijkel
Administration
Marieke van de Zandschulp

**MUSEUM
OF PHOTOGRAPHY
THESSALONIKI**

Director
Vangelis Ioakimidis
Artistic Consultant – International Relations
Alexandra Athanasiadou
Administrative Coordinator
Morfoula Zyga
Press and Communication Office
Barbara Basdeki

ACKNOWLEDGEMENTS

The co-producers, the curator and the Board of Advisors
wish to thank the following people and institutions:

the Belgian Ministry of Foreign Affairs, and the sponsors
Milo-Profi, Nikon, and ABN AMRO;

the Dutch Ministry of Education, Culture and Science,
the City of Rotterdam, BankGiro Loterij, and Wertheimer
Fonds;

the Greek Ministry of Culture and Sports, in particular
Lina Mendoni, Marios Kostakis, George Kalamantis,
Paraskevi Vassilaki, as well as Pericles Pilides, Arsen
& Roupen Kalfayan, Pantelis Arapinis and the Greek
Ministry of Tourism;

Vladimir Birgus, Ewa Borysiewicz, Gintaras Cesonis, Kurt
De Boodt, Kaat De Jonghe, Christine Frisinghelli, Stefan
Gronert, Barbara Hofmann, Curt Holtz, Barbara Honrath,
Claudia Küssel, Jean-Marc Lacabe, Hanne Lapierre,
Zuzana Lapitkova, Vesselina Nikolaeva, Christine Ollier,
Virginie Platteau, Rui Prata, Oliva Maria Rubio, Agnès
Sire, Roberta Valtorta;

and especially all the lenders:
M HKA, Antwerp
Zeno X Gallery, Antwerp
Studio Doreen Dierckx, Brussels
Galerie Conrads, Düsseldorf
Galerie Priska Pasquer, Cologne
Galerie Nagel Draxler, Berlin and Cologne
Centre Régional de la Photographie Nord –
Pas-de-Calais
Galerie RX, Paris
Museum of Photography, Thessaloniki
AD Gallery, Athens
Juergen Teller Ltd, London
Regina Gallery, London and Moscow
Paul Kasmin Gallery, New York

as well as those who wish to remain anonymous.

CATALOGUE

Edited by
Frits Gierstberg
Authors
Alexandra Athanasiadou (AA), Christophe De Jaeger
(CDJ), Paul Dujardin, Alicja Gescinska, Frits Gierstberg
(FG), Vangelis Ioakimidis (VI), Gautier Platteau (GP)

We are especially grateful to Till-Holger Borchert
and Koenraad Jonckheere for their much appreciated
contribution.

Coordination
Curt Holtz with Dorothea Bethke for Prestel
Gunther De Wit for BOZAR BOOKS
Translation
Translation from Dutch: Michael Robinson
Translation of the text by Alicja Gescinska:
Steven Lepez
Copy-editing and proof-reading
Danko Szabó
Graphic design
Jeroen Wille, Ellen Debucquoy, Stijn Verdonck,
Luc Derycke, Studio Luc Derycke, Ghent, Belgium
Printing
die Keure, Bruges, Belgium
Binding
Brepols, Turnhout, Belgium

Front cover
Thomas Ruff, *Portrait (Andrea Kachold)*, 1987. Chromogenic
print, 205 × 160 cm.
Courtesy the artist

Photo credits
© SABAM, Belgium / Pictoright / VG Bild-Kunst, Bonn for
Alberto García-Alix, Jitka Hanzlová,
Boris Mikhailov and Thomas Ruff
© Zeno X Gallery, Antwerp / Peter Cox, p. 230
© RMN-Grand Palais (Musée du Louvre) /
Michel Urtado, p. 232, left
© all artists and their galleries as mentioned
in the picture captions

www.hannibalpublishing.com
www.bozar.be
www.nederlandsfotomuseum.nl
www.thmphoto.gr

Prestel Verlag, Munich
A member of Verlagsgruppe Random House GmbH

Prestel Verlag
Neumarkter Strasse 28
81673 Munich
Tel. +49 (0)89 4136-0
Fax +49 (0)89 4136-2335

Prestel Publishing Ltd.
14-17 Wells Street
London W1T 3PD
Tel. +44 (0)20 7323-5004
Fax +44 (0)20 7323-0271

Prestel Publishing
900 Broadway, Suite 603
New York, NY 10003
Tel. +1 (212) 995-2720
Fax +1 (212) 995-2733
www.prestel.com

Library of Congress Control Number: 2014958096

British Library Cataloguing-in-Publication Data:
a catalogue record for this book is available from
the British Library; Deutsche Nationalbibliothek
holds a record of this publication in the Deutsche
Nationalbibliografie; detailed bibliographical data
can be found under: http://www.dnb.de

Prestel books are available worldwide. Please contact
your nearest bookseller or one of the above addresses
for information concerning your local distributor.

ISBN: 978-3-7913-4927-5